Washington's Government

EARLY AMERICAN HISTORIES

Douglas Bradburn, John C. Coombs, and S. Max Edelson, Editors

Washington's Government

Charting the Origins of
the Federal Administration

EDITED BY MAX M. EDLING AND PETER J. KASTOR

University of Virginia Press

CHARLOTTESVILLE AND LONDON

University of Virginia Press
© 2021 by the Rector and Visitors of the University of Virginia
All rights reserved
Printed in the United States of America on acid-free paper

First published 2021

9 8 7 6 5 4 3 2 1

Library of Congress Cataloging-in-Publication Data
Names: Edling, Max M., editor. | Kastor, Peter J., editor.
Title: Washington's government : charting the origins of the federal administration /
    edited by Max M. Edling and Peter J. Kastor.
Description: Charlottesville : University of Virginia Press, 2021. | Series: Early
    American histories | Includes bibliographical references and index.
Identifiers: LCCN 2021000461 (print) | LCCN 2021000462 (ebook) |
    ISBN 9780813946139 (hardcover) | ISBN 9780813946146 (epub)
Subjects: LCSH: United States—Politics and government—1789–1797. |
    Federal government—United States—History—18th century.
Classification: LCC E311 .W374 2021 (print) | LCC E311 (ebook) | DDC 973.2—dc23
LC record available at https://lccn.loc.gov/2021000461
LC ebook record available at https://lccn.loc.gov/2021000462

Cover art: *Sacred to Patriotism*, Cornelius Tiebout, engraving after Charles Buxton, 1798.
(Mount Vernon Ladies' Association)

Contents

Acknowledgments

One of the most rewarding features of an edited volume is its collaborative quality. That was even more so in this case because the collaboration was both interpersonal and institutional.

As editors, we remain profoundly grateful for the intellectual energy, constructive outlook, and patience that our contributors demonstrated throughout the process. Those qualities were abundantly on display at the April 2016 workshop where we gathered to discuss drafts, and it has remained through the revision and editing process that followed.

That workshop proved so fruitful through the participation of a number of other scholars who joined us to comment on the papers. Brian Balogh, Doug Bradburn, Johann Neem, and Rosemarie Zagarri participated, and the essays are all better as a result of their feedback. Rosemarie also generously agreed to write the afterword to this volume.

All of us owe a particular debt to George Washington's Mount Vernon, the institution that includes but is hardly limited to the plantation home of George and Martha Washington. Indeed, Mount Vernon has become a model of how best to support both public and academic history. The Fred W. Smith National Library for the Study of George Washington hosted the workshop. Stephen Mcleod and other members of the library staff provided crucial logistical support. The library was a magnificent site for this academic meeting, just as it excels in hosting public talks, teacher training, and other activities, all the while serving as home to researchers pursuing a variety of projects on George Washington and his time.

We especially want to thank Doug Bradburn. At the time of the workshop, he was serving as the founding executive director of the library. Since then, he has become president and CEO of Mount Vernon and as such supervises the entire operation of the estate on behalf of the Mount Vernon Ladies' Association. Kevin Butterfield, his successor as executive director at the library, has helped see this volume through to completion.

We are also grateful for the financial support we have received from our own institutions. The irony was not lost on us that we come from one university named for George Washington (Washington University in St. Louis) and another named for the title (King's College London) that Washington considered so inappropriate for the United States.

Finally, we want to thank the University of Virginia Press for publishing this volume. Dick Holway and Nadine Zimmerli served as editors for this volume. Dick is a legend among historians of the early American republic, having guided a generation of scholars through the publication process at UVA Press. While nobody can *replace* Dick, Nadine has *succeeded* him quite admirably.

Washington's Government

Introduction

Creating the Federal Government

In July 1792, George Washington was at a crossroads. Uncertain whether to pursue a second term as president, detecting strong disagreements within the nation's political class, he found that even a visit to his plantation, Mount Vernon, was no escape from public affairs. Writing to Alexander Hamilton, Washington explained that having met with local Virginians, "I have endeavoured to learn from sensible & moderate men—known friends to the Government—the sentiments which are entertained of public measures." Washington took pleasure in the fact that "these all agree that the Country is prosperous & happy; but they seem to be alarmed at that system of policy, and those interpretations of the Constitution which have taken place in Congress." Yet Washington was forced to acknowledge that "others, less friendly perhaps to the Government, and more disposed to arraign the conduct of its Officers . . . go further, & enumerate a variety of matters."[1]

Washington understood that this response was in part a political matter of emerging factionalism. He also feared that it might reflect ideological problems in the fabric of American republicanism. But in the paragraphs that followed, Washington listed a series of discrete government actions that the "other," "less friendly," observers of the government had fastened on. These actions had to do with taxation and, above all, with the management of the public debt, which the critics argued were undermining the republican system of government. Washington asked Hamilton to provide his "ideas upon the discontents here enumerated" at his earliest convenience to help him determine whether the policy measures had been executed effectively and were bringing good or bad results. In other words, at the end of the day George Washington saw the problems facing his administration as a matter of governance. In modern parlance we would say that Washington worried about the institutional capacity of the federal government; that he wanted to reconsider his policy-making priorities; and that he hoped to pursue a system of state building that was appropriate to the nation's needs and its resources.

This volume explores how those tasks of governance first came into being. Just how did the Washington administration go about converting the vague principles of the Constitution into viable institutions and effective policies? How did the government attempt to mobilize its resources—people, money, physical goods—to achieve its goals? And how did Americans respond to those actions? Answering these questions could not be more timely, as both George Washington's presidency and the realities of governance in early America generate growing interest in both academic and popular circles.

In the course of that exploration, the prevailing accounts of the Washington presidency are restructured in several crucial ways. First, the essays interrogate some of the most basic assumptions about Washington and his administration, revealing a new series of periodization schemes and constructing a new set of processes. Second, the essays do so by shifting the focus from the realm of electoral and constitutional concerns to a focus on administrative and institutional concerns. Thirdly, several of the essays try to approach the political history of the period by employing new methods based on quantitative rather than qualitative data.

What emerges from this analysis is a Washington administration that appears both more dynamic and more uncertain than was previously apparent. The administration appears remarkably experimental. Rather than creating in a straightforward manner a system promulgated by the Constitution, Washington, his advisors, and their cadre of subordinates constructed over time a series of possible mechanisms for doing the nation's business. The results were successful in some cases, disastrous in others. Yet at the end of Washington's second term, there was no denying that the federal government had achieved some remarkable results. Despite stumbles, false starts, and a growing opposition, the federal government had staked out its territory and was actively pursuing important policies in several key areas of governance thanks to an administrative organization that, while far from perfect, was reasonably efficient in implementing the goals formulated by Congress and the administration. In comparison to the lackluster administration of the central government under the Articles of Confederation, the American union had taken significant strides in a relatively short period of time.

The Washington administration has always enjoyed something of golden halo. After all, the prospects for disaster in 1789 seemed so numerous and imminent. This is true not only of the Washington administration but also of the Constitution itself. Yet for close to a quarter century now, much of the most dynamic work on public life during the early republic has concerned itself with political culture. While the boundaries of this work extend from the ferment of the American Revolution through the transition to the antebellum era, the 1790s often assume center stage. In particular, historians have often used the 1790s to identity the connections between public acts and political mobilization, between ideological disputes and party formation, between print culture and civic life.[2] This work has revealed a robust debate at work on the meanings of the Constitution, republican government, and participatory politics. So vast is this scholarship and so bright is its capacity to reveal the past that it often overshadowed another intellectual tradition that sought to make sense of governance.

That tradition of studying the history of governance begins with Leonard White, the touchstone for so many of the contributors to this volume. In his magisterial studies of public administration, White sought to tell a story of institutions, occasionally supplementing his close reading of correspondence with descriptive statistics of certain government offices.[3] White wrote at a specific moment and within an extended intellectual tradition that serves as a reminder that the history of state building was never an entirely academic concern. At the center of White's story was always an idealized notion of how government should operate: efficiently, well structured, well managed, and adequately resourced. This was a heroic story of what state building could do. It was fundamentally a progressive history of administration, and in a very specific way. This was not the progressive school of history (with its broad-reaching notion of inevitable progress) but rather a more specific tie to progressivism as a national movement beginning in the late nineteenth century that, among other things, championed the increase of state capacity and reform in government. At its core, progressives had argued that a modern, properly run government could achieve great things.[4]

White's own progressive claims about the early republic were eventually overshadowed both by different historical concerns and by a different history of the state. A later generation of scholars identified a normative "state" as defined by the bureaucratic procedures of the progressive era and the institutional capacities of western European social services. By these highly restrictive definitions, the era that White described did not, in fact, see a state emerge. The administrative history of the early republic was at best only a prelude to true state building. Comparing developments in the United States to the growth of the British state, a prominent historian of the early republic dismissed the federal government as "a midget institution in a giant land," a government that "had almost no internal functions" and whose "role scarcely went beyond . . . the use of port duties and the revenue from land sales to meet its own expenses." But the phrase that would come to embody this outlook for many scholars, and one that would eventually come under attack, was Stephen Skowronek's characterization of the early republic as an era of "Courts and Parties."[5]

Skowronek himself would later come to challenge this assumption, participating in a broad reconsidering of state building. This movement was, in part, a response to other scholarly changes, particularly the focus on social and cultural history that had rightly questioned whether public institutions— long the principal focus of scholars—should consume so much intellectual space.[6] Yet for all the discussion about state building, much of the scholarship retained a set of normative assumptions that excluded the early republic.

Scholars of the early republic both declared independence from and declared membership in the discussion of state building. They argued that prepogressive history did indeed contain a history of state building and of a state. But crucial to this work was the argument that the early state, while periodically familiar to scholars of the modern world, often worked by fundamentally different rules. The rallying cry for a new history of early state building first sounded after the publication of Richard John's *Spreading the News* and his important article on governmental institutions as agents of change. John's study of the postal service demonstrated the breadth of revelation that could emerge from studying federal operations. As much cultural history as institutional history, *Spreading the News* would become the point of departure for scholars attempting to fashion a new history of state building for a very old era in American history.[7]

But it would take a historian of modern state building to make sense of the discordant field. Brian Balogh's *A Government Out of Sight* synthesized the work on state building with a compelling interpretation for why American scholars and the American public had forgotten the era of robust state building during the early republic. In reality a powerful director of social development, the nineteenth-century American state had remained hidden from view because historians did not recognize the multifaceted and complex private-public partnership that characterized governance in the period as the activities of a modern state. But the nineteenth-century American state was an *associational state*—a polity where the federal government acted in partnership with local and state governments, voluntary organizations, the professions, interest groups, and even private corporations. In his book Balogh ascribed the act of forgetting this precursor to the modern state to the public political, as much as narrow academic, debates.[8]

Yet another reason why the central state dropped from the radar had to do with the remit of the federal government. Primarily designed to manage international relations, including so-called Indian diplomacy and foreign trade, the western territories, and intraunion relations, it seemingly had little impact on the concerns of a past generation of scholars who framed the nation's history as a narrative of modernization, of the nation's transition from a precapitalist and monarchical society to a market economy and liberal democracy. With the international turn of the historical discipline, this view is changing. In recent decades American historians have been drawn to global and Atlantic history, transnational and postcolonial studies, and other approaches that share the conviction that external relations and influences had a decisive impact on the nation's development. This perspective shift also opens for a reassessment of the role of the state in American history because what was once seen as marginal becomes of central importance. Of particular relevance to the study of the early federal government is the willingness to see the growth in United States' power as a major theme in the nation's history alongside traditional concerns with economic and political modernization.[9]

Drawing on the work of historians like John and Balogh, historians and political scientists alike have begun to construct an increasingly cohesive synthesis of state building in early America. First and foremost, they have reached the consensus that the early federal leadership was hardly the anti-state libertarians that they had so often been called. Federal leaders agreed that a properly funded, effectively managed, and aggressively deployed federal regime could achieve both foreign and domestic priorities. The principal disagreements concerned the scale of state capacity and its application. Of course, this was no minor disagreement and would play a key role in fueling political discord. By the time Washington was writing his anxious letter in July 1792, long before labels like Federalist and Republican had been attached to political organizations, factions within the political leadership were arguing over the proper extent of government capacity. Indeed, it is worth remembering that the first party split was to a large extent grounded in disagreement about the nature and extent of central state capacity in the fiscal, financial, and later military sphere, precisely the areas Washington worried about in his letter to Hamilton. Eventually, Federalists would face accusations of seeking government institutions that would bankrupt the country and create institutions of tyranny. Republicans would face accusations that they were providing inadequate resources to meet the nation's needs.[10]

Nowhere is the rising tide of interest in state building clearer than in a series of shifts within academic journals. *Studies in American Political Development*, which had rarely concerned itself with the decades before the Civil War, has published a series of articles on state building in the antebellum era and the early republic.[11] When *Diplomatic History* published an important forum in 2015 titled "American Indians and the History of U.S. Foreign Relations," the journal not only took an important step in situating native decision making within political and diplomatic history; it also acknowledged the significance of Native American policy as a fundamental feature of early policy making.[12] And most recently, both the major journals devoted to early America have highlighted the importance of the state. The *Journal of the Early Republic* ran a special issue focusing on state building, which considered both the extent and implications of recent work in the field, and the *William and Mary Quarterly* published an extensive and insightful essay on the new historiography of the early federal government.[13]

Today scholars show a much greater appreciation for the role of the federal government in conquering the West, in transforming public lands into private property, in manipulating the geography of race, and in binding the nation together through a network of communications than an older generation did. Nevertheless, despite a host of important new scholarship, we have yet much to learn about the governmental institutions that made such actions possible. For all the flurry about early state building, its primordial origins within the federal system remain something of a mystery. Lost in the focus on political culture, the formation of parties, the transition from republic to democracy, or the struggles between Hamilton and Jefferson lies the reality of a Washington administration struggling to create federal institutions that could respond to pressing challenges both numerous and profound.[14]

The contributors to this volume were drawn together by their shared commitment to exploring the federal government as a set of institutions populated by officials who were in varying ways engaged in institutional practices. But this project was made possible first and foremost by the Fred W. Smith National Library for the Study of George Washington at Mount Vernon. Max Edling and Peter Kastor approached the library about hosting a workshop in 2016 to develop a volume that would examine state building during the Washington administration. Douglas Bradburn, then the library's executive director (and now the president and CEO of Mount Vernon), generously offered to host the workshop and to provide staff and funding to support the event. The participants represented a wide range of institutions and career stages. Indeed, one of the functions of the workshop was to gather these scholars, most of whom had never met. Mount Vernon proved to be a perfect place for the event and not only for its connection to Washington. The Smith Library had magnificent meeting spaces, and the work of library staff served as a reminder of the ongoing efforts at Mount Vernon to understand both Washington and his world.

Certain key goals animated both the workshop and the volume it produced. The authors in this volume all seek to model alternative methodologies to studying the political history of the early republic. In contrast to the long-standing concerns with political theory, political culture, and party operations, it considers the Washington administration as a facet of American state building by focusing on the agencies and the personnel who faced the daily task of governance. This was no simple task. The United States faced extraordinary challenges both at home and abroad. Indeed, the story of American state building during the Washington administration emerges accordingly: from the confluence of the transition from confederation to federalism, from the specific external forces that shaped federal priorities, and from the internal dynamics of federal officials at all ranks of the policy-making structure.

As the early republic so clearly demonstrates, state building in the United States was often a reactive process, emerging in response to human and environmental forces that were beyond the control of American officials. So before exploring how Americans set out to govern themselves, it is essential to consider the forces that impelled them to action.

When the Washington administration began work in 1789, the United States was in crisis. Or, put more specifically, the United States faced a series of crises that were at once distinct and interconnected, foreign and domestic. It was these crises that had fueled the creation of the presidency by the Constitutional Convention in the summer of 1787 and, once the Constitution was adopted, would in turn shape the actions of the Washington administration. The federal leadership established a series of policy-making priorities: to preserve the union at a time when it appeared likely to disintegrate, to establish financial solvency and economic prosperity in a period of fiscal chaos and economic decline, to promote international relations in a period when few negotiating partners took the United States seriously, to extend civil administration onto the national domain in the trans-Appalachian West, and to promote racial supremacy at a time when many white observers feared a black revolt and when native peoples successfully repulsed white attempts at territorial dominance. As if these challenges were not daunting enough, policy makers worried about their capacity to do so without threatening the principles of republican government or the individual rights of white citizens.[15]

Understanding what state building would mean during the Washington administration begins by revisiting state building as practiced during the late colonial, revolutionary, and confederation eras. The decades immediately preceding 1789 established precedents that Americans eagerly followed or vehemently rejected, shaped the circumstances facing federal leaders, and created many of the formal institutions of governance that determined federal capacities. That uniform story presented here also serves as the prelude to each of the essays that follow. As these essays demonstrate, the Washington administration set to work in an era defined by a bifurcated, almost schizophrenic attitude toward governance. At one moment, the preceding decades had demonstrated an abiding fear of centralized power. At the other moment, constitutional ratification had reflected an emerging belief in institutional reform that many believed required both centralization and increased capacities.[16]

As commander in chief of the American army, Washington had witnessed the defects of the Articles of Confederation and the inability of the Continental Congress to organize and pursue the War of Independence in an efficient manner at close range. As Washington wrote in his resignation letter to Congress in early June 1783, the many and severe problems of fighting the War of Independence in an energetic way "in too many instances resulted more from a want of energy in the Continental Government, than a deficiency of means in the particular States." He added that "the inefficacy of measures, arising from the want of an adequate authority in the supreme Power, from a partial compliance with the requisitions of Congress in some of the States and from a failure of punctuality in others, while it tended to damp the Zeal of those which were more willing to exert themselves, served also to accumulate the expences of the War and to frustrate the best concerted plans." To Washington, it was "indispensable to the happiness of the individual States that there should be lodged somewhere, a supreme power to regulate and govern the general concerns of the confederated Republic." But unless the states would allow Congress "to exercise those prerogatives" invested in it by the Articles of Confederation, "every thing must very rapidly tend to Anarchy and confusion."[17]

Washington's words echoed a growing concern among a group of politicians who had been closely involved in directing the war against Britain that the American union was on the road to dissolution. "Anarchy and confusion" was eighteenth-century shorthand for the civil wars and domestic disturbances many observers foresaw should the union disintegrate into a North American state system of thirteen competing republics. Ultimately, disunion therefore spelled the end to both liberty and independence. Anarchy would make the people support any tyrant who promised to restore order, even at the cost of losing popular liberties. Independence could only be maintained if foreign predatory nations could be kept at bay. But without a strong and effective union the American states would become "the sport of European Politicks." Old World great powers would "play one State against another" to prevent the "growing importance" of America and "to serve their own interested purposes."[18]

The Articles of Confederation had been written to better organize the armed struggle against Britain and to signal to European powers that the American states were serious in their pursuit of independence. Providing for de facto union from 1777, the politics of state interest nevertheless delayed formal ratification to 1781, when the war was all but over. As Washington's circular pointed out, the articles fell considerably short of their intended aim. Once the war ended and Britain recognized American independence, securing state compliance with decisions of Congress proved even harder than during the struggle against Britain. By the middle of the 1780s, the United States faced a number of challenges that called into question the viability of the existing union. They can be summarized under three headings: the breakdown of the fiscal system created by the Articles of Confederation that left the public debt unpaid and the government unable to pay operating expenses, the management of the western lands that had been ceded to the union but had not yet been organized or settled, and the need to secure international trade agreements as an independent nation outside the common market of the British Empire.

The War of Independence had been fought primarily on borrowed money, and in 1783 both the states and the union were heavily indebted to soldiers, contractors, and foreign allies. Under the Articles of Confederation, Congress was expected to requisition money from the states, which were under obligation to meet congressional demands. The system never worked, and its failure became a principal reason for the confederation's downfall. Congress made six requisitions between 1781 and 1786 that together generated an income of slightly more than $5 million. A substantial figure, it was still no more than a third of the sum requested. To make matters worse, the returns on every requisition declined. By the summer of 1786, the financial situation was critical. Congress struggled to avoid default on its Dutch loans and stopped payments on its French and Spanish loans. It could pay neither its small army nor its handful of civil servants.

Several states tried to meet the demands of the union. In the middle years of the 1780s, taxes were three to four times higher than prewar levels, and many states, at least on paper, enforced harsh collection measures. Without ready money and faced with the threat of losing their property through foreclosure, the people protested. Their protests soon paid off when state after state abolished or postponed taxes and provided relief legislation that stayed court proceedings and issued paper currency. These relief measures preserved or restored the social peace but had negative consequences for Congress. When creditors lost faith in the union, they demanded that their home states step in to guarantee their investments, and many state governments answered the call. Out-of-state and foreign creditors had no such option, which led to tensions between states and between the union and other nations. Congress could pay its creditors in Amsterdam only by taking up a new loan to cover interest payments on the old. It was not a sustainable policy, and the credit of the United States plummeted.[19]

The risk of sovereign default had important implications for the ability of the United States to hold its own against other powers. Just as nations do today, eighteenth-century states financed wars and emergencies with borrowed money. As Alexander Hamilton, Washington's secretary of the treasury, pointed out, "In the modern system of war, nations the most wealthy are obliged to have recourse to large loans," and public credit was therefore of "immense importance" to "the strength and security of nations." But to borrow, a state had to have sufficient income to service its debts. Unless the system of state requisitions was reformed, Congress's credit was unlikely to recover. There was real danger that the young United States would be left to the mercy of stronger nations.[20]

But even if the United States could achieve fiscal reform, to what purpose would governing officials devote their resources? Most of their goals relied in one way or another on asserting white supremacy, and the means to do so reflected all the complexities of the nation's emerging political order. British colonists had declared their independence in part because they doubted the empire's commitment to preserving slavery and promoting western expansion. They feared the ability of African Americans—either enslaved or free—to secure support from colonial officials. They resented restrictions on the growth of the plantation system. They chafed at restrictions on settlement in the trans-Appalachian West, which British colonial officials had imposed as a means to prevent conflict between white settlers and indigenous residents.[21]

These concerns during the Revolution turned into policy-making objectives. Slaveholders demanded that governing officials preserve their human property against the chaos of war. Backcountry settlers joined a military campaign that sought to evict Native Americans.[22] George Washington himself supported these goals, and for multiple reasons. As a planter who speculated in western lands, enslavement and native displacement fueled his wealth. As commanding general during the Revolution, he helped coordinate efforts to preserve racial supremacy in the East and establish it in the West.[23]

White Americans were hard at work creating civil and military institutions that would preserve their racial goals. Courts and militias worked in concert to preserve African American enslavement, while legal systems also subordinated free people of color in all states, including those that had eliminated slavery. Those same militias worked in concert with the peacetime army to pursue a broad-based goal of subordinating native peoples on lands claimed by the United States and removing them from the lands most coveted by white settlers.

The Constitution did not change these priorities, but it did determine which agencies of government would be responsible for their enforcement. The effort to prevent federal interference meant that state building at the state level—involving courts and militias, governors and state legislators—managed the hierarchy between Euro Americans and African Americans.[24] In stark contrast to language that all but prohibited the federal government from regulating African American enslavement, the Constitution mandated that the federal government concern itself with Native Americans.[25] Federal leaders in turn immediately assumed upon themselves the sole authority over native policy.

One result of this constitutional arrangement is that African American enslavement, that fundamentally important feature of American life before 1865, remained absent from most areas of federal policy making. That hardly means enslavement was not an important feature of law and policy. To the contrary: it was foundational to both. Many officeholders at all levels of the federal government were personally committed to preserving slavery, often because they themselves were slaveholders. But the successful effort by white Americans in general to prevent slavery from becoming a divisive political issue and leaders in southern states in particular to preempt any federal intrusions on the institution meant that the slavery was rarely a central concern of federal policy making.[26]

In sharp contrast to African American policy, Native American policy was a driving source of federal action. Locating Native American policy within the federal government was so important because it overlapped geographically with the other great federal administrative challenge of managing the federal domain in the West. During the 1780s, a series of states had ceded their territory northwest of the Ohio River to Congress (the largest single cession came from Virginia). In July 1787 Congress passed the Northwest Ordinance, which established national authority over but also national responsibility for this land. Passage was secured only because members of the Constitutional Convention who were also delegates to Congress took time out of the convention to travel to New York and attend the congressional session. It was clear that the federal government under development in the convention would inherit this task.[27]

The Northwest Ordinance imposed immediate administrative requirements on the federal government. In the absence of state governments, the federal leadership would need to select civil officials to provide daily administration. In the decades that followed, territorial administration would remain perhaps the most demanding, resource-consuming activity in the federal government. Not only did territorial administration produce its own bureaucratic procedures and require its own budget, but it shaped the history of the US Army, much of which was stationed in the territorial periphery of the United States.[28]

At the other end of the nation, the American union had to safeguard its interests in a highly competitive Atlantic marketplace. Despite recurrent complaints about trade restrictions, the American colonies had flourished in the extensive common market of the British Empire. Independence and expulsion from the empire caused a severe economic shock when alternative trading partners failed to materialize. Exports fell by as much as a quarter compared to pre-Revolution volumes, despite a rapidly growing population. As a result, the economy slowed. According to one economic historian, the War of Independence may have set back gross domestic product per capita by as much as fifty years.[29]

After the Peace of Paris, Britain offered generous terms for American exports to the British Isles because it was in its best economic interest. However, Britain was much more restrictive about American trade with the West Indies, traditionally an important American export market. In 1783, Britain banned American ships from trading with its Caribbean possessions and also prohibited the importation of many American products that Britain hoped to secure from Canada and the maritime provinces of British North America. Meanwhile, in 1784 France prohibited the importation of US flour and wheat to the French West Indies and the exportation of sugar from the islands to North America. France also tried to corner the trade in fish from the Newfoundland fishing banks to the French West Indies, an action of particular concern to New England. Spain was not more forthcoming. Rather than opening markets, it closed the Mississippi River to American boats and goods, thereby imperiling the economic prospects of settlements in the continental interior. Although commercial agreements were signed with minor powers such as Prussia and Sweden, the major trading nations showed scant interest in commercial negotiations with the United States. With no new trading routes or trading partners, the American states remained stuck within the economic orbit of the British Empire but on terms considerably worse than in the colonial period. In 1783, the British politician Lord Sheffield brought this view home in his *Observations on the Commerce of the American States*, in which he argued that as long as disagreements between the states persisted, "it will not be an easy matter to bring the American states to act as a nation." Hence, he concluded, "they are not to be feared as such by us."[30]

The United States could improve its position only by punitive countermeasures that would force Europe's Atlantic powers to sign trade agreements. By 1783, members of Congress had realized that Britain and former allies France and Spain were intent on preventing the United States from acquiring a position of power in North America. Late in the year a committee proposed that ships from nations without a commercial treaty with the United States be banned from American ports. Foreign merchants operating in American ports would be allowed to import goods directly from their home countries only if their government had signed a trade agreement with Congress. But such restrictions required amendment of the Articles of Confederation, which in turn required the unanimous support of all thirteen member states. Such support was not forthcoming in either 1783 or 1785, when a more radical proposal was made. As Lord Sheffield had implied, in the eyes of Europe's empires, the American union seemed anything but a formidable enemy in a trade war.

In the Mediterranean trade, American ships suffered from raids by the North African Barbary states. Nominally part of the Ottoman Empire but in reality autonomous, these principalities had long claimed sovereignty over, and the right to intercept ships on, Mediterranean waters. European trading nations therefore paid tribute to Algiers, Tunis, and Tripoli to secure safe passage in the Mediterranean Sea. Cast out of the protection of the British Crown and lacking the funds to arrange treaty payments, US-flagged ships were fair game, and their cargoes and crew were often taken and held for ransom in North Africa. The spectacle of white Christians enslaved by African Muslims troubled Americans and was well publicized in early American plays and novels, such as Susanna Rowson's *Slaves in Algiers* (1794) and Royall Tyler's *The Algerine Captive* (1797). To Americans it seemed that European maritime empires were only too pleased to see American commercial activity in the Mediterranean stall. In a frequently quoted report, Benjamin Franklin claimed to have overheard a London merchant remark, "If there were no Algiers it would be worth Englands while to build one."[31]

The challenges of the postwar period had a clearly discernable impact on the Constitution. The document granted Congress the power to tax independently of the state governments, thus making it capable to both service the public debt and to fund the federal government's operating expenditures, including the cost of the army and a diplomatic establishment. The Constitution also gave Congress the "Power to dispose of and make all needful Rules and Regulations respecting the Territory or other Property belonging to the United States" (art. IV, §3) and these rules and regulations were fleshed out in the Northwest Ordinance. It also extended Congress's right to regulate commerce to include "the Indian Tribes" (art. I, §8). Finally, Congress was given the right to regulate commerce by passing an American Navigation Act. International treaties were made the "supreme

Law of the Land" (art. VI), thereby making it impossible for state courts to obstruct the implementation of international agreements such as the peace treaty with Britain.

But the sections of the Constitution that outlined the structure of the new federal government provided little guidance to future lawmakers. This was true of the judiciary as well as the executive. Although Article III defines federal jurisdiction, it says nothing about the federal court structure other than the vague reference to "such inferior Courts as the Congress may from time to time ordain" (§1). In its enumeration of presidential authority in Article II, Section 2, the Constitution implied the creation of an army and a navy, a diplomatic corps, and various other "executive Departments." But it refrained from listing the latter and from making any suggestion about their governance. Likewise, the Constitution assumed a federal workforce, with employees required to receive nomination by the president and confirmation by the Senate. Beyond that, however, it was left to the Washington administration to determine just what those departments would be.

In creating governmental institutions, Congress and the Washington administration did not operate from a clean slate. The Constitution not only shifted certain responsibilities; it shifted certain personnel. And it is the distinction between the two that goes a long way toward explaining the key concerns of this volume. Political theorists, constitutional scholars, and legal historians have long addressed the conceptual framework of federalism. But at the moment of its creation, what would the federal government mean for the institutional apparatus of government, for the state capacity of the United States, and for the individuals who populated the federal workforce?

The answers were, of course, more complex than the simple notion of a move from confederation to federalism might suggest. The Washington administration inherited institutions from the Confederation Congress, appropriated institutions from the states, and created institutions out of whole cloth to address the new demands of federal governance. Consider the first efforts to apply structure to the federal government. The Constitution may have referred to "executive Departments," but it had not specified them in any detail. Instead, Washington preserved for the executive branch those departments most directly responsible for the challenges facing the young republic. The State Department would address the nation's diplomatic challenges on the Atlantic; the War Department would address the nation's diplomatic challenges in the West; the Treasury Department would address the fiscal crisis.

Three institutions—the US Army, the diplomatic service, and the post office—made a relatively smooth transition from confederation to federal government, in no small part because there was no immediate leadership change. This was particularly true for the army, where Henry Knox spent a decade as secretary of war, beginning under the Confederation Congress in 1785 and concluding on New Year's Eve 1794. Ebenezer Hazard supervised the post office, and while Washington was eager to remove him from the post, it was not until September 1789 that he replaced him with Samuel Osgood. Finally, Thomas Jefferson's service as minister to France postponed his installation as secretary of state, so much so that John Jay, who had served as secretary of foreign affairs since 1784, continued to supervise foreign relations until March 1790.

In sharp contrast, the Treasury Department was a hybrid creature of federal consolidation. The first Treasury employees had been state revenue officials. Scattered throughout the nation's ports, these men immediately recognized what was afoot, and before the first revenue legislation was passed, they were already scrambling to preserve their jobs. Meanwhile, Treasury Secretary Alexander Hamilton was busy assembling a central office staff, promoting the creation of a national bank, and eventually establishing a revenue cutter service (the precursor to the US Coast Guard) to intercept smugglers and enforce the collection of trade duties. Much as Hamilton might embrace these powers, he complained to one of his subordinates, William Heth, "What law could ever define the details of the duty of a Secretary of the Treasury? It is evident these must be an endless variety of things unexpressed which are incident to the nature of his station & which he is bound in duty to perform at the call of the President."[32]

Only one institution—the federal court system—was entirely new. Established through the Judiciary Act of 1789, at first glance this system—with its assertions of judicial independence—hardly constituted a federal agency. But for every federal district judge there was also a US attorney, a marshal, and court clerk who reported to the executive. The act also established the attorney general, who in the person of Edmund Randolph would become an important player in the Washington administration.

What remained were a series of diffuse institutions with highly specific roles (the census office, the patent office, etc.) and most importantly the two territorial governments (in addition the Northwest Territory, the cession by North Carolina of its western lands precipitated the creation of the Southwest Territory in 1790). Plans floated around the federal capital of New York in 1789 to create an additional federal department to preside over these myriad tasks, what Jefferson referred to as "a separate minister for the domestic business." When Congress balked at the prospect, considering it too expensive to create another administrative staff, these agencies all fell under the State Department.[33]

The brief, unsuccessful history of the ministry for domestic business serves as an important cautionary tale. Biographers of Thomas Jefferson have commented on the fact that his supervision of the patent office and the census reflected his abiding interests in natural and social sciences. But those agencies came under State Department supervision for wholly political and administrative reasons. And while Jefferson may have lamented the added workload that came with those agencies, the result was to reinforce the State Department as an administrative fiefdom on par with the diffuse responsibilities of the Treasury Department.

The essays that follow tell the story of individual agencies, but always as a means to grapple with larger questions in the history of state building. They are arranged to paint an overall picture of the federal government from the inside out, from the president's cabinet to foreign and federal relations. There are some noticeable omissions. Some governmental institutions are not discussed here but have received intensive study elsewhere: the post office, the diplomatic corps, the army and navy.[34]

Among the most common virtues attributed to George Washington was his creation of the cabinet structure. But as Lindsay Chervinsky shows, the heads of department in the Washington administration could hardly be called a "cabinet." To begin with, the road to cabinet government was incremental and in no way preordained. Indeed, Washington resisted the notion of gathering his agency heads and called no more than nine cabinet gatherings between his initial appointment and the spring of 1793. It was only in the context of highly specific foreign policy challenges that Washington created the cabinet of luminaries to participate in a series of productive policy-generating meetings. Cabinet meetings then became frequent to the fall of 1794. The Constitution says very little about how the president should seek advice. Chervinsky shows that Washington did not rely on either colonial or British precedent in his conceptualization of the cabinet but rather on his experiences as commander in chief during the War of Independence, when important decisions were often preceded by councils of war. Yet for all the benefits he associated with cabinet government, Washington became decreasingly reliant on it during his second term, reverting back to his earlier process of reaching policy conclusions on his own or in consultation with a single advisor. Although Washington used cabinet gatherings to seek information on precedent-setting decisions, his abandonment of this form of decision making means that the cabinet did not become institutionalized during his presidency.

The decisions made by the president and his department secretaries were implemented by a federal field service. Because the government did not begin to publish a roll of personnel until 1816, the composition and size of the early federal workforce was a cause of concern to contemporaries and has remained a puzzle to historians. Using records of appointment, Peter Kastor provides the first complete census of the federal bureaucracy under Washington. In a careful examination of appointments and deployment, he shows how selecting and assigning federal personnel would prove to be a dominant concern of the Washington administration, with the emphasis shifting dramatically in a manner that coincided with Washington's two terms in office. During the first term, Washington and his department heads focused on initial appointments, with nominations flooding the Senate for advice and consent as federal capacities expanded. The institutions of government stabilized during Washington's second term. Although turnover remained a challenge, the number of personnel did not undergo dramatic change. In terms of deployment and function, there is considerable continuity in the federal workforce. These agents of government could be found in three geographic locations: clustered along the Atlantic seaboard, in the federal territories out west, and, in much smaller numbers, in foreign ports. As Kastor succinctly puts it, "George Washington's workforce consisted primarily of men located in the East who helped produce the funds that paid men in the West."

The source of those funds was the impost, which would continue to provide the main and often sole source of federal tax revenue for most of the nineteenth century. Considering that Americans had recently fought a Revolution sparked in no small part by opposition to taxation, the creation of a productive revenue system was a major achievement. Gautham Rao discusses how Congress and the nation's first treasury secretary drew on both American and British precedent in designing the customs service. The impost had long been held up as the most suitable form of central taxation in the American union. Its inobtrusive mode of collection made it a form of taxation palatable to the American public who readily protested against federal excise and property taxes. Like Britain's Navigation Acts, the 1789 Revenue Act was designed to raise revenue, to discriminate against the trade of other nations, and to provide some protection for American manufactures. The organization of customs collections in the ports was also influenced by British precedent, although the immediate model was a Maryland collection act. The federal government also continued the colonial practice of negotiation and accommodation in administration. Rao shows that rather than a strict enforcement of centrally adopted policy, the application of the revenue laws was the result of a continuous negotiation between the merchant community and local collectors. Collectors knew that the legitimacy of the revenue regime depended on their ability to accommodate the economic interests of importing ship captains and merchants. At first reluctant to accept what seemed a lax application of the law, Hamilton gradually came round to the view of the collectors when he realized that local discretion ensured that the revenue laws were productive. Early US revenue administration was thus governed by pragmaticism and local discretion. But far from a sign that the federal government was dysfunctional, Rao concludes that these features were what made the system work.

British precedent, local discretion, and pragmatism are also central to Kate Brown's account of the role of federal judges in the administration of the customs. It is an accepted view that the judiciary was an institution that existed outside governance and functioned separately from the other branches. Yet as Brown shows, federal district courts not only adjudicated important questions of foreign policy, neutrality, and commerce but also assumed crucial administrative and regulatory roles. Rather than serving as a check on the other branches of government, the early federal courts in fact collaborated with them in the administration of the law. The supervision of commercial disputes that fell to the courts under the Remitting Act of 1790 drew on a long English tradition of judges acting as both adjudicators and administrators. As part of the need to make the revenue service appear legitimate, Congress introduced legislation that allowed merchants liable for a fine for having breached the revenue laws to petition a district judge for a remission of the fine. After a hearing, the facts were transmitted to the treasury secretary, who had legal discretion of remission. When Hamilton made his decision, it was therefore made on the basis of the fact finding of a district court judge. Brown argues that far from an anomaly, such interbranch "collaborative state building" was a defining feature of the early federal government that persisted well into the nineteenth century.

The actions of customs collectors and district court judges on the Eastern Seaboard collected the money that financed a federal presence in the western territories. Stephen Rockwell's essay outlines the challenges that the United States faced in its trans-Appalachian domain. Although ceded by the states to the union and formally organized by the Northwest Ordinance of 1787 and the Ordinance of 1790, or Southwest Ordinance, this region was nominally in the US national domain but in reality controlled by powerful American Indian nations and confederations. Establishing effective sovereignty in the West was one of the most pressing policy matters to the Washington administration. The means to this end were the Indian treaty that combined land cessions with recognition of Indian territorial claims, on the one hand, and Indian war, on the other hand. From 1789 to 1794, federal troops waged almost continuous war with various native confederacies. Rockwell uses that conflict to consider the circumstances that fuel state building, institutional capacity, and executive authority in the United States. In the process, the wars of 1789–94 become a point of departure to establish a conversation between historians and political scientists as well as between scholars of the early republic and those of the twentieth century. Rockwell demonstrates that many of the principles that scholars have developed to explain state building and institutional capacity during the twentieth and twenty-first centuries are equally applicable to the eighteenth. Conversely, the example of the eighteenth century calls into question the commonplace assumption that institutional behaviors are a result of modern institutional structures.

St. Clair's defeat of 1791 features prominently in Rockwell's discussion of the Washington administration and American state building. So it does in Andrew Fagal's history of the early federal program for arms procurement. The need for the new nation to be self-sufficient in the production of military arms was an important lesson that American statesmen took away from their experiences in the War of Independence. It was shared by leaders as different in outlook as Hamilton and Jefferson. Fagal shows how the Washington administration followed in the footsteps of European states in formulating and implementing a system for arms production that would secure the nation's defensive capacity by minimizing foreign dependence. The manufacture of military stores was a central element in both Washington's 1783 "Sentiments on a Peace Establishment" and in the report of the same year from a congressional committee on the peace establishment chaired by Hamilton. As treasury secretary under Washington, Hamilton would lay out the administration's plan to establish a government-run military industry in his *Report on Manufactures*. But it was events on the frontier that set its implementation in motion. In the wake of St. Clair's defeat, a congressional committee came to the conclusion that the War Department's reliance on private contractors, who had failed to provide adequate arms, was a major cause of the disaster. The result was the creation of the national armory system with government-run manufactures at Springfield, Massachusetts, and Harpers Ferry, Virginia. Today these armories are best remembered for their contribution to the development of technology, but as Fagal reminds us, they are equally significant for contributing to the realization of US national self-determination. The development of a system for arms production was intended to bolster the military capacity of the US Army in both frontier forts and coastal fortifications.

Daniel Hulsebosch investigates how the United States' interactions with foreign powers and Indian nations in the Atlantic marketplace and the western borderlands were shaped by the law of nations. To an extent not always realized, the success of the American state-building project depended on the recognition of US independence by foreign powers. After the Peace of Paris, British governmental agents and merchants reported back to the British cabinet that conditions in the United States cast doubt on whether or not the new nation should be considered a functioning state. On the other side, American merchants, diplomats and politicians were only too aware of the low esteem in which their nation was held. Rectifying this reputational damage required the creation of a central government that could ensure that the nation and its citizens would abide by the law of nations that governed interactions between so-called civilized nations. International recognition would result in tangible benefits like foreign investments, commercial treaties, and permanent diplomatic missions from leading European powers. The Federalists drafted and promoted the Constitution with this in mind, and their ensuing statecraft invoked the law of nations both at home and abroad to mute criticism and to claim recognition. But the Washington administration was not merely a rule taker but also innovated the law of nations. As Hulsebosch shows, American statesmen used the law of nations to develop claims for free trade on the oceans and for a monopoly on diplomatic and trade relations with indigenous people in the continental interior. In the hands of the American government, the law of nations became a means to allow the United States to pass as a "civilized" nation conforming to European rules of engagement while retaining its revolutionary legacy of republicanism.

In the final chapter, Max Edling turns from the federal executive to the legislature. The chapter begins by comparing congressional legislation under the Washington administration with legislation passed by the British Parliament in the same period. In the late eighteenth century Parliament was primarily concerned with meeting demands for landed property regulation, improved transportation, and the promotion of agriculture through enclosure. In addition to this domestic agenda of what the British historians of Parliament have called Britain's "reactive state," there was also a powerful "fiscal-military" machinery that needed legislative support. The legislative agenda of Congress is very different. In the 1790s, Congress passed virtually no legislation regulating property, improving transportation, or promoting agriculture. Instead, the federal legislature focused on taxation, public finance, the military, shipping and international trade, intraunion affairs, and the administration of the western lands. In other words, Congress focused on tasks that correspond to the activities of the "fiscal-military" side of the British state, but it did little in areas that correspond to the activities of Britain's "reactive state." Yet it would be a mistake to conclude that in the United States there was no governmental direction of social and economic life. In the American union the domestic, "reactive," agenda of Parliament was pursued by the state assemblies and not Congress. Analysis of the legislation passed by the Pennsylvania state assembly in the 1790s shows the state legislature to be busy regulating society, promoting the economy, and developing transportation infrastructure in a manner that is similar to that of the British Parliament. Edling therefore concludes that "whereas the fiscal-military and the reactive state were merged in the same government in Britain, in the United States they existed at different levels of the federal structure. Congress was central to the American fiscal-military state. The General Assembly of Pennsylvania was central to the American reactive state." His study of legislative activity thereby serves as an important reminder that a full investigation of the American state in the era of Washington cannot be restricted to the federal level alone but has to take into consideration also institutions and activities at the state and local level.

These essays contain references to some of the political and diplomatic touchpoints of the 1790s (Jefferson's pursuit of international diplomatic recognition, Hamilton's *Report on Manufactures*, the Battle of Fallen Timbers, and the Treaty of Greenville). But those events are points of departure for considering how the federal structure came into being. And this is no celebratory account of federal success, nor is it an account of boundless visions of state capacity. To the contrary, this volume keeps state building located in its own time, with a vision of federal capacity bound by the ideas and organizational capacities of the late eighteenth century.

And that returns us to Washington's conundrums in 1792: how to build and manage a state apparatus effectively and how to assess public reaction. These difficulties are as old as the republic. But it fell to the Washington administration to first consider how best to respond within the structure of the US Constitution. In the pages that follow, we consider how a broad set of Americans sought to build a federal state and how those around them responded. While Washington often assumes center stage, he never stands alone. He is surrounded by men and women of varied status and multiple backgrounds. All of them asked how a federal government would operate, for all of them knew how much was at stake.

Notes

1. George Washington to Alexander Hamilton, 29 July 1792, *The Papers of George Washington: Digital Edition*, Presidential Series, ed. Dorothy Twohig, W. W. Abbot, and Philander D. Chase (Charlottesville: University of Virginia Press, 2008–), 10:588.

2. For examples of work on political culture during the 1790s, see Todd Estes, *The Jay Treaty Debate, Public Opinion, and the Evolution of Early American Political Culture* (Amherst: University of Massachusetts Press, 2006); Joanne B. Freeman,

Affairs of Honor: National Politics in the New Republic (New Haven, CT: Yale University Press, 2002); Nathaniel C. Green, "'The Focus of the Wills of Converging Millions': Public Opposition to the Jay Treaty and the Origins of the People's Presidency," *Journal of the Early Republic* 37, no. 3 (Fall 2017): 429–69; Sandra Moats, *Celebrating the Republic: Presidential Ceremony and Popular Sovereignty, from Washington to Monroe* (DeKalb: Northern Illinois University Press, 2010); Jeffrey L. Pasley, *The Tyranny of Printers: Newspaper Politics in the Early American Republic* (Charlottesville: University of Virginia Press, 2001); Jeffrey L. Pasley, *The First Presidential Contest: 1796 and the Founding of American Democracy* (Lawrence: University Press of Kansas); David Waldstreicher, *In the Midst of Perpetual Fetes: The Making of American Nationalism, 1776–1820* (Chapel Hill: University of North Carolina Press, 1997).

3. For examples of the qualitative methods deployed in some of the best work on early federal state building, see Brian Balogh, *A Government Out of Sight: The Mystery of National Authority in Nineteenth-Century America* (Cambridge: Cambridge University Press, 2009); Max M. Edling, *A Revolution in Favor of Government: Origins of the U.S. Constitution and the Making of the American State* (New York: Oxford University Press, 2003); Richard R. John, *Spreading the News: The American Postal System from Franklin to Morse* (Cambridge, MA: Harvard University Press, 1995); Jerry L. Mashaw, "Recovering American Administrative Law: Federalist Foundations, 1787–1801," *Yale Law Journal* 115, no. 6 (2006): 1256–1344; Gautham Rao, *National Duties: Custom Houses and the Making of the American State* (Chicago: University of Chicago Press, 2016).

4. Leonard Dupee White, *The Federalists: A Study in Administrative History* (New York: Macmillan, 1948); Leonard Dupee White, *The Jeffersonians: A Study in Administrative History 1801–1829* (New York: Macmillan, 1951); Leonard Dupee White, *The Jacksonians: A Study in Administrative History, 1829–1861* (New York: Macmillan, 1954). White's other scholarship provides a sampling of trajectory. See Leonard Dupee White, *The City Manager* (Chicago: University of Chicago Press, 1927); Leonard Dupee White, *Government Career Service* (Chicago: University of Chicago Press, 1935); Leonard Dupee White, *Introduction to the Study of Public Administration* (New York: Macmillan, 1939).

5. John M. Murrin, "The Great Inversion, or Court versus Country: A Comparison of the Revolutionary Settlements in England (1688–1721) and America (1776–1816)," in *Three British Revolutions: 1640, 1688, 1776*, ed. J. G. A. Pocock (Princeton, NJ: Princeton University Press, 1980), 425; Stephen Skowronek, *Building a New American State: The Expansion of National Administrative Capacities, 1877–1920* (Cambridge: Cambridge University Press, 1982). In a similar vein Richard Bensel claimed that the federal government "was not a directive force in social affairs." Richard Bensel, *Yankee Leviathan: The Origins of State Authority in America, 1859–1877* (Cambridge: Cambridge University Press, 1990), ix. For an analysis of how the post–Second World War intellectual climate encouraged scholars to turn away from the state, see David Ciepley, "Why the State Was Dropped in the First Place: A Prequel to Skocpol's 'Bringing the State Back In,'" *Critical Review* 14, nos. 2–3 (2000): 157–213.

6. Brian Balogh, "The State of the State among Historians," *Social Science History* 27, no. 3 (2003): 455–63; Peter B. Evans, Dietrich Rueschemeyer, and Theda Skocpol, eds., *Bringing the State Back In* (Cambridge: Cambridge University Press, 1985); Stuart S. Nagel, *The Substance of Public Policy* (Commack, NY: Nova Science,

1999); Julian E. Zelizer, *Governing America : The Revival of Political History* (Princeton, NJ: Princeton University Press, 2012).

7. John, *Spreading the News;* Richard R. John, "Governmental Institutions as Agents of Change: Rethinking American Political Development in the Early Republic, 1787–1835," *Studies in American Political Development* 11, no. 2 (Fall 1997): 347–80.

8. Balogh, *A Government Out of Sight;* Balogh, "The State of the State among Historians."

9. For the international turn see Peter S. Onuf, "A Declaration of Independence for Diplomatic Historians," *Diplomatic History* 22, no 1 (Winter 1998): 71–83; Ira Katznelson and Martin Schefter, eds., *Shaped by War and Trade: International Influences on American Political Development* (Princeton, NJ: Princeton University Press, 2002); David Hendrickson, *Peace Pact: The Lost World of the American Founding* (Lawrence: University Press of Kansas, 2003); Bernard Bailyn, *Atlantic History: Concepts and Contours* (Cambridge, MA: Harvard University Press, 2005); Thomas Bender, *A Nation among Nations: America's Place in World History* (New York: Hill and Wang, 2006); Jack P. Greene, "Colonial History and National History: Reflections on a Continuing Problem," *William and Mary Quarterly,* 3rd. ser., 64, no. 2 (April 2007): 235–50; David Armitage, *The Declaration of Independence: A Global History* (Cambridge, MA: Harvard University Press, 2007); David M. Golove and Daniel J. Hulsebosch, "A Civilized Nation: The Early American Constitution, the Law of Nations, and the Pursuit of International Recognition," *New York University Law Review* 85 (2010): 101–228. Recent attempts to analyze the nature of the federal government in light of the international turn and its significance in shaping the course of early American history are Andrew Shankman, "Toward a Social History of Federalism: The State and Capitalism to and from the American Revolution," *Journal of the Early Republic* 47, no. 4 (Winter 2017): 615–53; Max M. Edling, "'A Mongrel Kind of Government': The U.S. Constitution, the Federal Union, and the Origins of the American State," in Peter Thompson and Peter S. Onuf, eds., *State and Citizen: British America and the Early United States* (Charlottesville: University of Virginia Press, 2013), 150–77; Max M. Edling, "Peace Pact and Nation: An International Interpretation of the Constitution of the United States," *Past and Present* 240 (August 2018): 267–303.

10. Thomas Rodney to Hamilton, 10 February 1791, *The Papers of Alexander Hamilton: Digital Edition,* ed. edited by Harold C. Syrett (Charlottesville: University of Virginia Press, 2011), 8:21; Thomas Jefferson, Note of Agenda to Reduce the Government to True Principles, ca. 11 July 1792, *The Papers of Thomas Jefferson: Digital Edition,* Main Series, ed. Barbara B. Oberg et al.(Charlottesville: University of Virginia Press, 2008), 24:215.

11. William D. Adler, "State Capacity and Bureaucratic Autonomy in the Early United States: The Case of the Army Corps of Topographical Engineers," *Studies in American Political Development* 26, no. 2 (October 2012): 107–24; David F. Ericson, "The Federal Government and Slavery: Following the Money Trail," *Studies in American Political Development* 19, no. 1 (April 2005), 105–16; Karen Orren, "'A War between Officers': The Enforcement of Slavery in the Northern United States, and of the Republic for Which It Stands, before the Civil War," *Studies in American Political Development* 12, no. 2 (October 1998): 343–82; Eric Lomazoff, "Turning (into) 'The Great Regulating Wheel': The Conversion of the Bank of the United States,

1791–1811," *Studies in American Political Development* 26, no. 1 (April 2012): 1–23; Johann N. Neem, "Developing Freedom: Thomas Jefferson, the State, and Human Capability," *Studies in American Political Development* 27, no. 1 (April 2013): 1–15.

12. "American Indians and the History of U.S. Foreign Relations," *Diplomatic History* 39, no. 5 (November 2015), 926–66.

13. Ariel Ron and Gautham Rao, "Introduction: Taking Stock of the State in Nineteenth-Century America," *Journal of the Early Republic* 38, no. 1 (Spring 2018): 61–66; Hannah Farber, "State-Building after War's End: A Government Financier Adjusts His Portfolio for Peace," ibid., 67–76; Ryan A. Quintana, "Slavery and the Conceptual History of the Early U.S. State," ibid, 77–86; Rachel St. John, "State Power in the West in the Early American Republic," ibid., 87–94; Stephen Skowronek, "Present at the Creation: The State in Early American Political History," ibid., 95–103; Richard R. John, "The State *Is* Back In: What Now?," ibid., 104–18; Gautham Rao, "The New Historiography of the Early Federal Government: Institutions, Contexts, and the Imperial State," *William and Mary Quarterly*, 3rd. ser., 77, no. 1 (January 2020): 97–128.

14. These works include Katznelson and Shefter, *Shaped by War and Trade;* Stefan Heumann, "The Tutelary Empire: State- and Nation-Building in the 19th-Century United States" (PhD diss., University of Pennsylvania, 2009); Stephen J. Rockwell, *Indian Affairs and the Administrative State in the Nineteenth Century* (Cambridge: Cambridge University Press, 2010); William H. Bergmann, *The American National State and the Early West* (Cambridge: Cambridge University Press, 2012); Max M. Edling, *A Hercules in the Cradle: War, Money, and the American State, 1783–1867* (Chicago: University of Chicago Press, 2014); Bethel Saler, *The Settlers' Empire: Colonialism and State Formation in America's Old Northwest* (Philadelphia: University of Pennsylvania Press, 2014); Rao, *National Duties*, 25, n. 21; Paul Frymer, *Building an American Empire: The Era of Territorial and Political Expansion* (Princeton, NJ: Princeton University Press, 2017). Yet in his recent overview on literature on the American state in the early republic, Richard John notes that there are still many gaps to fill, among which he lists "the social background of government officers; the output of federal and state legislatures; corruption; the tariff; government printing; the management of intellectual property; economic regulation, especially at the state and municipal levels; and government-financed scientific projects—for example, state geological surveys" as well as central governmental departments such as the treasury. See John, "The State *Is* Back In," 117.

15. The most recent survey of the so-called critical period between the Peace of Paris and the establishment of the federal government is George William Van Cleve, *We Have Not a Government: The Articles of Confederation and the Road to the Constitution* (Chicago: University of Chicago Press, 2017). Jack N. Rakove, *The Beginnings of National Politics: An Interpretative History of the Continental Congress* (New York: Knopf, 1979), is essential reading for what was taking place in Congress in this period.

16. Edling, *Revolution in Favor of Government.*

17. "From George Washington to the States, 8 June, 1783," Founders Online, National Archives, http://founders.archives.gov/documents/Washington/99-01-02 -11404.

18. Ibid.

19. E. James Ferguson, *The Power of the Purse: A History of American Political Finance, 1776–1790* (Chapel Hill: University of North Carolina Press, 1961); Robert A. Becker, *Revolution, Reform, and the Politics of American Taxation, 1763–1783* (Baton Rouge: Louisiana State University Press, 1980); Roger H. Brown, *Redeeming the Republic: Federalists, Taxation, and the Origins of the Constitution* (Baltimore: Johns Hopkins University Press, 1993); Edwin J. Perkins, *American Public Finance and Financial Services, 1700–1815* (Columbus: Ohio State University Press, 1994); Stephen Mihm, "Funding the Revolution: Monetary and Fiscal Policy in Eighteenth-Century America," in *The Oxford Handbook of the American Revolution,* ed. Edward G. Gray and Jane Kamensky (New York: Oxford University Press, 2012), 327–51; Edling, *Hercules in the Cradle,* ch. 2.

20. Alexander Hamilton, "Federalist 30," in *The Federalist,* ed. Jacob E. Cooke (Middletown, CT: Wesleyan University Press, 1961), 192; Hamilton, "Defence of the Funding System," in *Papers of Alexander Hamilton,* 19:60.

21. Woody Holton, *Forced Founders: Indians, Debtors, Slaves, and the Making of the American Revolution in Virginia* (Chapel Hill: University of North Carolina Press, 1999); Gregory H. Nobles, *American Frontiers: Cultural Encounters and Continental Conquest* (New York: Hill and Wang, 1997); Alan Taylor, *American Revolutions: A Continental History, 1750–1804* (New York: W. W. Norton, 2016). For a comparative analysis showing how white supremacy, or a privileged status of "Creoles" relative to indigenous peoples, the enslaved, and "non-whites," was a central concern in all American independence struggles, see Joshua Simon, *The Ideology of Creole Revolution: Imperialism and Independence in American and Latin American Political Thought* (Cambridge: Cambridge University Press, 2017). An excellent overview of how the federal government managed the racial composition of the United States in the nineteenth century is Frymer, *Building an American Empire.*

22. Richard White, *The Middle Ground: Indians, Empires, and Republics in the Great Lakes Region, 1650–1815* (Cambridge: Cambridge University Press, 1991); Taylor, *American Revolutions;* Jeffrey Ostler, *Surviving Genocide: Native Nations and the United States from the American Revolution to Bleeding Kansas* (New Haven, CT: Yale University Press, 2019).

23. François Furstenberg, *In the Name of the Father: Washington's Legacy, Slavery, and the Making of a Nation* (New York: Penguin, 2006).

24. Sally E. Hadden, *Slave Patrol: Law and Violence in Virginia and the Carolinas* (Cambridge, MA: Harvard University Press, 2003); Christopher Tomlins, *Freedom Bound: Law, Labor and Civic Identity in Colonizing English America, 1580–1865* (Cambridge: Cambridge University Press, 2010); Gautham Rao, "The State the Slaveholders Made: Regulating Fugitive Slaves in the Early Republic," in *Freedom's Conditions in the U.S.-Canadian Borderlands in the Age of Emancipation,* ed. Tony Freyer and Lyndsay Campbell (Durham, NC: Carolina Academic, 2011), 85–108.

25. On the Constitution and Native Americans, see Leonard J. Sadosky, *Revolutionary Negotiations: Indians, Empires, and Diplomats in the Founding of America* (Charlottesville: University of Virginia Press, 2009), 119–47; Gregory Ablavsky, "The Savage Constitution," *Duke Law Journal* 63, no. 5 (February 2014): 999–1090. Many historians now argue that the Constitutional Convention guaranteed slavery by making the institution a state concern protected from interference from the federal government on the one hand and by providing guarantees for the continuation

of the slave trade and the apprehension of fugitives from slavery on the other hand. See most recently David Waldstreicher, *Slavery's Constitution: From Revolution to Ratification* (New York: Hill and Wang, 2009), 57–105; George William Van Cleve, *A Slaveholders' Union: Slavery, Politics, and the Constitution in the Early American Republic* (Chicago: University of Chicago Press, 2011), 103–83. Among legal historians Paul Finkelman has consistently argued for the importance of slavery in the Constitution, for example in "Slavery and the Constitutional Convention: Making a Covenant with Death," in *Beyond Confederation: Origins of the Constitution and American National Identity,* ed. Richard Beeman, Stephen Botein and Edward C. Carter II (Chapel Hill: University of North Carolina Press, 1987), 188–225. In the progressive tradition, Staughton Lynd was unusual in stressing the role of slavery in the making of the Constitution. His essays on the topic are collected in his *Class Conflict, Slavery, and the United States Constitution* (Indianapolis: Bobbs-Merrill,1967), 135–213.

26. On the federal government's interaction with slavery, see Don E. Fehrenbacher, *The Slaveholding Republic: An Account of the United States Government's Relations to Slavery* (Oxford: Oxford University Press, 2001), and David F. Ericson, *Slavery in the American Republic: Developing the Federal Government, 1791–1861* (Lawrence: University Press of Kansas, 2011).

27. Peter S. Onuf, "Liberty, Development, and Union: Visions of the West in the 1780s," *William and Mary Quarterly,* 3rd. ser., 43, no. 2 (1986): 179–213; Peter S. Onuf, *Statehood and Union: A History of the Northwest Ordinance* (Bloomington: Indiana University Press, 1987); Saler, *Settlers' Empire.*

28. Andrew R. L. Cayton, *The Frontier Republic: Ideology and Politics in the Ohio Country, 1780–1825* (Kent, OH: Kent State University Press, 1986); Andrew R. L. Cayton, *Frontier Indiana* (Bloomington: Indiana University Press, 1996); Peter J. Kastor, *The Nation's Crucible: The Louisiana Purchase and the Creation of America* (New Haven, CT: Yale University Press, 2004); Rockwell, *Indian Affairs and the Administrative State;* Walter L. Hixson, *American Settler Colonialism: A History* (New York: Palgrave Macmillan, 2013); Ablavsky, "Savage Constitution," 999–1088; Bergmann, *American National State;* Saler, *Settlers' Empire;* Ostler, *Surviving Genocide;* Rao, "New Historiography," 116–28.

29. John J. McCusker, "Estimating Early American Gross Domestic Product," *Historical Methods* 33, no. 3 (2000): 155–62.

30. John Holroyd, Earl of Sheffield, *Observations on the Commerce of the American States with Europe and the West Indies* (London: J. Debrett, 1783), 68.

31. Benjamin Franklin to Robert R. Livingston, July 22[–26], 1783, in *Papers of Benjamin Franklin,* ed. Ellen R. Cohn et al., vol. 40 (New Haven, CT: Yale University Press, 2011), 369.

32. Alexander Hamilton to William Heth, 23 June 1791, *Papers of Alexander Hamilton,* 8.

33. Thomas Jefferson to William Barton, 12 August 1790, *Papers of Thomas Jefferson: Digital Edition,* 17. The editors of *The Papers of Thomas Jefferson* chronicled the details of this issue in a lengthy editorial note following this letter.

34. John, *Spreading the News;* Jean Ann Bauer, "Republicans of Letters: The Early American Foreign Service as Information Network, 1775–1825" (PhD diss., University of Virginia, 2015); Francis Paul Prucha, *The Sword of the Republic: The United States Army on the Frontier* (New York: Macmillan, 1968); Richard H. Kohn, *Eagle and Sword: The Federalists and the Creation of the Military Establishment in America,*

1783–1802 (New York: Free Press, 1975); William B. Skelton, "Social Roots of the American Military Profession: The Officer Corps of America's First Peacetime Army, 1784–1789," *Journal of Military History* 54, no. 4 (1990): 435–52; William B. Skelton, *An American Profession of Arms: The Army Officer Corps, 1784–1815* (Lawrence: University Press of Kansas, 1992); Robert Wooster, *American Military Frontiers: The United States Army in the West, 1783–1900* (Albuquerque: University of New Mexico Press, 2009); Harold Sprout and Margaret Sprout, *The Rise of American Naval Power, 1776–1918* (Princeton, NJ: Princeton University Press, 1939); K. Jack Bauer, "Naval Shipbuilding Programs 1794–1860," *Military Affairs* 29, no. 1 (Spring 1965): 29–40; Howard P. Nash Jr., *The Forgotten Wars: The Role of the U.S. Navy in the Quasi War with France and the Barbary Wars 1798–1805* (South Brunswick, NJ: A. S. Barnes, 1968); David F. Long, *Gold Braid and Foreign Relations: Diplomatic Activities of Naval Officers, 1789–1883* (Annapolis, MD: Naval Institute Press, 1988); Kenneth J. Hagan, *This People's Navy: The Making of American Sea Power* (New York: Free Press, 1991), 21–160; Christopher McKee, *A Gentlemanly and Honorable Profession: The Creation of the U.S. Naval Officer Corps, 1794–1815* (Annapolis: Naval Institute Press, 1991); George Daughan, *If by Sea: The Forging of the American Navy—from the American Revolution to the War of 1812* (New York: Basic Books, 2008).

George Washington and the Cabinet

The Unlikely Development
of an Unintended Institution

LINDSAY M. CHERVINSKY

By the end of President George Washington's administration, the cabinet played a central, established role in the executive branch. Nearly every biography of Washington or study of his administration focuses on cabinet interactions as an integral part of his presidency. Yet despite its eventual position as a visible presidential governing tool, the cabinet's origins remain obscure. The Constitution contains no provision for the cabinet, and since 1789 Congress has passed no additional legislation to create an established executive advisory body. The constitutional omission was intentional. The delegates to the Constitutional Convention explicitly rejected all proposals for an advisory body, and they did not intend to provide the president with the power to create a cabinet of his choosing. After his inauguration, Washington strictly followed the constitutional guidelines contained in Article II, Section 2: he requested written advice from the department secretaries and consulted with the Senate on foreign affairs.

Washington quickly discovered, however, that the constitutional provisions were insufficient. Over the next few years, from 1790 to 1793, Washington increasingly favored individual consultations with his department secretaries. Washington convened a handful of cabinet meetings in 1791 and 1792. But the cabinet as we know it—an advisory body that meets and supports the president as a group—did not existing during the entirety of Washington's first term. The cabinet did not cement its integral role in the administration until 1793, and it took an event as important as the Neutrality Crisis to bring the cabinet into existence.

In the wake of the Neutrality Crisis, Washington established cabinet practices that best suited his needs. He summoned cabinet meetings when he required advice on diplomatic or constitutional issues that required him to establish precedent for the new nation. Accordingly, Washington called cabinet meetings to define neutrality policy in 1793, to determine the federal response to the Whiskey Rebellion in 1794, and to discuss whether to assert executive privilege in response to a congressional inquiry in March 1796. At the same time, he continued to meet with secretaries individually to discuss most domestic issues or departmental administration. In the final years of his administration, Washington continued to treat the cabinet as a personal advisory body to use, or not, as he saw fit. From 1795 to 1797, cabinet meetings declined as the administration faced fewer precedent-setting challenges and the more experienced Washington felt comfortable processing department business with the individual secretaries. Additionally, as Washington's original secretaries retired or resigned, their replacements failed to meet his expectations. Washington turned away from cabinet meetings because he no longer trusted the secretaries and preferred to consult loyal advisors outside of the cabinet.

The organic nature of cabinet development helps to explain why it lingers in the peripheries of scholarship on the early republic. Unlike the branches of government or the executive departments, the cabinet does not trace its origin to the Constitution or legislation.[1] Scholars observe the tense cabinet meetings of 1793 and assume that Hamilton and Jefferson interacted within the same institutional structure in 1790. Washington did not enter the presidency intending to create a cabinet. He did not even summon a cabinet meeting until the end of 1791. In fact, cabinet practice did not crystallize until spring of 1793 during the Neutrality Crisis. Instead, Washington methodically worked toward cabinet development in order to cope with the domestic and international demands of governing the United States. No further legislation ever codified the cabinet as an integral part of the executive branch. Instead, Washington's cabinet practices provided a strong precedent that his successors largely followed.[2]

The creation of the cabinet shapes how we study the rest of Washington's presidency. The cabinet's delayed emergence in 1793 requires us to reconsider Washington's interactions with the department secretaries in the early years of his administration. Washington's personal consultations with each secretary also take on more importance when we appreciate that he reserved cabinet meetings for issues of precedent or constitutional and diplomatic crises. Washington and an individual secretary handled the majority of departmental business. Finally, Washington's move away from the cabinet in the last years of his presidency shaped the precedent he left for his successors. Washington treated the cabinet as a personal advisory body to use when it suited his needs rather than an entrenched, institutionalized part of the executive branch. As a result, Washington's successors crafted their own relationships with the department secretaries and their advisors of choice.

Colonial History of the Executive Departments

Although Washington created a new type of advisory body when he adopted the cabinet in 1793, the executive departments had emerged to serve an important administrative role in the previous two decades. When Washington gathered the department secretaries to provide counsel, he broke with the administrative tradition established during the Revolutionary War. In the 1770s and 1780s, the Continental Congress had gradually adopted executive departments to meet the demands of waging the Revolutionary War and coordinating efforts between the thirteen states. Individually led departments solidified under the Confederation Congress, and the first federal Congress finalized the professionalization of executive government in the summer of 1789 when it passed legislation to create the War, Treasury, and State Departments. The evolution of the executive departments during the Revolutionary War suggested that the department secretaries would function as agency heads, not personal advisors to the president. Debates in the Constitutional Convention and the first federal Congress confirmed this interpretation.

After the Continental Congress gathered in Philadelphia on September 4, 1774, the delegates initially relied on committees for executive business. The delegates created committees to handle specific tasks, such as a committee to draft a statement of the rights of the colonies and a response to recent infringements upon those rights by the British government. These committees dissolved as soon as they completed their assigned task. In May 1780, Congress began the process of creating specialized departments. The delegates approved the first secretary position, the foreign affairs secretary, on January 10, 1781. On February 6, they approved additional secretary positions for the War, Marine, and Treasury Departments. On October 30, 1781, Congress filled the last of these positions when it elected General Benjamin Lincoln to be the secretary of the Department of War.[3]

The heads of the departments did not serve an advisory role during the Revolutionary War or the confederation period. The president of Congress wielded very little executive power and primarily oversaw congressional sessions. The department secretaries never gathered in any type of cabinet or council to advise the president of Congress. Instead, the secretaries operated as agency heads and administered the affairs of their departments, consulted with each other, and reported back to Congress when it was in session.[4]

The debates in the Constitutional Convention demonstrate that the delegates expected that the department secretaries would continue to operate as agency heads. Members of the convention did not intend for the department secretaries to gather in cabinet meetings to advise the president. Many of the delegates assumed at the beginning of the Constitutional Convention that the new Constitution would include some sort of council instead. In the 1780s, most states adopted constitutions that provided a council of state to advise (and often check) the governor. Unlike Washington's future cabinet, the state legislature appointed the councilors, and the governor was often required to obtain the council's approval before adopting policy. Additionally, the Anglo-American political tradition informed the delegates' assumptions. The British government included both a Privy Council and a cabinet council. The Privy Council was the larger, more formal body, composed of all the king's ministers. Because of its large size, political divisions frequently beset the Privy Council and prevented efficient governing. As a result, the king usually formed the cabinet council—a smaller, more intimate advisory group of his favorite ministers. Although no formal arrangements codified the cabinet council, both the British and American public knew of its existence and influence with the king.[5] As the delegates discussed councils and cabals in the convention, they kept these British examples in mind.

The initial proposals presented at the Constitutional Convention included various councils that would advise and assist the executive. The Virginia Plan, written by James Madison and presented by Edmund Randolph on May 29, 1787, included a council of revision. Madison had served on the Virginia Council of State from 1778 to 1780, and Randolph had worked closely with the council during his gubernatorial tenure (1786–88). The justices of the Supreme Court would sit on the proposed council of revision and would examine legislation and partner with the executive to check the power of the national legislature. On May 29, Charles Pinckney proposed a plan that also included a council of revision as well as an advisory council. Pinckney's plan authorized the president to create his own advisory council with the heads of the future departments.[6] In early August 1787, the Committee of Detail rejected the council of revision to prevent a similarly binding council from the proposed executive branch.

Charles Pinckney envisioned a different type of council than the council of revision rejected by the Committee of Detail or the Council of State in Virginia. His council included the president, the chief justice of the Supreme Court, the heads of the departments nominated by the president, and the president's personal secretary. The president was free to request advice at his leisure, however, and was not bound to follow the council's recommendation. Pinckney wanted to include a council in the Constitution to protect transparency at the federal level, not to limit the executive. He believed that by defining the council, each advisor would be required to take responsibility for his own advice, and the president could not hide behind the council.[7] The Committee of Detail continued to meet more or less regularly until the end of August and rejected Pinckney's proposal in one of its meetings.

The delegates omitted every version of a council from the final draft of the Constitution. They rejected George Mason's version of the council that would have imposed limitations on the executive similar to those that restricted the state governors. The delegates rejected a council of revision that would have aided the president to review and enforce legislation. Most importantly, the convention opposed Pinckney's proposed council, which strongly resembled the cabinet Washington gathered for the first time in November 1791.

Washington carefully followed the debates in the Constitutional Convention. As president of the Constitutional Convention, Washington attended every session and personally observed the progress of the cabinet throughout the course of the debates. After the end of the workday, Washington attended the theater, ate meals and drank tea with his friends, visited former army officers, and listened to music events with the best families in Philadelphia. The other delegates joined Washington at these events and used the social gatherings to discuss their positions on articles of the Constitution in a more private, informal setting. Washington left Philadelphia with a clear understanding of the delegates' rejection of a cabinet.

The Beginning of Washington's Presidency

Washington did not enter the presidency intending to create a cabinet. He planned to utilize the two options outlined in Article II, Section 2, of the Constitution: he visited the Senate to discuss foreign affairs and requested written advice from the department secretaries.[8] However, Washington discovered that these options were inadequate to respond to the pressures of governing and searched for additional methods of support. From 1790 to 1793, Washington slowly and deliberately increased interpersonal interaction with his secretaries and moved toward the creation of the cabinet. He convened the first cabinet meeting on November 26, 1791, but did not call frequent cabinet meetings until April 1793 when he embraced the cabinet as a central component of the executive branch.

Washington's August 1789 visit to the Senate demonstrated that he did not expect the department secretaries to serve as his primary advisors on foreign policy and treaties. Instead, he expected the Senate to provide prompt advice on such issues. On September 15, 1789, American commissioners planned to meet with representatives from North Carolina, the Cherokees, and the Creeks to negotiate a new treaty. After the end of the Revolutionary War, the Confederation Congress worked to establish peaceful relationships with Native American tribes that previously allied with Great Britain. By April 1789, the United States had signed treaties with the Wyandots, Delaware, Ottawa, Oneida, Cherokees, Choctaws, and Chickasaws, but relationships with the Creeks and Cherokees remained tense.[9] Washington needed to appoint commissioners and issue instructions for the upcoming summit. Following constitutional guidelines, Washington sought advice from the Senate about how he should direct the commissioners. On May 25, 1789, Washington submitted to the Senate all existing treaties with the Native American nations and relevant supporting documents in preparation for the meeting.[10]

Washington recognized that the first time he exercised his right to consult with the Senate would potentially set precedent for the rest of his administration and his successors'. Given these concerns, he initiated his first visit with caution. Both Washington and the Senate expected that their meetings laid the groundwork for the Senate to serve as the president's council of foreign affairs. In early August, the Senate created a committee to meet with Washington and his secretaries. The committee planned each detail of Washington's upcoming visit: they decided how Washington would enter the chamber, where he would sit, where the vice president would sit, and how the senators would address both the vice president and the president when both were present in the same space.[11] On August 20, Washington nominated commissioners to negotiate with the "southern" Indians and announced his upcoming visit in an official note on August 21.[12] When Washington arrived on the morning of August 22, he believed that he had provided all of the necessary information and expected the senators to be prepared to offer prompt advice.

On August 22, 1789, Washington and his secretary of war, Henry Knox, arrived at the senate chambers at eleven thirty in the morning. After the formal introductions, Washington handed Vice President John Adams a prepared speech. The speech offered a synopsis of the current diplomatic relationship between the United States, the Creeks, and the Cherokees and then posed a series of yes or no questions. John Adams quickly read through Washington's statement, but few senators heard the content of the speech. The Senate chambers occupied the ground floor of Federal Hall—located on one of the busiest corners of Wall Street. New York City sweltered in the customary August heat, and the doorkeeper had opened the windows in search of a faint breeze. As a result, all of the noise from the pedestrians, carriages, and horses from the street flowed into the room through the open windows. The clamor completely overpowered Adams's soft speaking voice. After a few complaints, Adams ordered the windows closed and repeated the speech.[13]

After the second reading, the chamber fell silent. A few senators awkwardly shuffled their papers or cleared their throats. William Maclay believed that Washington's presence intimidated his colleagues into silence. Always on the lookout for a conspiracy against the legislature, Maclay thought that if someone did not speak up, "these advices and consents [would be] ravish'd in a degree from us." Maclay shouldered the responsibility of defending the Senate's constitutional rights, stood up, and delivered a dramatic speech. He asserted that the treaties and the business between the Indians and the United States were new to the Senate—a bit of a disingenuous claim given Washington's efforts to provide the Senate with information prior to his arrival. Maclay requested a postponement of all questions until Monday and further suggested that all of the papers be referred to committee for a thorough examination before the Senate offered a recommendation. Washington lost his temper and shouted, "This defeats every purpose of my coming here!" Washington protested that he brought Knox to answer any questions and provide any necessary information. Washington objected that the delay would prevent him from taking further action but eventually acquiesced to returning a few days later.[14] Washington did return the following Monday, but the damage was done. On the way out of the building, Washington swore he would never return to the Senate for advice, and he kept his word.

Scholars have long recognized the importance of Washington's visit to the Senate, but they have usually utilized this dramatic moment to convey the widespread anxiety among public officials about republican virtue and constitutionalism. August 22, 1789, also proved to be a turning point in Washington's pursuit of advice and support.

Washington approached governing with a militaristic efficiency. He left the Senate chambers convinced that the Senate was too large and cumbersome to provide the meaningful, prompt advice he required. Washington believed that he had provided the Senate all of the information necessary to understand the diplomatic relationship between the United States and the Creeks and Cherokees and that he had done so in a timely manner. Furthermore, as the former secretary of war under the Confederation Congress, Knox possessed more knowledge about Indian affairs than almost any other American. Washington hoped that the Senate would take the opportunity to question Knox and then respond to the questions posed in the statement. As Washington developed his presidential leadership style, he sought the most efficient methods. The Senate's inability to provide ready advice convinced Washington that senators would not serve as suitable advisors in pressing diplomatic exchanges.

While navigating a new relationship with the Senate, Washington also initiated written correspondence with the department secretaries as suggested by Article II, Section 2, of the Constitution. Almost immediately after his inauguration on April 30, 1789, Washington exercised his right to request written advice. Before Congress created the new executive departments, Washington consulted with the acting secretaries of the leftover Confederation Congress. On May 9, 1789, Washington wrote to Henry Knox requesting a written report on the business of the War Department, and on June 9, 1789, he sent a similar letter to John Jay regarding the Office for Foreign Affairs.[15] For the next several months, Washington conducted the majority of executive branch business through letters. He solicited advice from the department secretaries, approved proposals, and issued orders all through written correspondence.[16]

Scholars have used these letters to piece together the behind-the-scenes activities of Washington's policy decisions. But these letters also shed light on Washington's method of governing. By corresponding with his department heads rather than meeting with them, Washington demonstrated the type of governance he believed to be most compatible with the Constitution.

As Washington's governing challenges grew, he sought additional support beyond the Senate and written advice. At first, he started with a small adjustment. On January 20, 1790, Henry Knox sent Washington an updated plan to organize the state militias and arranged to visit the president the following morning to receive further instructions. Knox arrived at Washington's house at nine in the morning. They discussed and amended the militia plans, which Washington then submitted to Congress.[17] After his meeting with Knox, Washington continued to conduct executive department business through letters whenever possible. He recognized the utility, however, of following up letters with in-person meetings when complicated issues required further discussion.

Washington grappled with the challenges of governing over a vast distance by inching closer to full cabinet gatherings. Washington left New York City at the end of August 1790 for his annual vacation to his home at Mount Vernon. During his absence, the department secretaries continued overseeing their respective departments. Prior to Washington's departure, he authorized Secretary of the Treasury Alexander Hamilton to negotiate a loan from the Dutch government to help pay off the foreign debt. Washington anticipated that the presence of a foreign minister might be needed in Amsterdam. Because the foreign minister would fall under the purview of the State Department, Washington instructed Hamilton to meet with Thomas Jefferson. Rather than consult with Hamilton and Jefferson separately and then wait for their individual responses, Washington ordered Hamilton and Jefferson to convene, come to an agreement about an agent, and send a report of their conversation.[18] In the name of efficiency, Washington stepped beyond the options technically outlined in Article II, Section 2, of the Constitution when he directed Hamilton and Jefferson to meet.

In March 1791, Washington again left Philadelphia, and his departure forced him to experiment with new methods of communicating with the department secretaries—just as he had done in April 1790. On Monday, March 21, 1791, Washington commenced his tour of the southern states.[19] Before departing, Washington forwarded his travel itinerary to the department secretaries. He instructed the secretaries to conduct their regular department business and to direct mail to his next destination for advice. Washington also authorized the secretaries to meet as a group if an urgent situation required more immediate feedback.[20] On April 9, Alexander Hamilton received a troubling letter from William Short. Short had negotiated a promising new loan from the Dutch, which the United States Treasury desperately needed to meet its upcoming debt payment due to the French. When the administration originally sent instructions to Short in August 1790, Washington instructed Hamilton not to accept a new loan until Washington himself approved the terms. The president, however, was making his way from Fredericksburg to Richmond and could not be reached for an immediate decision. Hamilton worried that any delay would threaten the new loan or timely payments to the French, so he followed Washington's instructions and shared Short's letter with the department secretaries and Vice President John Adams. The vice president and the department secretaries approved the new loan, and Hamilton forwarded the decision to Washington for final review. On May 7, 1791, Washington provided official authorization of Hamilton's meeting and the group's decision.[21]

On November 26, 1791, Washington convened his first cabinet gathering with all of the secretaries at his home at nine o'clock in the morning. Washington wished to consult with the secretaries on the current diplomatic relations with France and Great Britain. In particular, Washington wanted the cabinet to investigate the possibility of new commercial treaties with both nations. Because the topic meeting fell under Jefferson's purview as secretary of state, Washington asked him to draft discussion questions for the group. Jefferson also presented a proposed treaty of commerce with France. The cabinet initially approved the treaty during the November 26 meeting, but the administration later abandoned the treaty for being too restrictive to American interests.[22]

Washington found the in-person consultations to be helpful and convened a handful of cabinet meetings over the next year. Washington did not yet rely on the cabinet as a central part of the executive branch, however. Washington's interactions with his department secretaries in 1792 and early 1793 demonstrate that the cabinet continued to develop and crystallize slowly. Washington continued to request written advice whenever possible. For example, Washington returned to written advice in April 1792 when he considered exercising the presidential veto for the first time. On March 26, 1792, Congress passed "An Act for an Apportionment of Representatives among the Several States According to the First Enumeration." The legislation would have increased the House of Representatives to 120 members based on the first enumeration of the census. Washington ultimately vetoed the bill because he believed the method of apportionment to be unconstitutional. While debating this major step, he exchanged letters with the department secretaries and asked follow-up questions in individual conferences.[23]

The Neutrality Crisis

In the spring of 1793, the first major diplomatic crisis to face the new United States erupted. On February 1, France declared war on Great Britain and the Netherlands, and on April 5 news of the war finally reached Washington. While Washington wrapped up his stay at Mount Vernon, he asked Hamilton and Jefferson—both in Philadelphia—to brainstorm strategies to maintain American neutrality. Washington knew the outbreak of hostilities threatened to drag the United States into the European war. The American economy had recently shown signs of life, and industry was slowly recovering from the economic downturn of the 1780s. Washington and his secretaries believed another war would destroy the stability and progress of Washington's first term. Yet they found themselves in unchartered waters. The United States had never declared neutrality, or navigated the complications that go along with neutral policy. Washington and the secretaries also wanted to maintain a friendly relationship with France and preserve crucial trading partnerships with Great Britain. For the first time, Washington turned to frequent cabinet meetings over the next several months to address these challenges rather than relying on written advice and individual conferences.

On the evening of April 17, Washington arrived in Philadelphia. On the morning of April 18, he sent a message to the department secretaries requesting a meeting after breakfast the next day. Washington also included thirteen questions for the cabinet to consider in advance of their meeting.[24] The questions addressed three main issues: whether the administration should issue a proclamation of neutrality and if so, what terminology should be used; whether the administration should receive a minister from France and if any qualifications should be applied; and the conditions of the current treaties with France and Great Britain and how they might be amended. These three issues continued to plague Washington and dominated cabinet meetings for the duration of 1793. On April 19, the cabinet gathered at the President's House. They convened in Washington's private study on the second floor of the home.

Despite the obvious hostility between Hamilton and Jefferson, the cabinet initially made progress addressing Washington's questions. Question one asked, "Shall a proclamation issue for the purpose of preventing interferences of the Citizens of the United States in the War between France & Great Britain &ca? Shall it contain a declaration of Neutrality or not? What shall it contain?" The cabinet agreed that the administration would issue a declaration forbidding American citizens from participating in the hostilities for or against any of the belligerent powers. The second question posed, "Shall a Minister from the Republic of France be received?" The cabinet concluded that the government should receive a minister from France, but agreement broke down over whether the minister should be received absolutely or with qualifications.[25] Jefferson and Hamilton bitterly disagreed over the next several questions—which considered the United States' relationship with France. Hamilton argued that the French revolutionaries had abrogated the Franco-American alliance when they executed King Louis XVI. As a result, the United States was not obligated to support the French war against Great Britain and the Netherlands nor to accept the French minister without qualification until the United States established an official relationship with the new French government. Jefferson countered that the spirit of the alliance had been with the French state, not the king. Accordingly, the new minister should be received immediately and the United States should consider itself bound by all former treaties with France. Washington hoped that a brief respite would allow cooler heads to prevail, so he postponed a final decision and convened an additional meeting on April 22.[26] The secretaries agreed to language for the proclamation but remained steadfastly conflicted over the remaining issues of the reception of the French minister and treaties with France and Great Britain. Hoping to move forward, Washington requested written opinions from the department secretaries on questions three through thirteen. All of the secretaries submitted their opinions by May 6, but the issues covered in Washington's memo continued to plague the administration.[27]

Over the next eight months the cabinet met regularly, only pausing their frequent gatherings in the fall of 1793 when a yellow fever outbreak forced most government officials to flee Philadelphia. Most weeks, the cabinet met once or twice. At other times—including the last week of July, the end of August, and most of November—the cabinet met up to five times per week. The year 1793 therefore served as a turning point in executive branch development. The cabinet met to discuss regular affairs of business including Washington's annual address to Congress but primarily focused on ongoing issues with neutrality and the European war. How to respond to privateers in American ports particularly troubled the cabinet—especially those armed by the defiant French minister, Citizen Edmond Charles Genêt. Genêt defied American neutrality policy and immediately began issuing privateering commissions upon his arrival in Charleston. When Genêt arrived in Philadelphia, Jefferson warned him to cease all privateering activities. Genêt ignored these warnings, armed another French privateer—the *Little Democrat*—and ordered her to set sail. Genêt also threatened to go above Washington's head and appeal directly to the American people. Jefferson and Hamilton rarely agreed when discussing foreign policy, but on August 2, 1793, the cabinet unanimously agreed to request the recall of Genêt as French minister.[28] The cabinet met again the next day and finally established set rules of neutrality.[29] On June 4, 1794, Congress formalized these rules of neutrality in a bill, which served as the basis for neutrality policy throughout the nineteenth century.[30]

The Neutrality Crisis also shaped how Washington and the secretaries perceived their interactions. The cabinet participants recognized that their regular meetings formed a new institution. Jefferson described the gatherings as cabinet meetings in his memorandums. Individuals outside of the executive branch also labeled the group as the cabinet. After Washington issued his proclamation on April 22, 1793, James Madison wrote to Jefferson discussing the public's reaction to the statement. While the public response was overwhelmingly positive, some Virginians questioned the constitutionality of the proclamation. Madison shared these views and believed that the president's assertion of neutrality amounted to signing a treaty without the participation of the Senate. Madison then asked Jefferson, "Did no such view of the subject present itself in the discussions of the Cabinet?"[31]

Scholars tend to take for granted the cabinet's staying power and assume it served an integral role in Washington's presidency from the beginning. The reflections of the participants and the observers outside the administration challenge this interpretation. Jefferson and Madison's correspondence demonstrates that 1793 was a turning point for cabinet organization and public awareness of this new institution.

Ongoing Development of the Cabinet

The cabinet as an institution continued to develop after the tensions surrounding the Neutrality Crisis subsided. A quantitative analysis of the cabinet meetings demonstrates that Washington primarily convened the cabinet to discuss a diplomatic or constitutional precedent. Washington always treated the cabinet as a presidential tool at his disposal, however, and the cabinet meeting statistics suggest that he reduced his reliance on cabinet deliberations from 1795 to the end of his administration. As Washington's confidence in himself as president grew and the cast of characters in the cabinet evolved, he no longer believed he needed regular cabinet deliberations.

Washington called cabinet meetings when he could not resolve an administrative issue with just one of the department secretaries. Washington and the individual secretaries handled the majority of departmental administration in individual conferences. Washington summoned ninety-eight cabinet meetings during his presidency. Discussions on diplomacy, including relations with Native Americans, dominated sixty-three of the meetings, or 68 percent of the meetings. The executive's relationship with Congress and issues of constitutional interpretation account for another eighteen meetings, or 18 percent of meetings. Therefore, eighty-one out of the total ninety-eight cabinet meetings were devoted to issues of precedent.

Because Washington called cabinet meetings to discuss specific issues, the role of the cabinet evolved throughout his presidency. Figure 1 shows the cabinet meetings per year of Washington's administration. This graph is particularly revealing because it demonstrates the delayed emergence of the cabinet. Jefferson did not assume his position as secretary of state until early 1790 and the secretaries met in April 1791, but Washington did not convene a cabinet meeting until November 1791. Additionally, this figure demonstrates how 1793 represented a watershed moment for the cabinet, the executive branch, and the nation. Washington and his secretaries met forty-nine times to establish precedent-setting diplomatic policy and to determine how to enforce neutrality for the first time. In 1794, Washington continued to rely heavily on his cabinet. The bulk of meetings in 1794 focused on the Whiskey Rebellion in western Pennsylvania. Although the Whiskey Rebellion was not a diplomatic crisis, it still represented a first for the Washington administration. Washington and his secretaries used cabinet meetings to hash out how the federal government would respond to domestic insurrections—would they leave enforcement to the state or Congress? Washington and his secretaries seized the opportunity to establish a precedent of strong executive action in the face of rebellion. For the final twenty-six months of his presidency, Washington dramatically reduced his reliance on cabinet meetings.

Washington continued to use the cabinet as a tool to process difficult decisions, but he returned to handling the daily operations of each department as the responsibility of the individual agency head. Washington and the secretaries felt increasingly confident in their ability to execute policy. Consider the decision to impose an embargo in 1794.[32] In early 1794, the

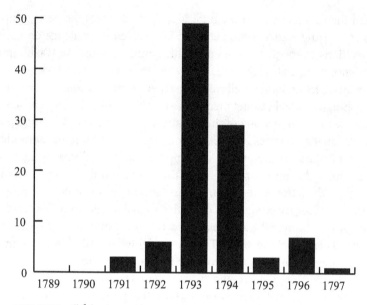

FIGURE 1. Cabinet meetings per year

United States appeared on the verge of another war with Great Britain. The British government refused to surrender control over western forts, citing American failure to comply with all of the terms of the Treaty of Paris, signed on September 3, 1783. On June 8, 1793, the British council passed an order requiring the detention of all neutral ships carrying corn, meal, or flour to French ports. Under this order, the British navy seized several American ships.[33] On March 26, 1794, Congress imposed a thirty-day embargo on all ships bound for foreign ports in order to protect American ships from further seizures. That same day, the cabinet met to discuss how best to implement the embargo, agreeing unanimously to authorize the state governors to utilize the militia to enforce the embargo.[34] On the other hand, by March 1794, the cabinet no longer met to decide on individual ships and whether to grant them passports to defy the embargo because they had already established the overall framework. Instead, Hamilton drew up passports and submitted them for Washington's approval. Washington granted or denied each passport using his own judgment rather than presenting the issue for cabinet deliberation.[35]

After 1794, cabinet meetings declined precipitously. Washington faced domestic and diplomatic challenges from 1795 to 1797, but few issues arose that required precedent-setting action. Washington and his cabinet had already navigated the treaty process, established neutrality policy, and defeated the insurrection over the whiskey tax in western Pennsylvania. Even when Washington frequently consulted with the department secretaries in person in 1793, he never totally abandoned written advice. Washington resorted to written opinions when he traveled or was at home at Mount Vernon. Washington returned to written advice from individual secretaries in the final years of his administration.

Cabinet meetings also declined after 1795 because Washington always intended for the cabinet to be an intimate advisory body to serve at his pleasure. Almost every single cabinet meeting took place in Washington's private study in the President's House in Philadelphia. The room was a generous size for a personal office—about fifteen by twenty-one feet—but the trappings of the room made it feel cozier. Washington's large French-style desk would have been the defining feature of the room. The desk measured sixty-two inches wide and thirty-five inches deep but sat out from the wall in order to provide access to locked compartments in the back. Washington's globe occupied additional space and a cast-iron stove resided in the corner to provide heat. Washington likely sat in his revolving desk chair—which he called the uncommon chair—while the other participants settled into other small chairs and tables around the room. The intimate setting provided privacy but also perhaps heightened tensions in the meetings.[36] Jefferson and Hamilton openly despised each other by April 1793, and given their close proximity in a confined space, it is no surprise Jefferson referenced the blood and gore of a cockfight when he described their meetings: "Hamilton & myself were daily pitted in the cabinet like two cocks."[37] Figure 2 depicts a re-creation of Washington's private study as it would have looked in 1793.

Washington continued to rely on the advisors that he had trusted for years. After Jefferson retired, Randolph assumed more responsibly in the cabinet as the new secretary of state. Washington appointed William Bradford as the new attorney general and continued to interact with the cabinet regularly. Bradford played an important role during the Whiskey Rebellion. On August 2, 1794, Washington convened a meeting with the department secretaries and governor of Pennsylvania Thomas Mifflin, Pennsylvania secretary of the commonwealth Alexander James Dallas, Pennsylvania chief justice Thomas McKean, and Pennsylvania attorney general Jared Ingersoll. Washington opened the meeting by declaring that "the circumstances which accompanied it were such as to strike at the root of all law & order; That he was clearly of opinion that the most spirited & firm measures were necessary to rescue the State as well as the General Government form the

FIGURE 2. Digital re-creation of Washington's private study

impending danger; for if such proceedings were tolerated there was an end to our Constitutions & laws." Washington explained that he hoped a peaceful outcome would be possible. If not, the administration secured approval from Supreme Court justice James Wilson to deploy federal forces. In the meantime, Washington asked Governor Mifflin to call out the Pennsylvania militia. The Pennsylvania officers disagreed with Washington's assertion of federal control. They insisted the state judiciary alone could punish the rioters.[38] After the meeting, Washington requested written opinions from the secretaries.[39]

On August 6, the secretaries met again to discuss their positions. Bradford suggested a middle path between Randolph's desire for peaceful negotiations and Hamilton's eagerness for a crushing military campaign. He encouraged Washington to send a peace delegation to meet with the insurgents but also to use that time to prepare for a military response when the negotiations likely failed. Although the personnel had changed, many of the cabinet dynamics remained the same. The secretary of state represented one extreme and the secretary of the treasury advocated the other. The attorney general tried to moderate between the two sides and chart a middle path. Bradford found himself in between Hamilton and Randolph because of a partisan divide rather than responsibilities assigned to the attorney general. Washington appreciated that Bradford's plan provided valuable political cover while he prepared a military response. Hoping that Bradford would have greater influence with his fellow Pennsylvanians,

Washington sent him to western Pennsylvania to represent the administration in the meeting with the insurgents.[40]

Hamilton and Randolph dominated cabinet deliberations and administrative procedures. During the summer and fall of 1794, they led the administration's response to the Whiskey Rebellion. Over the next few months, Washington and Mifflin sparred over the proper response to the insurrection. Washington received letters from Mifflin on August 5, August 12, and August 22. He relied on Hamilton and Randolph to draft the administration's reply to each letter. Hamilton created the first draft and then sent it to Randolph for review. Randolph included a few revisions and then sent the dispatches to Mifflin with Washington's approval. Each letter dismantled or refuted Mifflin's claims, including his proposal that the administration leave enforcement to the judiciary. All three letters also asserted the power and independence of the president. Randolph responded that Washington could not, "without an abdication of the undoubted rights and authorities of the United States provide, to a previous experience of the plan which is delineated in your letter."[41] Randolph essentially asserted that the Constitution required the president to lead a firm federal response to the rebellion.

The beginning of 1795 marked a major shift in the cast of characters in the cabinet. On December 31, 1794, Henry Knox retired as secretary of war, and Alexander Hamilton followed on January 31, 1795. On August 20, 1795, Randolph resigned as secretary of state, and on August 23, 1795, Bradford died. In early 1795, Washington promoted Timothy Pickering from postmaster general to secretary of war. After Randolph's resignation in August 1795, Washington again promoted Pickering, this time to secretary of state. He also promoted Hamilton's comptroller of the treasury, Oliver Wolcott Jr., to fill the secretary of the treasury position. Washington then struggled to fill the remaining openings. Washington refused to appoint men he suspected of sympathy with the emerging Republican opposition—he had endured enough partisan politics in the cabinet. Many leading statesmen—including William Paterson of New Jersey, Thomas Johnson of Maryland, General Charles Pinckney of South Carolina, John Marshall, Edward Carrington, and Patrick Henry all from Virginia—declined an appointment, so he eventually settled for James McHenry for secretary of war and Charles Lee as attorney general.[42] After his retirement, Washington admitted some of the replacements could not fill the shoes of the original secretaries. On August 9, 1798, Washington wrote to Hamilton regarding Secretary of War James McHenry, "Your opinion respecting the unfitness of a certain Gentleman for the Office he holds, accords with mine, and it is to be regretted, *sorely*, at this time, that these opinions are so well founded. I early discovered, after he entered upon the Duties of his Office, that his talents were unequal to great exertions, or deep resources."[43]

Before Randolph resigned in July 1795, Washington leaned heavily on the last remaining secretary from his original cabinet. Washington's management of the Jay Treaty starting in 1795 reveals his distrust of the cabinet as a whole and his preference for individual conferences with Randolph. On November 19, 1794, John Jay signed and sent the treaty with Great Britain to Washington.[44] In early March 1795, Washington received the package and shared the contents with Edmund Randolph but none of the other secretaries. Washington and Randolph determined to call a special session of the Senate and sent out messages calling the senators to Philadelphia by June 8, 1795.[45] Throughout the spring, the contents of the treaty remained a closely guarded secret. In April, Randolph wrote to John Adams and noted recent articles about the treaty in Benjamin Franklin Bache's paper, the *Aurora*. Randolph assured Adams that these articles were scandalous lies because "not one word of which [the treaty], I believe, is known thro' a regular channel to any person here, but the President and myself."[46] James Madison confirmed the secrecy surrounding the treaty in a letter to James Monroe on December 20, 1795: "I understand that it [the treaty] was even witheld from the Secretaries at war & the Treasury, that is Pickering & Wolcott."[47] Washington's efforts to keep Pickering, Wolcott, and Lee in the dark contrasted sharply with the robust cabinet deliberations that surrounded every aspect of the Neutrality Crisis in 1793.

Washington finally shared the contents of the treaty with the other department secretaries after the Senate had ratified it. On June 25, 1795, Randolph encouraged Washington to consult the other secretaries and provided a number of questions Washington could send to the other secretaries.[48] On June 29, 1795, Washington sent each of the department secretaries and the attorney general a letter asking for their written opinions. Washington's letter contained issues for the secretaries to consider, which were essentially the same questions Randolph had proposed, suggesting that the president consulted the other secretaries only at Randolph's encouragement. In particular, Washington requested advice about a conditional ratification. On June 24, the Senate had passed a resolution that suspended the twelfth article of the treaty, which granted commercial access to the British West Indies only to ships of seventy tons or less.[49] Washington also had reservations about Article XII and contemplated conditionally ratifying the treaty and sending an emissary to Great Britain to renegotiate that article. Washington questioned whether a renegotiation of Article XII would negate the Senate's ratification.[50] He asked his secretaries to advise whether he would need to resubmit a revised treaty for a new ratification.[51] Significantly, Washington did not convene a meeting to discuss this issue as he would have in 1793. Instead, Washington requested written opinions to keep the secretaries at an arm's length. Given the personal nature of the formative cabinet meetings in his private office in 1793, Washington convened fewer meetings in his personal space with agency heads whom he distrusted.

Washington also returned to written advice—but he looked outside the cabinet for advisors. Hamilton's role in the administration after his retirement in January 1795 further confirms Washington's preference for his former cabinet secretaries. Washington continued to request Hamilton's input on major issues facing the administration—often providing him with privileged information in the process. Not long after Hamilton's retirement from the Treasury, Washington requested his opinion on the recently published Jay Treaty.[52] Washington sent additional queries about the treaty to Hamilton as the public debated ratification. On July 13, 1795, Washington shared the same question with Hamilton that he previously sent to the cabinet secretaries—whether the treaty should be submitted to the Senate again for ratification if the British government agreed to amend Article XII.[53] On March 2, 1796, freshman New York congressman Edward Livingston introduced a hostile resolution regarding the Jay Treaty to the House of Representatives, and Washington again turned to Hamilton for help and advice. Livingston's resolution requested that Washington submit all of the papers relating to the negotiation of the Jay Treaty. Despite his burgeoning law practice, Hamilton replied to every one of Washington's requests for guidance. In March 1796, Hamilton even provided a draft for Washington to use in his response to the House of Representatives.[54] Washington did not always follow Hamilton's advice or use the provided materials. Their ongoing communications, however, suggest Washington preferred to consult with Hamilton instead of his cabinet secretaries after 1795.

Washington also continued an occasional correspondence with other trusted acquaintances. John Jay sent Washington private reports while serving as a special envoy to Great Britain, and Washington replied with domestic updates, especially regarding partisan tensions. On December 18, 1794, Washington wrote, "The business of the Session, hitherto, has been tranquil, and I perceive nothing *at this time*, to make it otherwise, unless the result of the Negotiation (which is anxiously expected by all) should produce divisions."[55]

Equally important was whom Washington chose not to consult. James Madison was initially one of Washington's trusted confidants. He helped Washington write his first address to Congress, provided guidance as

Washington used the presidential veto for the first time, and wrote the first draft of Washington's retirement address in 1792. But as Madison increasingly opposed the administration's policies and voted against Hamilton's fiscal legislation, his relationship with Washington frayed. By 1793, Washington no longer consulted him on important issues, and he was never invited into the cabinet.

Similarly, Washington kept Adams at arm's length. On May 10, 1789, Washington wrote Vice President John Adams and requested his opinion on several questions pertaining to how the president should conduct himself in public and in private social interactions, including "Whether a line of conduct, equally distant from an association with all kinds of company on the one hand and from a total seclusion from Society on the other, ought to be adopted by him? And, in the case, how is it to be done?"[56] In April 1791, when Washington left Philadelphia to conduct his tour of the southern states, he authorized the secretaries to meet in his absence if a pressing matter should arise. He instructed them to include Adams in the deliberations. Washington left no indication of why he suggested Adams be invited to this one cabinet gathering, but no future meetings. Because cabinet interactions evolved organically in response to governing pressures, Washington had not yet developed a standard cabinet meeting practice. Perhaps Washington wanted Adams to act as a stand-in for the president. Washington may have been reluctant to cede authority to the cabinet in his absence and felt that the vice president would serve as a check on the cabinet's power. Alternatively, it is possible that Washington simply believed five minds would make a better decision than four. After Hamilton convened a cabinet meeting on April 11, 1791, Adams never again participated in cabinet discussions. Washington occasionally forwarded a few documents for Adams to review and provide an opinion but never requested his advice in the heat of a crisis. For example, there is no record of Washington soliciting Adams's advice during the peak of the Neutrality Crisis. On January 8, 1794, after already establishing neutrality policy with the cabinet, Washington consulted with Adams about Genêt's ongoing privateer efforts.[57]

One explanation is offered by Kathleen Bartoloni-Tuazon, who argues that Adams found himself in a diminished role in the administration after his role in the Title Controversy tarnished his political reputation. Adams suffered widespread backlash from his central role as an advocate for a grand presidential title, earning insulting nicknames including "the Dangerous Vice" and "His Rotundity." Bartoloni-Tuazon argues that the public outcry forced Washington to distance himself from Adams and dashed any possibility of a close relationship between the president and the vice president.[58]

While the Title Controversy may have chilled the relationship between Washington and Adams, the president still ordered the department secretaries to include the vice president at the April 1791 cabinet meeting. Additionally, it is surprising that Washington did not consult with Adams in the final years of his administration. Adams had served as a minister to France and the Netherlands and had spent three years as the US minister to the Court of St. James in London. Furthermore, Washington had appointed Adams's eldest son, John Quincy Adams, to serve as the minister to the Netherlands. Adams could have provided valuable counsel on the Jay Treaty. Adams was also unquestionably loyal to the Federalist Party and the administration. Given Washington's sensitivities to partisan attacks, Adams could have provided a sympathetic ear. Washington remained circumspect as to why the vice president played a limited role in his administration, but the evidence suggests he relied on a select few advisors in the final year of his presidency and refused to go beyond that inner circle.

There are limitations to the statistical analysis of Washington's cabinet meetings. The surviving evidence frontloads a focus on Washington's presidency until 1794. After Jefferson retired in December 1793, partisan tensions in the cabinet waned. Randolph identified as a moderate Republican but often crumbled in the face of unified Federalist positions advocated by Knox, Hamilton, and Pickering. After Randolph's resignation in August 1795, the cabinet became unanimously Federalist. Jefferson recorded the cabinet deliberations in 1793 with incredible precision to document his disagreement with administration policies. It is possible additional meetings took place from 1795 to 1797, but none of the participants documented their conversations or left any evidence of gathering.

When Washington entered the presidency, he harbored no ambitions to create a new advisory council. He planned to treat the Senate as a council of foreign affairs and to engage with the department secretaries as agency heads. As the departments took on additional responsibilities, Washington and the secretaries began to meet individually to discuss specific issues under their purview. Washington continued this practice for the duration of his administration. Washington oversaw the institutional build-out discussed in the other essays in this volume, but he did so in individual conferences. In the spring of 1793, the cabinet developed as an institution in spite of itself. Washington could no longer rely on individual consultations and written opinions to solve the major diplomatic challenges facing the administration. The cabinet served as a central part of the executive branch for the next few years, before returning to pre-1793 status. During the final years of his presidency, Washington again treated the department secretaries as agency heads. He worked with them to process department business, requested written advice on most issues, and occasionally summoned a cabinet meeting if faced with a precedent-setting issue.

This essay examined two likely reasons why cabinet meetings declined from 1795 to 1797: Washington's increased comfort making diplomatic decisions without cabinet assistance and his distrust of the "B Team" of department secretaries that took office starting in 1795. Because Washington assiduously avoided discussing the cabinet in his private correspondence, there is no way to know for sure why he turned away from the cabinet in his finals years. Whatever the reason, Washington's use of the cabinet was consistent with his belief that the institution was an advisory body for him to use as he saw fit.

The cabinet is central to the study of the executive branch in the early republic for three reasons. First, understanding the development of the cabinet is necessary to understanding the expansion of other institutions. The interactions in the cabinet inform other aspects of state building. As the department secretaries built out more expansive institutions, they frequently met with Washington individually, not as a cabinet. Cabinet deliberations were reserved for questions of precedent. Understanding cabinet context for the development of departmental institutions provides a scope of reference to examine the secretaries' contributions. Hamilton undoubtedly spearheaded the creation of the new fiscal system, and Hamilton and Jefferson dominated cabinet deliberations starting in 1793, but Henry Knox played a much larger role in the administration than scholarship has suggested. Native American issues dominated the administration's attention, especially in Washington's first term. Washington and Knox worked together to coordinate administrative efforts in the western territories and cultivate good relationships with Native American nations. Washington and Knox took issues to the cabinet when they involved establishing precedent but not for daily administration. For example, on March 9, 1792, Washington convened a cabinet meeting to discuss an upcoming summit with a delegation from the Six Nations. Knox handled all of the communications and the details prior to sending an invitation to the Six Nations. Before welcoming a delegation, however, Washington wanted the entire cabinet to advise on the upcoming summit.[59]

Second, by ignoring the delayed emergence of the cabinet, scholars have assumed that the president and the secretaries interacted through the same cabinet framework in 1789 as they did after April 1793. When discussing interactions between Washington and his secretaries, scholars treat the cabinet as an institution that existed since the first day of the federal government.[60] Alternatively, scholars often reference cabinet meetings in 1790 and 1791, when these interactions either took place in individual meetings or written correspondence.[61]

Third, Washington established a cabinet precedent that guided future presidents. Had Washington's successors abandoned the cabinet and adopted a different governing model, history would remember the cabinet as a fluke or a relic of past era, like Washington's levees. Instead, his successors continued many of Washington's cabinet practices, ensuring that it remained a central part of the executive branch. Adams proposed questions in advance of cabinet gatherings and convened meetings in the face of domestic and international crises. Adams even retained all of Washington's secretaries in an attempt to provide continuity. Jefferson also modeled his cabinet practices on Washington's first term. On November 6, 1801, Jefferson wrote a circular to the heads of the departments. In this letter, Jefferson explained how Washington organized the first cabinet and why he intended to follow Washington's example:

> If a doubt of any importance arose, he reserved it for conference. By this means he was always in accurate possession of all facts & proceedings in every part of the Union, & to whatsoever department they related; he formed a central point for the different branches, preserved an unity of object and action among them, exercised that participation in the gestion of affairs which his office made incumbent on him, and met himself the due responsibility for whatever was done. . . . I cannot withhold recommending to the heads of departments that we should adopt this course for the present, leaving any necessary modifications of it to time & trial.[62]

Jefferson followed Washington's and Adams's examples and called meetings in response to constitutional issues, war with Barbary pirates, the Louisiana Purchase, and ongoing conflict with Great Britain. Adams, Jefferson, and their successors all introduced their own preferences into the cabinet, but Washington's precedent remains the core of the cabinet as an institution.

But Washington also left an institution in flux. The Adams cabinet almost imploded because of the department secretaries' loyalty to Alexander Hamilton. Rather than serving as the president's personal advisors, the secretaries continuously tried to undermine Adams's efforts to secure peace with France. Jefferson learned from both Washington and Adams. Emotionally scarred by the partisan battles in Washington's cabinet, Jefferson worked hard to avoid cabinet conflict in his own administration. He appointed Republicans loyal to both the party and his presidency. To ensure no one felt like a cabinet outsider as he did in 1793, Jefferson also cultivated good relationships with all of his secretaries to make them feel included and valuable. The Washington cabinet left a legacy that the relationship between the president and the secretaries would remain an individual choice for each administration. Depending on the president, the secretaries could serve as agency heads, personal advisors, or some combination of both. This legacy continues to shape modern administrations. Each president determines who will be the primary advisors and what their relation will be—with almost no oversight.[63]

Notes

1. A number of studies have evaluated the creation of the branches of government and the executive departments. Examples include Kenneth R. Bowling and Donald R. Kennon, eds., *Inventing Congress: Origins and Establishment of the First Federal Congress*(Athens, OH: Published by Ohio State University Press for the United States Capitol Historical Society, 1999); Noble E. Cunningham Jr., *The Process of Government under Jefferson* (Princeton, NJ: Princeton University Press, 1978); George Lee Haskins and Herbert A. Johnson, *Foundations of Power: John Marshall, 1801–1815* (Cambridge: Cambridge University Press, 2009); Maeva Marcus, ed., *Origins of the Federal Judiciary: Essays on the Judiciary Act of 1789* (New York: Oxford University Press, 1992); Stanley Elkins and Eric McKitrick, *The Age of Federalism: The Early American Republic, 1788–1800* (New York: Oxford University Press, 1993).

2. The emergence of the cabinet can perhaps be best understood through the institutional framework established by Leonard D. White in *The Federalists: A Study in Administrative History* (New York: MacMillan, 1948).

3. Worthington C. Ford et al., eds., *Journals of the Continental Congress,* December 15, 1780; January–February 1781; August–October 1781 (Washington, DC, 1904–37), 18:1154–56; 19:42–44, 123–24, 180, 203; 21:851–52, 1030.

4. Robert Morris, "Diary: December 3, 1781; December 10, 1781; December 17, 1781," in *The Papers of Robert Morris,* ed. E. James Ferguson, 8 vols. (Pittsburgh: University of Pittsburgh Press, 1977), 3:316, 356, 399. On December 3, 1781, Robert Morris invited the secretary of war (Benjamin Lincoln), the secretary of foreign affairs (Robert R. Livingston), the commander in chief (George Washington), and the secretary of Congress (Charles Thomson) to a meeting. He proposed that the secretaries meet every Monday evening for the purpose of "Consulting and Concerting Measures to promote the Service and Public Good."

5. Edmund Burke, *Thoughts on the Cause of the Present Discontents, 1770,* in Edmund Raymond Turner, *The Cabinet Council of England in the Seventeenth and Eighteenth Centuries* (Baltimore: John Hopkins University Press, 1930), 2:319–20.

6. "The Virginia Resolutions, 29 May 1787, Charles Pinckney's Plan, 29 May 1787," in *The Documentary History of the Ratification of the Constitution* (hereafter referred to as *DHRC*), ed. Merrill Jensen (Madison: State Historical Society of Wisconsin, 1976), 1:243–47.

7. James Madison, *Notes of Debates in the Federal Convention of 1787* (Athens, OH: Ohio University Press, 1984), 487–88.

8. US Constitution, art. II, sec. 2, cl. 2.

9. George Washington to the US Senate, 22 August 1789, *The Papers of George Washington*, Presidential Series (1987–), ed. W. W. Abbot, 3:521–27; Linda Grant de Pauw, ed., *Documentary History of the First Federal Congress of the United States of America* (hereafter *DHFFC*) (Baltimore: Johns Hopkins University Press, 1974), 2:137–53.

10. *DHFFC*, 2:5–6.

11. Senators addressed Vice President John Adams as "President" while he presided over the Senate. He forfeited this title when Washington was present.

12. George Washington to US Senate, 21 August 1789, *The Papers of George Washington*, Presidential Series, 3:515.

13. William Maclay, *The Diary of William Maclay*, ed. Kenneth R. Bowling and Helen E. Veit (Baltimore: Johns Hopkins University Press, 1988), 128–30. US Congress, *Senate Exec. Journal.*, 1st Cong., 2nd sess., 22 August 1789.

14. Maclay, *The Diary of William Maclay*, 128–30.

15. George Washington to John Jay, 8 June 1789, *The Papers of George Washington*, Presidential Series, 2:239, 455.

16. George Washington to Henry Knox, 4 September 1789; Henry Knox to George Washington, 15 February 1790; George Washington to Henry Knox, 8 March 1790, *The Papers of George Washington*, Presidential Series, 3:600; 5:140–47, 207–8.

17. Henry Knox to George Washington, 20 January 1790; George Washington to the US Senate and House of Representatives, 21 January 1790, *The Papers of George Washington*, Presidential Series, 5:24–25, 32.

18. Alexander Hamilton to George Washington, 26 August 1790; George Washington to Alexander Hamilton, 28 August 1790; Alexander Hamilton to George Washington, 3 September 1790, *The Papers of Alexander Hamilton*, ed. Harold C. Syrett (New York: Columbia University Press, 1961–87), 6:560–70, 579–80; 7:22–23.

19. George Washington, "March 1791," *The Diaries of George Washington*, ed. Donald Jackson and Dorothy Twohig (Charlottesville: University Press of Virginia, 1979), 6:99–107.

20. George Washington to Alexander Hamilton, Thomas Jefferson, and Henry Knox, 4 April 1791, *The Papers of Alexander Hamilton*, 8:242–43.

21. Tobias Lear to Alexander Hamilton, 26 August 1790; Alexander Hamilton to George Washington, 10 April 1791; Alexander Hamilton to George Washington, 14 April 1791; George Washington to Alexander Hamilton, 7 May 1791, *The Papers of Alexander Hamilton*, 6:566; 8:270–71, 288–89, 330.

22. George Washington to Thomas Jefferson, 25 November 1791, *The Papers of George Washington*, Presidential Series, 9:231–32; Thomas Jefferson to George Washington, 26 November 1791, *The Papers of Thomas Jefferson*, ed. Charles T. Cullen (Princeton, NJ: Princeton University Press, 1986), 22:344–46.

23. "I: From Henry Knox, 3 April 1792; II: From Alexander Hamilton, 4 April 1792; III: From Thomas Jefferson, 4 April 1792; IV: From Edmund Randolph, 4 April 1792," *The Papers of George Washington*, Presidential Series, 10:196–211.

24. Alexander Hamilton to George Washington, 5 April 1793; George Washington to Alexander Hamilton, 12 April 1793; George Washington to Thomas Jefferson, 12 April 1793; George Washington to the Cabinet, 18 April 1793, *The Papers of George Washington*, Presidential Series, 12:412–13, 447–48, 452–53.

25. George Washington to the Cabinet, 18 April 1793, *The Papers of George Washington*, Presidential Series, 12:452–53; Thomas Jefferson, "Minutes of a Cabinet Meeting" 19 April 1793," *The Papers of George Washington*, Presidential Series, 12:459.

26. "Minutes of a Cabinet Meeting, 19 April 1793," "Neutrality Proclamation, 22 April 1793," *The Papers of George Washington*, Presidential Series, 12:459, 472–73.

27. Thomas Jefferson to George Washington, 28 April 1793; Alexander Hamilton and Henry Knox to George Washington, 2 May 1793; Edmund Randolph to George Washington, 6 May 1793, *The Papers of George Washington*, Presidential Series, 12:487–88, 504, 534–47.

28. Edmond Charles Genêt to George Washington, 13 August 1793; Thomas Jefferson, "Cabinet Opinion on the Recall of Edmond Genet," 23 August 1793, *The Papers of George Washington*, Presidential Series, 13:436–37, 530. Alexander Hamilton, "Cabinet Meeting. Notes Concerning the Conduct of the French Minister," 2 August 1793, *The Papers of Alexander Hamilton*, 15:159–62.

29. George Taylor Jr., "Cabinet Opinion on the Rules of Neutrality," 3 August 1793, *The Papers of George Washington*, Presidential Series, 13:325–26.

30. *Annals of Congress*, 3rd Cong., 1st sess., 757.

31. James Madison to Thomas Jefferson, 13 June 1793, *The Papers of James Madison*, ed. Thomas A. Mason, Robert A. Rutland, and Jeanne K. Sisson (Charlottesville: University Press of Virginia, 1985), 15:28–30.

32. Congress enacted the embargo in response to British policy toward neutral shipping. British ships had been seizing all neutral ships carrying food supplies to ports under French control. This British policy was a major cause of anti-British sentiment in the United States. The embargo was intended as commercial relation for the British depredations on American trade. "Introductory Note: Alexander Hamilton to George Washington, 8 March 1794," *The Papers of Alexander Hamilton*, 16:130–34.

33. "Introductory Note: To George Washington, 8 March 1794," *The Papers of Alexander Hamilton*, 16:130–34.

34. "Cabinet Meeting. Opinion on the Best Mode of Executing the Embargo, 26 March 1794," *The Papers of Alexander Hamilton*, 16:198.

35. Alexander Hamilton to George Washington, March 28, 1794, *The Papers of Alexander Hamilton*, 16:207.

36. "The President's House in Philadelphia," Independence Hall Association, http://www.ushistory.org/presidentshouse/plans/; Stephen Decatur, *Private Affairs of George Washington: From the Records and Accounts of Tobias Lear* (Boston: Houghton Mifflin, 1933) 170; George Washington to Clement Biddle, 21 August 1797, *The Papers of George Washington*, Retirement Series, 1:311–12.

37. Thomas Jefferson to Walter Jones, 5 March 1810, *The Papers of Thomas Jefferson*, Retirement Series, 2:272–74.

38. Thomas Mifflin to George Washington, 5 August 1794, *The Papers of George Washington*, Presidential Series, ed. David R. Hoth and Carol S. Ebel (Charlottesville: University of Virginia Press, 2011), 16:521–22n1.

39. William Bradford to George Washington, 5 August 1794; Alexander Hamilton to George Washington, 5 August 1794; Thomas Mifflin to George Washington, 5 August 1794, *The Papers of George Washington*, Presidential Series, 16:472–78, 508–9, 514–23.

40. William Bradford to Alexander Hamilton, 23 August 1794, *The Papers of Alexander Hamilton*, 17:129–32.

41. Thomas Mifflin to George Washington, 5 August 1794, *The Papers of George Washington*, Presidential Series, 16:521n.

42. George Washington to Alexander Hamilton, 29 October 1795, *The Papers of Alexander Hamilton*, 19:355–63.

43. George Washington to Alexander Hamilton, 9 August 1798, *The Papers of George Washington*, Retirement Series, 2:500–502.

44. John Jay to George Washington, 19 November 1794, *The Papers of George Washington*, Presidential Series, 17:173–75.

45. Edmund Randolph to George Washington, 2 March 1795, *The Papers of George Washington*, Presidential Series, 17:606–7.

46. Edmund Randolph to John Adams, 2 April 1795, Founders Online, National Archives, http://founders.archives.gov/documents/Adams/99-02-02-1661.

47. James Madison to James Monroe, 20 December 1795, *The Papers of James Madison*, 16:168–71.

48. Edmund Randolph to George Washington, 25 June 1795, Early Access Edition, 18:691.

49. Carol Ebel, "Jay Treaty," *Digital Encyclopedia*, Mount Vernon, http://www.mountvernon.org/digital-encyclopedia/article/jay-treaty/.

50. "Notes from Edmund Randolph, 24 June 1795," Early Access Edition, 18:679–86.

51. Oliver Wolcott Jr. to George Washington, 30 June 1795, Early Access Edition, 18:738–42.

52. George Washington to Alexander Hamilton, 3 July 1795, *The Papers of Alexander Hamilton*, 18:398–400.

53. George Washington to Alexander Hamilton, 13 July 1795, *The Papers of Alexander Hamilton*, 18:461–64.

54. Alexander Hamilton to George Washington, 29 March 1796, *The Papers of Alexander Hamilton*, 20:85–86.

55. George Washington to John Jay, 18 December 1794; John Jay to George Washington, 25 February 1795, *The Papers of George Washington*, Presidential Series, 17:286–89, 577–80.

56. George Washington to John Adams, 10 May 1789, *The Papers of George Washington*, Presidential Series, 2:245–50.

57. George Washington to John Adams, 8 January 1794, *The Papers of George Washington*, Presidential Series, 15:32–34, 50,

58. Kathleen Bartoloni-Tuazon, *For Fear of an Elected King: George Washington and the Presidential Title Controversy of 1789* (Ithaca, NY: Cornell University Press, 2014), 8–10, 142–51.

59. "Thomas Jefferson's Memorandum of a Meeting of the Heads of the Executive Departments, 9 March 1792," *The Papers of George Washington*, Presidential Series, 10:69–73.

60. A few examples include T. H. Breen, *George Washington's Journey: The President Forges a New Nation* (New York: Simon and Schuster, 2016), 214–16; John Ferling, *Jefferson and Hamilton: The Rivalry That Forged a Nation* (New York: Bloomsbury, 2013), 226–27; Elkins and McKitrick, *The Age of Federalism*, 209.

61. George Washington to Alexander Hamilton, Thomas Jefferson, and Henry Knox, 4 April 1791; Alexander Hamilton to George Washington, 14 April 1791, *The Papers of George Washington*, Presidential Series, 8:59–60, 98–99; John Adams to Alexander Hamilton, 9 April 1791, *The Papers of Alexander Hamilton*, 8:258.

62. Thomas Jefferson, "Circular to the Heads of Departments," 6 November 1801, *The Papers of Thomas Jefferson*, 35:576–78.

63. To read more about Washington's cabinet legacy and the modern presidency, see Lindsay Chervinsky, "Donald Trump, George Washington, and the President's Cabinet," *Time*, 21 November 2016, http://time.com/4578694/president-cabinet -history/?xid=tcoshare.

Washington's Workforce

Reconstructing the Federal Government at the Moment of Its Creation

PETER J. KASTOR

William Short, Henry Carbery, and Thomas Melvill were at three very different points of the state-building process, and they never knew it. In all likelihood the three men never met. They certainly moved in different circles, and their public careers were worlds apart. Yet in 1789, they embodied the processes through which the federal workforce came into being during the administration of George Washington.

Short has always occupied a nebulous status for historians, but regardless of their opinion historians always locate Short squarely in the shadow of Thomas Jefferson. To some, Short is the loyal protégé, the first of many would-be sons who Jefferson recruited from the Virginia gentry. To others, he is the sycophant who hitched his career to Jefferson's, welcomed the offer to serve as his private secretary during Jefferson's tenure as minister to France, and considered himself entitled to subsequent diplomatic office.[1]

Melvill, like Short, was a public official, but his geographic and cultural circumstances could not have been different. A lifelong resident of the Boston area who fought in the American Revolution, in 1787 the Massachusetts state government selected him as naval officer, a job engaged in the lucrative but often adversarial role of revenue collection on the ships that populated the teeming harbor. Never the subject of substantive historical inquiry, Melvill nonetheless does figure in literary scholarship as the grandfather of Herman Melville.[2]

Short and Melvill have some claim to fame, albeit for their relationships to more famous Americans. Not so for Henry Carbery. A native of Maryland, he held neither prior office in 1789 nor has he mattered to historians since. But he did have problems—lots of them. Writing to Washington in July 1789, he explained that "I will not trouble You, Sir, with a detail of my Family, however antient . . . or the blood I have spilt, and property I have lost." He apologized not only for hinting at his suffering, but even for writing at all. "If You can Forgive me, Sir, for one single act of Indiscretion, for which I can never forgive myself, You will make me happy."[3]

For all these apparent differences, all three men were connected in the mad scramble to assemble the federal workforce. All three wanted federal jobs. And George Washington had to consider all three of them. In fact, Short was at the top of his list. On June 15, Short became the subject of Washington's first nomination to federal office. Washington had not even nominated men to run the major federal departments of State, Treasury, and War (he dispatched those nominations in September) when he wrote a letter to the US Senate that "Mr. Jefferson, the present Minister of the United States at the Court of France, having applied for permission to return home for a few months, and it appearing to me proper to comply with his request, it becomes necessary that some person be appointed to take charge of our affairs at that Court during his absence." After this preamble, Washington explained that "for this purpose I nominate William Short, Esquire, and request your advice on the propriety of appointing him." To this, Washington added, "There are, in the Office for Foreign Affairs, papers which will acquaint you with his character, and which Mr. Jay has my directions to lay before you, at such time as you may think proper to assign."[4]

The Senate immediately considered the case and in short order voted to confirm Short as chargé d'affaires in France.

On August 3, Washington nominated Melvill as surveyor for Boston and Charlestown, a federal office similar to his old state office of naval officer. Unlike Short, whose name stood alone in the president's business of the day, Melvill's was buried in a long list of commercial officials who Secretary of the Treasury Alexander Hamilton hoped would soon bring order to the chaos of fiscal planning.[5]

For Carbery there was no good news. The first federal appointments of the Washington administration came and went, and his name was nowhere to be seen.

With the creation of federal governance came the fundamental challenge of enforcing federal governance, and that required a federal workforce. The most oft-recounted appointees—cabinet members, Supreme Court justices, ministers to foreign countries—are also the most atypical. Instead, for over seven years the Washington administration was populated by the likes of Short and Melvill, and it rejected men like Carbery.

This essay constitutes a census of sorts, and the first of its kind. For decades, scholars have tossed around all sorts of estimates about the number of federal employees in the United States during the early republic. Pundits have joined that chorus from time to time because they recognize how much is at stake. What the Founding Fathers conceived of as the appropriate scope and scale of federal governance could be a tool for contemporary debates about the role of government in American life. But this debate rests on a rather flimsy foundation, because the specific numerical contours of the federal government, especially how it changed over time, has never been firmly established.

Quantitative analysis has long been the bread and butter of scholars in American political development, especially when studying the shifts toward modern bureaucracies from the late nineteenth through the mid-twentieth century. But historians of the early republic have been slow to respond. Worse still, the quantitative methods that so long characterized the scholarship in social history or the new political history of the 1970s have fallen from favor. The profoundly revealing essays in a 2013 special issue of the *Journal of the Early Republic* demonstrated the way that quantitative analysis—long a mainstay of political history but largely ignored in recent decades—could lead to a wholesale reinterpretation of the electoral facets of American politics.[6] Unfortunately, few scholars have taken a similar approach to the ranks of appointed officialdom.[7] I argue that a quantitative analysis of the appointed facets of American policy making is no less important.

My means to that end is as much a matter of writing as it is one of analysis. This essay deals principally in numbers rather than quotes. It also deploys different forms of quantitative analysis: the textual analysis of letters of application and recommendation, the chronological analysis of federal appointments over time, and the spatial analysis of the federal presence both at home and abroad.

What emerges is a story of federal operations that at times coincided with developments in other areas of American public life and at others is completely out of step with the fundamentally political periodization that scholars have imposed onto the Washington administration. Most importantly, the story of institutional development and institutional capacity really has two chapters: one extending from 1789 to 1793 and the other extending from 1793 to 1797. In the first chapter, federal leaders—including the supposedly antigovernment Thomas Jefferson—sought to expand the federal workforce, all the while struggling to respond to the instability that came as a result. In the second chapter, federal leaders sought to manage a stable but enlarged federal workforce with a more robust institutional capacity but a daunting mandate that often exceeded its operational limits. In both chapters of this story, federal governance remained administratively decentralized, and patterns of staff appointment in the capital often bore little relationship to the number of federal officeholders both at home and abroad.

This was a workforce defined not only by time but also by space. George Washington's workforce consisted primarily of men located in the East who helped produce the funds that paid men in the West. And in the end that spatial dimension underscores the functions of government under Washington. Washington's government was devoted first and foremost to an interconnected process designed to promote liberty for white citizens while establishing racial supremacy designed to subjugate nonwhites. Those whom Washington appointed were themselves part of this process. Day in and day out, those officials sought to maintain both opportunity and subjugation. But equally important, in their successful efforts to secure federal appointment, those who served in Washington's workforce were the embodiment of those possibilities and limitations.

Building and managing this workforce had implications beyond the execution of policy. It shaped the relationship between the executive and the Senate, it established the federal presence in disproportionate ways throughout the United States, and it made manifest the extent and limitations of freedom in the fledgling republic.

A Bureaucratic Census

I am not the first to go down this path. Members of the Washington administration also sought to make sense of the employment rolls of the federal government. But they only did so once, and it was not by choice. The challenge facing the administration over two centuries ago reflects the difficulties we face now in developing an accurate portrait of the federal workforce. And that is an important facet of state-building unto itself, for the absence of any cohesive, centralized accounting of federal employment resulted from the confluence of prebureaucratic notions of organizational management and the often unplanned, occasionally chaotic quality of building federal institutions. The urgency of state building imposed unique demands on each government agency, but all of them faced the pressure to move quickly.

The administration's moment of accountability came in May 1792, when Congress demanded that Treasury Secretary Alexander Hamilton produce "statements of the salaries, fees, and emoluments . . . of the persons holding civil offices or employments under the United States (except for judges)."[8] This action came about primarily in response to congressional concerns that Hamilton was building a fiefdom unto himself within the Treasury Department. But that immediate concern only reflected broader, more deep-seated anxieties about the power and cost of centralized government. For all these partisan and ideological concerns, the practical task of producing a concise listing of federal employees proved challenging.[9]

Hamilton delivered the results in February 1793. Congress welcomed the information and promptly released it to the public domain. The 1793 list is a rich source for historians of early federal institutions, but it certainly has its problems. First of all, it is incomplete, a fact that becomes quite clear in its extended title: "List of civil officers of the United States, except judges, with their emoluments." Not only are the judges missing, but so too are the officers of the US Army. Postmaster General Timothy Pickering appears on the list, but Pickering failed to provide Hamilton with a return of his own employees. Finally, the federal territories appear in the most cursory manner possible, listing only the two territorial governors and two territorial secretaries.

In addition to the gaps in the information, the 1793 list is fundamentally static. A snapshot in time, it reveals federal employment at specific moments that may or may not have been typical of broader trends. Nor can the list chronicle federal employment as a lived experienced for public officials. Selection and advancement, tenure in office and removal, geographic location and mobility; all of these experiences that occur over time are by definition missing from the isolated list of 1793.

Even more revealing are the documents that began rolling off the presses in later years. Congress requested a similar list in 1802, and the results were only marginally better. But in 1816, Congress passed a continuing resolution requiring the State Department to produce a published list of all federal employees on a biannual basis.[10] These federal registers provide for the later years of the early republic what remains altogether missing from the earlier years of the era: a single, complete, regularized, and accurate accounting of federal employment.[11]

In the absence of anything like the registers of the 1810s and 1820s, other sources must fill the gap. These are the sources that provide the data for the claims of this essay, and as a result those sources require some explanation, both in their capacity to reveal and their tendency to obscure.

The principal data source for the civil branches of government is *Journal of the Executive Proceedings of the Senate of the United States of America,* more colloquially referred to by historians as the *Senate Executive Journal.* The official record of Senate proceedings, interspersed throughout the *Senate Executive Journal* are presidential nominations and Senate discussions of advice and consent. Taking a "better safe than sorry" approach, Washington assumed that most public offices should undergo the scrutiny of advice and consent. This included all members of the cabinet and the federal judiciary, foreign ministers and consuls, principal revenue collection officials, and senior subordinates in the cabinet offices (i.e., the comptroller of the treasury or the paymaster of the army). Every commissioned officer in the US Army, from freshly minted second lieutenants through the major generals who occupied the highest rank, had his name submitted for advice and consent. The only offices that appear to be missing from the nomination and confirmation process are clerks in the central office staff, postmasters, and territorial officials below the senior leadership level.[12]

Although all commissioned officers in the US Army and Navy underwent advice and consent and are therefore recorded in the *Senate Executive Journal,* I used two different sources that offer more complete data on the career profiles of military personnel. For the army, I used Francis B. Heitman's *Historical Register and Dictionary of the United States Army, from Its Organization, September 29, 1789, to March 2, 1903.*[13] This venerable source contains brief career profiles of army officers, including state or nation of origin, state of residence when an officer was commissioned, and a list of promotions and unit assignments.[14] Although the Continental Navy was demobilized and its officers decommissioned after the American Revolution and Congress did not reauthorize the US Navy until 1794 and none of its ships put to sea until 1798, Washington did nominate four men to serve as captains in the reconstituted fleet. Biographical information and career profiles for these officers come from the digital edition of Edward W. Callahan's *List of Officers of the Navy of the United States and of the Marine Corps, from 1775 to 1900 . . .* compiled by the Naval Historical Center.[15]

It bears repeating that these results are exclusively for commissioned officers in the military. Enlisted personnel remain a black hole of historical research, especially for the 1790s. Data on enlistments, length of service, and movement within enlisted ranks remain almost nonexistent.[16]

The post office in general and local postmasters in particular have been the subject of much inquiry both for academic historians and individual enthusiasts. But no single machine-readable data set records the creation of post offices and the appointment of postmasters. For this essay, I used the *Preliminary Inventory of the Records of the Post Office Department Compiled by the National Archives.* Hardly a published collection, this material is instead a remarkable gathering of typescript compiled by the National Archives staff under the supervision of Arthur Hecht.[17]

In addition to the post office, federal territories constituted the other vital form of federal employment that existed almost entirely outside the realm of advice and consent. During the Washington administration the federal domain in the West was subdivided into two jurisdictions: the Territory Northwest of the Ohio River (the Northwest Territory) and the Territory South of the Ohio River (the Southwest Territory). The Northwest Territory remained both geographically and administratively cohesive during the Washington administration before being divided during the Adams administration in preparation for Ohio statehood. The state of Tennessee was created from the Southwest Territory in 1796, ending federal jurisdiction during the penultimate year of Washington's presidency. The executive branch enjoyed broad discretion in the selection and management of territorial officials. Appointments occasionally originated from the president, but most were issued by members of the cabinet or by the territorial governors, depending on the importance of the office. The principal source for these data is *Territorial Papers of the United States,* supplemented with additional material from the *Executive Journal of the Northwest Territory.*[18]

The greatest challenge to reconstructing the federal workforce remains the men physically closest to the president: the appointed officials in the nation's capital. Those men began with the cabinet, members of which underwent advice and consent. But the subordinate staff is more elusive. Consisting principally of clerks, these personnel did not require Senate approval, nor do they appear in other composite sources. The 1793 list of civil officers provides one of the only reliable enumerations of central office staff.

What follows is an analysis that considers these data as chronological, spatial, and institutional phenomena, each one telling a different story of functional realities of governance during the early republic.

The Chronology of Appointment

The experiences of William Short and Thomas Melvill, both of whom received appointment in 1789, were typical of many federal appointees. High-level personnel like Short were the subject of individual nominations, while men like Melvill found their names clustered with numerous other candidates for similar offices. Both men then joined a federal workforce that grew in a dynamic pattern throughout Washington's first term, only to stabilize during his second. In the first term, the seemingly chaotic quality of federal appointment was, in fact, a reflection of the shifting needs of government. In the second term, the relative stability of appointment constituted an institutional reflection of a broader national debate about the appropriate role of government. As a result, while Washington nominated men for office in consultation with his cabinet, the process was never entirely a product of their schedules and their opinions. Instead, the chronology of appointment emerged from the confluence of the administration's choices, the legislative calendar in Congress, and the intense national debate about republican governance.

The broad contours of nomination and appointment during the Washington administration are captured by the data contained within the *Senate Executive Journal* (table 1). High turnover and the creation of new offices combined to make this process a constant reality of the administrative and legislative calendar. Much of this activity came in the Treasury Department, which accounted for 51 percent of all civil appointments during

TABLE 1. Nominations and appointments to civil office by year

Year	Nominations	Change from previous year (%)	Confirmations	Change from previous year (%)
1789	175		174	
1790	114	-34.86	112	-35.63
1791	46	-59.65	43	-61.61
1792	150	226.09	152	253.49
1793	54	-64.00	49	-67.76
1794	58	7.41	56	14.29
1795	65	12.07	64	14.29
1796	65	0.00	62	-3.13
1797	30	-53.85	31	-50.00
Total	757		743	

Washington's Presidency, 66.22 percent of all civil appointments during his first term, and a whopping 87.50 percent during 1792 alone. Examined at a more granular level, these appointments, indeed like almost all appointments, occurred as a direct result of legislative action. Obviously, the large number of appointments in 1789 and 1790 were the direct result of landmark legislation that established federal functions and, in the process, mandated the selection of personnel to execute those functions.

Most of the Treasury Department appointments likewise came as a result of the Revenue Acts of 1789 and 1790, and the Excise of 1791. Likewise, consider the Judiciary Act of 1789. Scholars have long considered this act in limited terms, examining its impact on jurisprudence and federalism. But as Kate Brown demonstrates in her essay, this legislation created the system of lower courts and set in motion a process of collaboration between the judiciary and the executive. It also mandated the selection not only of thirteen federal district judges who represented the judiciary system but also the clerks and marshals who served those courts as well as the US attorneys who represented the executive branch before the court. Finally, the act expanded the cabinet itself through the creation of the office of attorney general. So in the process of establishing a legal system, the Judiciary Act both imposed on the president the task of populating those offices while also providing to the president the means to distribute patronage.

Although the number of nominations and appointments declined during Washington's second term, the number of civil officials certainly did not.[19] Instead, all those appointments had produced a civil workforce

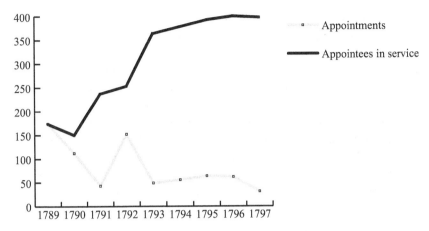

FIGURE 1. Appointments and appointees in service for civil officials

that grew over the course of the Washington administration, experiencing dynamic change during the first term before stabilizing during the second term. Figure 1 shows this simple relationship between appointments and workforce levels.

If nomination and appointment demonstrated a broad pattern divided between Washington's two terms, it was even more clearly delineated within the presidential and Senate calendar. March, August, and December were months consumed by personnel matters in the nation's capital. A full 56 percent of all nominations during the Washington administration (417) came during these three months. The largest single number of nominations came in March, when Congress began its new session. Meanwhile, the large number of August nominations no doubt reflected Washington's desire to settle appointments before Congress went into recess.

One final note on the Senate's role in the nomination process is particularly important. Throughout his administration Washington enjoyed nearly unchallenged authority in the selection of candidates for appointed office. The Senate confirmed 97.44 percent of his nominations, and members of the administration believed they were entitled to broad discretion in selecting administrative appointees.[20] This statistic stands in marked opposition to the conventional scholarly description of a Senate that during its first session sought to engage itself in bureaucratic management and bristled at any sign of executive intrusion, or the Senate that pushed back against executive control of foreign relations during the Jay Treaty debates of 1794–95.[21]

Rejections by the Senate were therefore few and far between. They also demonstrated no pattern in chronology, office, or cause. Indeed, Washington himself often struggled to determine the cause or response. He expressed thinly veiled frustration in an August 1789 letter to the Senate following the rejection of Benjamin Fishbourn, his nominee for a revenue post in Savannah. "Whatever may have been the reasons which induced your dissent, I am persuaded they were such as you deemed sufficient." To this Washington added, "Permit me to submit to your consideration, whether on occasions, where the propriety of nominations appear questionable to you, it would not be expedient to communicate that circumstance to me, and thereby avail yourselves of the information which led me to make them, and which I would with pleasure lay before you."[22] In time, he came to learn that these rejections were rare, unpredictable, and often connected to political realities beyond his knowledge. What's more, Washington apparently did not care. He rarely recorded any particular concern for rejected nominations, preferring instead simply to suggest a replacement. Of far greater concern throughout the administration was the task of filling high-level vacancies, especially when the likely list of nominees declined the offer. The administration faced no difficulty securing the service of revenue officials or consuls or army officers, but federal judges and foreign ministers were another matter.[23]

These patterns of growth and stabilization within the civil branches of government were reflected by the army officer corps. As the army met a series of defeats at the hands of Native Americans in the Northwest Territory that Stephen Rockwell chronicles in his essay, the Washington administration repeatedly sought to increase the army's ranks and restructure its organization. According to Heitman's copious records, exactly four hundred men held commissions in the US Army from 1789 to 1797. As William Skelton and other scholars have demonstrated, the army was perhaps the first branch of the federal bureaucracy to develop a truly cohesive professional culture, due in no small part to the long-term continuity of the officer corps.[24] From 1789 to 1790, most of these men were veterans of the Revolution who had remained in the army through the lean and unpredictable years of the confederation. Some of these men remained throughout the Washington administration, although their numbers were quickly diluted in 1791 and 1792 as the army commissioned a cohort of new officers during the expansion precipitated by the Indian wars. By the end of 1792, the army officer corps numbered approximately 208 men, close to the 222-man average that remained in place from 1792 to 1797.[25]

In addition to the hundreds of officers who received commissions during his administration, in June 1794 Washington also nominated four men to serve as captains in the US Navy. Congress dutifully confirmed the nominations. These men had neither ships nor men to command, but since Congress had authorized the construction of six new frigates,

Washington went about selecting men to supervise their construction and command them once they were ready for sea. In the absence of a separate naval administration, these four captains reported to Secretary of War Henry Knox, and neither Knox nor Washington paid them much attention.

When Washington left office in 1797, it appeared that the military establishment of the United States was on the decline, with the army demobilizing from the war in the West and no indication that the Navy would ever go to sea. But less than a year later the United States was engaged in a massive military employment program. The Quasi War motivated Congress not only to send the existing ships to sea but also to commission numerous other vessels. In addition to commissioned officers and enlisted personnel, Congress established the Navy Department, complete with its own civilian staff.[26] Meanwhile, the army went onto a wartime footing, with numerous officers flooding its ranks. Among the first to do so was George Washington, who revived his military commission as commanding general and immediately found himself once again considering the challenges of appointment as he struggled to select a new cadre of army officers.[27]

Washington personally selected only a small number of these civil and military nominees. Instead, he chose some in consultation with his cabinet or simply forwarded the names of people chosen by the chiefs of the State, Treasury, and War Departments. In addition to providing names that the president would submit for advice and consent, members of the cabinet hired and fired central office staff as they saw fit. The most famous (and infamous) example of an early federal staffer is Philip Freneau, whom Jefferson recruited as a State Department interpreter in a crass attempt to subsidize Freneau's work on the *National Gazette,* the newspaper that Jefferson hoped to become a journalistic outlet for the emerging opposition within the federal leadership.[28] Still other staffers would assume central policy-making roles during the administration. Oliver Wolcott Jr. served as auditor and comptroller in the Treasury Department before becoming the only staffer to join the cabinet proper when he succeeded Hamilton in 1795 as secretary of the treasury.[29] Tobias Lear—Washington's ever-loyal personal secretary—was not only an appointee himself but also became a crucial gatekeeper to the appointment process. He regularly responded directly to applicants and recommendations for public office.[30] These moments ranged from the mundane tasks of transmitting documents to more active engagement in the appointment process. An example of both occurred in June 1791. When the position of comptroller of the treasury was created, Lear received the commission "I had filled with the name of Mr Wolcott & after the seal was affixed to it & countersigned by the Secretary of State I delivered it to that Gentleman." This was the sort of straightforward

TABLE 2. Federal employees as reported by the administration, 1793

	Central office personnel	Other personnel	Total
State	8	15	23
Treasury	84	586	670
War	36	17	53
Judiciary		49	49
Cabinet	3	0	3
Total	131	667	798

act of administrative process typical of Lear and other central office staffers. But once he delivered the letter, Wolcott immediately engaged Lear in an extended discussion about his successor as auditor of the treasury.[31]

For every Freneau or Wolcott or Lear—staffers significant or infamous—there was a variety of more anonymous clerical personnel. It is on this one issue—estimating central office staff and subordinate personnel in federal offices outside the capital—that the 1793 "List of civil officers" ordered by Congress proves most useful. According to the administration's records, 131 staffers were employed in central offices, among a total of 798 federal employees, as shown in table 2.

The 1793 civil list indicates only one postal official: Timothy Pickering, who during the 1790s would amass more high-level appointments than any other public official in the early republic. But ever since Richard John first called our attention to the interpretive values of the postal service, scholars have long trumpeted the deep cultural impact and profound analytical importance of postal employees and the mail they carried.[32] That process began under the Washington administration, but it began slowly as Washington and his three postmasters general (Samuel Osgood, Pickering, and Joseph Habersham) selected the deputy postmasters throughout the United States. While the administration rushed to select diplomatic and commercial officials during Washington's first term, the effort to build out postal delivery only began during the second term, by which point those others government institutions had begun to stabilize. From 1789 to 1792, the administration appointed a total 169 postmasters. From 1793 to 1796, the total surged to 467, before tapering off to 23 during Washington's final perfunctory months in office.

In stark contrast to the post office, the other area of appointment that existed outside advise and consent—territorial administration—underwent the most dramatic vacillations over time of any government agency (see

TABLE 3. Territorial appointments

Year	Nonmilitia appointments	Militia appointments	Northwest Territory	Southwest Territory	Total
1789	7	9	16	0	16
1790	235	321	115	441	556
1791	68	28	36	60	96
1792	30	23	42	11	53
1793	30	21	35	16	51
1794	56	34	18	72	90
1795	110	116	95	131	226
1796	62	49	95	16	111
Total	598	601	452	747	1,199

table 3). The number of territorial appointments surged in 1790 and 1795, their numbers inflated by particularly large numbers of new militia commissions. But these numbers make sense for other reasons. After the initial scramble to assemble territorial institutions in 1789, territorial officials and their superiors in New York began to populate those institutions in 1790. Meanwhile, a growing number of white settlers and the increasingly complex systems of territorial governance further expanded the work roles in 1795. It bears repeating that territorial governments were a federal version of all the governing tasks that were usually left to states or localities.

This was a system of combined jurisdictions. A total of 1,199 men were appointed to territorial office during this period, 238 of whom held multiple offices. The record number of appointments goes to Robert Buntin of the Northwest Territory, who received a total of seven appointments. These offices ranged from clerk in various courts to land surveyor to recorder of deeds.

The federal workforce in all its forms both civil and military overwhelmingly—but not completely—consisted of men. For example, when Alexander Hamilton submitted a list of six lighthouses in Massachusetts and "the Officers appointed for their management," he included "the widow of the late General Thomas" for the lighthouse at Plymouth. Her appointment came with an annual salary of $233.50. It was the second-lowest salary but actually higher than one of the five men appointed to the other lighthouses.[33] The presence of women within the workforce presents an intriguing counterpoint to the all-male ranks of elected officialdom and an all-male electorate.[34] Female federal appointees consisted principally of lighthouse keepers, apparently widows of war veterans or public officials. And that goes a long way toward explaining Hamilton's reference to "the widow of the late General Thomas." Hannah Thomas had been married to Major General John Thomas, who died of smallpox while commanding troops in 1776. Maintenance of and residence in a lighthouse was a form of deferred pension for widows, and other women clearly imagined federal employment in similar terms. In December 1789, for example, Mary Katherine Goddard informed Washington that "she hath kept the Post Office at Baltimore for upwards of fourteen years." When Postmaster General Samuel Osgood removed her, she petitioned Washington to be reinstated, invoking the same sort of language that was so common among men applying for office. She pleaded dire necessity, adding that "she has sustained many heavy losses, well known to the Gentlemen of Baltimore, which swallowed up the Fruits of her Industry, without even extricating her from embarrassment to this day."[35]

So where does this leave us? Put another way, what is the composite picture of federal appointment during the Washington administration? The answer begins to emerge from the data in table 4. These figures need to be interpreted in two ways. First, they are an indication of the number of offices created under the federal system. In other words, this was a policy-making concern. But second, each of these positions also constituted both a challenge in recruitment and retention and an opportunity for patronage. In other words, this was a political concern, as policy makers considered the means of securing loyalty to themselves, to the nascent political factions they led, and to the nation as a whole.

Appointments for men and women—both as a means of generating institutional capacity and as means of distributing patronage—peaked from 1789 to 1792. Appointment was a task that consumed the administration and the Senate most intensively during Washington's first term. In his second term the attention shifted from the challenges of building a workforce to the challenges of managing its actions, both at home and abroad.

This was a process that clearly concerned Congress, and the demand for an accounting by Hamilton reflected long-standing fears about government corruption. Congress provided the impetus for appointment, either by approving the enabling legislation that required a workforce for its implementation or by passing a budget to pay the salaries of that workforce. Nonetheless, the Senate rarely challenged the administration's assumption that selecting and organizing the federal workforce was a function of policy making reserved to the executive branch.

As a result, the fact that the change in federal appointment coincided with the first list of federal employees released in 1793 was most likely more than mere coincidence. Nor was it simply a product of the pushback against

TABLE 4. Appointments by government department, 1789–1797

Year	State	Treasury	War	Judiciary	Army Officer Corps	Navy Officer Corps	Postmasters	Territorial (nonmilitia)	Other	Percent change	Total
1789	9	114	4	46	9	0	2	7	1		192
1790	27	68	1	16	12	0	4	235	0	89.06%	363
1791	5	22	0	13	91	0	4	68	3	–43.25%	206
1792	13	133	2	4	77	0	43	30	0	46.60%	302
1793	14	19	3	13	27	0	22	30	0	–57.62%	128
1794	27	12	0	14	76	4	29	56	3	72.66%	221
1795	6	44	5	7	17	0	37	110	2	3.17%	228
1796	26	17	3	14	19	0	24	62	2	–26.75%	167
1797	11	12	4	4	2	0	9	0	0	–74.85%	42
Total	138	441	22	131	330	4	174	598	11		1,849

Note: These figures do not include the following areas for which data are unavailable: central staff, low-level local officials, enlisted personnel in the US Army, postmasters outside the selected sample states. "Other" consists of miscellaneous appointees whose tasks and authority roles fell outside the standard parameters of the federal government's organization divisions.

Hamilton. Rather, members of Congress wanted to take stock of what kind of federal workforce they had created in Washington's first term. One thing is clear. Throughout Washington's second term, Congress was unwilling to consider any major increases to the federal payroll by expanding the capacity of individual agencies. They certainly wouldn't consider any new agencies.

The Geography of Governance

Thomas Melvill wrote his application from home in Boston; Henry Carbery wrote his during a visit to New York and hoped to join an army stationed principally in the Northwest Territory. These men hoped to serve in a government that was truly *national* in scope. But what exactly did national mean? For that matter, what did it mean for the United States to have a foreign service populated by men like William Short? Federal appointments might be located in every state and territory of the union, but few of them had broad geographic authority, and almost none of them had authority that was coterminous with state boundaries. Residents of the United States encountered the federal government in specific locations. These were occasionally in certain types of spaces: the customhouses and court buildings or the stores that often housed post offices. But federal officials themselves were likewise located in certain places, either clustered together alongside fellow employees or isolated both at home and abroad. The federal government that emerged during the Washington administration was concentrated on the Atlantic seaboard and throughout the territorial West. In between was land of limited federal contact and limited federal governance.

These two regions of federal employment—coastal and interior—were integrally connected. The coastal workforce concerned itself primarily with collecting federal revenue. The interior workforce consumed much of that revenue, in very specific ways. It was the interior workforce more than any other that expressed the fundamental role of government in the early republic: to secure liberty for white citizens and subordination for nonwhites.

The geographic realities of federal employment are best understood in spatial terms, represented both quantitatively and visually.[36] Before examining those realities in detail, however, one spatial factor remains both abundantly clear but frustratingly vague. The vast majority of the US Army was stationed in the West, principally in the Northwest Territory. But specific unit locations varied over time, and the data do not lend themselves either to analysis spanning the Washington administration or to the sort of specificity made possible by the fixed nature of other data points.

In the most general terms, the federal workforce was overwhelmingly focused on domestic responsibilities. The *Senate Executive Journal* records a total of 917 appointments in the United States and 97 (10.5 percent) overseas. The bulk of the 97 overseas appointees (79, constituting 81 percent) were in Europe, with the remaining 18 distributed throughout the islands of the Atlantic and Caribbean, the Barbary powers of North Africa, and a few consuls scattered to the four winds in places like Canton, China, and Calcutta, India.

The appeals for office and the distribution of appointment are best understood in relation to the following data points: applications to office, appointments as recorded by the *Senate Executive Journal*, the snapshot in time provided by the 1793 list of civil officers, and the returns from the 1790 census. Census results for adult white male numbers are the most revealing because officeholding was reserved to men (with the exception of the small number of women who supervised lighthouses). The results are shown in tables 5 and 6. It is worth noting that the federal leadership had settled on an administrative division of the country that did not align completely with formal constitutional divisions. Kentucky and Maine were both enumerated as separate census districts well in advance of their separation from Virginia and Massachusetts. Kentucky was already its own federal administrative district (for example, it received a judicial district separate from Virginia), while offices in Maine were occasionally treated as subdivisions of Massachusetts and occasionally treated as part of a separate jurisdiction.

The Mid-Atlantic is overrepresented among applications, most likely for two reasons. First, applicants often traveled to the capital before dispatching an application letter. This was most common in 1789 and 1790, when Washington personally received the largest number of applications, many of them involving situations where aspirants came to New York only to find that the president would not receive them personally. Second, if the Mid-Atlantic is overrepresented among applications, this is only an exaggeration of the existing population disparity, with the Mid-Atlantic constituting the most populace region in the country.

More striking than the Mid-Atlantic's overrepresentation among applications is its underrepresentation in other areas. The 1793 figures reveal New England as overrepresented and the South as underrepresented. In other words, there were more offices to be held in New England and a larger ongoing federal presence. But in terms of officeholders receiving appointments, the South was overrepresented, while New England was underrepresented. In other words, more men received appointments in the South, even though the actual number of offices was apparently less. This statistical incongruence was due in no small part to the far greater turnover in the South, especially in Virginia and South Carolina, where the administration was constantly responding to resignations, deaths in office, and

TABLE 5. Applications and appointments to federal office by state (percent of total)

State	Applications	Appointments	1793 list	Census
Connecticut	48 (2.92)	44 (4.80)	52 (6.56)	60,523 (7.50)
Delaware	43 (2.62)	19 (2.07)	8 (1.01)	11,783 (1.46)
Georgia	71 (4.32)	45 (4.91)	18 (2.27)	13,103 (1.62)
Kentucky	1 (0.06)	7 (0.76)	3 (0.38)	15,154 (1.88)
Massachusetts	120 (7.31)	80 (8.72)	112 (14.12)	95,453 (11.83)
Maryland	258 (15.71)	86 (9.38)	42 (5.30)	55,915 (6.93)
Maine	12 (0.73)	19 (2.07)	35 (4.41)	24,384 (3.02)
North Carolina	53 (3.23)	118 (12.87)	51 (6.43)	69,988 (8.67)
New Hampshire	12 (0.73)	28 (3.05)	21 (2.65)	36,086 (4.47)
New Jersey	72 (4.38)	32 (3.49)	14 (1.77)	45,251 (5.61)
New York	241 (14.68)	49 (5.34)	53 (6.68)	83,700 (10.37)
Northwest Territory	7 (0.43)	24 (2.62)	2 (0.25)	
Pennsylvania	307 (18.70)	26 (2.84)	86 (10.84)	110,788 (13.73)
Rhode Island	115 (7.00)	40 (4.36)	38 (4.79)	16,019 (1.98)
South Carolina	70 (4.26)	45 (4.91)	48 (6.05)	35,576 (4.41)
Southwest Territory	3 (0.18)	22 (2.40)	2 (0.25)	
Virginia	203 (12.36)	169 (18.43)	76 (9.58)	110,936 (13.75)
Vermont	6 (0.37)	24 (2.62)	4 (0.50)	22,435 (2.78)
Capital		40 (4.36)	128 (16.14)	
Total	1,642	917	793	807,094

Note: "Capital" refers to all personnel assigned to the central administration in the federal capitals of New York and Philadelphia.

the occasional refusal to accept office, which occurred before Washington learned the value of preclearing appointments to certain offices. Appointment was both an immediate governing reality reflected in the number of men appointed at any one time and a political reality in which presidents distributed patronage over time.

But what did these appointments actually look like? Put another way, how might these offices appear on a map or be represented through spatial representation? Two sets of illustrations provide an indication.[37] Figures 2–3 are simple point maps designed to represent the spatial distribution

TABLE 6. Applications and appointments to federal office by region (percentage of total)

Region	Applications	Appointments	1793 list	Census
New England	313 (19.06)	235 (26.80)	262 (39.40)	254,900 (31.58)
Mid-Atlantic	921 (56.09)	212 (24.17)	203 (30.53)	307,437 (38.09)
South	397 (24.18)	377 (42.99)	193 (29.02)	229,603 (28.45)
West	11 (0.67)	53 (6.04)	7 (1.05)	15,154 (1.88)
Total	1,642	877	665	807,094

Note: Regional definitions are as follows. New England: Connecticut, Massachusetts, New Hampshire, Rhode Island, Vermont; Mid-Atlantic: Delaware, Maryland, New Jersey, New York, Pennsylvania; South: Georgia, North Carolina, South Carolina, Virginia; West: Kentucky, Northwest Territory, Southwest Territory/Tennessee. These figures do not include personnel working in the federal capitals of New York and Philadelphia.

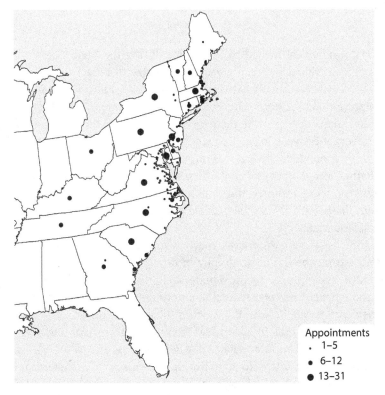

Appointments
. 1–5
• 6–12
● 13–31

FIGURE 2. Geographic distribution of federal appointees in the United States

Appointments
· 1–5
● 6–12
●13–31

FIGURE 3. Global geographic distribution of federal appointees

of appointments confirmed by the Senate during the Washington administration. Individual points are weighted by size to reflect the number of officeholders. Offices with state jurisdiction (mostly judicial appointments) are represented by a single circle in the geographic centroid of the state.

These maps demonstrate the degree to which most forms of domestic civil governance were located squarely along the Eastern Seaboard. This reality corresponded with but was not the result of population demographics. Rather, the majority of civil officials (especially Treasury Department appointees) were assigned not only to the major cities and towns of the Eastern Seaboard but also the isolated ports and dockyards that dotted the coastal landscape.

Figures 4–5 are cartograms, maps whose spatial features have been distorted from the literal geography in order to represent the number of appointments approved by the Senate. Weighted by adult white male population statistics and total federal appointments, respectively, these cartograms demonstrate how, in the existing states of the union, New England in general and Virginia in particular received the largest number of federal appointments, and populous states like Pennsylvania and New York lost out in the competition for patronage. But the reasons for this distortion have less to do with any form of regional preference than the reality of federal policy making. It bears repeating that the largest number of appointments were in federal revenue collection, most of it conducted in ports. With only

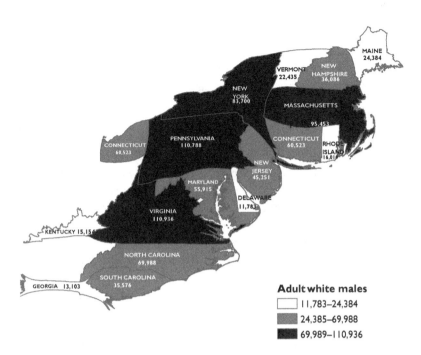

Adult white males

☐ 11,783–24,384

▨ 24,385–69,988

■ 69,989–110,936

FIGURE 4. US map weighted by state population (1790 census)

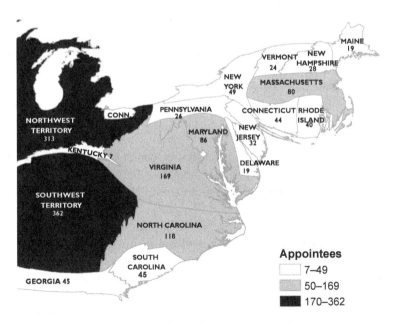

Appointees

☐ 7–49

▨ 50–169

■ 170–362

FIGURE 5. US map weighted by federal appointees from each state or territory

a few ports of entry or delivery, both New York and Pennsylvania had only a limited claim on federal patronage.

Equally important is the comparison between the existing states and the territories, where the cartograms visualize an important statistical reality: the territorial West might contain fewer white residents than the eastern states, but the federal presence was, by definition, far deeper. These maps and cartograms indicate a federal government whose offices within states (rather than federal territories) were located principally in close proximity to the Eastern Seaboard. These offices were heavily weighted toward but not entirely limited to the tasks of revenue collection in the Atlantic ports.

The revenue officials in the East and the territorial officials in the West were, at first glance, completely disconnected. They lived in profoundly different circumstances. They served different masters (most officials in the East took their orders from the secretary of the treasury or occupied the semi-autonomous status of the judiciary; most officials in the West reported to the secretary of state or the secretary of war). But they were inextricably linked, and not simply in their unified service to the Washington administration.

The greatest single expense facing the federal government during the Washington administration was western government. The largest single collection of federal employees—the US Army—was stationed principally in the territorial West. Add to that the expense of civil government. The only mechanism for funding that expense was the revenue system at work in the nation's ports of entry. As Max Edling has shown, Americans conceived of political economy through the model of the fiscal-military state established in Europe. During the Washington administration, the fiscal-military state served the specific purpose of western government.[38]

The government in the West functioned as both a specific bulwark and a general reminder of the function of government in the early American republic. At one moment, this was a government of liberty, nowhere more so than in the West. Territorial administration had at its core the goal of a rapid movement from territory to state, replacing European systems of the permanent subordination of colonial subjects with a newer model of coequal republics.[39]

But as in all aspects of governance within the United States, these opportunities for white citizens always assumed and required the subordination of nonwhites. And that role was usually bifurcated between federal and state leaders. During the Washington administration, federal officials took charge of Indian affairs, specifically the effort to subordinate Indian independence to federal sovereignty. At the same time, states took charge of preserving African American slavery and created legal restrictions for free people of color.[40] This goes a long way toward explaining why the federal legislation in Max Edling's essay so rarely addresses racial supremacy despite the crucial role that it would play in American public life.

But the workforce in the Southwest Territory stands out as an important reminder of the government's extensive role in all forms of racial supremacy, just as it provides an indication of things to come. The Northwest Territory usually assumes primacy of place over its southern partner. After all, it was the first federal territory, and the elimination of slavery in the Northwest has long intrigued historians as both a moment of opportunity and a road not followed. But the Southwest Territory was actually the first federal territory to enter the union, transforming into the state of Tennessee in June 1796. And slavery was alive and well in the Southwest Territory. As in other slave states, it fell principally to the militia to preserve African American enslavement. And those militia officers were part of a federal structure that reported through a clear hierarchy to George Washington.

The need to consolidate slavery, and the militia's traditional role in doing so, may well account for the large number of militia commissions in the Southwest Territory. The dual facets of the federal project of racial supremacy in the West involving both Indians and African Americans, would continue long after the Washington administration. Less than a year after Washington left office, John Adams would follow his lead, creating in the Mississippi Territory a structure that merged the Indian policy of the federal government with the African American policy usually left to states.

William Short, Thomas Melvill, and Henry Carbery each pursued different routes to the same destination of federal employment.

Short soared high but crashed hard. Although confirmed as chargé d'affaires, he never became minister to France, the office he clearly coveted. He spent two years as minister to the Netherlands, only to be replaced by John Quincy Adams, a man eight years his junior whose career already outshone Short's. Short ended his diplomatic career with a frustrating and unsuccessful tenure on the commission established in the wake of the Treaty of San Lorenzo. After spending much of the 1780s and '90s in Europe, Short disappeared from federal governance. He received a second shot at federal employment in 1808 when Jefferson selected him for a recess appointment as minister to Russia. But in one of those rare moments when the Senate rejected a presidential nominee, Short found himself left without a job. The globe-trotting diplomat he aspired to be was a job more easily filled by the likes of John Quincy Adams.

Henry Carbery eventually got his appointment but only after doggedly pestering the administration. In 1792, Washington nominated him for a commission as captain in the US Army, part of the growing cohort of officers in an army undergoing rapid expansion in response to the Indian victories in the Northwest Territory. After all that effort to secure a commission, Carbery soured on army life. He resigned his commission two years later, only to serve again during the War of 1812.[41]

Unlike either Short or Carbery, Melvill found that public service agreed with him. But this should hardly prove startling. Rather than seek the challenges of Atlantic travel and the competition for high office that faced Short or the dismal living conditions and threats to life and limb that faced Carbery, Melvill simply remained at home. Safely ensconced in Boston, he rode out the transition from administration to administration, serving in various revenue offices in the Boston area. Most importantly, he never acquired a reputation as a diehard Federalist, a career-ending label for a host of public officials whom Thomas Jefferson removed from office in a set of summary dismissals during 1801 and 1802. He finally left federal employment in 1830, but whether Andrew Jackson removed him for partisan reasons or because Melvill's work had declined by age eighty remains a mystery.[42]

Somewhere between Short, Carbery, and Melvill was a common experience for federal appointees. The standard tenure in office for men appointed to civil office during the Washington administration was 8.8 years, buoyed principally by Treasury Department employees like Melvill. And that brings us back to the question that began this essay: Are these case studies representative? In some ways, no. Short's foreign service made him unlike the vast majority of appointees who served at home, Carbery was unusual for the brevity of his service, and Melvill was unusual for the length of his. But they were like so many other public officials in the language they used to attain office and in the agencies in which they served. Senior diplomats were often drawn from the elite and semi-elite ranks that produced Short; the army in which Carbery served underwent high turnover during the 1790s; and revenue officials who did not immediately regret their appointments and resigned, or who managed to avoid Jefferson's campaign of removals in 1801–2, often stayed in office for decades. Equally important, the longest-serving federal officials did not see much in the way of promotion. Melvill may have received minor adjustments in his assignments, but these were lateral moves. Outside the military there were few hierarchies to climb, and the longest-serving appointees seemed perfectly happy to stay put.

These data also suggest that scholars need to rethink their understanding of the Washington administration. Too often any focus of the administration is driven by the first few years and especially by the emerging struggles between the titanic figures of Thomas Jefferson and Alexander Hamilton. Once Jefferson left the administration at the end of 1793, the story of politics and policy making during the early republic shifts gears, away from the internal operations within the administration and toward a set of discrete flashpoints. Events of 1794–95 tend to loom large, dominated by the Jay Treaty and the Whiskey Rebellion.

But the realities of state building suggest a specific chronology that runs over the extent of the Washington administration but is clearly divided into two periods. From 1789 to 1793, the administration concerned itself primarily with institutional organization and recruitment; from 1793 to 1797, the administration focused primarily on policy implementation and the institutional management. From 1789 to 1793, the federal workforce was relatively small but undergoing dynamic change. From 1793 to 1797, the federal workforce was relatively large but institutionally stable. The fact that this periodization scheme overlaps with the two terms of the Washington administration is coincidental but not irrelevant. Scholars have occasionally identified distinctions between Washington's two terms, but their discussion has focused primarily on political development and policy objectives. A focus on institutional development tells an equally revealing and potentially more important story. For all the heat generated by debates in New York and Philadelphia about the proper role of government, those debates remained purely theoretical. The recruitment and retention of federal employees made manifest the inchoate notions of what constituted a "large" or "small" federal government. In addition, those employees created the institutional capacity that determined what the federal government could actually do. Alexander Hamilton and Oliver Wolcott could not establish fiscal solvency without a stable and reliable cohort of revenue collection officials in the nation's ports. Thomas Jefferson, Edmund Randolph, and Timothy Pickering could not supervise foreign relations without the ministers who represented the United States in foreign countries or the consuls who provided the bulk of foreign intelligence. Samuel Osgood, Timothy Pickering, and Joseph Habersham could not make the post office an instrument of national unity without local postmasters. Finally, Henry Knox, Timothy Pickering, and James McHenry could not make progress on securing racial supremacy in the West without an army led by a growing officer corps.

In 1794, Washington made his own assertion of executive authority over the appointment process in stern terms. As Alexander Hamilton came under increasing criticism from the emerging Republican opposition, Washington wrote, "I *alone* am responsible for a proper nomination." Perhaps so, but populating the federal workforce was never entirely under Washington's control. Instead it emerged from a set of institutional demands and the self-interest of those who sought and received public office. The recipient of Washington's letter was none other than James Monroe, who expressed an abiding hatred for Hamilton.[43] Washington was clearly frustrated with Monroe, all the more so because he had just selected Monroe for the post of minister to France. Monroe spent much of the next twenty years in and out of federal employment, serving as a globe-trotting diplomat, secretary of state, and (for the briefest time possible) secretary of war. Thomas Melvill was still on the federal payroll when Monroe assumed office as the nation's fifth president. A generation after confronting Washington, Monroe would face Washington's challenge as he joined the cohort of presidents who, over the course of the early republic, sought to create and sustain the federal workforce.

Notes

The author wishes to acknowledge the invaluable assistance of the following individuals and institutions at Washington University in St. Louis: at the Humanities Digital Workshop (HDW), Douglas Knox and Steven Pentecost; in the Data Services division of the Washington University Libraries, Jennifer Moore and William Winston. The author also wishes to thank the numerous graduates and undergraduates who contributed data to this collection. Funding for this project was provided by the American Council of Learned Societies, a Mellon Foundation subgrant provided by Documents Compass at the Virginia Foundation for the Humanities, the Weidenbaum Center on Politics and the Economy at Washington University, and Arts and Sciences from Washington University.

1. George Green Shackelford, *Jefferson's Adoptive Son: The Life of William Short, 1759–1849* (Lexington: University Press of Kentucky).

2. Thomas Melvill to George Washington, 18 June 1789, *The Papers of George Washington: Digital Edition,* Presidential Series, ed. Theodore J. Crackel (Charlottesville: University of Virginia Press, 2008–) (hereinafter cited as *PGWDE-PS*), 3:44–45; *People of the Founding Era,* http://pfe.rotunda.upress.virginia.edu/.

3. Henry Carbery to Washington, 25 July 1789, *PGWDE-PS*.

4. Washington to the US Senate, 15 June 1789, *PGWDE-PS*, 2:498.

5. *Journal of the Executive Proceedings of the Senate of the United States of America* (Washington, DC: Duff Green, 1828) (hereinafter cited as *Senate Executive Journal*), 1:9.

6. *Journal of the Early Republic* 33, no. 2 (Summer 2013): 183–334.

7. Most of the historians who use quantitative methods to study state building during the early republic have tended to focus on military institutions and with revealing results. For examples, see Robert Gough, "Officering the American Army, 1798," *William and Mary Quarterly,* 3rd ser., 43, no. 3 (1986): 460–71; Christopher McKee, *A Gentlemanly and Honorable Profession: The Creation of the U.S. Naval Officer Corps, 1794–1815* (Annapolis: Naval Institute Press, 1991); William B. Skelton, "Social Roots of the American Military Profession: The Officer Corps of America's First Peacetime Army, 1784–1789," *Journal of Military History* 54, no. 4 (1990): 435–52; William B. Skelton, *An American Profession of Arms: The Army Officer Corps, 1784–1815* (Lawrence: University Press of Kansas, 1992); J. C. A. Stagg, "Soldiers in Peace and War: Comparative Perspectives on the Recruitment of the United States Army, 1802–1815," *William and Mary Quarterly,* 3rd. ser., 57, no. 1 (2000): 79–120.

8. *American State Papers: Documents, Legislative and Executive, of the Congress of the United States* (Washington, DC: Gales and Seaton, 1832–61), 1:57–68. *American State Papers* lists the report as 1792, and the list has often been attributed to that year. But even if the request originated in 1792, the information was not complete nor was it reported to Congress until 1793.

9. Alexander Hamilton to Thomas Jefferson, 6 October 1792, *The Papers of Thomas Jefferson: Digital Edition*, Main Series, ed. Barbara B. Oberg et al. (Charlottesville: University of Virginia Press, 2008) (hereinafter cited as *PTJDE-MS*), 24:445.

10. *The Public Statutes at Large of the United States of America* (Boston: Charles C. Little and James Brown, 1845), 3:342.

11. First published in 1816, this biennial publication had reached a stable form by 1820. See *A Register of Officers and Agents, Civil, Military, and Naval, in the Service of the United States . . .* (Washington, DC: Government Printing Office, 1816); *A Register of Officers and Agents, Civil, Military, and Naval, in the Service of the United States . . .* (Washington, DC: Government Printing Office, 1820). For the 1802 list, see *American State Papers*, 1:260–319.

12. The data for this analysis originate from the digital edition of the *Senate Executive Journal* placed online by the Library of Congress as part of the *Century of Lawmaking for a New Nation Project*. The Library of Congress produced a transcribed, machine-readable version of the *Senate Executive Journal* with SGML encoding. For information on the *Senate Executive Journal* and the digitization process conducted by the Library of Congress, see https://memory.loc.gov/ammem/amlaw/lwej.html. A team of undergraduate and graduate assistants supported by the HDW extracted all nominations from the *Senate Executive Journal* through a process of individual review assisted by keyword emphasis for terms such as "nominate" and "appoint." The workflow process included a preliminary process of data recording followed by two levels of review for accuracy. Each process was conducted by a different research assistant. The data were recorded in a MySQL database, which was exported to Excel for purposes of the analysis for this paper.

13. Francis B. Heitman, *Historical Register and Dictionary of the United States Army, from Its Organization, September 29, 1789, to March 2, 1903* (Washington, DC: Government Printing Office, 1903).

14. The data for this analysis originate from the 1903 edition of Heitman digitized by GoogleBooks. This digital edition contained scanned pages and limited, inaccurate optical character recognition. In order to produce a reliable, machine-readable data set, an outside provider was contracted to produce a transcription with limited XML tagging. An undergraduate research assistant, working under the supervision of the HDW, conducted further tagging to facilitate more robust and complex analysis. The data were exported to Excel for purposes of the analysis for this paper.

15. Edward W. Callahan, ed., *List of Officers of the Navy of the United States and of the Marine Corps, from 1775 to 1900 . . .* (New York: L. R. Hamersly), http://www.ibiblio.org/hyperwar/NHC/Callahan/.The digital edition was compiled by volunteers and placed online with basic HTML markup.

16. Stagg, "Soldiers in Peace and War," 79–120. The earliest reliable records for enlisted personnel in the US Army begin in 1802.

17. "Preliminary Inventory of the Records of the Post Office Department" (Washington, DC: National Archives Record Group 28). An undergraduate research

assistant photographed the entire collection using a digital camera. Undergraduate research assistants transcribed the information into Excel, and those Excel spreadsheets provide the data for this analysis.

18. Clarence Edward Carter, ed., *The Territorial Papers of the United States* (Washington, DC: Government Printing Office, 1934–75). The data for this analysis were compiled by a team of undergraduate and graduate research assistants working collaboratively on all pre-1830 federal territories. Working from the bound volumes of *Territorial Papers of the United States* and selected additional sources, the research assistants recorded all references to nominations and appointments to territorial office. The data were recorded in a MySQL database, which was exported to Excel for purposes of the analysis for this essay.

19. In the absence of a contemporary list of civil appointees, these data were compiled through the analysis of office creation, personnel appointments, and departures from office as recorded by the *Senate Executive Journal*. The decline from 1789 to 1790 was the result of several offices going vacant for extended periods as a result of near-immediate departures by some appointees.

20. Jefferson, Opinion on the Powers of the Senate Respecting Diplomatic Appointments, 4 April 1790, *PTJDE-MS*, 16:378–80.

21. Brian J. Cook, *Bureaucracy and Self-Government: Reconsidering the Role of Public Administration in American Politics* (Baltimore: Johns Hopkins University Press, 1996), 24–48; Todd Estes, *The Jay Treaty Debate, Public Opinion, and the Evolution of Early American Political Culture* (Amherst: University of Massachusetts Press, 2006).

22. Washington to the Senate, 6 August 1789, *PGWDE-PS*, 3:391–92.

23. Washington to Edmund Randolph, 30 November 1789, *PGWDE-PS*, 4:348; John Jay to Washington, 30 April 1794, *PGWDE-PS*, 15:683; Randolph to Washington, 14 May 1794, *PGWDE-PS*, 4:348; Robert R. Livingston to Washington, 15 May 1794, *PGWDE-PS*, 16:75.

24. Skelton, "Social Roots of the American Military Profession"; Skelton, *An American Profession of Arms*.

25. These figures were produced from a similar analytical method as the one used with the *Senate Executive Journal*, using Heitman's data on commission and departure dates to produce an average number of officers commissioned during a given year.

26. McKee, *A Gentlemanly and Honorable Profession*, 3–27.

27. For a revealing discussion of officer selection during the Quasi War, see Gough, "Officering the American Army, 1798," 460–71.

28. Jeffrey L. Pasley, *"The Tyranny of Printers": Newspaper Politics in the Early American Republic* (Charlottesville: University Press of Virginia, 2001), 73–76.

29. Leonard White, *The Federalists: A Study in Administrative History* (New York: Macmillan, 1948), 123–25.

30. Tobias Lear to Hamilton, 28 December 1790, Harold C. Syrett, ed. *The Papers of Alexander Hamilton: Digital Edition* (Charlottesville: University of Virginia Press, 2011), 7:384; Washington to Lear, 15 June 1791, *PGWDE-PS*, 8:268–69; Hamilton to Lear, 17 February 1792, *The Papers of Alexander Hamilton: Digital Edition*, 11:37; Lear to Hamilton, 18 February 1793, *PGWDE-PS*, 12:92.

31. Lear to Washington, 23 June 1791, *PGWDE-PS*, 8:294–96.

32. Richard R. John, *Spreading the News: The American Postal System from Franklin to Morse* (Cambridge, MA: Harvard University Press, 1995).

33. For example, see Hamilton to Washington, 3 January 1790, *The Papers of Alexander Hamilton: Digital Edition*, 6:44.

34. Sean Wilentz, *The Rise of American Democracy: Jefferson to Lincoln* (New York: W. W. Norton), 201–2.

35. Mary Katherine Goddard to Washington, 23 December 1789, *PGWDE-PS*, 4:426–28.

36. Jo Guldi, "The Spatial Turn in History," Scholas' Lab, Spatial Humanities: A Project of th Institute for Enabling Geospatial Scholarship, http://spatial.scholarslab.org/spatial-turn/the-spatial-turn-in-history/index.html.

37. All illustrations were produced by Jennifer Moore and William Winston in the Data Services division of the Washington University Library.

38. Max M. Edling, *A Revolution in Favor of Government: Origins of the U.S. Constitution and the Making of the American State* (New York: Oxford University Press, 2003).

39. Peter S. Onuf, "Liberty, Development, and Union: Visions of the West in the 1780s," *William and Mary Quarterly*, 3rd. ser., 43, no. 2 (1986), 179–213; Peter S. Onuf, *Statehood and Union: A History of the Northwest Ordinance* (Bloomington: Indiana University Press, 1987).

40. Brian Balogh, *A Government Out of Sight: The Mystery of National Authority in Nineteenth-Century America* (Cambridge: Cambridge University Press, 2009); Robin L. Einhorn, *American Taxation, American Slavery* (Chicago: University of Chicago Press, 2006).

41. The Maryland Executive Council to Washington, 18 February 1792, *PGWDE-PS*, 1:114; *Senate Executive Journal*, 1:114; Heitman, *Historical Register and Dictionary of the United States Army, from Its Organization, September 29, 1789, to March 2, 1903*, 281.

42. Carl E. Prince, "The Passing of the Aristocracy: Jefferson's Removal of the Federalists, 1801–1805," *Journal of American History* 57, no. 3 (1970): 563–75; *Senate Executive Journal*, 4:46.

43. Washington to James Monroe, 9 April 1794, *PGWDE-PS*, 15:551.

The Theory and Practice of Federalist Political Economy

GAUTHAM RAO

The ratification of the US Constitution of 1788 gave President George Washington and his Federalists command of the new federal government at the moment of its creation. The first years of the Washington administration would be consumed with creating the institutional infrastructure of federal governance. Political economy was a particularly important area for this project of building a new American state. Political economy, or the science of the wealth of nations, chiefly concerned how the state could channel "the annual labour of every nation" toward the accumulation of national wealth and resources.[1] To be sure, during the preceding decade elite Americans had embarked on a sprawling dialogue about the problem of national political economy. The location of political authority, the nature of governmental institutions, and the scale and scope of taxation were debated in newspapers, pamphlets, broadsides, to say nothing of coffeehouses and city commons. The Constitution seemed to settle these questions by creating the federal government and setting forth how it would function. Yet as witnessed by the experiences of Washington and Alexander Hamilton, his chief aide on political economy, the Constitution had merely enclosed the discussion of national political economy within the narrower confines of Federalist ideology and federal administration.

This chapter recounts the theory and practice of Federalist political economy in the first few years of the new federal government's operations. It centers on customhouses, the federal government's most significant institution in the realms of taxation and regulation. In an era long before the advent of the income tax, customs revenue was intended to be the federal government's chief source of revenue. Article I, Section 8, of the new Constitution granted Congress the power to levy duties. Moreover, customs duties were far preferable to other forms of taxation because of their unobtrusiveness. The federal government would assess taxes on imported goods, importing merchants would pay the duty to customs officers, and then the merchants would pass along the cost of the tax into the price of goods en route to the marketplace. Customs duties thus limited the institutional footprint of taxation to the venue of the customhouse. By way of contrast, property taxes would require officers to assess individuals' holdings while also raising the specter of taxing one type of property—the human kind—that would make them unpalatable for southern slaveholders. Customhouses, then, would channel the government's cut of Atlantic commerce into federal coffers to pay the interest on the newly consolidated federal debt, to bankroll federal operations, and defray the cost of the new civil list.[2]

Yet the elegant design of this branch of federal political economy would pose hoary questions about the relationship between the state and the marketplace in the shadows of the American Revolution. First, Congress faced a hypothetical crisis of governance as it would struggle to determine what commodities to tax and regulate and to what extent to do so. With the revolutionary experience looming in the background, congressmen pondered whether federal customs officers would be able to successfully insert the appendages of the state into the notoriously ungovernable Atlantic marketplace.[3] These same problems seemed all the more challenging as the new government sprang into operation. How exactly would federal customs men collect revenue? How would they tell merchants—long accustomed to doing as they pleased—what they could or could not traffic, to which ports? In short, it would fall on customs officers to determine in practice the limits and capabilities of the new federalist political economy.

Ultimately, this chapter argues, Congress and federal customs officers managed to align the tumultuous tides of Atlantic commerce on their shores with the national purpose of federalist political economy during the Washington administration. On one hand, Congress solved the riddle of customs governance by abandoning grand visions of high republican governance through the virtue of officeholders and merchants. Instead, it created statutory rules of officeholding and customs regulation that mirrored familiar British precedent. On the waterfront a similar phenomenon occurred as federal customs officers found that the best way to establish the authority of a distant central government was to do as British imperial customs officers had done for decades past, by negotiating their authority with the merchants that passed through their port. In identifying how Congress and officeholders put into practice the Federalists' political economy, this chapter offers a different perspective from accounts that have typically privileged political culture and ideological dimensions of federal governance in the first years of the new republic.[4] While understandings of institutions and citizenship were undoubtedly significant, the problem of connecting the new federal government with the world of Atlantic capitalism posed pressing demands and required immediate if seemingly ad hoc solutions.

Political economy was a central topic of political dialogue in the 1780s because the United States emerged from the War of Independence awash in debt. Although political leaders throughout the United States entertained different and sometimes competing visions of how the government should fund itself, there was widespread agreement that the Continental Congress's fiscal methods were no longer viable. During the war, Congress relied on three approaches to funding itself and the war effort: loans from banks and foreign nations, "requisitions" of funds from the states, and so-called paper money that it printed on its own authority. That the United States secured independence from Great Britain suggests that Congress succeeded in its fiscal endeavor. That the states and federal government owed upward of $70 million suggested the opposite, though, and the fiscal precariousness of the first federal government pushed political economists of considerable talents to rethink the status quo.[5]

Robert Morris and Alexander Hamilton were the two political economists that most vociferously advocated a customs revenue system in these years. Both agreed that in theory customs duties were the optimal solution to the nation's fiscal crisis. As Robin Einhorn explains, the customs or the impost offered "several advantages" because it limited tax collection to the locale of the customhouse. Since merchants paid the tax to the government upon the act of importing goods, customs duties also bound the commercial elite and their merchant capital to the spine of the new state. Moreover, the colonies and states had routinely relied on imposts for revenue.[6] Morris's advocacy of the impost was indeed dramatic. As the first and only superintendent of finance, Morris was tasked by Congress with restoring public credit, and he believed that impost revenues were crucial to doing so by creating "a Funded Debt" with which to pay the interest on the nation's loans. Yet the political obstacles to a national impost proved impossible and led to Morris's ouster in 1784.[7] Hamilton contemplated customs duties beginning in his sprawling letter at the end of the 1770s—most likely addressed to James Duane—as part of a "vigorous system of taxation" that would shore up government finance and convince "the monied and trading men within ourselves" to loan funds to the United States. Yet Hamilton's efforts—as author of the *Continentalist*, as a requisition tax collector, as a congressman, and a New York assemblyman—to convince Congress to adopt a customs revenue system went the same way as Morris's had.[8]

Yet the Constitutional Convention furnished a more welcoming stage for Hamilton's preferred political economy. He did not shy away from the potential problems that would face a federal customs duty system, especially the dilemma of what would happen to nascent federal taxing authority as it traveled to the nation's peripheries, at the water's edge. "Distance has a physical effect upon mens minds," he explained, most ominously.[9] He more forcefully advocated for the benefits of a customs system in *The Federalist*. Broken federal finance had wrought the terror of Daniel Shays, he explained in *Federalist* 1. As he built a more nuanced case for his vision, he explained that the collection of customs revenue from the movement of "commerce" would defray the cost of military expansion and procurement, federal institutional development, and of course, "for the payment of the national debts." The argument would prove persuasive for the time being.[10]

The federal taxing power came into existence with the ratification of the Constitution of 1788 and specifically with the inclusion of Article I, Section 8. The first Congress thus turned its attention in 1789 to fashioning the statutory foundation of the customs revenue system. After it became immediately clear that there was little precedent to stand upon, James Madison and other congressional leaders proposed adopting the failed 1783 impost only to find it missing the actual rates of taxation on commodities.[11]

The subsequent debate about what imported goods Congress should tax or regulate revealed the persistence of regional parochialism and biases under the new Constitution.[12] A related if more fundamental doubt about the viability of federal customs duty collection also received a great deal of discussion. Connecticut's Jeremiah Wadsworth, who had once been a sea captain and merchant, warned his colleagues in Congress that if a duty on liquor, for example, was perceived to be too high for the importing merchants, "it can never be collected."[13] Counteracting this sentiment was the reality of successful state imposts that Hamilton and Morris had raised just years before. Pennsylvania, Virginia, New York, Maryland, and Massachusetts, for example, all were evidence that impost collections could work.[14] Courts and legislatures also seemed to be moving toward strengthening the impost systems. In 1784 Maryland imposed new central controls on impost collections, while Virginia offered more widespread enforcement the following year.[15] In the Philadelphia Court of Common Pleas in 1787, Judge Edward Shippen explained that importation revenue laws "are of a harsher nature than any others, and necessarily so; for, the devices of ingenious men, render it indispensable for the Legislature to meet their illicit practices with severer penalties."[16] Between 1785 and 1788, the New York Court of Admiralty saw twenty-three condemnations out of twenty-seven impost enforcement cases.[17]

But could federal customs officers do as well as their state counterparts? The recent revolutionary past clouded the problem. "From the experience we have had of the opposition of our people to the British acts of Parliament," explained Massachusetts's Fisher Ames, "if the same opinion is entertained with respect to our ordinances, that . . . will be defeated in a similar manner."[18] Putting aside this uncomfortable history, there simply would not be enough customhouses or customs officials to police the coasts. "We have an extensive sea-coast, accessible at a thousand points, and upon all this coast there are but few custom-houses where officers can be stationed," warned Thomas Tudor Tucker. The only way "to render us perfectly secure in the collection of our duties" would be to establish so great a "number of custom-houses, on those parts of the coast most assailable." But this would ultimately undermine the entire rationale of the impost, he concluded, for "it would require more revenue to support such a system than all we shall derive from the impost."[19]

The United States would in fact have to rely upon the people themselves to sustain the law. For Fisher Ames, the nation's abject dependence on the obedience of the people underscored the dangers posed by a class of smugglers who had emerged into the light during the Revolution. According to Ames, speaking now with not a little condescension, the law could only work if "the merchants are to associate, and form a phalanx in our support" and if the merchants' "private honor is to be called in aid of public measures." Even supposing that "the most respectable merchants will disdain to smuggle," did not the law place the United States at the mercy of the "inferior characters, I care not what you call them, infamous parricides, ready to defraud your revenue by evasion, or any other means in their power"?[20] There were three pointed answers to Ames's pessimistic view of human nature. James Madison believed that mere passage of the law would inform "the citizens of America . . . that their individual interest is connected with the public." Roger Sherman of Connecticut took a far more sanguine view. "I think we ought to rely a great deal on the virtue of our constituents," he argued, because "they will be convinced of the necessity of a due collection of the revenue" and "will give all the assistance in the execution of the law that is in their power." The merchants were part and parcel of the people too. "The mercantile part of the people," he concluded, "will submit themselves to our ordinance, and use their influence to aid the collection." There would of course be some slack in the system—"some characters concerned in an illicit trade, acting without principle," but "we can restrain them" by attaching a stigma "of infamy" to smuggling. Alexander White of Virginia believed that the spirit of the nonimportation movements of the 1760s and 1770s would now rise again to support the new government. "Something like this," he was sure, "may be expected to take place now."[21]

Then came the grueling debates about specific articles and rates of duty as an already cantankerous Congress struggled to the point of exhaustion.[22] During these debates Senator Arthur Lee of Virginia distinguished himself in his willingness to protract discussion with histrionics—"so tremendous an accent, and so forlorn an aspect, as would have excited even Stoics to laughter"—until his wishes were met. Pierce Butler of South Carolina took his seat in the Senate "and flamed like a Meteor" with the repeated charge that the impost, and anything like it, would "ruin South Carolina." Though they had given observers a preview of the tenor of debates over the tariff for decades to come, Lee and Butler would eventually lose their epic rhetorical battles as the Senate and House reconciled their bills by late June.[23] The impost, or tariff, as it would thereafter be called, that President George Washington signed into law in 1789, had been at the center of American political and political economic debate of the 1780s. It was now law.

Within the span of a few months in 1789, Congress enacted a revenue system that mirrored the British navigation laws that had so recently inflamed colonial anger. Both were primed to generate revenue. The intent of the Sugar Act of 1764, for instance, was "for Granting Certain Revenues in the British Colonies," while that of the 1789 tariff was "for the support of government, for the discharge of the debts of the United States."[24] In both instances, too, the state took particular aim at deriving revenue from taxing West Indian luxury goods such as rum, molasses, Madeira, and sugar. Here, then, Congress and Parliament contemplated the American as a cosmopolitan consumer who enjoyed the great luxuries of colonial plantations. Fashionable though it may have been to speak of the virtuous republican farmer, Americans' penchant for the finer things was a foundation of central finance for both the British Empire and early United States. In short, after a decade-long, tortuous experiment with central government, Americans imposed upon their commerce and their waterfront virtually the same extractive system of taxation and regulation that had ruled under the British Empire.[25]

Like the Navigation Laws, the first tariff also discriminated against rival nations' trade. Since the end of the War of Independence, Great Britain had barred American vessels from trading in the British West Indian colonies. The United States now returned the favor. Congress placed high duties on British West Indian produce with the hopes of channeling American merchants toward other European powers.[26] Congress also embraced a secondary level of commercial discrimination by distinguishing between the rights and duties of foreign and domestic vessels. The Registering Act of 1789 essentially Americanized the dusty statutory foundation of British mercantilism, the Navigation Act of 1660. The Navigation Act had created two tracks of commerce: foreign and domestic. The law sought to encourage British participation in domestic trade by limiting it to vessels owned by British subjects. The Registering Act created precisely the same system for the United States, though trade between the states would be called "coastwise" trade.[27]

Whether it was because of the undeniably British influence on the first federal tariff legislation or some other impetus, Congress seems to have reconsidered its blind trust in the idea that the virtue of the people would make the federal impost a self-executing law. In May 1789, a handful of congressmen, led, it seems, by the Maryland delegation, approached that state's impost collector, Otho Holland Williams, and asked him to write what would come to be known as the "Collection Bill." Williams was a strong choice to draft this type of legislation. He had been a general in the Continental Army and a confidant of George Washington. With the peace, Williams returned to Baltimore "to accept an office in the customs in the State of Maryland." It turned out to be a most disagreeable post. Maryland's revenue laws were "ambiguous and exceedingly diffused," he confided to George Washington in 1789. For instance, Maryland required shipowners to register their vessels with the state by securing a special permit from the governor, yet the council provided no template for the permit. Williams took it upon himself "to get [the laws] revised, and after preparing new Bills which were presented to the Legislature, I succeeded in the design." Williams's "design" for Maryland's "customs" borrowed heavily from the British Empire's customs system. Most importantly, Williams centralized taxation and regulation of commerce in "one person, in each port of entry," with "all the several Powers, duties and perquisites, which in most other States have been separated and executed by several persons." The product of Williams's labor was Maryland's lengthy 1784 "ACT respecting the commerce of this state, to prevent frauds in the customs, and to direct the duty of naval officers, and to regulate the conduct of masters and mariners of merchant vessels."[28]

Williams's 1784 bill, after substantial changes by "principal draftsman" New York's John Laurance, became the foundation of the Collection Act of 1789.[29] Customhouses would have three principal officers: the collector, naval officer, and surveyor. Each officer had specific tasks regarding regulation, revenue collection, and paperwork.[30] That the same set of officers had inhabited British colonial customhouses was just one piece of evidence that the US Congress had produced a basic customs revenue system that closely resembled that of the same British Empire that had departed the colonies less than a decade previous. Both systems also divided territory into a grid wherein each square became a jurisdictional district with its own office-holders. For both the British Empire and the federal government, vessels with imported goods were restricted to designated "ports of entry" before arriving at smaller points of disembarkation known as "ports of delivery."[31] The British Empire thereby offered a convenient blueprint for how the fledgling federal government could bundle tranches of Atlantic capitalism into government revenue. But the United States also had developmental visions that surpassed those of distant previous rulers in London. Thus a group of smaller ports would also be designated as ports of entry as Congress wagered on future prosperity.[32]

Early federal customs legislation also aimed to streamline a process of compensating officeholders that had been haphazard and disconten-ting under the British Empire. A "table of fees" would dictate how officers would be compensated in lieu of the more antiquated reliance on "custom-ary" compensatory traditions at a single port.[33] Just as the legislation sought to tighten the formal relation between merchants and officeholders, it also prescribed a more direct relationship between officeholders and the secre-tary of the treasury. Under the British Empire the structure that governed customs regulation was subject to overlapping authority from Parliament, the Board of Trade, the Commissioners of Customs, regional surveyors of customs, governors, and customs officials themselves. In the United States, customs officers reported directly to the secretary of the treasury in order, it was hoped, to strengthen the administrative bonds of the customs revenue system.[34]

Early statutes also established a sound foundation for customs law. The entire system was held together by the customs bond or the individual mer-chant's promise to obey by customs regulations and to pay customs duties. The customs bond dated back to the British Navigation Act of 1660 and, in numerous iterations over subsequent decades, was a pledge of mercantile good behavior to the state. American merchants were well versed in post-customs duty and other bonds, so this aspect of customs law reflected the persistence of a familiar taxing and regulatory mechanism.[35] The logistics of prosecuting customs crimes also borrowed heavily from British prece-dent by prioritizing "*in rem*" suits against seized vessels and cargo instead of "*in personam*" suits against individuals.[36] Jurisdiction marked one notable departure from British customs law, though, because of the presence of a federal court system in the United States. The British Empire had struggled to prosecute customs cases in local colonial courts and, during the Amer-ican Revolution, in the Vice-Admiralty Court in Halifax. The lack of a jury in these admiralty proceedings also spurred colonial ire. Yet in the early United States, customs cases would be tried in the lower federal courts that the Judiciary Act placed in districts throughout the country. Customs cases were thus simultaneously local and national. They would also be tried in front of local juries in service of the federal court.[37]

By the summer of 1789, then, the first US Congress had created the legal architecture of a federal customs system that was intended to fund the new government and implement a Federalist political economy. In the months that followed, this legal architecture would endure a stress test as the customhouses opened for business. As had been the case so often in western modernity, Congress's laws on the books would come to appear very differently when put into practice.[38]

The administrative correspondence between the secretary of the treasury and customhouses on the nation's maritime frontier during the Washington administration tells the story of a struggle over the location of federal authority. Initially, Secretary of the Treasury Alexander Hamilton would assert his right to define how customs law should be interpreted and implemented through a series of detailed "circulars" that contained precise instructions for customs officers to follow. Yet customs officials proved resistant to Hamilton's central authority because as they attempted to make sense of federal customs laws they felt a countervailing pressure that emanated from the men who had business at the customhouse: the nation's Atlantic merchants. In port after port, these merchants demanded that customs officials shirk Hamilton's punitive directives in favor of practices that proved more generous to merchant capital. More often than not, these merchants got their way. Hamilton, though initially uncomfortable with customs officers' use of discretion to innovate governing practices on the waterfront, gradually acquiesced to this administrative system once he was confident that customs duties were producing a reliable revenue stream for the federal government.

The story of customhouse administration in these years can be understood by tracking the content and circulation of Hamilton's preferred means of communication with customs officers on the waterfront: the "circular." These were formal letters from the secretary to customs officers that outlined Treasury policy on fine points of policy. Since congressional statutes tended to be brief and statutory language was often subject to multiple interpretations, Hamilton used the circular to attempt to fill in the administrative gaps of understanding.[39] Yet from Hamilton's very first Treasury circular, his instructions reflected an ambivalence between requiring specific administrative behavior on the one hand or urging customs officers to innovate administrative policies for themselves on the other hand. In his circular to collectors of customs of September 14, 1789, Hamilton thus demanded that officers inform him "of the amount of Duties which have accrued in the several States, and of the Monies which have been already received in payment of them." Yet in the very next sentence Hamilton opened the door for the collectors to interpret the meaning of "Duties which have accrued" and "Monies which have been already received" because, he explained, "in this absolute precision is not expected, but a General Statement accurate enough in the main to be relied on." This pattern would repeat itself throughout his tenure as secretary and provide customs officers with the administrative space to determine practices of governance.[40]

Hamilton's ambiguity between demanding specific figures and a "General Statement" of the customhouses' cash on hand would also trigger a more immediate crisis that revealed how difficult it was for customs officials to administer coercive policies on the merchants in their ports. In short, different customs officials had followed different rules for collecting duties. The problem stemmed from the language of the first tariff law of 1789, which specified that duties could be collected on specified goods "from or after the first day of August" of that year. Yet many customhouses had not been apportioned or staffed by the first of August. Should officers seek to collect duties in this period "prior to the organisation of the Custom houses in the respective districts"? Hamilton believed so. "After mature reflection on this point, I am of opinion that those duties are demandable, and that it is incumbent upon the officers of the customs to claim them, and if disputed, to prosecute the claim to a legal determination," he explained. Hamilton was aware that the "Remedy" he proposed—mass litigation against importing merchants—would cause "inconveniences," but he strictly prioritized the rule of law and the rule of revenue over all else.[41]

The idea that customs officials were to track down unpaid duties and sue for them in federal court would have struck many officers as unwise as it was impractical. For one thing, in the months between enactment of the tariff and the "organization" of customhouses, officers struggled without adequate resources. For instance, collector William Heth in Bermuda Hundred, Virginia, complained that he lacked "official forms for their business" and that his port "never had a naval officer before and he has not even an official seal."[42] Logistical problems aside, Hamilton's directive also flouted an early modern Anglo-American officeholding culture in which relationships between officers and subjects were mediated by the politics of honor, reputation, and respect. In this culture, a suit for debt besmirched the reputation to say nothing of the credit of the debtor and could boomerang back to tarnish the reputation of the rapacious creditor.[43] Thus a few of the collectors balked. Otho Holland Williams in Baltimore refuted Hamilton's interpretation of the statute because "Congress had no executive powers here at the time," while Maryland "had no right then to impose the duty." Thus, he counseled that "the Merchants" in question would "protest against payment" and warned that "payment cannot be enforced." In Philadelphia, collector Sharp Delany was "much embarrassed" by Hamilton's order. Congressman Thomas Fitzsimons, a merchant turned politician who would later be president of the Philadelphia Chamber of Commerce, warned of "the great difficulty that would Arise in Endeavoring to make goods under these Circumstances pay dutys to the United States."[44]

Hamilton gradually relented from pursuing duties presumably owed to the United States between August 1, 1789, and mid-September. On December 30, 1789, he suggested that collectors pursue a single test case in the federal courts to bring the question to a final "legal determination" that would "probably form a rule." He then ceased to press the issue, and in no instance did collectors of customs prosecute scores of local merchants. A few months later he advised Congress to drop the matter altogether.[45] That quiet settlement of the matter was indicative of a broader pattern in administrative governance during Hamilton's tenure as secretary of the treasury: Hamilton's attempt at strict enforcement would meet resistance from customs officers seemingly shielding local merchants. At stake in this struggle was the broader question of where the line resided between federal officeholders and the merchants they were to collect duties from or, even more broadly, between the state and merchant capital. Hamilton was attuned to this potentially vexing problem, for in his second circular to the collectors he took pains to address commercial resistance to customs law. "Though the complaints of the Merchants will not always be infallible indications of defects," he wrote, "yet they will always merit attention, and when they occur, I shall be glad to be particularly informed of them." Self-interest compelled the merchants to criticize the laws that taxed and regulated them, yet they required close attention if only because the merchants were the source of the government's revenue. On the other hand, though, there were fears of the federal government becoming a captured mercantile state. Massachusetts merchant and Federalist extraordinaire Stephen Higginson, for example, warned Hamilton that "a good Officer" of the customs might "be borne down by the combined [w]eight of people in trade." Higginson saw a pressure from commercial peoples that "may in general press" the officer and force "a dependence" that would subvert the rule of law. And yet Higginson too knew that "the great Object is, first, to get a revennue" and that customs taxes were among "the only Sources that can be relied upon."[46]

Among the collectors, William Heth of Bermuda Hundred was perhaps the most outspoken critic of Hamilton's administrative approach. In mid-November 1789, Heth promised to speak his mind to the "*Lord of the*

Treasury" on paper and in person. "The Collection and Coasting acts are unjust, inequitable and subject to abuse," he wrote.[47] Additionally, William Smith, who had been so influential in shaping the initial impost law, urged the other key figure in the bill's drafting, Otho Holland Williams, to camp out in New York for "a fortnight" if Congress took to revising the laws.[48] But there were many complaints from other quarters about the necessity of using their location-specific knowledge and administrative discretion to implement an inchoate system. An official in Maine insisted he had "discretion to dispense" funds as the customhouse business demanded. From Boston "the merchants are in opinion that some allowance, in weighing" sugar should be allowed to account for natural decomposition. Ship captains were causing "no small trouble & difficulty" to the Philadelphia customs officials by demanding a lax interpretation of taxes on tonnage.[49]

Overdue customs duties continued to pose the most significant divergence between the federal law and collectors' practice. While Hamilton eventually gave up on the missing duties of August 1789, he took a far less forgiving view toward merchants who failed to pay duties thereafter. In most cases, these merchants had taken out a bond, or a promise to pay the duty at a later date. But what was to be done if the merchant failed to honor the terms of the customs duty bond? Hamilton requested that "if the Bonds are not paid, *as they fall due* they be immediately put in suit. On this point, the *most exact punctuality* will be considered as *indispensable.*" Hamilton had learned that in previous years state impost collectors, fearing the demise of their reputations, had caused "relaxations" of suits for overdue duties and now colored his instructions with an "air of rigor." But he nonetheless demanded "*strict observance*" in mid-December 1789, as the first customs duty bonds were coming due.[50] In Philadelphia collector Sharp Delany expressed trepidation over Hamilton's strict enforcement policy. He now thought he might soften the blow by distributing "a notice . . . to every person indebted, five days before the bond is due." But Delaney pledged that he undertook "the disagreeable necessity of putting a Bond in suit" and now awaited the outcome.[51]

It would take a few years for Hamilton to recognize that many customs officials failed to implement his policy of strict enforcement. By the end of 1791 overdue customs duty bonds totaled almost $2 million. Baltimore merchants owed $142,235, Charleston merchants owed $172,625, Boston merchants owed $175,651, and New York merchants owed $423,700.[52] Customs officials' reluctance to sue for customs duty bonds would continue for a few decades to come until repeated congressional investigations in the wake of serious financial panics brought statutory changes and, eventually, enforcement changes. Despite Hamilton's vociferous insistence to the contrary, customs officials in the first years of the new republic had chosen en masse not to prosecute for overdue customs duty bonds in order to shield from mass litigation the local merchants that did business at the customhouse.[53]

Although Hamilton would begin to learn the extent of the customs duty bond problem in the following year, already by April 1790 Hamilton had come to fear that his central authority over the collectors was coming unglued. In a lengthy report to Congress on the "defects" of existing revenue laws, Hamilton counted off a list of areas in which customs officials had interpreted laws as they pleased, the most egregious of which was allowing vessels that were supposed to report to the customhouse to roam about and raise the suspicion of smuggling or charging fees for services as was customary at their local port instead of what was specified in relevant statutes and circulars.[54] The most important section was the conclusion, wherein Hamilton called on Congress to create a new class of federal officer within each state who would answer directly to the secretary of the treasury and supervise the collectors of customs in his purview. This measure would have simplified the onerous process of drawing currency in "the most remote parts" of the union, but there were "other reasons of perhaps still greater weight for the measure." Above all, his experience as secretary of the treasury taught him that customs officers were liable "to receive a tint from the personal interests of the individuals and the local interests of districts." This "tint" left customs officials "at present unreliable." They "serve rather to distract, than to inform the judgment" of the secretary. Hamilton believed the new officer was "essential to a due supervision of the conduct of the particular officers engaged in the collection of the revenues, and to the purposes of exact and impartial information, as to the operations which relate to them." This measure would help Hamilton overcome the problem of drift and "distance" between himself and the numerous officers that resided on relatively distant shores. Hamilton's proposed intermediary class of officers between the Treasury and the customhouses would thus relocate administrative authority back to the nation's capital.[55]

Less than a year after the federal government's customs system began operations, the Treasury Department and Congress were already contemplating substantial reforms because the practices of this new engine of political economy had begun to diverge sharply from its original designs. Hamilton's struggles with collectors of customs over the location of administrative authority portended continued drift away from the nation's capital and toward the waterfront.

Congress never acted on Hamilton's request for a solution to the customs officials that had fallen under the sway of "individuals and the local interests of districts." This was not because customs officials suddenly began hewing their practices to the letter of statutes and circulars. Nor was it because they suddenly began to prosecute the many custom duty bonds that had fallen overdue. It was because Hamilton and Congress lost their political will to undertake administrative reform.

The single most important impetus for this seemingly new trajectory was the fact that, despite all the difficulties that plagued customs enforcement and regulation in the months since September 1789, the customhouses were collecting adequate revenue. The revenue numbers began to become clear in the summer of 1790 as Hamilton reported to Congress a likely "surplus of about One Million of Dollars accruing from the duties now in operation." Hamilton believed that this surplus would best be used for "purchases of the public debt in the Market." For the moment, customs revenue thus seemed adequate to support a prized pillar of Hamilton's political economic vision for the new nation. A few months later Hamilton's numbers fixed customs revenue from August 1, 1789, to December 31, 1791, at about $6.5 million. A year later Hamilton's Treasury reported $3.9 million in customs revenue for 1792.[56] Customs officials were using their discretion and deviating from the letter of federal law, and yet the Federalists found themselves relatively flush with revenue.

Or perhaps the Federalists came into this money *because* of how officials were playing fast and loose with the rules of customs law? There is no single document that provides an answer. But a story of the federal government's customs collector in Providence, Rhode Island, suggests that Hamilton and the Treasury had more than made peace with customs officials' deviation from the letter of the law. Jeremiah Olney was a fairly comfortable merchant who had served in the Continental Army and become a confidant of Hamilton's during Rhode Island's protracted discussion of the ratification of the Constitution. George Washington likely had little reason to look at anyone other than Olney for the post of collector of customs for the important port of Providence.[57] But by 1791 Olney found himself at war with the merchants of Providence because he had followed Hamilton's 1789 circular and penalized a merchant with overdue customs bonds. By 1793, the Providence merchants, led by the merchant prince of Rhode Island, John Brown, took their remonstrance public by criticizing Olney for his "vigorous and severe execution of the Revenue law."[58]

Olney's troubles in Providence would continue to spiral, leading to a series of competing lawsuits and appeals that culminated in the 1796 US Supreme Court case *Olney v. Arnold*.[59] For the purposes of understanding Federalist political economy, however, the matter was decided three years before in a letter from Hamilton to Olney. This was not a circular letter that detailed the specifics of the case but rather a more personal message from Hamilton to a trusted confidant who had fallen on rough times. "Some good men, who esteem you and think highly of your conduct," wrote Hamilton, "have expressed to me an idea that it has been in some instances too punctilious, and not sufficiently accommodating." He concluded, "The good will of the Merchants is very important in many senses, and if it can be secured without any improper sacrifice or introducing a looseness of practice, it is desirable to do so."[60]

For Hamilton, it seemed, the lesson of customhouse governance in the first years of the 1790s was that local administrative practices that "secured" the "good will of the Merchants" were more beneficial for the ends of Federalist political economy than practices that may have alienated these same merchants. There was an irony to these proceedings since their critics believed that the Federalists had been captured since their birth by merchant capital. Instead, Hamilton began his tenure as secretary of the treasury seeking to take a coercive posture toward the merchants whose capital was to become the foundation of the federal government's revenue. Yet customs officials on the waterfront instead took a more conciliatory approach toward local merchants as they devised practices to put into motion Congress's revenue laws. Hamilton seemed to relent from his initial policy of strict enforcement as early as 1791, but the Olney saga suggests that the secretary of the treasury's conversion was complete by April 1793. Federalist political economic theory and practice may not have aligned under the Washington administration. Yet at least in terms of the story of customhouses and revenue, this gap is in part what made it work.

Notes

1. Adam Smith, *An Inquiry into the Nature and Causes of the Wealth of Nations,* ed. Edwin Cannan (Chicago: University of Chicago Press, 1976). On concepts of political economy that would migrate to the early United States, see Steven Pincus, "Rethinking Mercantilism: Political Economy, the British Empire, and the Atlantic World in the Seventeenth and Eighteenth Centuries," *William and Mary Quarterly,* 3rd ser., 69, no. 1 (January 2012): 3–34; Pincus, *The Heart of the Declaration: The Founders Case for an Activist Government* (New Haven, CT: Yale University Press, 2016).

2. US Constitution, art. 1, sec. 8, cl. 1. On the comparative unobtrusiveness of customs duties, see Gautham Rao, *National Duties: Custom Houses and the Making of the American State* (Chicago: University of Chicago Press, 2016), 53–74; Max M. Edling, *A Revolution in Favor of Government: Origins of the U.S. Constitution and the Making of the American State* (New York: Oxford University Press, 2003), 209–10. On southern slaveholders' resistance to property taxes, see Robin L. Einhorn, *American Taxation, American Slavery* (Chicago: University of Chicago Press, 2006), 155.

For a discussion of the new federal debt, see Max M. Edling and Mark D. Kaplanoff, "Alexander Hamilton's Fiscal Reform: Transforming the Structure of Taxation in the Early Republic," *William and Mary Quarterly*, 3rd. ser., 61, no. 4 (October 2004): 713–44. For a sense of the size of the new civil list, see Leonard White, *The Federalists: A Study in Administrative History, 1789–1801* (New York: Free Press, 1948); Carl E. Prince, *Federalists and the Origins of the U.S. Civil Service* (New York: New York University Press, 1977); Peter S. Onuf, ed., *Establishing the New Regime: The Washington Administration* (New York: Garland, 1991).

3. See among others, Eliga Gould, "Zones of Law, Zones of Violence: The Legal Geography of the British Atlantic, circa 1772," *William and Mary Quarterly*, 3rd. ser., 60, no. 3 (Jul., 2003): 470–510; Denver Brunsman, *The Evil Necessity: British Naval Impressment in the Eighteenth-Century Atlantic World* (Charlottesville: University of Virginia Press, 2013); Marcus Rediker and Peter Linebaugh, *The Many-Headed Hydra: Sailors, Slaves, Commoners, and the Hidden History of the Revolutionary Atlantic* (Boston: Beacon Books, 2000); Wim Klooster, *Illicit Riches: Dutch Trade in the Caribbean, 1648–1795* (Leiden: KITLV, 1998); Linda M. Rupert, *Creolization and Contraband: Curacao in the Early Modern Atlantic World* (Athens: University of Georgia Press, 2012).

4. For leading studies of federal political culture, citizenship, and ideology, see for instance Stanley Elkins and Eric McKitrick, *The Age of Federalism* (New York: Oxford University Press, 1993); Joanne B. Freeman, *Affairs of Honor: National Politics in the Early Republic* (New Haven, CT: Yale University Press, 2002); François Furstenberg, *In the Name of the Father: Washington's Legacy, Slavery, and the Making of a Nation* (New York: Penguin Books, 2006). Some notable exceptions are Edling, *Revolution in Favor of Government*, on the problem of statecraft; Richard R. John, *Spreading the News: The American Postal System from Franklin to Morse* (Cambridge, MA: Harvard University Press, 1995), on communications policy; Harold D. Langley, *George Washington's Coast Guard: Origins of the U.S. Revenue Cutter Service, 1789–1801* (Annapolis, MD: Naval Institute Press, 1978), on the maritime frontier.

5. On the range of political economic thought in the 1780s, see Max M. Edling, *A Hercules in the Cradle: War, Money, and the American State* (Chicago: University of Chicago Press, 2014), 17–80; E. James Ferguson, *The Power of the Purse: A History of American Public Finance, 1776–1790* (Chapel Hill: University of North Carolina Press, 1961); Roger H. Brown, *Redeeming the Republic: Federalists, Taxation, and the Origin of the Constitution* (Baltimore: Johns Hopkins University Press, 1993). Notably, scholars such as Benjamin Irvin argue that, despite their fiscal demise, paper bills did important cultural work. Benjamin H. Irvin, *Clothed in the Robes of Sovereignty: The Continental Congress and the People Out of Doors* (New York: Oxford University Press, 2011), 75–96.

6. Einhorn, *American Taxation, American Slavery*, 133.

7. Robert Morris to Samuel Huntington, 14 May 1781, *Papers of Robert Morris*, ed. E. James Ferguson, 8 vols. (Pittsburgh: University of Pittsburgh Press, 1973–99), 1:62–64. On the failure of the continental impost, see Brown, *Redeeming the Republic*, 23–24; Einhorn, *American Taxation, American Slavery*, 119.

8. Hamilton to James Duane, *The Papers of Alexander Hamilton*, ed. Harold C. Syrett, 27 vols. (New York: Columbia University Press, 1961–87), 2:245, 247, 244 (hereafter *PAH*); Hamilton, *Continentalist* 4, August 30, 1781, *PAH*, 2:669–71. For the other entries, see Hamilton, *Continentalist* 1, 12 July 1781, ibid., 2:649–53;

Continentalist 2, 19 July 1781, ibid., 2:654–57; *Continentalist* 3, 9 August 1781, ibid., 2:660–65. See one of Hamilton's most significant engagements with the issue in Continental Congress, Unsubmitted Resolution Calling for a Convention to Amend the Articles of Confederation, n.d. [July 1783], ibid., 3:420–26, esp. 423.

9. Max Farrand, ed., *The Records of the Federal Convention of 1787,* 4 vols. (New Haven, CT: Yale University Press, 1966), 1:305. For a broader discussion of Hamilton's performance at the convention, see Rao, *National Duties,* 58–61.

10. Hamilton, "Number XXX," *Federalist,* https://guides.loc.gov/federalist -papers/text-21-30; Brewer, *Sinews of Power,* 118; Edling and Kaplanoff, "Hamilton's Fiscal Reform," 713–44.

11. *Annals of Congress,* 1st Cong., 1st sess., 108–9 (9 April 1789).

12. Jacob E. Cooke, *Tench Coxe and the Early Republic* (Chapel Hill: University of North Carolina Press, 1979), 134–39.

13. Jeremiah Wadsworth, in ibid., 1:203 (24 April 1789).

14. M. E. Kelley, "Tariff Acts under the Confederation," *Quarterly Journal of Economics* 2, no. 4 (July 1888): 473–81; Robert A. Becker, *Revolution, Reform, and the Politics of American Taxation, 1763–1783* (Baton Rouge: Louisiana State University Press, 1980).

15. "An Act respecting the Commerce of this state, to prevent frauds in the customs, and to direct the duty of naval officers, and to regulate the conduct of masters and mariners of merchant vessels," in *Laws of Maryland . . . ,* ed. Alexander Contee Hanson (Annapolis: Frederick Green, 1785), n.p.; Drew R. McCoy, "The Virginia Port Bill of 1784," *Virginia Magazine of History and Biography* 83, no. 3 (July 1975): 298. See also "An act for better securing the revenue arising from customs," (October 1785), *The Statutes at Large . . . of Virginia,* ed. William Waller Hening, 13 vols. (1823; Charlottesville: University Press of Virginia, 1969), 12:46–47.

16. *US Reports: Phile Qui Tam v. The Ship Anna,* 1 US (1 Dall.) 197 at 205–6 (1787).

17. The tabulation is made from the twenty-seven case files in Case Papers of the Court of Admiralty of the State of New York, 1784–1788, RG 21, M948, Archives I.

18. Speech of Fisher Ames, *Annals of Congress,* 1st Cong., 1st sess., 311 (9 May 1789). For a description of Ames's position during this debate, see Winfred E. A. Bernhard, *Fisher Ames: Federalist and Statesman, 1758–1808* (Chapel Hill: University of North Carolina Press, 1965), 83–84. On the long shadow smuggling cast over the coming of the Revolution, see John W. Tyler, *Smugglers and Patriots: Boston Merchants and the Advent of the American Revolution* (Boston: Northeastern University Press, 1986).

19. Thomas Tudor Tucker, *Annals of Congress,* 1st Cong., 1st sess., 304 (8 May 1789). See also speech of Jackson in ibid., 326 (9 May 1789).

20. Speech of Fisher Ames, ibid., 312 (9 May 1789). Ames, though, would become an ardent defender of the customs revenue system. See Herbert E. Sloan, *Principle and Interest: Thomas Jefferson and the Problem of Debt* (New York: Oxford University Press, 1995), 136.

21. Speeches of Fisher Ames, James Madison, and Roger Sherman, *Annals of Congress,* 1st Cong., 1st sess., 312, 315, 317 (9 May 1789). For a similar sentiment to Sherman's see speech of Thomas Fitzsimons, in ibid., 320 (18 May 1789).

22. See, for instance, ibid., 323–50.

23. Kenneth R. Bowling and Helen E. Velt, eds., *The Diary of William Maclay and Other Notes on Senate Debates* (Baltimore: Johns Hopkins University Press, 1988), 57, 65, 72.

24. Though it is worth noting that the Tariff of 1789 was also partially a protectionist measure, what with the phrase in the preamble "the encouragement and protection of manufactures." To the extent that it was protectionist, the law aimed to shelter nascent American manufactures against goods commonly imported from Great Britain, for instance: glass, stone and earthenware, gunpowder, oil paints, shoe buckles, gold lead and lace, blank books, writing paper, wrapping paper, buttons, saddles, gloves, millinery, haberdashery, iron casting, rolled iron, clothing, brushes, and playing cards. US Congress, *The Public Statutes at Large of the United States of America, from the Organization of the Government in 1789, to March 3, 1845*, ed. Richard Peters (Boston: Little and Brown, 1845), 1:24–27 (1789) (hereafter *Statutes at Large*), 24–27 (1789). See William Hill, "Protective Purpose of the Tariff Act of 1789," *Journal of Political Economy* 2, no. 1 (December 1893): 54–76.

25. 1 *Statutes-at-Large*, 24 (1789). Thomas Barrow, *Trade and Empire: The British Customs Service in Colonial America* (Cambridge, MA: Harvard University Press, 1967), 181–85. On the importance of Americans' luxury consumption in political economic design, see Allan Potofsky, "The Political Economy of the French-American Debt Debate: The Ideological Uses of Atlantic Commerce, 1787 to 1800," *William and Mary Quarterly*, 3rd ser., 63, no. 3 (July 2006): 497.

26. The desire to facilitate American commerce with France burgeoned after the Treaty of Amity and Commerce in 1778. See Paul B. Cheney, "A False Dawn for Enlightenment Cosmopolitanism? Franco-American Trade during the American War of Independence," *William and Mary Quarterly*, 3rd ser., 63, no. 3 (July 2006): 463–88. American commerce with Saint-Domingue during this period is explored by Michelle Craig McDonald, "The Chance of the Moment: Coffee and the New West Indies Commodities Trade," *William and Mary Quarterly*, 3rd ser., 62, no. 3 (July 2005): 441–72. On British discrimination against American trade, see Alice B. Keith, "Relaxations in the British Restrictions on the American Trade with the British West Indies, 1783–1802," *Journal of Modern History* 20, no. 1 (March 1948): 1–2.

27. 1 *Statutes at Large*, 55 (1789). See Drew R. McCoy, "Republicanism and Foreign Policy: James Madison and the Political Economy of Commercial Discrimination, 1789 to 1794," *William and Mary Quarterly*, 3rd ser., 31, no. 4 (October 1974): 633–46; R. G. B. Hutchins, *The American Maritime Industries and Public Policy, 1789–1914: An Economic History* (Cambridge: Cambridge University Press, 1941), 164; Barrow, *Trade and Empire*, 1–11.

28. Otho Holland Williams to George Washington, May 12, 1789, George Washington Papers, Series 7, Applications for Office, Library of Congress; A. C. Hanson, *Laws of Maryland, Made since M, DCC, LXIII . . .* (Annapolis, MD: Frederick Green, 1787), 428–37. On the problem of issuing registers, see ibid., 261. According to William Maclay, the House had begun debating a similar law in May 1789 but voted it down once it became known that "Mr. Williams of Baltimore is making One, of his own motion." Bowling and Velt, *Diary of William Maclay*, 47.

29. Bowling and Velt, *Diary of William Maclay*, 47. Maryland Historical Records Survey Project, *Calendar of Otho Holland Williams Papers in the Maryland Historical Society* (Baltimore: Maryland Historical Records Survey Project, 1940), 189. My thanks to Professor Aaron Knapp for pointing out that Laurance's bill supplanted Williams by the summer of 1789, in contravention of my assertion in *National Duties*, 64.

30. See Rao, *National Duties*, 64–68 and table 65.

31. 1 *Statutes at Large*, 145 (1789); Barrow, *Trade and Empire*, 10–18, 77–78.

32. 1 *Statutes at Large*, 24 (1789).

33. 1 *Statutes at Large*, 29 at 45 (1789); Barrow, *Trade and Empire*, 178–79, 189–90. On the "fee system" in nineteenth-century America, see Nicholas R. Parrillo, *Against the Profit Motive: The Salary Revolution in American Government, 1780–1940* (New Haven, CT: Yale University Press, 2013), 221–54.

34. On the contrast, see Theodore Sedgewick to Benjamin Lincoln, 1 August 1789, Reel 9, Benjamin Lincoln Papers, Massachusetts Historical Society.

35. Navigation Act of 1660, 12 Charles II, ch. 18, p. 1. Barrow, *Trade and Empire*, frequently notes the importance of the bond in sustaining the Navigation Acts. On the concept of bonds to secure "good behavior," see Joshua M. Stein, "Good Behavior: The Abuse and Demise of a Preventative Justice Tool," private MS in author's possession.

36. On the *in rem* system, see Barrow, *Trade and Empire*, 76; William R. Casto, "The Origins of Federal Admiralty Jurisdiction in an Age of Privateers, Smugglers, and Pirates," *American Journal of Legal History* 37, no. 2 (April 1993): 117–57.

37. 1 *Statutes at Large*, 145 at 176–77 (1789); L. Kinvin Wroth, "The Massachusetts Vice Admiralty Court and the Federal Admiralty Jurisdiction," *American Journal of Legal History* 6, no. 3 (July 1962): 268. On the Judiciary Act, see 1 *Statutes at Large*, 73–93 (1789); Akhil Reed Amar, "The Two Tiered Structure of the Judiciary Act of 1789," *University of Pennsylvania Law Review* 138, no. 6 (1990), 1499–1567.

38. On this theme in legal history, see for instance Hendrik Hartog, "Pigs and Positivism," *Wisconsin Law Review* 4 (1985), 899–935; Laura F. Edwards, *The People and Their Peace: Legal Culture and the Transformation of Inequality in the Post-Revolutionary South* (Chapel Hill: University of North Carolina Press, 2009); Risa Goluboff, *Vagrant Nation: Police Power, Constitutional Change, and the Making of the 1960s* (New York: Oxford University Press, 2016).

39. On Hamilton's administrative style, see Rao, *National Duties*, 75–102; Jerry L. Mashaw, "Recovering American Administrative Law: Federalist Foundations, 1787–1801," *Yale Law Journal* 115, no. 6 (April 2006): 1256–1344; Richard T. Green, "Alexander Hamilton and the Study of Public Administration," *Public Administration Quarterly* 13, no. 4 (Winter 1990): 494–519; Harvey Flaumenhauft, *The Effective Republic: Administration and Constitution in the Thought of Alexander Hamilton* (Durham, NC: Duke University Press, 1992); Gerald Stourzh, *Alexander Hamilton and the Idea of Republican Government* (Palo Alto, CA: Stanford University Press, 1970).

40. Alexander Hamilton, Circular to Collectors of Customs, 14 September 1789, Circulars of the Office of the Secretary of the Treasury, Reel 2.

41. "An Act for Laying a Duty on Goods, Wares, and Merchandises Imported into the United States," 1 *Statutes at Large*, 24 at 24 (1789). Alexander Hamilton, Circular to Collectors of Customs, 31 October 1789, Circulars of the Office of the Secretary of the Treasury, Reel 2.

42. William Heth to Otho Holland Williams, September 1789, in Williams Catalog, 192.

43. On this early modern moral economy, see Craig Muldrew, *The Economy of Obligation: The Culture of Credit and Social Relations in Early Modern England* (New York: St. Martin's, 1998); Bruce H. Mann, *Republic of Debtors: Bankruptcy in the Age of American Independence* (Cambridge, MA: Harvard University Press, 2002);

Peter J. Coleman, *Debtors and Creditors in America: Insolvency, Imprisonment for Debt, and Bankruptcy, 1607–1900* (Madison: State Historical Society of Wisconsin, 1974).

44. Otho Holland Williams to Alexander Hamilton, 7 November 1789, *PAH*, 6:500. Thomas Fitzsimons to Alexander Hamilton, November 18, 1789, *PAH*, 6:521.

45. Alexander Hamilton, Circular to Collectors of Customs, 20 December 1789, Circulars of the Office of the Secretary of the Treasury, Reel 2; Alexander Hamilton, "Report on Defects in the Existing Laws of Revenue, April 22, 1790," *PAH*, 6:373.

46. Alexander Hamilton, Circular to Collectors of Customs, 2 October 1789, Circulars of the Office of the Secretary of the Treasury, Reel 2; Stephen Higginson to Alexander Hamilton, 11 November 1789, *PAH*, 6:507, 508, 511.

47. William Heth to Otho Holland Williams, 19 November 1789, *Catalogue of the Otho Holland Williams Papers in the Maryland Historical Society* (Baltimore: Maryland Historical Records Survey Project, 1940), 196.

48. William Smith to Otho Holland Williams, 9 February 1790, Williams Catalogue, 202. See also Otho Holland Williams to Alexander Hamilton, October 23, 1789, *PAH*, 5:459.

49. Alexander Hamilton to Stephen Smith, 4 December 1789, ibid., 6:5; Benjamin Lincoln to Alexander Hamilton, 9 December 1789, ibid., 6:9; Sharp Delaney to Alexander Hamilton, 21 December 1789, ibid., 6:25.

50. Alexander Hamilton, Circular to Collectors of Customs, 18 December 1789, ibid., 6:18.

51. Sharp Delany to Alexander Hamilton, December 24, 1789, ibid., 6:33.

52. Alexander Hamilton, Report on the Receipts and Expenditures of Public Monies to the End of the Year 1791, ibid., 13:39; Frederick Dalzell, "Taxation with Representation: Federal Revenue in the Early Republic" (PhD diss., Harvard University, 1993), 204–6, 208–9.

53. See Rao, *National Duties*, 167–96.

54. Alexander Hamilton, "Report on Defects in the Existing Laws of Revenue," 22 April 1790, *PAH*, 6:396.

55. Ibid. 6:396–97.

56. Alexander Hamilton, "Report on Additional Sums Necessary for the Support of the Government," 5 August 1790, ibid., 6:542. Alexander Hamilton, Public Funds: Revenue, Income, Appropriations, and Expenditures, 1791–1792, February 14, 1793, *American State Papers: Documents, Legislative and Executive; Selected and Edited under the Authority of Congress*, 38 vols., Class III, *Finance*, 5 vols. (Washington, DC: Gales and Seaton, 1832–1861), 1:219. The *Historical Statistics of the United States of America* estimates revenue between 1789 and 1791 to have been $4,399,000. The same source provides a precise number for every year thereafter, beginning with $3,443,000 in 1792. Susan B. Carter et al., eds., *Historical Statistics of the United States: Millennial Edition*, 5 vols. (New York. Cambridge University Press, 2006), http://dx.doi.org/10.1017/ISBN-9780511132971, table Ea588–593. On the importance of the funded debt to Hamilton's vision of political economy, see Edling and Kaplanoff, "Alexander Hamilton's Fiscal Reform."

57. For an example of Olney's correspondence with Hamilton, see Olney to Alexander Hamilton, November 3, 1788, Reel 4, Alexander Hamilton Papers, Library of Congress. For Olney's background, see Frederick Dalzell, "Prudence and the Golden Egg: Establishing the Federal Government in Providence, Rhode Island,"

New England Quarterly 65, no. 3 (September 1992): 355–88; Dalzell, "Taxation with Representation," 216–18; Rao, *National Duties,* 95.

58. Memorial of the Merchants of Providence, 31 January 1793, Jeremiah Olney Papers, Rhode Island Historical Society.

59. *US Reports: Olney v. Arnold,* 3 US (3 Dall.) 308 (1796); Maeva Marcus et al., "Olney v. Arnold; Olney v. Dexter," *Documentary History of the Supreme Court of the United States, 1789–1800,* 8 vols. (New York: Columbia University Press, 1986–2007) 8:575; Mary Sarah Bilder, *The Transatlantic Constitution: Colonial Legal Culture and the Empire* (Cambridge, MA: Harvard University Press, 2008), 194; Robert P. Frankel Jr., "Judicial Beginnings: The Supreme Court in the 1790s," *History Compass* 4, no. 6 (2006): 1009–1110.

60. Alexander Hamilton to Jeremiah Olney, April 2, 1793, *PAH,* 16:277.

Creating Interdepartmental Collaboration

Federal Judges, the Remitting Act, and Cooperative State Building

KATE ELIZABETH BROWN

The drafting of the US Constitution in 1787 commenced an ambitious phase of American state building. The framers aimed to create durable republican institutions to separately house the three distinct and indispensable functions of government. While the final draft of their efforts provided precise directions about the broad contours of the federal government and its powers, the US Constitution omits crucial details about the day-to-day business of governing. For example, the Constitution establishes the depth and breadth of Congress's Article I powers, but it vests the president with the energy and prerogatives necessary to fulfill his Article II responsibilities through a generic, somewhat controversial grant of executive power.[1] And Article III's outline of the federal judicial power is vaguer still; the framers established the US Supreme Court and its jurisdiction within the text, but left it up to Congress to establish the practical scope of the powers and processes of any other judicial institutions, including lower courts. With so many practical particulars left out of the final text of the nation's founding document, the task fell to the officials who opened the federal government for business to initiate a second phase of American state building: the creation and implementation of rules for daily governance.

While scholars have paid close attention to the annals of congressional debates and, to a lesser extent, to the everyday happenings in the executive branch, they frequently ignore the federal courts' participation in the daily business of governing the early republic. And yet federal judges became indispensable administrators, as well as adjudicators, in the early state-building project. Federal judges supervised many of those mundane but essential functions that sustained and legitimated both abstract republican principles and the blueprint for governmental power enacted through the Constitution. They simultaneously acted as administrators executing law and policy and sat in judgment on the federal bench. Therefore, focusing on the judges' dexterity and interbranch cooperation while serving in both capacities reveals the impactful, yet interstitial, work accomplished by these unsung operatives of American state building.

Congress legislated the lower federal courts into being in 1789. While Article III of the US Constitution established the US Supreme Court, the highest federal court, "An Act to Establish the Judicial Courts of the United States" further created thirteen district courts and three circuit courts as the lower and middle tiers of the federal judiciary.[2] The act divided and assigned trial-level and appellate jurisdiction to the new courts. For example, Congress gave the district courts trial-level cognizance over admiralty matters and limited criminal and civil jurisdiction. In sharp contrast, the circuit courts served as trial courts for most federal criminal and civil cases, with appellate jurisdiction overseeing admiralty cases. Congress assigned judges to the various federal benches through the act as well. A single appointed judge staffed each district court, but the local district judge, combined with two Supreme Court justices "riding circuit"—that is, traveling around their particular geographical assignment—comprised each circuit court. Both Supreme Court justices and district court judges did double duty, simultaneously sitting on two federal benches.

Although the lower federal courts and their caseloads proved crucial to the daily functions of the national government, the federal district and circuit courts languish at the periphery of scholarly attention. When historians do take note of the lower federal courts, they tend to overlook the variety of cases on the courts' bustling dockets. Legal and political scholars choose instead to focus on isolated exercises of judicial review or to emphasize the Supreme Court's caseload rather than focus on the more routine litigation tried in the district or circuit courts.[3] This amounts to a substantial oversight, particularly because the district courts presided over the nation's admiralty docket and, with it, cases involving weighty questions of foreign policy, neutrality policy, and national commerce.[4] Congress also enhanced the federal judges' duties by assigning various administrative and regulatory tasks to the lower federal courts.[5] Despite these extensive responsibilities, scholars have ignored the ways in which federal judges served as key administrative personnel during the Washington administration.

This essay recaptures the significance of lower federal courts' involvement in early republic state building by examining one type of reoccurring, interstitial transaction: the process by which the federal government remitted or mitigated penalties incurred under federal revenue laws. Congress first outlined the broad contours of this remitting process in 1790 through "An Act to provide for mitigating or remitting the forfeitures and penalties accruing under the revenue laws" (hereafter the Remitting Act). Under the statute,

Congress involved district judges in the administrative process by which the treasury secretary adjudged and mitigated statutory penalties relating to coasting-trade violations.[6] In so doing, Congress initiated a process that was dependent on cooperative engagement between the Treasury Department, run by Alexander Hamilton, and the first cohort of federal judges. In the case study below, I will examine how this remitting process worked, in detail, to foster a collaborative relationship—a cooperative process of state building—between the executive and judicial branches in Washington's administration.

These combined administrative/adjudicator duties simultaneously conducted by federal judges facilitated the practical business of day-to-day governance as well as the abstract but crucial state-building goal of legitimizing governmental institutions and actions. Judges did so by working closely with executive officials to administer law. In contrast to the pervasive scholarly narrative focused on judicial review, the federal courts did not function principally as a constitutional "check" on the other branches of government (or the states). Rather, the daily workings of the lower federal courts demonstrate that instead of interbranch clashing, the courts actively fostered interbranch collaboration. In fact, this interstitial cooperation between departments formed a key element of state building during Washington's administration.

In studying early republic state building through this transactional approach, I examine litigation and case law, the typical fodder for studying courts, but I also rely on business-related correspondence generated by the particular executive-judicial collaboration that Congress inaugurated under the 1790 Remitting Act. The letters, testimonies, and treasury memos circulating among Hamilton's desk, the federal courts, and the customhouses located at ports across the young nation illustrates the variety and scope of the collaborative state-building activities undertaken by executive and judicial administrators. The remitting process reveals one common, reoccurring example of federal judges implementing executive policy and carrying out the functional realities of governance.

In the pages below, I consider the federal judges' extensive role in state building, first by exploring the origins of the 1790 Remitting Act, followed by a close examination of the remitting process in action. After detailing the federal district judges' transactional involvement in the remitting process, I then demonstrate how, through adjudication, the district and circuit courts legitimized the very remitting process they helped to implement. Their involvement in state building thus became a self-fulfilling cycle: as federal judges legitimized the new constitutional republic incrementally, through cooperative and equitable remitting transactions, they then used the power bestowed on them by these new republican institutions to sanction the remitting process itself, as well as their authority as judges, to make such decisions.

Cooperation with Oversight:
The Origins of the Remitting Act

When Congress first assembled in the spring of 1789, it had its work cut out for it. Part of its inaugural duties included creating a system of lower courts, an effort initiated in the Senate. But another set of Congress's pressing tasks was to resolve the outstanding business left by the late Confederation Congresses. This included the consideration and disposal of various claims submitted to Congress by individual petitioners—an administrative undertaking that the busy, deliberative houses of Congress could not address efficiently. When Congress instead asked Treasury Secretary Hamilton to resolve some of these claims, he in turn suggested that Congress establish an alternative process that would ultimately become the basis for the Remitting Act. After considering Hamilton's advice, Congress opted to assign administrative duties to the federal judges and quasi-judicial powers to the treasury secretary, while requiring the two separate departments to cooperate with each other. The process established by the Remitting Act thus borrowed from an older English magistracy tradition in which judges presided simultaneously as adjudicators and administrators.

The remitting process emerged from the Confederation Congress's unfinished business. During its first few years in operation, the newly created federal government fielded scores of petitions from soldiers, merchant suppliers, and widows who applied to the first federal Congresses requesting pensions, restitution for damages, backpay, reissued government securities, and compensation for contracted goods and services.[7] To dispose of each petition, Congress often referred the matter to the treasury secretary and occasionally to the secretary of war. These executive officers would then research the claim (if at all possible) before submitting their decisions to Congress, who ultimately decided on whether or not the claimant deserved payment (and if so, for how much). After considering one such petition referred to him, Hamilton suggested to Congress that an alternate process would be more expedient for disposing of claims arising from the revenue laws.

On January 19, 1790, Hamilton submitted his proposal to Congress along with his thoughts on the petition of Christopher Saddler. Saddler, a British mariner, asked Congress for relief from "the forfeiture of his vessel and cargo, which have been seized in the port of Boston, for a violation of the impost law of the United States; of which law the petitioner was wholly ignorant." Hamilton was alarmed that the nation's brand-new impost laws were taking merchants by surprise. Through no fault of their own, shippers would be penalized by the federal government's new customs laws—"from which heavy and ruinous forfeitures ensue"—that they did not yet know existed.[8] Such a predicament not only inequitably antagonized merchants, Hamilton noted, but penalized those who conducted the lucrative carrying trade, which threatened the federal revenue and relied heavily on duties collected through customs and port transactions.

In response to "the necessity," which was "peculiarly great in the early stages of new regulations," Hamilton suggested that these novel circumstances required "vesting somewhere a discretionary power of granting relief." He continued, "The Secretary begs leave to submit to the consideration of the House, whether a temporary Arrangement might not be made with expedition and safety, which would avoid the inconvenience of a Legislative Decision on particular Applications."[9] After considering Hamilton's report in committee, the House took Hamilton up on his suggestion.

Four months later, "An Act to provide for mitigating or remitting the forfeitures and penalties accruing under the revenue laws, in certain cases therein mentioned" went into effect on May 26, 1790.[10] The Remitting Act gave the secretary of the treasury the discretionary power to determine whether or not merchants should receive remissions or mitigated penalties when they unintentionally and nonfraudulently violated a revenue law. As part of the remitting process, Congress also recruited federal district court judges to report to and to advise the treasury secretary before he made his decision. Less than a year after the Judiciary Act of 1789 had created the lower courts, and with barely enough time for judges to undergo the process of the president's nomination and the Senate's advice and consent, Congress was already putting the district court judges to work. Rather than create a federal court of claims to handle those petitions requesting statutory forbearance, Congress conferred the power to adjudicate revenue penalties to an executive official (the secretary of the treasury) acting on the advice and fact-finding abilities of a federal judicial official (the district court judges). Through a cooperative effort waged by district judges, customs collectors, and the treasury secretary, they ensured that the federal revenue, as well as the nation's commercial viability, remained equitable and intact.

The Remitting Act established a collaborative process among the branches of the federal government that harkened back to English practices. For centuries, English judges, including common law judges and justices of the peace, served at the pleasure of the king, who, sitting squarely at the center of the English constitutional model, united the overlapping executive, judicial, and lawmaking functions of his realm. Judges were kingly surrogates, spread across the realm, dispensing his justice and—particularly for local justices of the peace—executing the king's law. These local magistrates had extensive administrative authority, including the duty to quarantine during plague outbreaks, to implement efforts to repair local infrastructure, to administer the poor laws, to oversee a general commission to keep the peace, and to levy, at his discretion, taxes among the community. English justices of the peace, therefore, served the king in combined judicial and executive capacities.[11]

Colonial British America also inherited this English magistrate model to govern at the local level. Although the US Constitution gave the appearance that federal magistrates would be strictly separated from the duties of the executive branch, years of colonial practice and English inheritance suggested a more flexible approach to governing and thus legitimized Congress's remitting process. The US Constitution might have been a bold experiment in republican political science, but the Congress was too accustomed to its Anglo-American legal heritage to simply reject those time-tested English and colonial practices if they could prove useful to the new republic.

The Remitting Act was not the only example of judicial oversight of administrative action contemplated during the early years of the republic. Already, courts provided for judicial oversight of administrators through common law actions against the government's officials, a method of supervision also used by colonial courts. Leonard D. White, who pioneered the study of bureaucratic process in the early republic, noted that through this inherited, common law process, Congress expected judicial oversight to be "an ultimate protection against error, bad judgment, partiality, or venality of the customs officers."[12] But legal accountability in the early republic did not just include lawsuits against administrators; judges supervised administrators through their inclusion, as individuals, on administrative tribunals as well.[13] The Remitting Act provided a perfect example of this form of judicial collaboration with oversight.[14]

Congress deliberated on collaborative judicial-executive arrangements on multiple occasions in its early years, and those debates, recorded in the Annals of Congress, reveal a general approval for judicial involvement in or oversight of administrative tasks. When discussing an early version of the Remitting Act, for example, Congressman Michael Jenifer Stone (Maryland) questioned whether or not remissions decisions should be made without judicial oversight. Fearing "an arbitrary determination, independent of the principles of law," Stone wanted the judiciary to be somehow involved in the remitting decisions.[15]

Around the same time, Congress also discussed assigning to the federal courts the nonjudicial task of naturalizing citizens. During this discussion, Congressman Peter Silvester (New York) suggested that district judges be involved in the naturalization process because Congress could rely on the judges' good judgment and fairness. The United States should not "admit aliens to the rights of citizenship indiscriminately," noted Silvester, who was "clearly in favor of a term of probation, and that [the aliens'] good behavior should be vouched for." As for who could be trusted to do the vouching, Silvester "suggested the idea of lodging the power of admitting foreigners to be naturalized in the District Judges."[16]

James Madison voiced more evidence that Congress expected the courts to provide oversight to administrative actions. Concerned that the Treasury's routine claims process seemed to "partake of a judiciary quality as well as executive," Madison proposed that some judicial participation be adopted into the treasury process. He noted that "making [the Comptroller, an executive officer] thus thoroughly dependent [on Congress, which could impeach the Comptroller], would make it necessary to secure his impartiality, with respect to the individual." Madison's solution was to get the federal courts involved: "This might be effected by giving any person, who conceived himself aggrieved, a right to petition the Supreme Court for redress, and they should be empowered to do right therein; this will enable the individual to carry his claim before an independent tribunal."[17] Although Congress did not adopt Madison's suggestion regarding the Treasury Department's claims process (after all, Congress provided a check on the Treasury's discretion by controlling the public purse), but a variation of Madison's proposal reappeared in the Remitting Act a few months later.

In the final version of the statute, the procedural particulars of the Remitting Act protected any person who could be liable, or had already been found liable, for any fine, forfeiture, or penalty arising under federal revenue statutes that imposed impost or tonnage duties. Under the act, the unfortunate penalized shipper would petition a district judge for a remission or mitigation of the fine, penalty, or forfeiture he incurred. The judge would then give notice to the petitioner, as well as to the US district attorney, to show cause for or against forbearance. After this summary hearing, the judge would then transmit the facts of the hearing to the secretary of the treasury. Per the statute, the secretary had complete legal discretion to remit or mitigate the penalty incurred: "[The secretary of the treasury] shall thereupon have power to mitigate or remit such fine, penalty or forfeiture, or any part thereof, if in his opinion the same was incurred without wilful negligence or any intention of fraud, and to direct the prosecution, if any shall have been instituted for the recovery thereof, to cease and be discontinued, upon such terms or conditions as he may deem reasonable and just."[18] Note, however, that the secretary did not have the power to overturn a decision regarding the breach of the impost laws; he merely had the authority to lessen the penalty imposed by the law.

Congress could have structured the remitting process differently. Because the president already possessed a prerogative power to issue pardons, Congress might have directed the remitting process to the president rather than to the treasury secretary as the final arbiter of remission requests. In fact, years after Congress passed the Remitting Act, at least one petitioner, William Martin of Maine, ignored its statutory protocol and opted to ask President Washington for a pardon instead of initiating the formal remitting process through a federal district court. Even with the Remitting Act on the books, pardoning, as well as submitting a petition to Congress, remained alternate routes to remissions and other nonjudicial reprieves in the early republic. Martin's pardon request reveals, however, that though Martin petitioned the president to remit his penalty, Washington still deferred to the treasury secretary—the congressionally appointed remissions adjudicator— to make the final decision.[19]

Also, by the time Congress passed the Remitting Act, it was already common for the lower federal courts to cooperate with members of the executive branch. On a daily basis, Hamilton issued instructions to his team of customs collectors as they worked with portside district attorneys across the district courts to prosecute those who violated revenue laws. Hamilton wrote to Jeremiah Olney, the customs collector stationed at Providence, Rhode Island, because rum, molasses, sugar, and salt was "said to have been fraudulently landed" from a sloop that evaded another collector stationed in Barnstable, Massachusetts. Hamilton directed Olney to be on the lookout for the sloop, asking, "I have to request that you will cause her to be seized, if she should be found in your District."[20] Once found, the treasury officials would contact local US attorneys to cause the offending vessel to be libeled in federal district court.

As the Treasury Department filled the federal district court dockets with cases involving revenue violations, the district judges regularly interacted with these customs officials. Through the normal course of these revenue law prosecutions, the district judge and trial provided the ultimate legal disposition of the matter. Yet under the remitting process, the judges and the executive had their respective roles inverted; judges presented facts to the treasury secretary, and the secretary had the final word on whether or not the statutory penalty would be forgiven.

By placing the secretary of the treasury at the head of the Remitting Act's decision-making process, Congress also had policy considerations in mind: to encourage trade by providing the least cumbersome method for forbearing inadvertent penalties. The treasury secretary oversaw the personnel and process that enforced revenue and coasting laws. He was also best positioned to investigate remissions requests (or to investigate fraud, as the case might be). But Congress did not give the treasury secretary complete discretionary authority over remissions and mitigations; it deliberately included district court judges in the remissions process so that the treasury secretary had some legal accountability to the petitioner and to the courts.

The logic behind cooperative judicial-executive oversight made sense in the context of the early republic. Many congressmen, judges, and executive officials were not only trained lawyers in the traditions of the English common law but were comfortable with the inherited English model of judge as administrator. Furthermore, the treasury secretary was best positioned to ensure consistent outcomes that aligned with the administration's policy goals. If the collectors only prosecuted noncompliance with revenue laws in court, then penalties computed by juries might be too lenient toward shippers (thus jeopardizing the national revenue) or unforgiving juries might adhere to the letter of the law too strictly (which, in turn, could discourage trade). Also, if noncompliant merchants had only legal remedies available to mitigate duty and tonnage penalties, then the extra cost and hassle incurred through litigation might also stifle trade. The Remitting Act thus borrowed from an inherited colonial practice and created an equitable way to balance the three crucial state-building goals under consideration by the young republic: collecting revenue, imposing law, and encouraging trade. Trade would not suffer because of inequitable outcomes, penalty forbearance would be consistently applied, and the cost of doing business with the United States would be lessened (at least Congress and the treasury secretary hoped this to be true).

As we will see, Hamilton fully embraced the district judges' participation in the remitting process, involving them intimately in what he viewed as serious policy-oriented business. Hamilton used the judges' comments on the truth of the evidence in order to make a decision—but he would not be content unless all factual inconsistencies had been resolved and enough evidence had been gathered for him to make a decision. Hamilton also accepted and, when he thought necessary, challenged the testimony and facts offered by the district judges who reported to him.

Interbranch Collaboration through the Remitting Process

President Washington nominated the first cohort of judges to the federal bench immediately following the passage of the 1789 Judiciary Act, and these men willingly engaged with their combined judge/administrator roles. Like Washington, his nominees served in an unchartered territory of newly created offices in a bold experiment in republican governance—circumstances that required that they establish precedent rather than adhere to it. Fortunately for these judges, their past experiences as public servants, common lawyers, and judges gave them some common ground as well as common perspective as they embarked on their precedent-setting task of adjudicating and administering federal law. How these federal judges collaborated with Secretary Hamilton to implement the day-to-day particulars of the remitting process is explored below.

By assigning administrative duties to judges, the Remitting Act borrowed from the English example and gave the first federal judges, who were all trained in Anglo-American law, a familiar model for their own administrative responsibilities. Judges in the early republic learned the law through an autodidactic process known as "reading law," whereby would-be lawyers immersed themselves in reading from the legal libraries owned by their friends, the local lawyer in town, or occasionally, a college professor. A select few American lawyers trained at the eighteenth-century equivalent of law school, which required traveling to London to read and debate law at the Inns of Court. Though a few Washington appointees enjoyed this privilege—including William Paca, a district judge involved in the remitting process who read law at London's Inner Temple—most provincial lawyers turned judges read law privately, sometimes in conjunction with attending an American college.

In addition to their legal training, which was steeped in the traditions of English and colonial common law, most of the first cohort of federal judges also had prior government or military experience at the national level. Washington's appointees tended to have past army experience serving in the Revolutionary War, to have served as delegates to the Continental or Confederation Congresses, to have governed as state legislators or even as state governors, and to have extensive experience as attorneys or judges at either the state or confederation level. Thus the federal judges conducting cooperative state building through the remitting process shared a common perspective; they tended to be nationally oriented, steeped in the Anglo-American common law, and well-versed in the English judge-as-administrator model. (Hamilton, a lawyer whose résumé also included past military and government service, shared this common experience and perspective as well.)

Under the Remitting Act, Congress required federal district judges to interact and collaborate with multiple parties—from petitioner to customs agent to treasury secretary—scattered across the nation. The process therefore relied on a network of written communications between executive and judicial personnel, only part of which has survived. Moreover, most of the extant remitting correspondence generated during Washington's administration comes from the treasury secretary's desk; therefore, reconstructing the district judges' particular contributions to the remitting process requires inferring the judges' actions or opinions from the secretary's responses or his subsequent actions or from the questions that the secretary put to the district judges. Nevertheless, the remitting process, pieced together through partially preserved transactions reveals the extensive collaboration and mutual deference exhibited by the district court judges and the Treasury Department.

The remitting process began at port, when a treasury official determined that a shipper had violated US customs law. Then, either before or after the Treasury initiated prosecution in federal district court, the merchant opted to submit his petition to the district judge, thus commencing an investigation. The judge then forwarded the statement of facts to the secretary of the treasury.[21]

For example, in the spring of 1790, Christopher Hillary, the customs collector stationed at Brunswick, Georgia, refused to offload cargo onboard the schooner *Swift* because the ship's captain did not have a manifest for the goods.[22] The owner of the cargo, Duncan Manson, petitioned the US District Court for Georgia under the Remitting Act and attested that "no fraud was intended and that the duties were paid or secured to be paid in Charleston [South Carolina]."[23]

Nathaniel Pendleton, the district court judge for Georgia, heard the case. Pendleton, a former lawyer from Savannah, Georgia, had served in the Continental Army before accepting Washington's appointment to the federal bench.[24] Pendleton presumably took a deposition outlining the facts alleged by Manson, inquired about Hillary's version of the story, and forwarded both to Hamilton for his review.

Hamilton responded to Pendleton in April 1791 and granted Manson his remission. In his correspondence with the judge, Hamilton surmised that, due to a personnel problem onboard the *Swift*, timing and miscommunication caused the vessel's new captain to assume he had the necessary manifests when, in fact, he did not. As a condition of the remission, however, Manson had to pay court costs and other claims that arose from the forfeiture.[25]

Although Congress vested Hamilton with the ultimate authority to decide whether or not to remit or mitigate revenue penalties, the district judges also enjoyed discretion and room to shape the outcome of the petition. Some judges attempted to convey just the facts, without alerting Hamilton to their private opinions on the petitioner's claims. Judge Henry Marchant of Rhode Island, a former attorney general and state representative in Rhode Island who had also served as a delegate to the Continental Congress, took this approach. In the case of the *Rising Sun,* Marchant presided over the US District Court for Rhode Island and meticulously described to Hamilton the "Truth of the Facts set forth by the said Petitioner [Thomas Hazard Jr. of St. Johns]" without suggesting whether or not he thought that Hazard had intended to commit fraud. Marchant summarized the proceedings: "The said Vessell . . . was seised by [Jeremiah Olney, the collector stationed at Providence] . . . having on Board a Cargo of Fish." The problem, however, was the schooner's registry: "In Said Schooner appears by the British Register to be of the Burthen of Thirty two and three Quarter Tons, but upon remeasurement Her actual Burthen is only Twenty three Tons and sixty one Ninety fifths of a Ton." Because tonnage measurement differed between the US and foreign jurisdictions, when Olney remeasured the *Rising Sun,* her tonnage was less than the thirty tons requisite by law to import foreign goods.[26]

After this narrative, Marchant offered his assessment. To the judge, even though "it appears to me that, the said Schooner was, once or twice previous to the adoption of the present Constitution by this State particularly in the Year 1789, entered at the sd. Port of Providence, and paid Light Money agreably to Her Tunnage by the British Register," Hazard had not captained the *Rising Sun* before, and he did not realize that her British tonnage would differ from American tonnage requirements. Marchant concluded: "All which I do hereby certify to the Secretary of the Treasury of the United States."[27]

Marchant believed that Hazard's pending forfeiture demonstrated the exact kind of predicament that warranted the remitting process. When Hazard's family first entered Rhode Island's ports in the *Rising Sun,* the state had not yet entered the union. Now, in August 1792, the schooner returned to the port of Providence, but the customs law in force had changed, and this time the new captain of the *Rising Sun*—Thomas Hazard Jr.—had never been captain of this or any other vessel before. An equitable remission was in order, and a few weeks later, the treasury secretary sent Jeremiah Olney a note conveying his decision: Hamilton remitted the penalty, though Hazard, like Manson, still owed an unspecified fee to other parties for costs and charges.[28]

Perhaps because Thomas Hazard Jr. seemed naïve and unfortunate rather than cunning and dodgy, Judge Marchant declined to expound on whether he thought Hazard fraudulent. But other judges were not so circumspect. In an undated note, Hamilton enclosed documents relating to Timothy Savage's petition, where the Federal District Court for Connecticut clearly suspected Savage of intent to defraud the US government and alerted the secretary to his suspicions.[29] And in another, unrelated case, after Judge Cyrus Griffin of the District Court for Virginia submitted his statement of facts to the treasury secretary regarding the petition of John

McRae and John Morrison, Hamilton was convinced that the petitioners' claims were "in an *extremely questionable shape*" (Hamilton's emphasis).[30]

Like Marchant, Griffin practiced privately before serving in multiple state and national capacities. Before his appointment to the federal bench, Griffin represented Virginia in the both the Continental and Confederation Congresses, and he adjudicated prize cases on the Court of Appeals in Cases of Capture. Griffin's affidavit tipped off Hamilton to the possibility of a fraudulent transaction—exactly the reason that federal district judges made excellent fact finders for the remitting process—because in response, Hamilton initiated a flurry of investigation. Along with the judge's summary, Hamilton also received depositions from another importer and from Daniel Delozier, the deputy collector at Baltimore. But these documents did not include sufficiently specific information for Hamilton to feel comfortable adjudging the situation, and therefore, Hamilton complained to Judge Griffin that despite their suspicions, "There is no legal proof that the goods have ever paid duty." In other words, sufficient proof had not yet been collected to prove the petitioners' fraud. Hamilton suggested that Griffin order the collection of more evidence.[31]

As Hamilton declared to Otho Williams, the ranking collector at Baltimore, "I am very far from being satisfied, that there has not been more than inadvertence in this case." But even though Hamilton and Judge Griffin suspected fraud, the treasury secretary was "unwilling nevertheless to precipitate a forfeiture as long as there is a chance of new light to evince innocence." Therefore, he continued, "I have concluded to give you [Williams] the trouble of a further investigation." Hamilton instructed Williams to collect a better, legally binding deposition from the importer and to recheck the Treasury's records against the suspicious marks and numbers found on the seized cargo. When all of this was complete, Hamilton instructed Williams to resubmit his findings to Judge Griffin, who would then submit a "supplement" to the secretary.[32]

As these examples of the remitting process suggest, district judges did not grudgingly or dismissively report to the treasury secretary's office. Instead, they actively collaborated with the Treasury in a dialogue, submitting and resubmitting facts and opinions to assist the treasury secretary in making his final decision. True to his overactive, meddling nature, Hamilton drove the process, but in the surviving correspondence between the Washington administration and the federal district courts, there is no hint that the district judges refused to cooperate with the investigations inspired by the Remitting Act. In fact, the judges seemed particularly willing to collaborate with the Treasury—especially when the secretary requested more information when he determined that important questions remained unanswered.

For example, in April 1793, Hamilton heatedly wrote to Judge James Duane, an old colleague from New York City's legal scene who now sat on the bench of the District Court for New York. Duane had extensive experience in New York's colonial government, holding positions such as clerk of the New York Court of Chancery and attorney general of the colony, before becoming a delegate to the Continental Congress. In 1784, Hamilton famously persuaded the New York Mayor's Court, which was then presided over by then Mayor James Duane, to accept Loyalist Joshua Waddington's law of nation's defense in defiance of New York's Trespass Act in the case *Rutgers v. Waddington*.[33] Almost a decade later, Hamilton worked with Duane under the terms of the Remitting Act to better understand the circumstances surrounding the case of Samuel (Lemuel) Toby and the Ship *Lydia*.

Hamilton returned Duane's original statement of facts "in order that a further enquiry & statement may be had." Hamilton was not pleased: "I am not at present satisfied of the innocence of the transaction, as it respects all the parties, who may be concerned, and as it is a shape in which fraud may present itself with great success, I am solicitous for a pretty strict scrutiny." But the treasury secretary was still deferential to his old friend and colleague in admitting, "It is with reluctance, I at any time give the trouble of a revision or restatement," but Toby's petition was "in my opinion of a nature to require particular vigilance & circumspection." Hamilton "doubt[ed] not that additional attention requisite will be chearfully bestowed." In between his expressions of displeasure and deference, Hamilton included a list of five specific questions that "for different reasons appear to me desirable to be known." Duane's reply has not survived, but it must have been satisfying to Hamilton, for he ultimately issued a warrant of remission in May 1793.[34]

Hamilton never shied away from requesting more information, and the district judges seemed ever willing to oblige.[35] Following the petition of George Tyler, Hamilton asked Judge David Sewall of the District Court for Maine in November 1790 to collect more information about Tyler's situation, as well as to clear up an inconsistency between the judge's version of Tyler's trial, and the Penobscot collector's account. Hamilton would not grant or deny a mitigated fine or lessen the imprisonment penalty until Judge Sewall, a former delegate to the Massachusetts constitutional convention, clarified the omissions and discrepancies that existed in the case.[36] How Sewall responded to Hamilton has not been recovered, but it is noteworthy that before presiding on the Superior Court of Massachusetts, Judge Sewall was a justice of the peace in Maine. Because of this past experience as a local magistrate, Sewall would have been particularly comfortable with the judge-as-administrator role required of him under the Remitting Act.

And the judges asked questions of Hamilton too. On one such occasion, an unidentified district judge asked whether or not he should release any vessel or goods forfeited on proper surety to the shipper who had instigated the remitting process. Hamilton generalized from this specific inquiry. In a circular memo to all federal district judges, Hamilton responded carefully, as he was unwilling to claim that he could authoritatively interpret the statute. Nevertheless, he suggested that such a measure would be "expedient . . . if such a proceeding should appear to the Judge, before whom the matter is brought, legal." Hamilton also noted that the judge should ensure the "competency of the sum" taken as surety. Behind his question to the treasury secretary, the unidentified district judge most likely had a policy consideration in mind: if the confiscation penalty would be remitted in all likelihood, then the merchant's ability to trade should not be further hampered while pending the secretary's decision. Hamilton seemed to agree with this logic; as long as a sufficient surety was in place, awaiting merchants should have access to their confiscated goods and vessels.[37]

While the district judges shaped the initial presentation of facts that eventually landed on the treasury secretary's desk, Hamilton drove the investigation from that point forward. What resulted was a conversation and collaboration among judges, customs officials, and the treasury secretary to resolve points of fact as well as points of law. Although Alexander Hamilton was a well-respected lawyer, he did not pretend to have the authority to tell these district court judges, all accomplished jurists and statesmen, what the law meant. Hamilton rarely sought to interpret federal statutes and impose his readings on federal judges. To the contrary, through the course of investigation, Hamilton sometimes asked the judges to resolve points of law for him.

There is evidence that Hamilton opened dialogues with his colleagues when legal questions arose throughout the remitting process. He did so with William Paca, the district judge presiding over the District Court for Maryland, and John Lowell of the District Court for Massachusetts, both distinguished legal jurists with impeccable credentials. Lowell practiced law privately in Massachusetts before serving as a state representative, a delegate to the Massachusetts constitutional conventional, and to the Continental Congress. Paca, a signer of the Declaration of Independence, sat in Maryland's assembly and senate. Before accepting Washington's recess appointment to the federal bench in 1789, Paca was also a judge in Maryland's General Court and a governor of the state from 1782 to 1785. Like Cyrus Griffin, both Lowell and Paca adjudicated prize cases on the Court of Appeals in Cases of Capture before accepting their federal district court judgeships.

In March 1794, Hamilton had made a decision on the separate, unrelated petitions of Henry Jackson and Samuel Carr, who each had their casks of distilled spirits confiscated at Boston and Baltimore, respectively. When William Paca and John Lowell sent their statements of facts to Hamilton, both questioned the applicability of the remitting process to their corresponding petitioners.

When replying to Hamilton, Paca seems to have given his opinion outright that the forfeiture and remission which generated Carr's petition was unlawful. In response, Hamilton treaded carefully and gently suggested that he thought it within the spirit of "An Act concerning the Duties on Spirits distilled *within* the United States" that its regulations also applied to spirits *imported* into the United States.[38] Also, Hamilton admitted that he thought that the remitting process operated prospectively to revenue laws passed after Congress enacted the Remitting Act (the 1790 original, as well as subsequent statutory updates to it). Hamilton was convinced that, because Congress had continually renewed the original Remitting Act, and because it had such a favorable, equitable function, the act applied retrospectively, to those laws in force before the remitting acts were passed, as well as prospectively. But in his letter to Paca—which did not include Hamilton's decision on Carr's remission—Hamilton asked the judge to reconsider his opinion on "whether the Act of May 90 for mitigating &c, having an aspect to future as well as to the then existing laws, does not extend to the case in question?"[39]

Paca's response has not be found, but just a few weeks later, Hamilton confidently stated to Lowell—who had questioned the applicability of the Remitting Act to Jackson's petition—that the 1790 Remitting Act "continued in force by subsequent Acts, having an aspect to future as well as to the then existing laws, extends to the case in question." Although Lowell cast doubt on this point initially, he seemed to have accepted Hamilton's decision on the matter in the end; the Massachusetts District Court ultimately recorded Hamilton's remission.[40]

Just as Hamilton respected the opinions he received from district judges, they in turn respected the integrity of Hamilton's decisions as well. When, for example, William Gerrish received a fine for violating an unspecified customs law, he attempted to recover in the District Court for Maine. He also initiated the remitting process, which raised suspicions for Hamilton and presumably also for Judge David Sewall, who would have prepared Gerrish's petition. After reading over the petition, Hamilton generated a list of questions raised by the suspicious nature of Gerrish's circumstance, sent them to Nathaniel Fosdick, the collector at Portland, and ultimately denied Gerrish's remission request. Subsequently, Gerrish lost his lawsuit in the District Court for Maine to recover the fine incurred. The court ruled against Gerrish, indicating that "the decision of the Secretary of the Treasury being received, not to remit the penalty, nor any part thereof," along with Gerrish's nonappearance in court, persuaded Judge Sewall in the matter.[41]

The Remitting Act served a policy purpose specific to the circumstances of a new federal government dependent on maritime revenue and working to establish its legitimacy as a sovereign nation. During Washington's administration, federal officials continued the process of refining the powers of government and implementing new and effective methods of governing. To balance the sometimes conflicting goals of collecting revenue without impeding trade, and of enforcing federal law vigorously but with equity and fairness, executive officials and federal district judges cooperated under the Remitting Act. Through the remitting process, as outlined by statutory law but elaborated by an ongoing, collaborative conversation among district judges, customs collectors, and the treasury secretary, the federal courts and Washington's administration began to work cooperatively to achieve national policy goals. This collaboration continued on the dockets of the lower federal courts.

The Remitting Act in the Courts

When legal questions arose from both the original and the various iterations of the Remitting Act, federal judges reviewed and upheld the legality of the very remitting process they helped to implement.[42] Under these iterations, district judges still acted as administrators, reporting to and investigating for the treasury secretary, all the while helping to ensure that business conducted at American ports remained vibrant and equitable. At the same time, an examination of their decisions on remitting questions demonstrates that federal judges consistently upheld and deferred to the treasury secretary's discretionary power to forgive revenue law penalties, while simultaneously reaffirming their own authority to adjudicate federal policy concerning coasting, embargo, and neutrality laws.

Federal courts considered legal questions arising from the validity and procedural requirements of the Remitting Act, as well as from the terms of federal neutrality and revenue laws. Federal judges were therefore constantly in position to engage in state building, legitimizing both the institutional processes established by the Remitting Act (the collaboration between an energetic executive and a fact-finding judge) and the sitting administration's policy agenda. This in turn helped to formalize the federal courts' authority as constitutional umpire and definitive arbiter of federal law.

In the 1794 case of *US v. The Hawke*, for example, Judge Thomas Bee, a former South Carolina assemblyman, senator, and lieutenant governor, approved Congress's neutrality policy while upholding the federal courts' jurisdiction under the Remitting Act. This case arose in admiralty when the collector at Charleston initiated a suit in the South Carolina District Court, alleging that the claimant, Mr. Bolchos, purchased the vessel in violation of the 1793 Enrollment Act.[43] Congress had passed this statute to enforce US neutrality during the early years of the maritime wars between France and Britain, as well as to enforce a short-lived trade embargo to any foreign port.[44] The complaint (libel) alleged first, that the *Hawke* embarked on a foreign voyage without surrendering its American trade license, and second, that the captain of the schooner sold the vessel to Bolchos, a foreigner. Both of these alleged acts were in violation of the 1793 statute.[45]

After argument, Bee decided that the *Hawke*'s complicated voyage was nothing but a "fraudulent contrivance" meant to evade Congress's embargo. Bee determined that the vessel violated the licensing provision of the Enrollment Act but not the foreign-sale clause. Furthermore, Bee ruled that because of the fraudulent nature of its voyage, the *Hawke*'s sale to Bolchos was illegal, and so the ship retained its American character. With this decision, Bee upheld the embargo as national foreign policy.

Interestingly, Thomas Parker, the US attorney for the district of South Carolina, prosecuting the libel tried to argue that the district court lacked jurisdiction over the case. First, he argued that since the United States had proof of the vessel's Enrollment Act violations, the court could not look into the motives behind the violation. The court should, instead, simply approve the libel. He then claimed that under terms of the Remitting Act, only the secretary of the treasury had the power to investigate whether or not fraud was intended. If the treasury secretary thought not, then he could mitigate or remit the penalty. Bee rejected these claims, however, and construed the claimant's violations of the Enrollment Act through the lens of his fraudulent motives.

The *Hawke* libel underscores, again, the multivalent role of the district judge in the early republic. The judge, collector, and US attorney represented the judicial and executive authority of the federal government, each taking part in the investigation and prosecution of Congress and the Washington administration's foreign policy. Although Bee took part in the administrative side of revenue law remissions, he was cloaked with judicial power—which he strongly defended—when presiding over his courtroom. Bee maintained the district court's jurisdictional authority by refusing to concede that only the treasury secretary had the power to determine the case. Bee also resisted the US attorney's argument that, because the Remitting Act was concurrently in force, the district court should only defer to the executive, confine itself to fact finding, or simply rubber-stamp violations of federal law.

US v. The Hawke also demonstrates how, in addition to collaborating on administrative matters, the executive and judicial branches coexisted as two separate jurisdictions, both adjudicating federal customs law. Revenue law violations could be brought to either the district court (for a legal determination) or to the treasury secretary (under the remitting process) for adjudication. Bee would not follow the US attorney's argument to seize and forfeit the *Hawke* because, even though the claimant *could have* petitioned the secretary for a mitigated penalty, he had not done it. Because the schooner was in a judicial venue, rather than within the executive's jurisdiction, the district judge and the federal admiralty court would properly and judicially adjudicate the libel.

Although the Remitting Act created a concurrent, nonjudicial forum to which merchants could petition and thus "compete" with federal district courts, federal judges still sustained and deferred to the treasury secretary's alternative jurisdiction. This state of affairs continued long after Hamilton and the first set of district court judges had established the practices for implementing the Remitting Act. In the *Case of the Cotton Planter,* a libel originating in the District Court for New York but appealed to the New York Circuit Court, the claimant shipowner violated President Jefferson's 1807 embargo by sailing to the West Indies in January 1808.[46] The claimant originally petitioned the treasury secretary—this time Albert Gallatin—for a remitted penalty, claiming ignorance of the law. Gallatin refused to remit the penalty, and so the collector and district attorney for New York successfully libeled the *Cotton Planter* in the district court.

On appeal, Supreme Court Judge Henry Brockholst Livingston reversed the forfeiture. Livingston was appointed to the US Supreme Court by Thomas Jefferson in 1806 after a long, accomplished career as lieutenant colonel in the Continental Army, private secretary to minister to Spain John Jay, and an associate justice on the New York Supreme Court. As was the practice at the time, Associate Justice Livingston heard *The Cotton Planter* while traveling the federal appellate circuit. Livingston reasoned that, even though ignorance of the law was not a valid legal excuse, the embargo did not specify a commencement date; moreover, Livingston thought the shipowner's home port had not received timely news of the embargo.

The court thus granted relief to the shipowner for these mitigating circumstances. In his opinion for the court, however, Livingston noted, "That there is a power in the secretary of the treasury to relieve in case of an unintentional violation of laws relative to trade, and therefore the less occasion for the interposition of the judiciary; that the secretary has refused relief here, because he considered the alleged ignorance of the claimant a mere pretence." But did the secretary's decision preclude the federal court's jurisdiction? No, wrote Livingston, because the original libel and its appeal "is a question purely of judicial cognizance, and may be decided without interfering with any other department of government."[47] In other words, Livingston acknowledged that two separate processes coexisted under Congress's Remitting Acts. And so, since the treasury secretary did not halt the district court's proceedings, the libel could continue.

Livingston continued by recognizing the integrity of the executive's jurisdiction to remit revenue penalties: "Nor is there any doubt that the secretary of the treasury would have remitted the forfeitures, if any had accrued, if he had been satisfied of the bona fides of the transaction." Because Gallatin's decision occurred before the libel began in federal district court, however, did circuit court adjudication interfere with the executive's remitting powers? Again, Livingston decided no. He wrote, "As the decision of that gentleman has been incorporated with the proceedings in this cause . . . it may be thought by some that this court thinks itself competent to reverse what he has done. The court disclaims any such right."[48]

Finally, Chief Justice John Marshall—the chief combatant for the federal courts in the traditional narrative of executive-judicial relations—weighed in on the legality of the remitting process. Becoming chief justice of the US Supreme Court in 1801 was the capstone to a long career in national service. Previously, he fought as a lieutenant in the Revolutionary War, attended Virginia's ratification convention in 1788, and between 1797 and 1801 served as minister to France, as US representative from Virginia, and finally, as secretary of state. A staunch Federalist, Marshall would spend decades crafting nationally minded Supreme Court decisions. And like his brethren in *The Cotton Planter*, Marshall deferred to the treasury secretary's remitting powers.

When Marshall considered the provisions of the 1813 Remitting Act, he expounded on how the concurrent district court and treasury jurisdictions worked with each other in practice, much like the ways Hamilton interacted with district judges like Marchant and Sewall in the 1790s. Marshall described the collaborative remitting process as it stood under an 1813 customs law:[49]

The legislature seems to have intended that the act of the Treasury Department should be final and conclusive and that all the facts should be placed before him before he performs that act. Those articles, the forfeiture of which is remitted, are of course restored to the proprietor. The prosecutions, if instituted, are to cease. It would seem to be a part, and an essential part, of the duty of the secretary, to define the articles on which this remission operates, or if it be only on a certain interest on those articles, to define that interest.[50]

Marshall also described the part of the process used so often by the treasury secretaries: "If the statement of facts made by the court, did not enable the secretary to ascertain this interest, it would seem to be his duty, to require a more full statement; and the case should go back to him for a final decision."[51] And so, if district judges failed to provide all of the particulars to explain the petitioner's remission request, then the treasury secretary could request a more complete report from them—a precedent set by the first treasury secretary and the first district court judges, decades before. Also, Marshall described another collaborative part of the remitting process. If the treasury secretary chose to remit only a portion of the petitioner's seized property, then he should hand off the rest of the forfeiture to be adjudicated in federal court. Marshall thus confirmed that both departments could administer and adjudicate violations of the law for the same petitioner.

Harkening back to the ministerial versus political duty distinction he articulated in his famous 1803 *Marbury v. Madison* decision, Marshall noted that the Treasury's properly employed statutory remission powers fell within the executive's prerogative sphere—a realm of discretion that was not reviewable by federal judges.[52] He asked: "Could the court in which the prosecutions were depending, have proceeded to an investigation of the extent of the interest of the petitioners, after receiving this instrument of dismission from the treasury department? I believe it could not." Marshall concluded his opinion by declaring, "The secretary acts . . . and his acts cannot be revised by the court."[53]

When the federal courts considered legal questions arising from the validity and procedural requirements of the Remitting Act, they upheld the process they had consistently implemented from the second year of Washington's terms in office. Moreover, the courts ratified the quasi-judicial powers of the treasury secretary, as well as their own administrative roles in the process, which Congress had adopted under the original Remitting Act, to address the functional realities of governing. If the new federal government was going to effectively enforce customs law while at the same time encouraging foreign and domestic trade in American ports, it seemed necessary to find some mechanism to equitably mitigate those penalties arising from the novel circumstances of a brand-new government opening for business with new and changing revenue laws. The remitting process was successful, then, both because it worked and because it represented the collaborative state building implemented during the early republic.

Cooperation and Conflict in the Early Republic

The 1790 Remitting Act fostered a relationship among federal court judges and the executive branch that persisted well into the third decade of the nineteenth century. In addition to this collaborative exercise, the remitting process allowed federal judges to accomplish the business of state building in increments, in the interstices of federal governance, and on a day-to-day basis. Federal judges, who were steeped in common law training and who came to the bench with extensive experience as statesmen and soldiers, readily adopted the old English magistracy model (the judge as both adjudicator and administrator) to effectuate and endorse commercial policy and executive remitting decisions. In turn, these judges were also able to legitimize their own jurisdictional authority as concurrent with the remitting process.

The remitting process, and the cooperative state building it nurtured, reveals how flexible the American constitutional framework was to incorporating elements of English constitutionalism in order to make the republic—a brand-new, experimental state—work. This suggests that the framers of the US Constitution created a government that permitted give and take in the separation and delegating of power. The remitting process also demonstrates that the first US Congresses were not afraid to borrow from the English model in order to make their own republican government work more effectively.

Cooperative state building, therefore, created synergy across all three newly created branches of the federal government. When lawmakers, executive officials, and judges collaborated across surprisingly blurred departmental boundaries to fact-find, adjudicate, and endorse national policy, the result was successful governance and, in turn, legitimacy conferred upon these new institutions of state. Collaboration, it turns out, was the key to state building in the early republic.

Yet the 1790s also ushered in a period of divisive, partisan political battles between Federalists and Jeffersonian Republicans to determine the ultimate meaning of the founding and direction of the new republic. Could cooperative state building still persist amid such conflict? What would happen when, after Washington's terms in office, the Federalists lost political ground to their opposition, the Jeffersonian-Madisonian faction?

Despite the fact that the Remitting Act fostered cooperative state building among Federalist Congresses, the arch-Federalist Alexander Hamilton, and a cohort of mostly nationally minded Federalist judges, the remitting process persisted even after Republicans had swept control of the Congress, the White House, and even some federal judgeships. But conflict inevitably arose. In addition to congressional battles over the Judiciary Act of 1801 and its repeal, as well as the impeachment of Supreme Court Justice Samuel Chase, Federalists and Republicans occasionally sparred in the federal courts. Chief Justice John Marshall, for example, famously upheld a prerogative sphere for executive action that did not include the Jefferson administration's denial of William Marbury's commission in *Marbury v. Madison*.[54] And in a lesser known dispute, the Jefferson administration chafed at an 1808 South Carolina Circuit Court decision about the limits of executive discretion and judicial oversight. The case, *Gilchrist et al. v. the Collector of Charleston*, ignited a politically charged debate about the relationship between the executive and judicial branches.[55]

In *Gilchrist*, the South Carolina Circuit Court narrowly interpreted the administrative discretion granted by statute to customs collectors and found the collector stationed at Charleston to have detained a vessel in error. The case was politically sensitive, however, because both President Thomas Jefferson and Treasury Secretary Albert Gallatin had advised the collector to detain the vessel in the first place. The court had denied the discretionary prerogative claimed by the administration to interpret and execute customs laws—and the administration fired back with a strongly worded public letter written by Attorney General Caesar A. Rodney criticizing the court's decision.[56] Conflict between the courts and the executive was an inescapable and formative part of interbranch relations in the early republic as well.

And yet through the partisanship, Federalist judges continued to defer to and uphold the Republican administration's authority to remit or mitigate revenue penalties. Political sniping and disagreements among the branches occurred, but this did not end the interstitial cooperation that still occurred, transaction by transaction, between federal judges and a succession of treasury secretaries. Cooperative, interbranch state building persisted despite the political enmity of the 1790s and the Federalists' permanent transfer of national power to Republicans at the turn of the nineteenth century.

Cooperative state building was therefore a pervasive force in the creation of the nation, even if the collaborative work accomplished by federal judges and executive officials was drowned out by partisan vitriol. In the early republic, cooperative state building was also lasting and successful. For the institution-building efforts of the federal judiciary, combined with the collaborative relationships that judges developed with the executive branch, transformed what was merely a blueprint for government, existing only on parchment, into a vibrant, effective state.

Notes

1. Saikrishna Bangalore Prakash, *Imperial from the Beginning: The Constitution of the Original Executive* (New Haven, CT: Yale University Press, 2015), 69–73.

2. "An Act to establish the Judicial Courts of the United States," ch. 20, 1 Stat. 73 (1789).

3. See, for example, Julius Goebel Jr., "The Oliver Wendell Holmes Devise: History of the Supreme Court of the United States," in *Antecedents and Beginnings to 1801*, vol. 1 (New York: MacMillan, 1971); William R. Casto, "James Iredell and the American Origins of Judicial Review," *Connecticut Law Review* 27 (1995): 329–63; Casto, *The Supreme Court in the Early Republic: The Chief Justiceships of John Jay and Oliver Ellsworth* (Columbia: University of South Carolina Press, 1995); Robert P. Frankel Jr., "Before *Marbury*: *Hylton v. United States* and the Origins of Judicial Review," *Journal of Supreme Court History* 28 (2003): 1–13; and Larry D. Kramer, *The People Themselves: Popular Constitutionalism and Judicial Review* (New York: Oxford University Press, 2004).

4. For scholarly treatments of the lower federal courts, see Jerry L. Mashaw, *Creating the Administrative Constitution: The Lost One Hundred Years of American Administrative Law* (New Haven, CT: Yale University Press, 2012); Maeva Marcus, ed., *The Documentary History of the Supreme Court of the United States: 1789–1800*, 8 vols. (New York: Columbia University Press, 1985–2007); and Gautham Rao, *National Duties: Custom Houses and the Making of the American State* (Chicago: University of Chicago Press, 2016).

5. See, for example, "An Act for the government and regulation of Seamen in the merchants service," ch. 29, 1 Stat. 131 (1790), and Mashaw, *Creating the Administrative Constitution*, 73–74. Also see *Hayburn's Case*, 2 US (2 Dall.) 409 (1792), for Congress's ultimately unsuccessful attempt to recruit federal judges in the administration of pensioner's claims.

6. "An Act to provide for mitigating or remitting the forfeitures and penalties accruing under the revenue laws, in certain case therein mentioned," ch. 12, 1 Stat. 122 (1790).

7. The first Congress received hundreds of petitions, which ranged from citizens' unsolicited advisory opinions to Congress on policy to protests against slavery. See William C. diGiacommantonio, "Petitioners and Their Grievances: A View from the First Federal Congress," in *The House and Senate in the 1790s: Petitioning, Lobbying, and Institutional Development*, ed. Kenneth R. Bowling and Donald R. Kennon (Athens: Ohio University Press, 2002), 29–56.

8. Alexander Hamilton, "Report on the Petition of Christopher Saddler" (19 January 1790), in *The Papers of Alexander Hamilton*, ed. Harold C. Syret, 27 vols. (New York: Columbia University Press, 1961–87), 6:191–92, including n. 2 (hereafter *PAH*). During the 1790s, Congress enacted, repealed, and modified tonnage, duty, and excise acts numerous times. See *Statutes at Large* for statutes enacted on 20 July 1789 (ch. 3, 1 Stat. 27), 4 July 1789 (ch. 2, 1 Stat. 24), 16 September 1789 (ch. 15, 1 Stat. 69), 20 July 1790 (ch. 30, 1 Stat. 135), 4 August 1790 (ch. 35, 1 Stat. 145), 3 March 1791, (ch. 15, 1 Stat. 199; ch. 26, 1 Stat. 219), 2 May 1792 (ch. 27, 1 Stat. 259), 5 June 1794 (ch. 49, 1 Stat. 378), and 29 January 1795 (ch. 17, 1 Stat. 411).

9. Alexander Hamilton, "Report on the Petition of Christopher Saddler" (19 January 1790), *PAH*, 6:191, 192.

10. "An Act to provide for mitigating or remitting the forfeitures and penalties accruing under the revenue laws, in certain case therein mentioned," ch. 12, 1 Stat. 122 (1790).

11. Norma Landau, *The Justices of the Peace, 1679–1760* (Berkeley: University of California Press, 1984), 21; Michael Dalton, *Countrey Justice* (1619), Classical English Law Texts (London: Professional Books Limited, 1973), 34–36, 58–64, 79–90, 118–22, 128–35.

12. Leonard D. White, *The Federalists: A Study in Administrative History* (New York: Macmillan, 1948), 455.

13. Jerry L. Mashaw argues that "legal control of administration by courts included not only post hoc review of the legality of official action but also the insertion of courts into administration—sometimes making them the administrators." Mashaw, "Recovering American Administrative Law: Federalist Foundations, 1787–1801," *Yale Law Journal* 115 (2006): 1321.

14. Ibid., 1331–33.

15. *Annals of Congress,* House of Representatives, 1st Congress, 2nd Session, 1168 (8 February 1790).

16. Ibid., 1164 (4 February 1790).

17. Ibid., 636 (29 June 1789).

18. "An Act to provide for mitigating or remitting the forfeitures and penalties accruing under the revenue laws, in certain case therein mentioned," ch. 12, 1 Stat. 122, 123 (1790).

19. Martin had violated a 1790 duty and tonnage statute, then requested a pardon from the president in 1794; before granting or denying the pardon, Washington asked Hamilton to review the petitioner's request. Hamilton reported back to Washington, noting that "upon the whole as Mr Martin is undoubtedly an innocent sufferer, I incline to the opinion that a pardon may be adviseable which would operate to remit one half the penalty incurred." The president then granted Martin's pardon two days later. See Alexander Hamilton to George Washington, 9 June 1794, *PAH,* 16:472.

20. Hamilton to Jeremiah Olney, 31 July 31, 1792, in *PAH,* 12:140.

21. See, for example, Alexander Hamilton to Sharp Delany, 22 January 1795, *PAH,* 18:173–74n1, and Judge Henry Marchant to Alexander Hamilton, 31 August 1792, *PAH,* 12:299–300.

22. By not providing a manifest for his goods, Duncan Manson violated section 11 of "An Act to provide more effectually for the collection of the duties imposed by law on goods, wares and merchandise imported into the United States, and on the tonnage of ships or vessels," ch. 35, 1 Stat. 145, 156 (1790). Section 11 mandated that US importers must "produce such manifest or manifests in writing, which such master or other person is herein before required to have on board his said ship or vessel, to such officer or officers of the customs, as shall first come on board his said ship or vessel, for his or their inspection."

23. US District Court Case Files, District of Georgia, Federal Records Center, East Point, Georgia, as quoted in Hamilton to Nathaniel Pendleton, 11 April 1791, *PAH,* 8:274–76n2.

24. All biographical details about the federal judges included in this essay come from the "Biographical Directory of Federal Judges, 1789–Present," *History of the Federal Judiciary,* http://www.fjc.gov, website of the Federal Judicial Center, Washington, DC.

25. Hamilton to Nathaniel Pendleton, 11 April 1791, *PAH*, 8:274–76.

26. See section 70 of "An Act to provide more effectually for the collection of the duties imposed by law on goods, wares and merchandise imported into the United States, and on the tonnage of ships or vessels," ch. 35, 1 Stat. 145, 177 (1790). Discrepancies existed between foreign regulations of tonnage and the American method of measuring tonnage, which resulted, in the case of the *Rising Sun*, in a vessel that was too light to meet the American tonnage requirement for importation. Henry Marchant to Alexander Hamilton, 31 August 1792, *PAH*, 12:299–300, including n. 4, and Jeremiah Olney to Alexander Hamilton, 25 August 1792, *PAH*, 12:273.

27. Henry Marchant to Alexander Hamilton, 31 August 1792, *PAH*, 12:299–300.

28. Alexander Hamilton to Jeremiah Olney, 13 September 1792, *PAH*, 12:376.

29. Alexander Hamilton to——, undated, *PAH*, 6:41.

30. Alexander Hamilton to Otho H. Williams, 4 June 1791, *PAH* 8:437–38.

31. Hamilton lectured the judge, "The Deposition moreover should have been that the goods were the contents or part of the contents of certain *specified packages* under *specified marks* and *Numbers* imported in *specified vessels* the same on which the official documents shews the duties had been paid or secured. . . . It is observable that the deposition and manifest given as it is presumed after the seizure do not say when the goods were shipt, and that there is no proof or statement of the time of said seizure." Alexander Hamilton to Cyrus Griffin, 15 February 1791, *PAH*, 8:38–39.

32. Alexander Hamilton to Otho H. Williams, 4 June 1791, *PAH*, 8:437–38. Also see Otho H. Williams to Alexander Hamilton, 10 June 1791, *PAH*, 8:462–64.

33. Rutgers v. Waddington (N.Y. Mayor's Ct., 1784).

34. Alexander Hamilton to James Duane, 5 April 1793, *PAH*, 14:284–86.

35. For an example of Hamilton expressing his extreme displeasure not to a district judge, but to Sharp Delany, the collector of Philadelphia, and for how Delany handled his part in the remitting process, see Hamilton to Delany, 22, 28, and 30 January 1795, *PAH*, 18:173–74, 203, 210–11.

36. Alexander Hamilton to David Sewall, 13 November 1790, *PAH*, 7:150–52.

37. Alexander Hamilton, "Treasury Department Circular to the District Judges," 17 October 1791, *PAH*, 9:402.

38. "An Act concerning the Duties on Spirits distilled within the United States," ch. 32,1 Stat. 267 (1792).

39. Alexander Hamilton to William Paca, 5 March 1794, *PAH*, 16:118.

40. Alexander Hamilton to John Lowell, 19 March 1794, *PAH*, 16:184–85.

41. Federal District Court, District of Maine, Federal Records Center, Boston, as quoted in Alexander Hamilton to Nathaniel Fosdick, 23 January 1795, *PAH*, 18:178n2.

42. The original Remitting Act passed on 26 May 1790 (ch. 12, 1 Stat. 122) and was extended, renewed, or revised on 8 May 1792 (ch. 35, 1 Stat. 275), 3 March 1797 (ch. 13, 1 Stat. 506), and 2 January 1813 (ch. 7, 2 Stat. 789). On 11 February 1800, Congress passed an amendment to the 1797 Remitting Act that removed the sunset provision on the treasury secretary's remitting powers (ch. 6, 2 Stat. 7). Congress also inserted remitting clauses in subsequent revenue acts that authorized or slightly altered the remitting process under those particular statutes. See section 3 of "An Act further to regulate the entry of merchandise imported into the United States from any adjacent territory," ch. 14, 3 Stat. 616, 617 (1821). Also, in an

1823 tonnage act amendment, Congress gave the treasury secretary a remitting-like power to admit entry of foreign goods or persons if he did not suspect fraud. In this provision, district judges are not involved in the secretary's adjudication process. See section 10 of "An Act supplementary to, and to amend an act, entitled 'An act to regulate the collection of duties on imports and tonnage,' passed second March, one thousand seven hundred and ninety-nine, and for other purposes," ch. 21, 3 Stat. 729, 734 (1823).

43. US v. The Hawke, 26 F. Cas. 233 (D.C.D. S.C., 1794). See "An Act for enrolling and licensing ships or vessels to be employed in the coasting trade and fisheries, and for regulating the same" (1793 Enrollment and Licensing Act), ch. 8, 1 Stat. 305 (1793).

44. On 26 March 1794, Congress passed a joint resolution declaring "That an embargo be laid on all ships and vessels in the ports of the United States," res. 2, 1 Stat. 400 (1794).

45. See sections 8 and 32, at 1 Stat. 305, 308, 316 (1793).

46. The Cotton Planter, 6 F. Cas. 620 (C.C. D. N.Y., 1810) and the 1807 embargo, "An Act laying an Embargo on all ships and vessels in the ports and harbors of the United States," ch. 5, 2 Stat. 451 (1807).

47. Ibid., 620, 621.

48. Ibid., 622.

49. "An Act directing the Secretary of the Treasury to remit fines, forfeitures and penalties in certain cases," ch. 7, 2 Stat. 789 (1813).

50. Gallego et al. v. US, 9 F. Cas. 1105, 1108 (C.C. D. Va., 1820).

51. Gallego et al. v. US, 9 F. Cas. 1105, 1107 (C.C. D. Va., 1820).

52. 5 US (1 Cranch) 137 (1803).

53. Gallego et al. v. US, 9 F. Cas. 1105, 1108 (C.C. D. Va., 1820).

54. Marbury v. Madison, 5 US (1 Cranch) 137 (1803).

55. 10 F. Cas. 355 (C.C.D. S.C., 1808).

56. Gilchrist et al. v. Collector of Charleston, 10 F. Cas. 355, 357 (C.C.D. S.C., 1808).

Indian Affairs and
the Relentless American State

STEPHEN J. ROCKWELL

When President George Washington heard that General Arthur St. Clair and the bulk of the US Army had been overrun and defeated by a pan-Indian alliance on the banks of the Wabash River in the old Northwest Territory, he was *mad*. Our image of the stoic, unflappable, self-controlled Washington is blown apart, if only for a moment, as we imagine him storming around his office yelling epithets at the distant, and wounded, St. Clair. "To suffer that army to be cut to pieces, hacked, butchered, tom-ahawked, by a surprise. . . . O God, O God, he's worse than a murderer!" Washington's anger focused on the warning he had given St. Clair: "BEWARE OF A SURPRISE! You know how the Indians fight us. He went off with that," Washington asserted, "as my last solemn warning, thrown into his ears."[1]

Washington had reason to be upset. St. Clair's defeat in December 1791 came after years of planning and diplomacy involving dozens of Indian nations, years of inching toward a stable negotiated peace or a decisive US military victory. Instead, diplomacy failed and a national military disaster followed, with significant ramifications on the prospects for the fledgling nation's survival. St. Clair's defeat was the third failure by the young national government to secure the safety and peace of the new settlers and pioneers in the territory, and the third time US troops had been bested by Indians. It came even as the United States pursued delicate negotiations with the Creek and other powerful Indian nations in the South, who knew of the new nation's futile efforts in the territories to the north. The defeat made fast news to the European powers still present on the United States' borders—England around the Great Lakes and the Old Northwest, Spain in the South, and French settlements to the north and west. St. Clair's defeat made the United States look weak and vulnerable, hardly the sturdy new state that Washington and so many others had envisioned at the Constitutional Convention less than five years earlier.

And yet a year and a half later, General Anthony Wayne reversed St. Clair's loss at the Battle of Fallen Timbers, and 1795 saw the landmark Treaty of Greenville put order to the area north of the Ohio River. By the end of his second term, Washington's administration would effectively manage affairs in the South and encourage Congress to pass intricate, considered legislation aimed at regulating land purchases from Indians, limiting conflicts between whites and Indians, and augmenting military strength and organization.

For a political scientist, the movement during Washington's two terms from near chaos on the new nation's borders, to the relative calm brought by victories in war and policy, is critically important. This essay examines lessons about the presidency and the American state that emerge from studying Indian affairs during Washington's two terms. Following a brief overview of Indian affairs during Washington's presidency, we will see that the nation's first president pushed a coherent legislative agenda in Indian affairs, that bureaucratic autonomy developed quickly, that the president fought undeclared wars, and that presidential use of public rhetoric and communication to support policies dates back to the office's earliest days. Together, these dynamics suggest that the notion of a "modern" presidency characterized by these features, and distinct from a "traditional" presidency, is a myth. At the level of the American state, a study of Indian affairs in Washington's two terms dramatizes how state building was driven by war, how complex issues led to sophisticated, interrelated public policy governance, how the federal government immediately became a focal point for public demands, and how a "sense of the state" developed in the nation's earliest years. At this level, studying Indian affairs in Washington's presidency adds to our growing understanding of the scope, influence, and intrusiveness of the early American state. Indian affairs were of major significance under President Washington, and a study of US–Indian relations reveals important lessons about the early development of the presidency and the American state.

Relentless Expansion

The United States faced threatening, complicated, and violent prospects of war and fragmentation across its borders at the start of George Washington's first term. A quick overview of this environment will help bring the development of the presidency and the American state in these years into bolder relief.

To the northwest, especially north of the Ohio River, the British maintained influence over well-organized alliances of Indian nations. Still in charge of important posts in the Old Northwest such as Detroit and

Sandusky, and in control of Niagara and the Great Lakes, Britain was patron to powerful Indian nations like the Shawnee and Miami. Standing poised to pounce on any mistake by the new American government, Britain hoped to use the Indians in the Northwest as a buffer against the Americans, particularly to stop American settlement at the Ohio River. The Indian nations themselves resented American efforts to claim lands after the Revolution, and they rejected the trespasses of white squatters.

Under the Articles of Confederation, Congress failed to muster much effect on the region. In 1785 Congress dispatched General Josiah Harmar to remove whites who had crossed the boundary line at the upper Ohio River, and he burned cabins and forced whites back across the river. His three-hundred-man force was overmatched in 1785 and 1786, though, by Indians defending their territory and raiding contested areas, and by whites pushing illegally across boundaries.[2] He was sent out again in 1787, but 1787 and 1788 witnessed increasing Indian attacks.[3]

St. Clair arrived in 1788 as the first governor of the new Northwest Territory, with instructions to induce the Indians to cede lands to the United States. White migration had increased as the region reached territorial status, as noted in a June 1788 report from Harmar that counted more than six thousand people and close to three thousand horses moving in that spring. More than 250,000 Americans had moved west of the Appalachians by the late 1780s, increasing conflicts and exacerbating the likelihood of breakaway states. Focused on bringing order and dominion to the area, St. Clair arranged a large negotiating conference in December 1788 at Fort Harmar. The January 1789 Treaty of Fort Harmar reaffirmed cessions to the United States north of the Ohio River, prompting St. Clair to declare the negotiations a success, but with a divided Indian population the agreement was tenuous at best.[4]

In the Old Southwest, Spain had closed the Mississippi to all but Spanish navigation in June 1784, and it controlled New Orleans, Florida, and many of the trade routes through the Gulf of Mexico and past Cuba. Spain developed alliances with southern Indian nations, particularly the Creek, with the goal of using the Indians as a buffer between Spanish territory and the United States.[5] The Creek leader Alexander McGillivray delicately calibrated and recalibrated relations with Spain, the United States, and the British trading firm of Panton Leslie, seeking the best security and trade accommodations for the tribe.

At the same time, North Carolina and Georgia had declared the extension of their territories deep into Creek lands, and Georgia had signed the Treaty of Augusta in 1783—an illegitimate treaty because it was signed by only a small number of unauthorized Creeks. The Confederation Congress sent federal treaty commissioners into the area in 1785, but overlapping and competing jurisdictions rendered their authority dubious and their actions largely ineffective. Another federal effort to negotiate peace with the Creeks, this one by Dr. James White, failed in early 1788; McGillivray rebuffed White's successor, Richard Winn, as well, as Creek ties with Spain tightened. The Cherokees were also rejecting American overtures, and Congress asked Secretary of War Henry Knox what force might be required to impose peace in the Southwest.[6]

Caught in the middle, thousands of new settlers demanded protection and empowerment. In his 2008 book *The Political Mind,* cognitive linguist George Lakoff defines the role of "progressive government" as providing for protection and empowerment: "Protection is there to guarantee freedom from harm, from want, and from fear. Empowerment is there to maximize freedom to achieve your goals."[7] This modern framework fits the earliest days of the republic, as westerners made protection and empowerment the prerequisites for loyalty.

Indian harassment of trade and settlements in the North and the South, and the looming threat posed by the European powers, disrupted safety and security throughout the years of the confederation and into the Washington administration. A federal district judge estimated that fifteen hundred Kentuckians had been killed by Indians in the six years following the end of the Revolution, while another study found thirty-six hundred deaths from roughly 1775 to 1795. White settlers were dying in new villages, along the Wilderness Road, and while flatboating on the rivers. Historian Dale Van Every estimates that 450 deaths per year might have been the norm in the late 1780s.[8]

Legal disorder created chaos for settlers, too, as disputes over land titles multiplied between early settlers and later settlers, among land companies, and between Indians and squatters on Indian lands. Problems of overlapping land titles, new and old settlers, eviction notices, and legal dispossessions exacerbated uncertainty throughout the 1780s, especially in Kentucky.[9]

Finally, it's worth noting that these westerners weren't necessarily going to wait until the United States got its act together, established legal order, and mounted an effective defense against Indians and their European patrons. The new settlers would side with whatever power protected them from threats and empowered them to develop communities, secure land titles, and increase trade. The West was the scene of ongoing schemes by individuals like John Sevier, James Robertson, and James Wilkinson, and communities like Franklin, Holstein, and Cumberland, to organize outside of the United States, to ally with England or Spain, or even to declare independence.[10] People moving west demanded the benefits of a state's power, demanded protection and opportunity. If the United States couldn't provide them, they would look elsewhere.

The absence of effective governmental authority in the late 1780s encouraged such projects, and new settlers constantly reexamined their options. Meanwhile, US Indian policy in the late 1780s remained "so irrational as to seem incoherent": the government made aggressive moves in the North against well-organized Indians backed by Britain, yet it offered surprising concessions and acted with surprising restraint in the South, where Spanish support for native populations was less committed.[11] Populations in both areas became increasingly frustrated and angered by US ineffectiveness.

Washington's first term strategy was a relentless effort to avoid war and a relentless effort to win the wars that the nation did fight.[12] To this end, Washington and Secretary of War Knox pursued a two-track strategy to bring coherence and effectiveness to Indian policy in the Northwest and in the South. While there were important differences and variations, the United States would try to reduce costs and enhance stability and order by securing diplomatic and treaty agreements with Indian nations, delineating boundaries, and establishing reciprocal trade and criminal justice relationships. At the same time, though, the United States would prepare for war and fight when necessary, with a steadily increasing ability to punish those who refused to negotiate and cede lands and to remove those whites who crossed illegally into Indian territory. By the end of Washington's first term, these goals had not been met—but the administration and a compliant Congress had established a commitment to eventual success, laying firm foundations for the development of the American state behind a strong executive branch.

In the North, Harmar went out again in the fall of 1790 with a force of 320 regulars and more than 1,100 militiamen. As the Indians receded and refused to engage, Harmar ruthlessly burned native towns and crops. When Colonel John Hardin was sent out to find the Indians and force them to engage, Miamis led by Little Turtle destroyed Hardin's forces. Harmar returned homeward having lost 183 men, including 79 regulars. St. Clair told Knox that the mission had been a success—much like his overly optimistic review of the Treaty of Fort Harmar—but the evidence suggests that the Indians saw it as a successful engagement with a heretofore untested American force, which they now knew could be defeated. In early 1791, Indians stepped up their attacks on American settlements—Harmar's efforts had encouraged, not dissuaded, the Indians. US military efforts continued to meet with frustration, and the Indians continued to outsmart, outmaneuver, and outfight the combined forces of American militia and regulars.[13]

Demands on the government increased, now from easterners who had moved west recently, not just from veteran Kentuckians.[14] St. Clair began preparing the invasion force that Washington hoped would finally put an end to the chaos, even as the government, true to the two-track policy, continued to try to negotiate agreements. Congress sent Revolutionary War veteran John Proctor to the Iroquois to enlist their good offices as mediators with the western tribes. The Iroquois, bothered by ongoing demands for land from New York State and Pennsylvania, balked at the approach at the same time as St. Clair was preparing his major offensive in summer 1791.[15]

Negotiations failed again, and when St. Clair finally engaged, after lengthy preparations and long delays, he met with spectacular and catastrophic defeat. Three thousand Indians, in an effective alliance of Miami, Delaware, Shawnee, Kickapoo, Wyandot, Ottawa, Ojibwa, Potawatomi, Conoy, Nanticoke, and a few Mohawk, Creek, and Cherokee met St. Clair's forces. Little Turtle, Blue Jacket, and Buckongahelas led the native forces, with support from French and British traders and officials including Simon Girty, Alexander McKee, and Matthew Elliott. The US military lost roughly two-thirds of its personnel, with 630 US officers and enlisted men killed and another 250 or so wounded. Fifty women accompanying the troops were killed, and roughly 150 were taken captive. Historian Colin Calloway tallies other losses, including six cannons, more than three hundred horses, close to four hundred tents, and twelve hundred muskets and bayonets, plus swords, pistols, axes, spades, blacksmith's tools, medicine, provisions, official papers, and all the army's drums.[16]

The catastrophe engrossed the public attention, generating newspaper articles, reports, and even songs. Calloway concludes that the battle "was the biggest victory Native Americans ever won and proportionately the biggest military disaster the United States ever suffered." He adds that "the destruction of the army . . . threatened the very existence of the infant United States."[17] This is no exaggeration—historians now, and citizens and officials then, recognized in the disaster a grave threat to the American future.

At the same time that the Washington administration increased its efforts in the Northwest, with disastrous consequences, renewed efforts were also under way in the South. There, McGillivray and the Creeks harried American settlements and aligned politically and militarily with the Spanish and economically with the British. Washington's first delegation to the Creeks reflected the significance he attached to the Creeks' strength and importance to southern affairs. Benjamin Lincoln, the Revolutionary War general who had accepted Cornwallis's sword in surrender and who had also led the tactical effort to put down Shays' Rebellion, led the team. Also at the mission's head were Cyrus Griffin, the last president of the Continental Congress, and David Humphreys, soon to be minister to Portugal and then to Spain. But like the Confederation Congress's emissaries, Lincoln was rebuffed, and raids on American settlements continued.[18]

Jurisdictional tensions between white governments eased when North Carolina ceded its western lands to the United States in February 1790, clearing the way for the federal government and its agents to exercise clear and credible leadership in negotiations. Congress established the Southwest Territory just three months later, and Washington's persistence paid off when McGillivray finally hit it off with an American emissary, this time New York merchant and Anti-Federalist Marinus Willett. Willet took McGillivray north to New York City, where he was wined and dined by Henry Knox and his wife, Lucy. A happy and flattered McGillivray signed the Treaty of New York (and its secret protocols for US rank and payments to McGillivray) in August, just six months after North Carolina stepped out of the way of the federal government's efforts. In 1792, Knox sent new emissaries on a friendship mission to the Cherokees, Choctaws, and Chickasaws, and Congress increased Cherokee annuities by 50 percent in an effort to maintain the unstable peace.[19]

By the end of Washington's first term Indian affairs remained problematic. Indians still harassed white settlements, the divisions of authority between the federal and state governments remained contested, and Spain continued to control the Mississippi River, New Orleans, Florida, and the Gulf Coast.[20] The demands of the era were pushing the constitutional office of the presidency to become something very familiar to twenty-first-century political scientists.

Part of the reason for Washington's unremitting effort to woo McGillivray, and for his anger with St. Clair after the 1791 defeat, was Washington's understanding of the demands made by westerners for protection and the frustration felt by those westerners at years of disappointment and uncertainty. Having waited five years for Washington and the new government under the Constitution to secure the West, St. Clair's defeat and continuing tensions among the players in the South signaled that that process remained unfinished. After St. Clair's defeat, western opposition to US troops became vehement, as did eastern opposition to the cost; southern tensions tightened.[21]

Even so, the Washington administration stuck to its two-track plan. Washington and Knox worked Congress for more money and a reorganization of the military, and as Wayne prepared the *next* invasion force, Knox sent multiple and diverse peace delegates west in the hopes that somebody would find a way to avert further violence by negotiating a settlement.[22]

Four Things Indian Affairs Reveal about the Presidency

From the standpoint of a political scientist, the first and second terms of the Washington presidency are interesting because they show just how much of the "modern" presidency is present from the very beginning. Political scientists have for many years drawn an unnecessary and overly broad distinction between a "traditional" presidency and a "modern" one. A study of President Washington's approach to Indian affairs and related western policy matters demonstrates just how misguided such a distinction is. The nature of presidential action is a product of constitutional design, and the play in that design, far more than it is the result of developments in media and communications, in bureaucratic growth, or in personality.

Presidency scholars have been caught up in arguments about traditional and modern presidencies for years.[23] Scholars have, for example, argued that traditional presidents were not legislative leaders, that they lacked defined legislative agendas and the willingness to push Congress to adopt presidential measures and policy suites.[24] Other scholars have seen a relationship between the absence of presidential legislative leadership and the primitive state of national administration. Without a strong executive branch and robust administrative capacity, this argument suggests, there was little need or opportunity for the president to put together and press for a legislative program.[25] Scholars and the public have sometimes interpreted the apparent twentieth-century rise in undeclared wars as a modern development brought on by expanded executive powers and a weakening Congress.[26] Finally, scholars have argued that the nation has witnessed dramatic changes in forms of presidential communications and in the audiences for those communications.[27]

Each of these four points—the president as legislative leader, the development of national administrative capacity, presidential war making, and popular communication—are erroneously seen as "modern."[28] In fact, each tracks directly back to the Washington presidency, as President Washington quickly filled the gaps and gray areas in the constitutional design with executive action. Recognizing a relentless executive branch in action from the republic's earliest days erases the artificial and erroneous divide between a "traditional" and a "modern" presidency.

1. *The president pushed a coherent legislative agenda in Indian affairs.* The image of the president taking the reins of public policy and leading Congress and the public by initiating and then pursuing a coherent legislative program is something decidedly associated with the "modern" presidency.

Yet Washington's team led Congress to support a robust legislative agenda, much of which focused on Indian affairs and the West. While the broadbrush review above gives a small sense of the diplomatic and military action, most such summaries overlook the coherent interbranch approach orchestrated by Washington's administration.

Washington's legislative agenda in Indian affairs was immediate and important, and his leadership secured passage of legislation that continues in many ways to govern US practice today.[29] The 1790 Indian Trade Act is a good example. Its passage begins with Washington's first annual message of January 8, 1790, and the attached report by Secretary of War Knox. The act asserted federal preeminence over the states by requiring federal participation in all land sales from Indians, and it delegated to the president and his subordinates vast authority over Indian trade and a host of other matters. The act's first clause stated that "no person shall be permitted to carry on any trade or intercourse with the Indian Tribes without a license for that purpose under the hand and seal of the Superintendent of the department, or of such other person as the President of the United States shall appoint for that purpose." The clause mandated that a $1,000 bond be offered by an applicant for such license, payable to the president and binding the licensee to abide by whatever "rules, regulations and restrictions, as now are, or hereafter shall be made" by the president. The president was granted discretion to get around the licensing requirement by allowing people to conduct trade with Indians whose communities were surrounded by US citizens "without license if he may deem it proper." Further, Congress granted superintendents "full power and authority" to rescind licenses, through a trial process; merchants found to be violating the regulations or trading without a license would see their goods and merchandise seized and split fifty-fifty between the United States and the person prosecuting.[30]

In October 1791, Washington laid out a careful plan for Indian affairs in his third annual message. The specific details now ran to ten short paragraphs. Following up a year later, Washington's fourth annual message in November 1792 reminded Congress that the 1790 Trade Act was about to expire and explained the necessity for congressional action. The fourth message opened directly with discussion of Indian affairs in the Northwest, it expanded to twelve (no longer short) paragraphs, and it now explained context and background and requested increasingly specific provisions for managing Indian affairs. For example, Washington recommended that Congress provide for agents to be sent to specific tribes or regions, and for plans to allow the president to promote "civilization" among the Indians and carry on trade with them. Each of Washington's first four annual messages, then, increased in length, in specificity, and in the emphasis placed on congressional action in Indian affairs.

In March 1793, Congress expanded the 1790 law with "a considerably stronger and more inclusive piece of legislation." The law itself grew from seven sections to fifteen, with a particular focus on the federal role in the acquisition of land and on enforcing policies that would prevent whites from intruding on Indian lands (punishable in the 1793 act by a $1,000 fine—equal to about a $25,000 fine in 2017 dollars—or a year in prison). Crimes committed by whites in Indian country or against Indians would be punished sharply. Such laws reinforced provisions in treaties that made many of the same points, treating crimes against Indians with the same severity as crimes against whites even over the objections of many in Congress. Historian Francis Paul Prucha concludes that "a good part of Washington's program was written into these laws." President Washington was charting the course for a raft of interconnected policies passed into law by Congress.[31]

Two important pillars of US Indian policy emerged from the president's legislative leadership during Washington's second term: trade and intercourse legislation and the government trading house policy known as the factory system. Washington pressed Congress for a network of agents to be assigned to diplomatic and other duties among the Indian tribes, for "civilization" initiatives like farming and vocational training to help calm the frontiers and lead to peaceful and just relations, and he pushed for indemnities and compensation programs for Americans who lost property to Indians. Washington also pressed Congress for legislation authorizing and funding a system of government trading houses. These initiatives were codified by Congress, with many of them organized into a series of comprehensive acts that regulated trade and intercourse with Indian tribes as well as acts such as that creating the trading house network known as the factory system.[32]

Anthony Wayne's 1795 Treaty of Greenville and the 1795 Jay Treaty solidified the nation's military gains, anchoring a future characterized by treaties, trade agreements, and American-style diplomacy and negotiation. During the height of conflict, and then with peace settling in, Washington and Knox together led Congress to build out an integrated legislative agenda that relied on federal law, ratified treaties, and executive administration.

2. *Bureaucratic autonomy and discretionary authority were forged early.* Congressional debate on various Indian bills, the Militia Bill, the Land Office Bill, the Military Establishment Act, and others relied on extensive reports produced by top cabinet advisors like Treasury Secretary Alexander Hamilton and Secretary of War Henry Knox, submitted to Congress to guide

congressional action. Hamilton's leadership on tax, debt, and finance policy, for example, led to the 1789 Impost Act and the deals on the public
debt. His 1790 Treasury Department report on lands suggested that "no
land shall be sold, except such, in respect to which the titles of the Indian
tribes shall have been previously extinguished"—language included verba-
tim in House resolutions of January 4, 1791, and then carried with minor
changes into the final House bill in February.[33] Henry Knox's reports on
Indian affairs in the North and South, at the very opening of the Washington administration, profoundly influenced congressional action.

This leads us to the second "modern" aspect of the presidency evident
even in Washington's first term: the role of the independent and autonomous
executive branch bureaucracy. Executive departments forged autonomy
quickly, becoming the source of information and expert advice driving congressional decisions, becoming imbued with broad discretionary authority
delegated by Congress to the president and his agents, and becoming an
independent force of action outside of congressional oversight or control.[34]

Knox's work as secretary of war exemplifies the way in which administrative experts provide guidance, innovation, and policy advice for elected
leaders. In 1789, at the outset of the Washington administration, Knox articulated detailed plans for Washington and Congress that spelled out exactly
how much money and how many troops would be necessary to pacify the
Northwest and the South militarily. Knox also recognized and outlined the
constraints imposed by cost and by debt. Knox's report to Washington on
subjugating the northern Indians detailed the need for twenty-five hundred
men—Harmar had four hundred available at the time—and $200,000, an
enormous and impractical sum. Even more impractical was Knox's estimate for enforcing peace in the South: in July 1789 Knox proposed that
such an effort would require twenty-eight hundred men and $450,000—
the equivalent of more than twelve billion dollars in 2017—for just the
first nine months. The cost and the manpower required in both cases were
prohibitive.[35]

But Knox provided a practical alternative to such costly war plans, one
that would guide American land acquisition policy and Indian relations for
the rest of US history. Knox argued that peace was more economical than
war, and he laid out for Washington and for both houses of Congress the
morality and justice required in Indian affairs. He argued that peace, diplomacy, fairness, and justice should be guiding lights of American policy—
war would be a costly last resort, engaged only when absolutely necessary.
He argued that fighting unnecessary wars was unbecoming a great nation,
and that the United States must dispossess the Indians legally. He also

pointed out that if the government listened only to disaffected, angry, and bitter white settlers, the United States would surely attack Indians—but he added that the Indian perspective must be heard, too. Knox's statements on Indian right to soil influenced the shift in US policy from its initial and often counterproductive postwar stance, as he argued for backing off the nation's aggressive post–Revolutionary War land claims and returning to land purchases and negotiated agreements. It was Knox, with Washington's support, who designed the two-track early policy that defined American Indian affairs.[36]

The act creating the War Department in August 1789 delegated broad authority to the president to delegate authority to the secretary of war. Congress argued about, but understood, exactly what it was doing in these early days. Congress explicitly chose to delegate discretion rather than spell out details in the case of the post office, for example. Representatives hoped that administrators like surveyors, receivers, and land office officials would check and balance each other in the field, preventing abuses. The rapid drain of authority from Congress to the executive branch even sparked sarcastic remarks, with one member of the House noting the prominent roles of the Treasury Department and the Senate in the introduction of legislative proposals: "Have we, in truth, originated this money bill? Do we ever originate any money bill? . . . Why so little jealousy of the Executive Department, separated by the constitution with so much care from us?"[37]

Executive branch administrators often acted without significant oversight from Congress. Military leaders and treaty commissioners received detailed instructions written by Knox.[38] Simultaneously, the pace and volatility of borderland affairs quickly encouraged the civilian and military field services to exercise broad discretionary authority. St. Clair, for example, negotiated different terms with different Indians in 1788 than he had been instructed to do, because he found unforeseeable constraints (and opportunities) when he operated in the field.[39] In all of this, administrators in the capital and in the field were independent forces exercising autonomous decision making.[40]

The treaty process is a terrific example. Many of us are familiar with the tale of Washington going to the Senate early in his first term for the "advice and consent" part of treaty making. Washington visited the Senate in August 1789 to discuss negotiations of a treaty with the southern Indians. As Lindsay Chervinsky's essay shows, Washington's first instinct was to seek advice and consent during the discussions of the treaty and see what the senators had to say. He submitted a detailed list of questions and showed up to get answers and engage in discussion. And like many an executive forced to go to a committee meeting, he decided during that meeting that he'd wasted his time. The senators were unsure what to do, lacked essential information about the treaty and the circumstances surrounding it, and were unable to come to clear conclusions about what their advice, as a body, was. Washington left in a huff, vowing never to return.[41]

Henceforth, Washington and his delegates in the executive branch would negotiate and sign treaties in the field without getting much prior advice or consent from the Senate. The Senate often worked with the president to authorize treaty commissions and set the parameters of negotiations and available resources, but the actual work would be done by the executive branch and submitted to the Senate when it had reached a very advanced stage. That stage was often reached by going far beyond, or far afield, of what Congress had authorized at the outset.

In this, treaty making with Indian nations mirrored treaty making with European nations. This is an important point for our understanding of the fast development of the presidency and its administrative capacity. In practice, treaty making with Indian and European nations helped expand the presidency's authority and the bureaucracy's autonomy. Legally, too, Indian treaties functioned much as treaties with European nations did—they quickly came to be official agreements among distinct political communities, important enough to demand ratification by the Senate, and which codified reciprocal obligations among the participants. Even as the nature and practice of Indian treaty making evolved in US history, and as the practice came under increasing fire in the Jacksonian era as a relic and an absurdity, John Marshall's Supreme Court sanctioned and reinforced the lasting significance of the treaties upon signatories. It was only in the specific terms of the agreements that significant differences began to separate Indian treaties from treaties with European nations, particularly in the Indian treaties' common statements regarding Indian nations' dependence upon the United States—the root of the Indian nations' continuingly ambiguous status as semisovereign, domestic dependent nations. Beyond the nature of the treaties' terms, the treaty making *process* with American Indian nations, and the legal status of the results, enhanced the unilateral authority of the presidency in the Washington administration's earliest days.[42]

Thus when Washington told the Senate in 1790 that "the treaty with the Creeks may be regarded as the main foundation of the future peace and prosperity of the south-western frontier of the United States"—and when he said that he was working to uphold agreements with the Cherokees and the congressional ban on encroachments into Indian lands by removing white squatters, that there were five hundred families illegally squatting in the French Broad and Holstein areas, and that he wondered if he should uphold older agreements or work to negotiate new ones as circumstances on the ground evolved in the wake of North Carolina's land cession to the United States—when Washington presented all of this to the Senate and asked for direction, the Senate told him to use his discretion.[43]

These are remarkable grants of authority. They become significant for the study of the presidency and state building when married with the significance and complexity of affairs in the old South and the old Northwest. What the Senate was ceding to Washington was not marginal power related to distant frontiers—they were ceding to the president the power to make policy across the frontier, affecting thousands of people: new and old settlers, natives and newcomers. They were conceding the authority of executive branch officers to make decisions on the ground on policy issues from physical boundaries to criminal justice adjudication, from rules governing traders to the ability to settle disputes and punish offenders. The president was instantly in position to lead, to be entrepreneurial, when it came to directing the course of national policy. Executive branch officials could set policy and expect Congress to sanction those decisions later.

Delegation continued, even advanced, into Washington's second term. The 1796 Trade and Intercourse Act enacted Washington's legislative agenda in Indian affairs, but it also delegated authority for detail, design, and implementation to the executive branch. Congress evinced little interest in administrative detail or management, preferring instead to give Washington and his executive branch broad latitude for creating these policies on the ground, deciding how to allocate resources, and realizing the gains of the initiatives. Despite congressional *debates* about the details, the wisdom of the measures, the expense, and the extent of the authority they were delegating to the president, Congress nevertheless returned again and again to a posture of delegation and repose. Congress was made interested in policies by Washington's messages, debated details, delegated actual authority, and then fell back to passive, intermittent oversight of the measures as they were realized and implemented by executive branch administrators.[44]

In the South, where Washington had less experience and state governments were more active, one might expect to see less deference from Congress to presidential discretion and authority. This was not the case. Washington did have difficulty early, until Georgia and North Carolina ratified the Constitution and ceded their western land claims to the federal government. In those early years, the federal government's ability to dictate affairs in those regions was limited. But once the states entered the union and ceded western lands, the institutional leadership situation quickly came to resemble that in the Old Northwest—territorial leadership belonged to the federal government, often delegated to the president and the executive branch and its officers, free from the pushback presidents faced when dealing with established state governments.

Examples abound. Members of Congress, particularly from southern states, were upset with the Washington administration's secret 1790 treaty with Alexander McGillivray, yet Congress accepted it and funded it. Southern representatives continually complained about federal exclusion of southern state interests during treaty negotiations in the South, and yet they were largely unable to prevent federal agents from controlling discussions, leading negotiations, and even physically barring state officials from treaty negotiations. Often complaining of what they saw as Washington's dismissal of the significance of the threats facing southern US citizens on the western frontiers, and jealous of the attention he paid US interests in the Ohio valley, southern members in Congress were unable to get Washington to change course. The president remained the locus of action and authority.[45]

As Washington moved into his second term, the president's discretionary authority in the South only increased. The trade and intercourse laws, particularly the 1796 act, included vast policy domains delegated by Congress to the president and the executive branch. The factory system, lynchpin of the Indian agent system and of the nation's effort to manage and regulate trading relations, was placed almost entirely under presidential control, and it was Washington's executive branch team that decided to establish factories in the South and Southwest, beginning with Colerain, Georgia, and Tellico Blockhouse in Tennessee. The president's delegated authority to oversee and manage border relations, criminal justice protocols, military maneuvers, and trade relationships quickly became largely unbound, and his ability to allocate monetary and human resources as he saw fit followed the same path. Congress often debated, often assessed, often argued, but rarely acted in any way other than to support and sanction Washington's moves and his team's treaties and agreements.

3. The president fought undeclared, unpopular wars. The United States was at war with the Indian nations of the Northwest for thirty years, from the end of the Revolution in 1783 to William Henry Harrison's victory over Tecumseh in 1813. Congress never declared war, despite the fact that these conflicts extended for decades, involved many of the same places and participants, and witnessed ongoing tactical and strategic adjustments and diplomatic interludes. Later in the nineteenth century, the United States would fight two long wars with the Seminoles in Florida, extended wars with Indian nations of the upper Midwest, the Southwest, California, and the Pacific Northwest, and of course long wars with the Sioux and other Indians of the Dakotas and Great Plains. Many of these wars, like the war in the Old Northwest, were deeply unpopular with large segments of the American public.[46]

It is important to recognize these conflicts as long, coherent, and significant to the life and treasury of the nation. They were not sidelights or minor policing actions but—as illustrated by St. Clair's defeat—of major significance as the nation struggled to move west. These undeclared wars with Indians were a more persistent feature of US policy than the two times the new nation *did* declare war—against Britain in 1812 and against Mexico in 1848—and a more regular part of American policy making than the war scares that occasionally challenged US relations with European powers.

In the wake of St. Clair's defeat, for example, Congress entered into a long, detailed, and acrimonious debate in the House of Representatives over the propriety of supporting another effort to pacify or subjugate the Indians of the Old Northwest. Some members castigated the administration's policies in the wake of St. Clair's defeat: "The mode of treating the Indians in general was reprobated as unwise and impolitic," reports the record of congressional debate. Other representatives called for a halt to expansion, and better enforcement of established borders with the Indians: "It is only exposing our arms to disgrace, betraying our own weakness, and lessening the public confidence in the General Government, to send forth armies to be butchered in the forests, while we suffer the British to keep possession of the posts within our territory." Some highlighted the importance of dislodging Britain from the western posts, while others worried that previous losses didn't augur well for a fourth try; others still debated the strengths and weaknesses of a large force of regular soldiers compared with an asymmetric war engineered by individual and largely independent militia forces. Some believed the problem wasn't strategy, but preparation: "Collected at length at the head of the Ohio, they [St. Clair's forces] fruitlessly loitered away their time, till they finally erected a monument to our eternal disgrace and infamy." Some argued that scarce resources demanded smarter allocation—why spend the money on the military, when the Treasury couldn't adequately fund lighthouses?[47]

Popular attention was riveted, evidenced by complaints from members that the debate was unfocused, wide ranging, and aggressive precisely because the galleries were open. Debate continued, though, with representatives in turn blaming and exonerating white settlers, defending the United

States' efforts to negotiate peaceful agreements and cessions, highlighting the forbearance of frontier settlers when constrained by Congress or the president, even in the face of increasingly brutal Indian attacks. Some argued to stop fighting before the nation got in too deep and committed too many resources; others argued that that point had long since been passed and that it was too late to stop now; others tied the debate into broader issues of taxes, freedom, and the risks posed by a large standing army.[48]

About the only thing Congress did not debate was the Constitution's explicit grant to Congress of the power to declare war.

For better or worse, since Washington's first term wars have been led by the executive and supported by Congress without a formal declaration of war. By examining the actual practice of the Washington administration and the first Congresses, scholars have recently begun to fill out our knowledge of the founders' understanding of war making under the Constitution. Robust detail in these debates is wrapped inside the broad question of which branch has authority to initiate war and, at the end of the day, control the course of that war. The debate's best recent protagonists— Saikrishna Bangalore Prakash, John Yoo, Robert Delahunty, and William Adler—include Indian affairs during the Washington administration to make competing points about the relationship of Congress to the president in the realm of declaring war, initiating war, deploying troops, and so on.

What's revealing is how these authors use the Indian affairs history to develop competing conclusions. Yoo, Delahunty, and Adler tend to focus their attention on President Washington's earliest efforts in the Old Northwest, arguing that the deployments of Harmar and St. Clair, in particular, were primarily executive-planned and -initiated actions taken with minimal support or authorization from Congress.[49] Prakash tends to focus much of his attention on relations with the Creeks in 1792–93 and on congressional action taken in 1793, 1794, and afterward, arguing that the president's powers to wage war and deploy troops were constrained by Congress and that they are, at the end of the day, concurrent and residual, subordinate to express congressional mandates.[50]

While this essay cannot delve deeply into what is an extensive historical and philosophical debate, the inclusion of the Indian cases pushes our knowledge further than earlier treatments that excluded these actions.[51] The Indian affairs contexts tilt the debate over war powers decidedly toward Prakash's pro-Congress position, even as they keep Yoo's and Adler's perspectives intriguingly relevant. Prakash's arguments list extensive congressional actions to conclude that Congress exercised authority over minute details of war making and deployments in the Washington years. Prakash is correct that, since the days of Josiah Harmar and Arthur St. Clair, Congress has acted to limit and manage the actions of the president in war making. But Yoo and Adler are correct, too, to see in our history numerous examples in which the president and his officers have taken discretionary, offensive war making action that had not been explicitly authorized by Congress.[52] Yoo's notion that the president has considerable latitude for action is true, as is Adler's conclusion that "rhetorical presidential support for Congress's role did not accord with their practical readiness to initiate and manage hostilities unilaterally. The willingness of presidents to act against congressional wishes is therefore not necessarily a historical aberration."[53] Prakash wins out, however, given how quickly and easily President Washington deferred to congressional control when Congress acted clearly and decisively. At the end of the day, Prakash is correct to see the president's powers as ultimately bounded and even superseded by congressional authority under the Constitution.[54]

For our purposes here, it is enough to highlight the critically important role of Indian affairs in uncovering the framers' intent and practice regarding such a centrally important government activity as waging war. The history of the nation's early wars with American Indians contributes mightily to our understanding of this fundamental issue, and excluding the Indian contexts does little other than distort and mislead.

4. Presidential rhetoric and public communication developed rapidly. Jeffrey Tulis's leading work on the subject of nineteenth-century presidential communication sees a "rhetorical presidency" that speaks directly to the public about hard-core policy matters arising only in the twentieth century. Moreover, Tulis's argument continues, rare efforts by nineteenth-century presidents to speak directly to the public, or directly influence the course of legislation, sparked quick backlash, as angry voters and legislators acted to curtail the breach of etiquette created by active, communicative presidents. This interpretation has been echoed in numerous textbook and scholarly treatments of the office's public communications.[55]

Yet President Washington addressed core public policy issues in public rhetoric. His inaugural address encouraged serious consideration of the amendments that would become the Bill of Rights. The president's annual message was a critical factor in legislative developments, and Congress acted swiftly and directly to put the president's suggested initiatives into effect, as we have seen. The legislative histories of the Indian Trade Bill and the Indian Treaties Bill indicate that congressional action on these efforts was largely sparked by the president. The legislative history of the Militia Bill begins with Washington's first annual message, and the legislative history of the 1791 Military Establishment Act begins with Washington's second annual message.[56] The second annual message framed congressional discussion on a host of issues.[57] After St. Clair's defeat and after ardent congressional debate, Washington secured a second enlargement of the military and a five-thousand-man-strong American Legion, with "Mad" Anthony Wayne in charge.[58]

Washington understood and capitalized upon the public nature of his communications. With the policy-heavy and influential third annual message in October 1791, for example, Washington staked out specific positions on important issues and laid out a detailed policy agenda to Congress and the public. Newspapers reprinted the speech in its entirety and, according to Tulis, in the early republic the annual messages and veto messages "received the most scrutiny and were the most carefully crafted presidential remarks."[59] Washington crafted these messages with the explicit purpose of influencing public opinion.[60]

About half of the third message focuses on Indian affairs and the need to address such important matters with specific and carefully designed efforts. The fourth message is proportionately even more concerned with Indian affairs, and it opens directly with the situation in the Northwest.[61] Washington reflected on St. Clair's efforts, the outcome of which at that point were unknown, but which Washington contextualized as part of an ongoing effort to secure the West to the United States. The president called for government action and order in alienating Indian lands and for trade regulations and experiments in efforts to civilize the Indians. He asked Congress to allow the president the freedom of action necessary to proceed shrewdly and effectively, including calling for "provision" to be made to punish encroachments and to deal with those who acted so as to endanger the peace of the union. In the 1793 Trade and Intercourse Act, Congress authorized the president to provide animals, tools, goods, money, and other items to promote civilization, and it authorized him to assign "temporary," eventually permanent, agents to specific tribes or areas. Twenty thousand dollars per year was allocated.[62]

Washington thus discussed significant policy matters in his first inaugural address and first annual message, and by the third and fourth was regularly recommending specific policies to Congress and, indirectly—but intentionally and knowingly—the public. He supplemented these public comments by regularly making direct and indirect policy statements to private individuals and to public groups.[63] Early presidents did not, and could not, speak directly to the public as often and as directly as they can today. But Washington rapidly expanded his use of public communication to aim directly at the details of important and controversial policy issues.

Four Things Indian Affairs Reveal about Early State Building

Executive branch dynamism and the push for westward expansion created a relentless American state under President Washington.

1. *War and conflict drive state building, even in America.* Max Edling writes, in *A Hercules in the Cradle*, "It is difficult to conclude other than that the remarkable growth of the physical size of the nation, and the growth in population and wealth that this made possible, were to a large extent the result of state-organized and state-directed violence." He continues: "If war and violence made America great, that greatness rested on the ability of the American government to pay for soldiers, warships, military equipment, and supplies."[64]

Edling examines the state's growth from the early republic through the Civil War, and the lesson holds in the more narrow confines of Washington's two terms as president. The early American state was nurtured by war and the necessities of fighting successfully. And as the United States improved its fighting abilities, the two-track strategy of the Washington administration simultaneously enhanced and improved the nation's abilities related to diplomacy—where treaty conferences lasted for weeks and involved thousands of people, requiring great organized effort for planning, provisioning, and policing.

As such, then, state building in the early United States presents not a puzzle but a familiarity. Scholars have long associated military conflict and war with state building. The United States prepared for wars and fought them, and in the process—like so many other nations—developed command and control systems, executive prerogative, and field discretion. The nation, like so many others, launched early along a path of increasing military expenditures to meet, and defeat, the expected next threat. Following historian Alan Taylor, Calloway writes that $5 million were spent fighting the Indian confederation in the North from 1790 to 1796—close to $130 million in 2017 dollars, and almost five-sixths of total federal expenditures for that period. The commitment seemed clear: if Harmar's resources and supply systems and chain-of-command organization were inadequate, boost them all for St. Clair. If St. Clair's proved inadequate, boost them again for Wayne. Boost them relentlessly until the goal was achieved.[65]

Each of the early defeats in the Old Northwest brought executive leadership aimed at increased resources and improved organizational abilities. In particular, the investigation into St. Clair's defeat laid the blame on an inefficient and debilitating contracting and provisioning process, encouraging not just military reform but reform in government supply chains and other public-private partnerships. Each step sent power and authority to the executive, as did laws like the trade and intercourse acts.[66] By the end of Washington's second term, resources and administration would succeed in gaining dominion over broad areas, largely putting to rest concerns about Spanish conspiracies and western independence movements.

2. Complex governance means there are no discrete policy categories. It is always tempting to divide government operations into discrete categories. Indian affairs, land policy, diplomacy, finance, the military—we think in such categories, just as we think of today's policy in its own modern silos—education, immigration, energy, defense, homeland security. But just as these silo walls quickly break down today, with immigration and defense, for example, entangled in questions of homeland security, education, refugees, and health care, public policy in the 1790s also broke out of its silos.

Indian affairs had its own budget categories and appropriations, its own offices, its own officials, its own rhetoric in presidential speeches. It can be, and was, discussed as though it existed as a discrete entity. But scratch the surface, and Indian affairs quickly intertwine with other issue areas. The military and its spending and appropriations are involved, because the army might be used to fight Indians or to remove white squatters from unceded Indian lands. The land offices are involved, because they and the nation's surveyors and explorers exchanged information with the Indian service and treaty commissioners about valuable lands, geographical features, and the best way to ensure a peaceful and effective expansion. Indian policy overlapped with policy on land acquisition and sales; land policy overlapped with policy on the public debt; the public debt invoked questions about the size and strength of the federal government, which in turn implicated questions of the standing military and its relations to a militia system, which raised the issue of federalism, which ran back to Indian affairs and conflicts between the federal government and state and territorial jurisdictions.[67] Indian affairs in the Northwest had clear and quick impacts on Indian affairs in the South, as Spain, the Creeks, and others took advantage of the government's focus, expense, and ineffectiveness in the North, and Indian affairs in the Southwest impacted the United States' boundary negotiations with Spain.[68] Indian annuities paid from the executive involved the War Department and its agents but were paid out of the Treasury Department, which supervised purchases under a 1792 law and which would, in 1795, see the creation of the office of Purveyor of Public Goods.[69] It was all connected.

The interconnected nature of policy in the early republic confounds efforts to examine the presidency or state building by examining discrete policy areas. Our understanding of the early presidency is distorted by dividing too sharply the office's functions into separate, discrete parts. For example, in an essay aimed at maintaining the distinction between the modern and the traditional presidency, Thomas Engemann and Raymond Tatalovich place Indian affairs mostly within the president's responsibilities as chief diplomat. This, however, overlooks the aspects of Indian policy that required the president to act as commander in chief, as executive branch and administrative leader, as legislative leader, and as policy/opinion leader, leading the authors to overlook the president's activities in these areas.[70]

The absence of policy silos in the early republic also complicates efforts to separate out state and federal responsibilities and to distinguish between "internal" and "international" affairs. In Indian affairs, these lines overlapped. States challenged the federal government for on-the-ground control of treaty negotiations, the extension of laws, and the exercise of force. The case of John Proctor's mission to enlist the Iroquois as mediators in the conflict with the northwestern Indians, noted above, is a good case in point. This is in some ways a story about the borderlands conflict with the Miami and others in the Northwest—but it overlaps continuing Indian affairs and land acquisition efforts in the heartlands of New York and Pennsylvania. Indian affairs, with its relationships to land, debt, and other issues across and beyond US possessions, might be viewed as international by native and federal leaders believing they were dealing with Indian nations on unceded Indian lands, as state internal matters by states claiming that those lands belonged to the state, and as both in tension by white settlers and squatters.[71] Indian affairs makes the drawing of bright lines between policy issues, or between domestic and international affairs, very problematic. Drawing artificial lines and truncating debate has generally been used to minimize the role of the federal government and its officers. But in the early republic, the sum is greater than its parts. The state's scope and effectiveness fade when we break them down too far; they appear in bold relief when we understand the complex interconnectedness of that government's activities.

3. The early national government was a focal point for public demands. Demands for government assistance rained down upon Congress and the presidency during Washington's two terms. The public quickly came to see the national government as responsible for taking action. Appeals to the president came from all quarters, from public officials and homesteaders, from traders and saloonkeepers, and from whites, Indians, slaves, and anyone else. J. P. Nettl asks this question about a "state": "To what extent have

individuals generalized the concept and cognition of state in their percep-
tions and actions, and to what extent are such cognitions salient?"[72] Citizen
demands for action and citizen reactions to government intrusions suggest
a high level of salient cognition during Washington's presidency.

Some citizen demands were for bigger, better government, particularly
in the defense and development of western settlements. Some were complaints about big, bad government, particularly when federal restrictions
restrained purchases, settlement, and retaliation. Still others were mixed—
demands for benefits then going to others, demands that attention be paid
to the writer instead of being lavished on another person, another town,
or another region. As the historian Henry Steele Commager wrote, "What
they wanted was land; what they wanted was protection against the Indians;
what they wanted was stable government."[73] As soon as they could, citizens
and others made it very clear that they would make demands and that they
would complain.

Washington received notes like this one, sent in late 1789 from frazzled
and embattled citizens in the Old Northwest: "Suffer us further to assure
you, that we, on the behalf of our bleeding country, look up to you, and to
you only, for that assistance that our necessities require, and shall conclude
with praying that the great Parent of the universe may conduct you under
the eye of his special providence enabling you to fill the exalted station to
which he hath called you, as well for the good of your fellow citizens, as
also for the happiness of mankind, so far as they come within the bounds
of your administration."[74] Rufus Putnam put it more succinctly in 1791:
"Unless Government speedily send a body of troops for our protection, we
are a ruined people."[75]

Matters were the same in the South. As just one example, consider how
bent out of shape Representative James Jackson of Georgia got at the president, when Washington in his second annual message explained the dire
situation of the Old Northwest but failed to mention the need to protect the
South from the Creeks. "He [Jackson] then expatiated on the sufferings of
the people of Georgia, and asked, what must be their feelings when they
reflect on the preparations made to chastise the Wabash banditti, while the
exertions of Congress have not been called forth to their relief." Jackson
closed with exasperation at the white glove treatment Alexander McGillivray had received from the Washington administration, describing how "a
savage of the Creeks" had been brought to the seat of government "and
there loaded with favors, and caressed in the most extraordinary manner."[76]

Knox summarized the complementary views of westerners and the
administration in January 1791:

The population of the lands lying on the Western waters is increasing rapidly. The inhabitants request and demand protection; if it be not granted, seeds of disgust will be sown; sentiments of separate interests will arise out of their local situation, which will be cherished, either by insidious, domestic, or foreign emissaries.

It therefore appears to be an important branch of the administration of the General Government, to afford the frontiers all reasonable protection, as well in their just rights as against their enemies; and, at the same time, it is essential to show all lawless adventurers that, notwithstanding the distance, Government possess the power of preserving peace and good order on the frontiers. It is true economy to regulate events instead of being regulated by them.[77]

Knox endorsed the classic government mandate for protection—accompanied by a classic statement that government would act forcefully upon those who would challenge its authority.

4. A sense of the state developed during Washington's presidency. The early American state was not weak, and it was not ineffective.

One of the great unstudied aspects of the early American state is the deference paid to it by individuals and communities, even those on the US frontier. Often passed quickly by in political studies, the dominant message for many years has been that the federal government could not control the frontier. With this image often comes the assumption that individuals ignored the federal government's authority. As we have seen, though, this is untrue—folks on the borders (or over them) sought protection and empowerment and searched pragmatically for governing authorities that would support their interests. In the South, as in the Northwest, people made choices informed by the boundaries and rules set by the US government. So while there are plentiful examples of families and communities ignoring treaty boundaries and attempting to settle on unceded Indian lands, there are numerous examples of federal officers removing white settlers from Indian lands. And there are numerous examples of populations deferring patiently and respectfully to the limits and boundaries set by the government. Consider those old photos of the Oklahoma Sooners, lined up, waiting for the gun to start their rush into opened territory. Who drew that line in the middle of the plains? Who fired the shot? This classic American image of expansion *restrained* is built on decades of popular respect for government regulation of lands and settlement, born during the Washington administration.

Any study of state building needs to recognize the key role played by individual members of that state, and what scholar Stephen Skowronek famously called "the sense of the state." Our histories of American political development have long been distorted by Skowronek's largely unfounded assertion that the early state "failed to evoke any sense of the state." Yet not only did the early state provide a "sense of an organization of coercive power operating beyond our immediate control and intruding into all aspects of our lives,"[78] but that state was called into existence and beckoned forward by the demands of western Americans.

As early as the summer of 1789, Henry Knox pointed out that the state would be imposed:

> The angry passions of the frontier Indians and whites, are too easily inflamed by reciprocal injuries, and are too violent to be controlled by the feeble authority of the civil power.
>
> There can be neither justice or observance of treaties, where every man claims to be the sole judge in his own case, and the avenger of his own supposed wrongs.
>
> In such a case, the sword of the republic only, is adequate to guard a due administration of justice, and the preservation of the peace.[79]

Knox went through a list of necessary actions, including restraining white movement across boundaries, utilizing missionaries, and demonstrating to whites on the frontier that the government was more than merely a paper authority.[80]

The United States began immediately to dominate land sales, regulate trade through licensing and bonding requirements, police boundaries with troops who removed squatters and destroyed illegal settlements, pressure frontier folks not to antagonize the Indians or initiate their own efforts at justice or retaliation, and intrude on Indians existing in tension between their own communities and the enforcement abilities of the United States.

Much of the discussion of this centers on the North, as the series of military missions sought to pacify the Indians and enforce treaties and boundaries. But the federal government intruded upon southerners, too. Just before the Treaty of New York was signed, Washington sent three companies of troops to Georgia to make sure that Georgia did not provoke the Indians and wreck the deal. After the treaty was ratified, Washington issued two proclamations requiring Georgians to respect the federal government's position, even inducing the Georgia state officials to support the federal position by finding a legal loophole that helped constrain local and individual actions. Southerners and the federal government continued at odds with each other through 1792 as Blount's mobilization of troops to go after the Indians was quashed by stern warnings from Knox in late 1792 and early 1793.[81]

The federal government did indeed remove white squatters from Indian lands, it did sign treaties, and it did distribute land to states and land companies and individual settlers. Even in Washington's first term, it removed Indians and it removed whites, it protected property rights, it restricted and regulated land purchases, it extended federal adjudicatory authority, it expanded criminal justice protocols, it established and enforced boundaries, and it protected and promoted trade. It managed affairs in the South, and it defeated the Northwest Indians in Washington's second term. Its diplomats saved the country from another major war with European powers in its early years, just as Washington had set out to do. The early American state was not *potential;* it was real, active, and effective.

By the end of his second term, George Washington's efforts had developed core aspects of the modern presidency and the modern American state.

Between the unsettled shudders of the 1780s and the relative peace and stability of 1797, when Washington turned the presidency over to John Adams, the independence dreams of Sevier and the Spanish conspiracies of Wilkinson had faded, as the clarity of policy planning and the increasing real effectiveness of the US government satisfied new western settlers. The Treaty of New York quieted the South, and after St. Clair's defeat the relentless leader of a relentless state continued to hammer at the Indians of the Old Northwest. US government officials brought Iroquois leaders to Philadelphia to mediate between the United States and western Indians. Knox hired popular traders to go West to negotiate; John Hardin and Captain Alexander Trueman were sent out from Fort Washington to negotiate, only to be killed; Hendrick, a Stockbridge Indian, was employed but failed to attend major negotiations; Brigadier General Rufus Putnam was sent west with minor success; and the United States continued to try to use Joseph Brant as a mediator.[82] Anthony Wayne geared up the military to win the battlefield at Fallen Timbers in the summer of 1794, and the groundwork was laid for the landmark diplomatic agreements of 1795: the Jay Treaty declared the Mississippi River open to England and the United States and promised the removal of the British from their northern forts; the Treaty of San Lorenzo established peace and formal boundaries with Spain in North America; and the Treaty of Greenville stabilized peaceful relations with the Indians of the Northwest.[83] The new American state did what was necessary to protect and empower its people and their interests.

Between Washington's first inaugural and his farewell speech is a rich history of presidential and state development, as the United States moved from paper potential to reality. Long forgotten in the public mind is the crisis of Arthur St. Clair's defeat in the middle of Washington's eight years as president. Washington was angry when St. Clair allowed his troops to be surprised and crushed in 1791. But we know Washington was nothing if not persistent. He reinforced his relentless dedication to national goals in his message to the House and Senate reporting the disaster. Rather than focus on the tragedy, Washington focused coolly and confidently on the future. "Although the national loss is considerable, according to the scale of the event," Washington announced, "yet it may be repaired without great difficulty, excepting as to the brave men who have fallen on the occasion, and who are a subject of public as well as private regret. A farther communication will shortly be made of all such matters as shall be necessary to enable the Legislature to judge of the future measures which it may be proper to pursue."[84] From his private anger at St. Clair's defeat, Washington had returned to his public confidence in the inevitable success of a careful and organized American state.

Notes

The author gratefully acknowledges the support of a Faculty Summer Research Grant from St. Joseph's College, New York.

1. The quotations are attributed to Tobias Lear's reports of the incident. The first quotation is from Theodore Roosevelt, *St. Clair's Defeat, 1791*, reprint by the Public Library of Fort Wayne and Allen County, 60; the second is from Colin G. Calloway, *The Victory with No Name: The Native American Defeat of the First American Army* (Oxford: Oxford University Press, 2015), 130.

2. Dale Van Every, *Ark of Empire: The American Frontier, 1784–1803* (New York: Mentor, 1964), 31–32, 69–74, 115–16; *Papers of George Washington: Presidential Series,* ed. Dorothy Twohig (Charlottesville: University of Virginia Press, 1987), 2:294n10.

3. Gayle Thornbrough, introduction to *Outpost on the Wabash, 1787–1791*, ed. Gayle Thornbrough (Indianapolis: Indiana Historical Society, 1957), 7–17; Josiah Harmar to Henry Knox, 7 August 1787, in Thornbrough, *Outpost on the Wabash,* 34–40; Van Every, *Ark of Empire,* 170, 185.

4. Calloway, *The Victory with No Name,* chs. 1 and 2 and 58–60; Van Every, *Ark of Empire,* 203, 205, 206, 190–92; Francis Paul Prucha, *The Great Father: The United States Government and the American Indians* (Lincoln: University of Nebraska Press, 1984), 62; Frank T. Reuter, *Trials and Triumphs: George Washington's Foreign Policy* (Fort Worth: Texas Christian University Press, 1983), 75. St. Clair owned a thousand acres of Ohio Company land: Calloway, *The Victory with No Name,* 52. The Washington administration was also working at this time to normalize relations with Britain: Reuter, *Trials and Triumphs,* 76.

5. See Van Every, *Ark of Empire,* 183. See also Reuter, *Trials and Triumphs,* ch. 4.

6. Van Every, *Ark of Empire,* 80, 83, 192–93; Reuter, *Trials and Triumphs,* 109–38; *Papers of George Washington,* 2:326n1. For Knox on McGillivray's influence and on

the fight between Georgia and the Creeks, see *American State Papers: Indian Affairs,* vol. 4, part 1 (Washington, DC: Gales and Seaton, 1832), 15–38.

7. George Lakoff, *The Political Mind: A Cognitive Scientist's Guide to Your Brain and Its Politics* (New York: Penguin, 2009), 48. See also Barthelemi Tardiveau to Harmar, 6 August 1787, in *Outpost on the Wabash,* 26–34; Harmar to Knox, 7 August 1787, in *Outpost on the Wabash,* 34–40; and John Hamtramck to Harmar, 3 November 1787, in *Outpost on the Wabash,* 44–46.

8. Van Every, *Ark of Empire,* 167 and 167n4; see also, for example, the list of depredations communicated by Benjamin Lincoln, *American State Papers: Indian Affairs,* 77; *The Diaries of George Washington,* ed. Donald Jackson and Dorothy Twohig (Charlottesville: University Press of Virginia, 1979), 6:91. Van Every also uses deaths of colonels as a rough estimate, arguing that these elected officials served as county lieutenants and militia commanders. Van Every writes that colonels were "the most prominent figure of any locality" and that thirty-seven were listed as killed in action in the twenty years from 1774 to 1794.

9. Van Every, *Ark of Empire,* 50–52, and see 206. Title issues are discussed at 100–101 and 111 and described as "a state of perpetual confusion throughout the 1780's" (101). See also Harmar to Knox, 24 November 1787, in *Outpost on the Wabash,* 48–49.

10. See Van Every, *Ark of Empire,* 37–38, 181–207, and generally. On Franklin, see ibid., 190 and ch. 7, and Kevin T. Barksdale, *The Lost State of Franklin: America's First Secession* (Lexington: University Press of Kentucky, 2010). On Robertson and Cumberland, see Van Every, *Ark of Empire,* 90, 95, and ch. 6. On Wilkinson, see ibid., chs. 8 and 9 and Andro Linklater, *An Artist in Treason: The Extraordinary Double Life of James Wilkinson* (New York: Walker, 2009).

11. Van Every, *Ark of Empire,* 190. See also Thornburgh in *Outpost on the Wabash,* 9, 15.

12. See, for example, Prucha, *Great Father,* 44–61; Calloway, *The Victory with No Name,* 25.

13. Prucha, *Great Father,* 63, 64; Reuter, *Trials and Triumphs,* 88, 90; Van Every, *Ark of Empire,* 228–32, ch. 14; *The Diaries of George Washington,* 6:72–73.

14. Reuter, *Trials and Triumphs,* 91.

15. Van Every, *Ark of Empire,* 231–32.

16. Calloway, *The Victory with No Name,* 108, 125.

17. Calloway, *The Victory with No Name,* 5. On reports, poems, and public attention, see Calloway, *The Victory with No Name,* 24, 130–39.

18. Van Every, *Ark of Empire,* ch. 5, 215. See also Prucha, *Great Father,* 54–56; Reuter, *Trials and Triumphs,* 75–77, 120–38. Lincoln acted under authority from Massachusetts governor James Bowdoin. See Leonard L. Richards, *Shays's Rebellion: The American Revolution's Final Battle* (Philadelphia: University of Pennsylvania Press, 2003), 23–36.

19. Van Every, *Ark of Empire,* 218; Prucha, *Great Father,* 55–56, 68; Reuter, *Trials and Triumphs,* 123–27. Willet went as a private agent but in reality acted as a proxy for the government, so that the government, in Washington's words, "might not appear to be the Agent in it, or suffer in its dignity if the attempt to get him [McGillivray] here should not succeed." *The Diaries of George Washington,* 6:22–23, 41, 80, 85.

20. Prucha, *Great Father,* 68–70; Reuter, *Trials and Triumphs,* 136–38.

21. See letter from James Seagrove to Washington, 27 July 1792, quoted in Van Every, *Ark of Empire*, 263.

22. Knox prevailed on Congress for reforms that would appear in a 1792 act providing for more regular infantry and militia cavalry: Prucha, *Great Father*, 64; Calloway, *The Victory with No Name*, 142–44. See Van Every, *Ark of Empire*, 264–68; Calloway, *The Victory with No Name*, 73–76, 140–42. Wayne, delayed, would be at least six months preparing and training. The United States offered to drop its insistence on the border line set by the Treaty of Fort Harmar but met intransigence from the Indians as negotiations eventually yielded no progress. See Prucha, *Great Father*, 65; Reuter, *Trials and Triumphs*, 98.

23. The delineation of a "traditional" and a "modern" presidency is a staple of textbooks and introductory works about the presidency. See, for example, James P. Pfiffner, *The Modern Presidency*, 6th ed. (Boston: Wadsworth, 2011); Sidney M. Milkis and Michael Nelson, *The American Presidency: Origins and Development, 1776–2002*, 4th ed. (Washington, DC: CQ Press, 2003), 202–19; George C. Edwards III and Stephen J. Wayne, *Presidential Leadership: Politics and Policy Making*, 7th ed. (Belmont, CA: Thomson, 2006), 6–11; William D. Adler, "'Generalissimo of the Nation': War Making and the Presidency in the Early Republic," *Presidential Studies Quarterly* 43 (2013): 414–15. For a policy-centered and institutionalist approach, see Lance T. LeLoup and Steven A. Shull, *The President and Congress: Collaboration and Combat in National Policymaking*, 2nd ed. (New York: Longman, 2003), 6–28.

24. For example, Milkis and Nelson, *American Presidency*, 209–12; Edwards and Wayne, *Presidential Leadership*, 410–12; Shirley Anne Warshaw, *The Keys to Power: Managing the Presidency*, 2nd ed. (New York: Longman, 2005), 54–55.

25. For example, LeLoup and Shull, *The President and Congress*, 38–40; Edwards and Wayne, *Presidential Leadership*, 414; Kenneth R. Mayer, *With the Stroke of a Pen: Executive Orders and Presidential Power* (Princeton, NJ: Princeton University Press, 2001), 113; Peri E. Arnold, *Making the Managerial Presidency: Comprehensive Reorganization Planning, 1905–1996* (Lawrence: University Press of Kansas, 1998), xiv, 10–11; Peri E. Arnold, "Effecting a Progressive Presidency: Roosevelt, Taft, and the Pursuit of Strategic Resources," *Studies in American Political Development* 17 (2003): 70.

26. For example, see the discussions in David Gray Adler, "The Constitution and Presidential Warmaking: The Enduring Debate," *Political Science Quarterly* 103 (1988): 1–3 and particularly the list of sources offered at n. 2; Simeon E. Baldwin, "The Share of the President of the United States in a Declaration of War," *American Journal of International Law* 12 (1918): 1–14; Norman A. Graebner, "The President as Commander in Chief: A Study in Power," *Journal of Military History* 57 (1993): 111–32; Cass R. Sunstein, "An Eighteenth Century Presidency in a Twenty-First Century World," *Arkansas Law Review* 48 (1995), 10–11.

27. Jeffrey A. Tulis, *The Rhetorical Presidency* (Princeton, NJ: Princeton University Press, 1987); see also Milkis and Nelson, *American Presidency*, 204–9; Edwards and Wayne, *Presidential Leadership*, 9–10.

28. A number of recent works have challenged the traditional-modern dichotomy, including a general challenge by David K. Nichols in *The Myth of the Modern Presidency* (University Park, PA: Pennsylvania State University Press, 1994). Other works have challenged select pieces of the "traditional presidency" model: see, for example, Adler, "'Generalissimo of the Nation'"; Ryan L. Teten, "Evolution of the Modern Rhetorical Presidency: Presidential Presentation and Development of the

State of the Union Address," *Presidential Studies Quarterly* (2003): 333–46; Jon C. Rogowski, "Presidential Influence in an Era of Congressional Dominance," *American Political Science Review* 110 (2016): 325–41; Raymond T. Williams, "Unilateral Politics in the Traditional Era: Significant Executive Orders and Proclamations, 1861–1944," *Presidential Studies Quarterly* 50 (2020): 146–62; Graham G. Dodds, *Take Up Your Pen: Unilateral Presidential Directives in American Politics* (Philadelphia: University of Pennsylvania Press, 2013); Mel Laracey, *Presidents and the People: The Partisan Story of Going Public* (College Station: Texas A&M University Press, 2002); Jeffrey E. Cohen, *The President's Legislative Policy Agenda, 1789–2002* (Cambridge: Cambridge University Press, 2012). See also the list of sources in Adler, "'Generalissimo of the Nation,'" 414–15.

29. Including Indian affairs lends support to the argument Nichols made more than twenty years ago in *The Myth of the Modern Presidency*. Nichols argued that Washington's presidency exhibited characteristics we usually ascribe to a "modern" presidency, one of which was his role as legislative leader. See also *The Diaries of George Washington*, 6:6. For a critique of Nichols's approach, see Thomas Engemann and Raymond Tatalovich, "George Washington: The First Modern President? A Reply to Nichols," in *George Washington and the Origins of the American Presidency*, ed. Mark J. Rozell et al. (Westport, CT: Praeger, 2000). For discussion of Washington's legislative policy agenda, see Cohen, *President's Legislative Policy Agenda*, especially 13–18, 104–5, 151–52.

30. *Documentary History of the First Federal Congress*, ed. Charlene Bangs Bickford and Helen E. Veit (Baltimore: Johns Hopkins University Press), 5:984–97 (hereafter *DHFFC*).

31. Prucha, *Great Father*, 91; see also 89–114. These provisions would be repeated and expanded in subsequent years; see, for example, the 1796 Act for Establishing Trading Houses with the Indian Tribes (11 February 1796; *US Statutes at Large* 1:452–53), built upon Washington's efforts in 1795. In general, see Francis Paul Prucha, *American Indian Policy in the Formative Years: The Indian Trade and Intercourse Acts, 1790–1834* (Lincoln: University of Nebraska Press, 1970), 147–65. The inflation calculation is based on Oregon State University Inflation Conversion data, available at http://liberalarts.oregonstate.edu/spp/polisci/research/inflation -conversion-factors-convert-dollars-1774-estimated-2024-dollars-recent-year.

32. For example, An Act to Regulate Trade and Intercourse with the Indian Tribes (22 July 1790; *US Statutes at Large* 1:137–38); An act for establishing Trading Houses with the Indian Tribes (11 February 1796; *US Statutes at Large* 1:452–53); An act to regulate trade and intercourse with the Indian tribes, and to preserve peace on the frontiers (19 May 1796, *US Statutes at Large* 1: 469–74); see *Abridgment of the Debates of Congress from 1789 to 1856* (Memphis: General Books, 2012) (hereafter *Debates*), 1:560–61, 606–7 (January–February 1796); *Annals of Congress: Debates and Proceedings in the Congress of the United States*, 4th Cong., 1st sess. (Washington, DC: Gales and Seaton, 1849), 229–32, 240–43, 283–87, 401–7, 893–904. The acts themselves appear at 2889–91 and 2909–16 (Trading House Act, approved 18 April 1796, 19 May 1796).

33. *DHFFC*, 5:1234, 1237, 1239. The report also multiplies federal functionaries in the field to survey, track deeds, and manage the process. See also the discussion of Hamilton's leadership on taxes and finance policy, leading to the Impost Act of 1789, in Max M. Edling, *A Hercules in the Cradle: War, Money, and the American*

State, 1783–1867 (Chicago: University of Chicago Press, 2014), chs. 1 and 2. The independent role of the Treasury Department and its officers—together with similar autonomy at offices like the General Land Office and the Patent Office—suggest that the War Department's autonomy was not a function of the context of race or of territorial status. In fact, many activities of Washington's War Department took place within the established states, from treaty making in places like New York and Pennsylvania to the expansion of the factory system in the South.

34. The standard work on bureaucratic autonomy is Daniel Carpenter's excellent *The Forging of Bureaucratic Autonomy: Reputations, Networks, and Policy Innovation in Executive Agencies, 1862–1928* (Princeton, NJ: Princeton University Press, 2001). The book offers little analysis of bureaucratic autonomy before the Civil War, but Carpenter's theoretical approach and his explication of what we mean by bureaucratic autonomy fit the earliest years of the republic. On delegations of authority generally, see, for example, Reuter, *Trials and Triumphs*, 36–43, 51–77. For the "traditional" interpretation of the presidency as administrative leader and the status of the administrative bureaucracy, see, for example, Milkis and Nelson, *American Presidency*, 74–77.

35. Van Every, *Ark of Empire*, 213, 193–94; *American State Papers: Indian Affairs*, 25. Inflation calculation based on Oregon State University Inflation Conversion factors.

36. See *American State Papers: Indian Affairs*, 13, 60–61; *DHFFC*, 5:1283. See also Prucha, *Great Father*, 44–60.

37. *DHFFC*, 6:2028–29; *Debates*, 1:235, 106, 330. See also 306, noting necessity of "devolving much of the Legislative power upon the Executive Department."

38. *American State Papers: Indian Affairs*, 65–68, 70, 71.

39. *Papers of George Washington*, 2:196–98; see also Calloway, *The Victory with No Name*, 71. St. Clair toured the Northwest Territory in 1790, establishing county governments in places like Vincennes, Kaskaskia, and Cahokia. Van Every, *Ark of Empire*, 217.

40. Cf. Carpenter, *Forging of Bureaucratic Autonomy*, esp. ch. 2.

41. *Debates*, 1:12–15; Kenneth R. Bowling and Helen E. Veit, eds., *The Diary of William Maclay and Other Notes on Senate Debates* (Baltimore: Johns Hopkins University Press, 1988), 128–32. One can also consider Washington's creation of a consular service as an example of policy entrepreneurship and eventually bureaucratic autonomy. Washington built on earlier precedents for consuls, and since consuls were unpaid, he did not need congressional appropriations to expand the service. Reuter, *Trials and Triumphs*, 54–55.

42. See, for example, Prucha, *Great Father*, 44–58; *Cherokee Nation v. Georgia*, 5 Peters 16; *Worcester v. Georgia*, 6 Peters 559. For a broader discussion of Washington's use of unilateral directives, see Dodds, *Take Up Your Pen*, 86–119, especially 97, 101, 104–5, 107–8.

43. *Debates*, 1:163. Interestingly, the Senate even delegated to the president the authority to ratify treaties by his own actions. After an early treaty had been signed and gone into practical effect, with both US and Indian communities following its terms, Washington asked the Senate whether or not further "ratification" by the Senate was necessary. The Senate wrote Washington that the treaty could presume to have been "ratified" as it went into practice, by executive branch action alone. No further action, no two-thirds vote, was needed. See *Debates*, 1:14–15, 125;

Papers of George Washington, 2:200n4; *American State Papers: Indian Affairs* 58–59, 123; *DHFFC*, 2:42; George Washington to the Secretaries of State, Treasury, and War, and the Attorney General, 29 June 1795, in *Writings of George Washington*, ed. John C. Fitzpatrick (Washington, DC: US Government Printing Office, 1940), 34:224–25. Cf. Prucha, *Great Father*, 52–53.

44. See, for example, the sixth annual message, reprinted in *Writings of George Washington*, vol. 34, especially at 28–37; also, in the same collection, George Washington to Edmund Pendleton, 22 January 1795 (99–100); George Washington to the secretary of war, 10 March 1795 (140–41) ("Congress having closed their late session without coming to any specific determination with respect to the Georgia sale of Lands and the application for the extinguishment of the Indian rights to those lands; and not having expressed any sentiment respecting the predatory war between the Southern Indians and the Southern and Southwestern frontiers of these United States, and the desire of the latter to institute offensive measures; it has become indispensably necessary for the Executive to take up the subject upon a full and comprehensive scale, that some systematic plan may be resolved on and steadily pursued during the recess"). Cf. with the following letter to the secretary of war, 11 March 1795, focused on executing actions Congress *did* take: 141–42; George Washington message to the Senate, 25 June 1795 (218–20); and the seventh annual message, 8 December 1795 (386–87). See also the text of the 1796 Act for Establishing Trading Houses with the Indian Tribes, Annals of Congress, 2889–91 and 2909–16. For a detailed review of these matters, see Prucha, *Great Father*, 89–177.

45. See, for example, *Debates*, 1:372, 383, 393, 494–95, 567.

46. On St. Clair, see Van Every, *Ark of Empire*, 245. In the South, Arthur Campbell, a North Carolina legislator linked to the state of Franklin, had told Washington as early as May 1789 that war would be unpopular in the South. Like others, he advocated for a cheaper and more judicious policy toward the Indians, encouraging trade and restraint on the parts of the federal government as well as the states of Georgia and South Carolina. *Papers of George Washington*, 2:254.

47. *Debates*, 1:323–32.

48. *Debates*, 1:323–32.

49. See, for example, Robert J. Delahunty and John Yoo, *Making War*, 93 *Cornell Law Review* (2007), 123–67; John C. Yoo, "War and Constitutional Text," *University of Chicago Law Review* 69 (2002): 1639–84; Adler, "'Generalissimo of the Nation.'"

50. Saikrishna Bangalore Prakash, "The Separation and Overlap of War and Military Powers," *Texas Law Review* 87 (2008): 299–386, for example at 315n57, 322–24, 330, 334–40; Saikrishna Prakash, *A Two-Front War*, 93 *Cornell Law Review* 197 (2007): 204n47, 213–17.

51. Studies that begin with Washington's Neutrality Proclamation or debates surrounding wars with France and England miss critically important, and significant, examples of how war-making powers were understood and realized at the time. See, for example, Adler, "Constitution and Presidential Warmaking," especially 17, 26–27, 35–36; Baldwin, "Share of the President," 2–3; Abbot Smith, "Mr. Madison's War: An Unsuccessful Experiment in the Conduct of National Policy," *Political Science Quarterly* 57 (1942): 232. Graebner mentions Indians but sees them as exceptions—places "where the threat was too trivial to require congressional approval"—an assessment that would have surprised Washington, St. Clair, Congress, and, of course, the northwest Indians. Graebner, "President as Commander

in Chief," 116. William Adler calls these early conflicts "small wars," and Delahunty and Yoo call them "smaller conflicts." Adler, "'Generalissimo of the Nation,'" 413; Delahunty and Yoo, *Making War,* 123. It is important to note how little significance seems to have been attached to race as a factor in the United States' early wars. Despite the occasional use of terminology like "savages" in congressional debates and other papers, these debates, presidential and War Department records, and the like overwhelmingly present Indian affairs from the standpoint of power and territory more than they present them as differences based on racial characteristics. There is an extensive literature on race and the frontier, of course, but regarding declarations of war, the early presidents and Congresses rarely declared war regardless of the opponent with which the United States was fighting—examples include the Quasi War with France and the United States' efforts against European powers around the Great Lakes and down to Florida, none of which produced a declaration of war. In the one early instance in which Congress did declare war, the War of 1812, that declaration was hesitant, hard won by President Madison, and generally seen as a failure that weakened the country and the presidency. This all suggests that the absence of declarations of war when fighting Indians had causes other than race. See, for example, Robert M. Owens, *Mr. Jefferson's Hammer: William Henry Harrison and the Origins of American Indian Policy* (Norman: University of Oklahoma Press, 2007), 81–82; Wilbur R. Jacobs, *Dispossessing the American Indian: Indians and Whites on the Colonial Frontier* (Norman: University of Oklahoma Press, 1972), 124–25; cf. Reginald Horsman, *Race and Manifest Destiny: The Origins of American Racial Anglo-Saxonism* (Cambridge, MA: Harvard University Press, 1981); Richard Drinnon, *Facing West: The Metaphysics of Indian-Hating & Empire-Building* (New York: Schocken, 1990), 70–98.

52. Delahunty and Yoo's argument is often marred by misrepresentations and misstatements. For example, Delahunty and Yoo misstate Prakash's argument when they write, "Furthermore, if *only* Congress can authorize *any* of the actions that *might* be taken to be 'declarations' of war, then even diplomatic decisions that are unquestionably within the Executive's constitutional authority, such as President George Washington's 1793 decision to have the French Ambassador 'Citizen' Genet recalled, would have been 'declarations of war'—and would thus have fallen *outside* the President's power" (*Making War,* 151; italics in original). Prakash's argument about residual power does not argue anything close to this. Elsewhere, Delahunty and Yoo write, "The Washington administration developed a political and military strategy toward the Indians without consulting Congress," but they add that "Washington did not seek authorization from Congress for further offensive operations or his strategy, but he knew he would need legislative cooperation for the further expansion of the military. Washington sent Congress a flood of information about the failed St. Clair expedition" (*Making War,* 158, 161). Even if Delahunty and Yoo are trying to draw a line between Washington's early foray with St. Clair and his later effort with Wayne, congressional debates did not draw such a sharp line between developing strategy and increasing the size of the army. In fact, congressional debates in the era consistently examined a variety of angles on the larger issues, with consideration of strategy and goals intertwined with debates over the best means to achieve them. See, for example, Washington's message to Congress in October 1791, laying out information on the then in-progress St. Clair mission, recommending measures to Congress, and asking Congress's assistance and action

for a list of items prefaced by the phrase "In order to do this, it seems necessary"—following which Washington suggests regulations for alienating lands, managing commerce, promoting civilization, "enabl[ing]" the executive to take action, and providing for penalties upon those "who, by violating their [Indians'] rights, shall infringe the treaties, and endanger the peace of the Union" (October 1791, *Debates*, 1:293–94; see also 23–30 January 1792, *Debates*, 1:323–32). To suggest, as Delahunty and Yoo do, that Washington did not consult with Congress is misleading. Finally, Delahunty and Yoo state that, after St. Clair's defeat, "The regular American Army ceased to exist and no organized military stood in the western United States to protect the frontiers, which were laid open to attack" (*Making War*, 161). This is wildly overstated; see, for example, Robert M. Owens's account of the young William Henry Harrison arriving in the region with his commission and then getting to work with the remaining parts of the army. Owen, *Mr. Jefferson's Hammer*, 16–18.

53. Adler, "'Generalissimo of the Nation,'" 413–14.

54. The fact that the authors train their focus on different events, for the most part, raises the intriguing possibility that they are both right—that Washington's early actions directing Harmar and St. Clair were largely executive driven, with minimal involvement or direction from Congress—yet after the administration's repeated failures in the Old Northwest, Congress took a stronger hand in directing details ever afterward. If true, and it would require further research to get at this more decisively, this may suggest a reversal of our usual understanding of Congress's power in the early republic. We usually think of the early republic as featuring a president largely unfettered in war making and defense, but one in which Congress is minutely in charge of the nascent civilian bureaucracy. A close look at contexts relating to Indian affairs suggests that the opposite might be true—the Washington years appear to have seen a short leash set by Congress on President Washington's military endeavors, even as Congress quickly fell back to passive and intermittent oversight of civilian administration. See, for example, the debate in the House of Representatives following Washington's announcement of the St. Clair disaster: *Debates*, 1:323–32.

55. Notably, Tulis's quotation in the introduction to *The Rhetorical Presidency*, used to illustrate Abraham Lincoln's unwillingness to discuss detailed policy matters with a public audience, is taken sharply out of context. The rest of the original quotation shows Lincoln quickly moving into exactly the kind of detailed policy discussion that Tulis argues did not take place. *Rhetorical Presidency*, 5.

56. *DHFFC*, 5:1433; Calloway, *The Victory with No Name*, 33–34, 71. The 1790 act is similar to an act of 1786: *American State Papers: Indian Affairs*, 14.

57. *Debates*, 1:158–70.

58. Van Every, *Ark of Empire*, 246. There were cases, of course, where congressional leadership prevailed over the president's wishes. The best example may be the 1789 Tonnage Act, which Washington opposed and which Reuter reports made the president "furious." Reuter, *Trials and Triumphs*, 45.

59. Tulis, *Rhetorical Presidency*, 55. In *The Rhetorical Presidency*, Tulis argued that presidents rarely discussed major issues publicly until the twentieth century. Tulis drew a bright line between the traditional presidency, which chose to speak only in general terms (and not often even then), preferring platitudes and friendly talk to careful public discussion of issues and details. Tulis writes that Washington almost filled his first inaugural address—a draft of which ran to seventy-three pages—with

policy ideas, but instead he ultimately offered general statements about providence and nonpartisanship. "Washington refused to talk policy," Tulis writes, overlooking Washington's encouragement for amending the Constitution to include what became the Bill of Rights. Tulis also misconstrues Washington's use of the annual message to "talk policy." Tulis examines Washington's first annual message, asserting that Washington did not discuss deep policy issues. The analysis then turns to the form of delivery of the annual message and the attention to formalities and procedures in the early presidency. Tulis's analysis goes no farther on content, thus overlooking Washington's discussion of Indian affairs and other topics and leaving the erroneous impression that Washington never got around to "talking policy." See also Ryan L. Teten, "'We the People': The 'Modern' Rhetorical Popular Address of the Presidents during the Founding Period," *Political Research Quarterly* 60 (2007): 669–82.

60. See, for example, many of Washington's letters reprinted in *Writings of George Washington,* vol. 34, such as George Washington to the secretary of state, 16 October 1794 (2–3); George Washington to John Jay, 1 November 1794 (18: "I shall be more prolix in my speech to Congress, on the commencement and progress of this [whiskey] insurrection, than is usual in such an instrument . . . but, as numbers (at home and abroad) will hear of the insurrection, and will read the speech, that may know nothing of the documents to which it might refer, I conceived, it would be better to encounter the charge of prolixity, by giving a cursory detail of facts (that would show the prominent features of the thing) than to let it go naked into the world, to be dressed up according to the fancy or the inclination of the readers, or the policy of our enemies"); George Washington to the Towns of East Hampton, Southampton, etc., 7 September 1795 (301); George Washington to William Falkener, 14 September 1795 (303); George Washington to Jesse Sanders, 30 September 1795 (320); George Washington to Alexander Hamilton, 29 October 1795 (351–52); George Washington to the Citizens of Frederick County, Virginia, 16 December 1795 (395–96).

61. Van Every, *Ark of Empire,* 216.

62. Prucha, *Great Father,* 140, 161. Washington touted his administration's treaties with the Cherokees and the Six Nations of New York, and he called for the sale of vacant lands held by the United States. *Debates,* 1:294–95.

63. See, for example, *Papers of George Washington,* 2:78–79, 179–80, 84–85, 86–87; Reuter, *Trials and Triumphs,* 172–73, 199; Philip Abbott, "Do Presidents Talk Too Much? The Rhetorical Presidency and Its Alternative," *Presidential Studies Quarterly* 18 (1988): 360–61n8. Cf. Mel Laracey, who writes that Washington's speeches during his tours did not refer to current events or issue, and were largely ceremonial. Laracey writes that while nineteenth century presidents often went public more than is generally thought, Washington preferred to use Jefferson and Hamilton as proxies to communicate to the public through newspapers. Laraecy, *Presidents and the People,* especially 49–53, 55–57, 140.

64. Edling, *A Hercules in the Cradle,* 12; see also 221–51.

65. Calloway, *The Victory with No Name,* 25–26; Calloway cites Alan Taylor, *The Divided Ground: Indians, Settlers, and the Northern Borderland of the American Revolution* (New York: Knopf, 2006), 238. See also Calloway's discussion of the March 1791 and March 1792 acts expanding and organizing American military forces: *The Victory with No Name,* 71, 142–43.

66. Calloway, *The Victory with No Name,* 5–6, 20–22, 77–92, 134, 136–39, 25–26.

67. For another example, see Edling's explanation of how tax, debt, and finance policy influenced military, defense, and western policies. *A Hercules in the Cradle,* e.g., 80, ch. 3, and conclusion; also Reuter, *Trials and Triumphs,* 38–39; Calloway, *The Victory with No Name,* 9, 23–26.

68. For example, Reuter, *Trials and Triumphs,* 128–30; Robert M. Owens, *Red Dreams, White Nightmares: Pan-Indian Alliances in the Anglo-American Mind, 1763–1815* (Norman: University of Oklahoma Press, 2015).

69. Prucha, *Great Father,* 169–73.

70. Engemann and Tatalovich, "George Washington: The First Modern President?" To use Indian affairs to help make the argument that Washington as president really had few responsibilities in areas other than diplomacy is incorrect, a misunderstanding of the complex and complicated nature of policy even in Washington's first term.

71. See Reuter, *Trials and Triumphs,* 30, for example. In contrast, consider the drawing of relatively sharp lines by Edling in *A Hercules in the Cradle,* 19–31. It is instructive that Edling's usual focus on specific data and policy information falls back to a review of political philosophers to describe the bright lines between "internal" and "international" affairs rather than focusing on the diplomats and policy makers at federal, state, and tribal levels in the years of the early republic; see 22–23.

72. J. P. Nettl, "The State as a Conceptual Variable," *World Politics* 20 (July 1968): 566.

73. Henry Steele Commager, foreword to Van Every, *Ark of Empire,* x; see also 41; Reuter, *Trials and Triumphs,* xxi–xxiii.

74. *American State Papers: Indian Affairs,* 86; see also Calloway, *The Victory with No Name,* 60.

75. Rufus Putnam to Washington, 8 January 1791, *American State Papers: Indian Affairs,* 122; see also Putnam to Knox, 8 January 1791, *American State Papers: Indian Affairs,* 122; and Reuter, *Trials and Triumphs,* 90. See also *American State Papers: Indian Affairs,* 84–88, for demands for help and protection aimed at Washington; 88, 91, for some references to depredations, the need to organize, and need to restore faith in the government; *Debates,* 1:91 for demands for lands and general assessments: "It will take prudent management to prevent the fatal effects of a commotion in that country [Kentucky]." On the Ohio memorials and Knox's report to Washington, which Washington forwarded to the House and Senate, see *American State Papers: Indian Affairs,* 107–22. On Spain as a viable threat, see *Debates,* 1:105–6; Van Every, *Ark of Empire,* 200n11; *The Diaries of George Washington,* 6:14–16, 21, 38, 46; Calloway, *The Victory with No Name,* 60, 68–71.

76. *Debates,* 1:242. Jackson also expressed anger at the secret provisions included in the Treaty of New York, anger that the three commissioners sent to the Creeks didn't include a citizen of Georgia, and anger that the treaty—rather than protect the rights of Georgians—sacrificed them instead.

77. *American State Papers: Indian Affairs,* 113.

78. See the discussion in Stephen Skowronek, *Building a New American State: The Expansion of National Administrative Capacities, 1877–1920* (Cambridge: Cambridge University Press, 1982), 3, 5.

79. *American State Papers: Indian Affairs,* 53.

80. *American State Papers: Indian Affairs,* 53, 83–84.

81. *The Diaries of George Washington,* 6:70, 72, 73; Prucha, *Great Father,* 69–70; Reuter, *Trials and Triumphs,* 127–28. Against federal protestations, Blount, Sevier, and others mobilized their own attacks and invaded Indian country in 1793. Prucha, *Great Father,* 68–70; Reuter, *Trials and Triumphs,* 137–38.

82. Van Every, *Ark of Empire,* 251–55; Calloway, *The Victory with No Name,* 73–76, 140–42; examples of Washington's concern for ongoing western dissatisfaction, including concern for Spain, appear at *The Diaries of George Washington,* 6:73, 14–16, 31–33, and 40–41.

83. For review of these agreements, see for example Reuter, *Trials and Triumphs,* ch. 6.

84. *Debates,* 1:312–13.

"The Next Great Work to Be Accomplished"

American Armament Policy

ANDREW J. B. FAGAL

During the American Revolution the Continental Congress and the state governments were constantly beset by shortages of funds and arms, and the persistence of these fiscal and military weaknesses into the 1780s were of prime concern for American policy makers. At the end of that decade Alexander Hamilton and Thomas Jefferson, two men whose ideological differences would help define the country's political debates in the 1790s, were in broad agreement over the major policy goals for the newly instituted federal government. Both believed that the first objective should be to revitalize the public credit, previously weakened by nonpayment of Revolutionary War debt. Hamilton's financial system, including the assumption of state debts, a sinking fund, and a nationally chartered bank, is a well-known testament to the seriousness with which the Washington administration approached this problem.[1] But Jefferson also desired that the new government should regain its ability to borrow money by paying down debt.[2] In a 1788 letter, Jefferson opined that the new government would have to "make provision for the speedy paiment of their foreign debts. . . . This will give them credit."[3] The next objective shared by both men, and born out of the experience of the revolution, was the creation of a domestic arms industry. In that same letter, Jefferson informed his correspondent that a "concomitant" goal of the federal government "should be magazines and manufactures of arms." Hamilton, for his part, agreed in principle and in his 1791 *Report on Manufactures* told Congress that after stabilizing public credit the development of an arms industry was "the next great work to be accomplished."[4]

This consensus between Hamilton and Jefferson on the importance of public credit and armament policy might appear odd given the deep divisions that arose between them during George Washington's presidency. In fact, the two men had very different ideas on how the federal government could best pursue these goals, and the final form that the United States' fiscal and military powers should take. Their disagreement, of course, helped shape national political discussion during the 1790s. But the importance that postindependence Americans placed on the armaments industry was unsurprising given world historical trends. Virtually all polities in the early modern period, particularly those asserting independence or undergoing industrialization, attempted to ensure that they would not have to rely upon foreign sources of arms and munitions in a time of war. Access to weapons was, and is, a sine qua non of state formation. It is axiomatic that without arms there is danger of coercion from a sovereign power. Beginning in the eighteenth century (although there were certainly precedents dating back to the sixteenth), a number of European countries began a process whereby the state took on an increasing role in the design, production, and maintenance of weapons systems, from small arms and munitions to warships.[5] But this state involvement in the production of armaments was by no means relegated to the West. Governmental oversight and direction in all stages of the weapons acquisition process was present across Asia in the Chinese Qing dynasty, the Japanese shogunate, the various polities in South Asia, and the Ottoman Empire.[6] Even though West Africa was largely dependent upon European sources of arms via the Atlantic slave trade, newly formed states in the nineteenth century, such as Muhammad Ali's Egypt and Queen Ranavalona's Madagascar, also pursued policies that supported the domestic production of weapons.[7] In this, the United States was no different than any other early modern polity.

An examination of American armament policy during the critical years of state formation in the early republic, with special attention to Washington's administration, is instructive for showing the ways in which the United States both underwent institutional mimesis and diverged from larger historical trends. During the Revolution, all Americans could readily agree that the newly independent United States had to develop a domestic arms industry. The main question that confronted policy makers was how to do this in a manner consistent with republican government. Based off of their experiences during the revolution, Washington, Hamilton, and most other Federalists with a military background agreed that the United States should follow the path of European countries and manufacture small arms and munitions at nationally owned and operated factories. Jefferson and his political allies, who often had diverging experiences during the revolution, disagreed with the Federalist assessment and argued instead that the government should ensure that private enterprise would fulfill this important role in the polity. Despite the election of 1800 and the institutionalization of Jeffersonian governance in favor of private armaments, the Washington administration played a crucial role in the development of the American weapons industry in two precedent-setting ways.[8] First, in a 1790 speech to Congress, Washington asked the legislature to develop policies that would render the United States self-sufficient in the production of war materiel. Regardless of the actual policies taken after Washington's tenure, the federal government would seek to promote the domestic manufacture of arms. Second, in response to the demand necessitated by the Northwest Indian War, Washington was able to convince Congress to finally establish a national armory system modeled after those of Europe. The dual institutions of the Springfield and Harpers Ferry armories would shape American state power, industrialization, and technological development well into the twentieth century. Washington's presidency, ultimately, supported key aspects of the weapons acquisition process that would shape American governance in the decades to come.

Despite its importance, weapons acquisition has been generally neglected in the historiography on American politics and state formation, even if it has played a central role in the history of technology.[9] In the larger picture of state building and institutional development, the mutually supporting connections between war making and centralization are well known in the literature on the development of modern states—including in the early American context.[10] The relationship among these historical processes are so well known that important recent works in early American history have turned away from war and have looked elsewhere for signs of leviathan.[11] The experience of the Washington administration, in particular the defeats of Generals Josiah Harmar and Arthur St. Clair in 1790 and 1791 during the Northwest Indian War, demonstrates that the government's ability to actually function as a successful state was in question. The effectiveness of native arms successfully challenged, at least for a time, the autonomous power of the early United States.[12] The federal government's initial inability to project power into the Northwest Territory was due in part to the fact that it was unable to effectively raise, train, and most importantly, equip, an army that could express its will in the tramontane West. The lessons that Washington, Hamilton, and other members of the administration applied from the American Revolution to the problems of governance in the 1790s would shape a national debate over arms procurement and lead the federal government to adopt policies that would ensure that "the next great work" was actually accomplished.

Armament Policy in the Critical Period

The great lesson coming out the War of Independence was that *dependence* upon foreign sources of arms and munitions undermined national self-determination. From its beginning, access to weapons had played a crucial role in the conflict. General Gage ordered his troops to Concord to seize cannon, gunpowder, and small arms, while Lord Dunmore plundered the Williamsburg armory of the same.[13] In both instances, hostilities broke out. Although the American militias were generally well armed at first, especially in New England, the colonies did not have the industrial infrastructure to rapidly replace losses, arm soldiers with weapons based upon a uniform pattern, or produce in large enough quantities the necessary gunpowder.[14] Further compounding the problem, British naval supremacy could hinder any importation from abroad. The reality of the situation was first felt at the 1775 Battle of Bunker Hill when the New England militia's insufficient supply of gunpowder and lack of bayonets forced them to cede the field. The situation generally did not improve from there on out. Despite major attempts by Congress and the state governments to alleviate the problem by promoting domestic industry, as well as a clandestine operation run by Hortalez and Company to import arms from Europe, the Continental Army faced periodic shortages of essential supplies until French intervention in 1778 and even then continued to face deficits as the country's fiscal situation collapsed.[15]

During the war George Washington and others in his immediate circle came to the conclusion that the national and state governments would have to adopt similar institutions to those created by other early modern states to meet the army's demand for weapons. In this vein, in late 1775 the Virginia Convention allocated money toward a state-run arms factory in Fredericksburg to replace the weapons seized by Dunmore.[16] Over the course of the next several months Fielding Lewis, Washington's brother-in-law and the superintendent of the factory, kept the general apprised of the slow but steady progress in producing arms.[17] The armory's main breakthrough came when Thomas Harris, a skilled gunsmith, escaped from Lord Dunmore's fleet in the Chesapeake and offered his services to Virginia. By the end of 1775, Harris had overseen the construction of a mill for "boreing grinding and polishing the work" and instructed "Common blacksmiths In the aforesaid branches."[18] Although the Fredericksburg Manufactory struggled throughout the war, its success in producing arms demonstrated to Washington that the state was fully competent to run and manage military production.

In addition to the example provided by his native Virginia, the Continental Congress's military stores department also showed Washington that nationally directed manufacturing could be a success if adequately funded. With manufacturing centers at Springfield, Massachusetts, and at Philadelphia and Carlisle in Pennsylvania, Quartermaster Generals Benjamin Flower and Samuel Hodgdon provided the army with a steady stream of cannon, muskets, and ammunition, even if it was never enough to meet Washington's expectations. Although the flow of arms to the Continental Army was largely dependent upon the ability of Congress to fund the military stores department, the agency demonstrated to Washington and other officers in his orbit that the national government was fully competent to manage a national workforce.[19]

At the termination of hostilities in 1783 American political and military leaders were faced with a conundrum: what actions should Congress take to promote military industry during peacetime? French intervention had been critical for supplying the Continental Army, and in the closing years of the war the industrial enterprises still run by the states had all shut down as cost-saving measures while the military stores department had dramatically scaled back its operations. In this void, a series of military and political leaders—all associated with the nationalist school—offered a solution. Plans authored by George Washington, Alexander Hamilton, Henry Knox, Benjamin Lincoln, and Baron von Steuben all encouraged the Continental Congress to foster the production of war matériel. In a memorandum written before the termination of hostilities, Secretary at War Lincoln stressed the crucial role that would be played by military manufacturing in the forthcoming peace. According to Lincoln, "The modes which shall be adopted to complete the magazines with a full supply of stores—and the manner of keeping up the supply will, in my opinion, mark the future character of the new Empire."[20] Relying on France to supply weapons in the future was foolish, as "it would be idle for a people to talk of Independence who were indebted for the means of their existence to any nation on Earth—since, in that case, they would hold their freedom on the uncertain tenure of the pacific disposition of such a power."[21] In the secretary's estimation, state sovereignty was predicated upon military preparedness, and military preparedness was determined by stockpiles of arms and munitions as well as the capacity to manufacture more.

Reacting to Lincoln's memorandum, one of the first problems that Congress tackled after the Treaty of Paris was what to do regarding its peacetime military establishment. Hamilton, chairing the congressional committee tasked with finding an answer to this problem, sought advice from Washington, Lincoln, and others on what to include in his report.[22] Washington's reply, the 1783 "Sentiments on a Peace Establishment," has long been a fixture of scholarship on the early US military and has principally been used by historians to show how militia reform and manpower mobilization were key elements of the federalist state-building program.[23] Largely unremarked upon in the historiography is the extent to which Washington linked economic development, and particularly that of arms manufacturing, to the health of the state. Washington laid out four goals in his report: a standing army to protect the frontier, a well-organized militia, arsenals to store military goods, and military academies to train engineers and artillerists and provide artisanal training for "Manufactories of some kinds of Military Stores." Not only did Washington's goals prescribe how the military forces should be composed, but he also noted that the national government had a vested interest in manufacturing ample supplies of war matériel.

According to Washington the future security of the United States was tied to its manufacturing capacity: "The Establishment of Military Academies and Manufactures, as the means of preserving that knowledge and being possessed of those Warlike Stores . . . are essential to the support of the Sovereignty and Independence of the United States."[24] The United States' very *sovereignty* and *independence* was predicated on a military establishment that produced its own war matériel. Unlike Lincoln's ardent opposition to importations, Washington argued that arms and munitions from Europe could be preferable in the short run, as the country lacked the fiscal and military institutions necessary to encourage domestic manufactures.[25] Realizing the financial plight of the republic, Washington knew that finance minister Robert Morris and the Continental Congress could, and would, quash any military plans that were not immediately necessary for maintaining independence. While it was not financially feasible for the state to establish its own domestic manufacturers of military wares in the short run, the long-term "reference to such establishments" was of great importance to the future of the union.

If Washington offered Hamilton a broad overview of the necessity of arsenals and armories, his former subordinate took the plan and radically expanded it and presented to Congress an all-encompassing, comprehensive, vision for state-run military manufacturing.[26] Like Lincoln and Washington, Hamilton also emphasized the importance of war matériel for the security of the republic. "Every country," he explained, "ought to endeavor to have within itself all the means essential to its own preservation."[27] Congress should therefore endeavor to set up foundries, armories, and gunpowder mills as well as stockpile goods at strategically located arsenals. Additionally, the national legislature should establish a corps of artificers to oversee and staff these facilities. Far from mere enlisted positions, Hamilton's proposed corps of artificers was an expansive national workforce. Each arsenal would contain masters in all the relevant trades, such as gunsmithing, as well as over 180 journeymen and apprentices at each location, all serving as enlisted men and subject to military discipline. This highly skilled national military workforce could then instruct common soldiers on how to produce weapons, in the hopes that controlling their labor would allow the government to obtain weapons at a cheaper price than importation or contracts with private suppliers.

The financial situation of the United States following the Revolutionary War meant that Hamilton's report was effectively dead on arrival. The collapse of paper currency in 1779 strained continental finances, and the inability to tax at a national level only compounded the problem. To restore the United States to a firm fiscal footing and pay for the national arsenals and the corps of artificers, Hamilton and other nationalists championed a tariff that would fund the government via a 5 percent ad valorem tax on imported goods.[28] The tariff failed in two subsequent years when Rhode Island, and then New York, refused their assent to the tax. Far from spurring on a state-run system of industry, superintendent of finance Robert Morris ordered the sale of military stores at a loss on the open market just to raise funds for the national government.[29] Hamilton's vision would go nowhere as long as Congress lacked the power to tax.

Arms Production and the Report on Manufactures

The US Constitution addressed a wide variety of national concerns through the institutional framework of a fiscal-military state.[30] The immediate fiscal aspects of the compact were quite clear. In 1789 Congress passed a tariff to fund the government and service the national debt. Other than adopting the Confederation army and establishing a department of war, the path forward on the military side of the fiscal-military ledger was less clear. Secretary of War Knox suggested that once the "infant state of the finances" was remedied, the public ought to establish "manufactories of the implements and materials of War."[31] Washington, of course, agreed with Knox's assessment and at the opening of the second session of the first Congress in January 1790, Washington asked the assembled representatives to consider measures that would "promote such manufactories, as tend to render [the United States] independent on others, for essential . . . military supplies."[32] In this, Washington announced that his administration made it a priority to tackle the problem of armaments that had faced the country since the opening of the American Revolution. The day following Washington's speech, the House asked Treasury Secretary Alexander Hamilton to prepare a report on how to render the United States self-sufficient in the production of war matériel.[33] This request would ultimately lead to Hamilton's *Report on Manufactures*, the third of his major policy papers. While Hamilton's earlier *Reports on Public Credit* laid out his fiscal program for the United States, the *Report on Manufactures* spelled out the Washington administration's plan to establish a state-run military industry.[34]

The final document, which Hamilton returned to Congress in December 1791, went well beyond Congress's request for a report on military manufacturing. Instead, Hamilton introduced the final plank of his vision for effective governance. While he designed the reports on debt assumption and the national bank to stabilize the country's credit, the *Report on Manufacturers* served several goals. Hamilton proposed modest tariff increases to provide the fiscal resources necessary to support the expenditures of the national state, export bounties to support those industries involved in foreign trade, provided a robust defense for the importance of large manufacturing establishments in the country's political economy, and endorsed government-owned production facilities to render the United States independent of other countries for military goods.[35] The fiscal and financial issues implicit in the *Report on Manufacturers* notwithstanding, Hamilton reinforced the arguments made in the 1780s that the only reliable measure for ensuring a successful military mobilization was national control over the weapons acquisition process.

In constructing the *Report on Manufactures* Hamilton first turned to his subordinate, Tench Coxe, the assistant secretary of the treasury. During the 1780s, Coxe had arrived at roughly the same conclusions as Thomas Jefferson regarding a preference for private contracting as opposed to public ownership in arms acquisition. Both men were also closely involved with the arms trade, Coxe as a representative of his mercantile firm and Jefferson as an agent for Virginia while serving as the US minister to France. Their experience as arms merchants demonstrated to them that the best way forward would be for the national government to encourage entrepreneurs to set up shop in the United States in order to work as private contractors.[36] Their view clearly came to the fore in Coxe's draft for the *Report on Manufactures*. In order to create a national market for American-produced military goods, Coxe proposed protective tariff duties, prohibitions on critical imports, an abolition of the duties on the coastal trade, government-assisted internal improvements, and direct loans and land grants to manufacturing entrepreneurs to aid in capital creation. For Coxe, privately owned American manufacturers should supply the United States with weapons in a time of war. Because of the elastic shifts in supply and demand during periods of peace, the government would have to step in and encourage private producers though favorable contracts.[37]

Hamilton mostly rejected Coxe's suggestions out of hand and included his, Washington's, and Knox's own favored policies in the report submitted to Congress.[38] Far from a report that focused solely on the armaments industry, as Congress had originally intended and as Coxe had actually done, Hamilton authored a wide-ranging white paper weighing the pros and cons of different forms of governmental intervention in the American market. But the *Report on Manufactures* did include four key provisions that reflected his earlier 1783 committee report on the military peace establishment. First, Hamilton addressed the fact that even though the arms industry had flourished during the Revolution, during the 1780s it "diminished for want of demand."[39] Second, the industry was so essential for national security that "every nation . . . ought to endeavor to possess within itself all the essentials of national supply."[40] Third, Congress should remember the experience of the Revolution when the Continental Army mostly relied on the private contract system: "The extreme embarrassments of the United States during the late War, from an incapacity of supplying themselves, are still matter of keen recollection: A future war might be expected again to exemplify the mischiefs and dangers of a situation, to which that incapacity is still in too great a degree applicable, unless changed by timely and vigorous exertion. To effect this change as fast as shall be prudent, merits all the attention and all the Zeal of our Public Councils; 'tis the next great work to be accomplished."[41] Finally, Hamilton suggested a solution: create nationally owned factories.

According to Hamilton, the armament industry was too important for the security of the country to leave in the hands of private contractors. Support for domestic producers of firearms through contracts could work in the short run. In the long run, though, the federal government would have to create its own armories that would operate in peacetime in order to ensure a steady supply during war. Hamilton then asked Congress "whether manufactories of all the necessary weapons of war ought not to be established, on account of the Government itself. Such establishments are agreeable to the usual practice of Nations and that practice seems founded on sufficient reason."[42] Hamilton wished to shape the United States in the mold of the major fiscal-military states of Europe, where arms and munitions manufacturing was concentrated in royal arsenals such as the Tower of London, Woolwich, Waltham Abbey, and Faversham in Great Britain; the Tula Arsenal in Russia; and St. Etienne, Charleville, and Essone in France.

Hamilton's rationale in support of government-owned facilities was that the public simply could not trust private producers of military arms to provide for national defense. "There appears to be an improvidence, in leaving these essential instruments of national defence to the casual speculations of individual adventure; a resource which can less be relied upon, in this case than in most others."[43] Harkening back to classical republican ideals, Hamilton insisted that private interest simply could not be trusted to coincide with that of the public during wartime. Hamilton rejected Coxe's firm protectionist measures to channel the armament industry into private hands because military goods were not "objects of ordinary and indispens-able private consumption or use." Instead, Hamilton classed military goods as items that government should seek to manufacture for itself. "As a general rule, manufactories on the immediate account of Government are to be avoided; but this seems to be one of the few exceptions, which that rule admits."[44] With the *Report on Manufactures,* Hamilton had authored the most significant early policy paper for American military industry.

The Crises of the 1790s and the Genesis of Military Manufacturing

Shortly after Hamilton delivered his report on the importance of military manufacturing to Congress, the first in a series of domestic and international crises confronted the Washington administration. On November 4, 1791, a force of Miami, Shawnee, and Delaware Indians, all well versed in the maintenance and operation of firearms, decimated an American army headed by Arthur St. Clair as it advanced on native villages on the Wabash River.[45] The effects of St. Clair's defeat upon the development of military institutions in the United States have long been understood in American historiography.[46] Less well understood is the relationship between American military defeat on the frontier and the resulting push for institutional mimesis in the production of arms at the national level. The congressional investigation into St. Clair's defeat propelled the politics of the country's arms supply away from the white papers of elite policy makers and into the actual practice of governing a country with diverse political and economic interests.

In the immediate aftermath of the disaster in the Northwest Territory, two narratives competed for national prominence.[47] The first, argued by Secretary Knox, put the blame on St. Clair's strategic failures. The general's decision to conduct a campaign in the late fall and winter was inadvisable, as it compounded any number of military problems from supply lines to tactical maneuvering in a forested area. The second narrative, pushed by St. Clair, was that the failure was a result of War Department misman-agement. The entire system of private contractors—including merchants, manufacturers, and quartermasters overseen by Knox and Quartermaster General Samuel Hodgdon—had failed to provide the army with necessary supplies or functional weapons. The army was doomed without proper equipment. Of these interpretations regarding the army's failure, St. Clair's became widely accepted in the public sphere, even if a number of army officers accepted that the true causes of the defeat were likely a combination of the two explanations. For example, one widely distributed (fictional) captivity narrative, *The Remarkable Adventures of Jackson Johonnet of Massachusetts,* implicitly took St. Clair's side when it depicted the army throwing down ineffective muskets.[48] The press was relentless in its condemnations of Knox once word emerged that the expedition's chief contractor, William Duer, had extensive land dealings with the secretary. Such was the appearance of impropriety that several congressmen refused to appropriate any funds until the situation was addressed.[49] Contrary to the public opinion expressed in print and in the legislature, experienced army officers understood that the "true causes of the defeat" were likely a combination of strategic blunder and administrative incompetence.[50]

Given the competing narratives explaining the outcome of St. Clair's expedition, the House of Representatives authorized a select committee to investigate the causes of the defeat and came to the conclusion that Henry Knox's War Department had failed to properly supply the army.[51] Among the evidence collected by the inquest, Arthur St. Clair's memorandum largely shaped their ultimate findings.[52] One of his most damning arguments was that in the summer of 1791 he had to turn Fort Washington into "a large manufactory on the inside" to make up for the deficiencies of the war department's contractors.[53] None of the munitions forwarded to the army had been manufactured into cartridges, and the muskets that Hodgdon forwarded to the army, taken from the Revolutionary War surplus stored in Philadelphia, were of such poor quality that St. Clair ordered the construction of an armory in the fort where they could be repaired. It took all summer to manufacture cartridges and repair the arms at Fort Washington, which cut into the campaign season. In September, Knox had ordered St. Clair to move out, which the general followed despite his reservations.[54] By the time the army faced the Miami, Shawnee, and Delaware on the banks of the Wabash on a snowy November morning, they had working weapons, no thanks to the contractors. According to the congressional investigation, the defeat was due to the fact that the army was delayed over the summer at Fort Washington doing the job that Knox and Hodgdon should have overseen in the first place. The troops had fought bravely, even if they had been beaten on the field of battle. Defeat was a result of incompetence in the War Department.

The formal report issued by the select committee and the laws passed by Congress in the spring of 1792 marked an important development in the United States' move toward the European system of state-centered arms acquisition. The committee found that the quartermaster had supplied the army with poor quality and expensive goods purchased from vendors in Philadelphia. Likewise, the goods that were produced did not make it into the army's hands in a timely manner, so that when the secretary of war ordered the army to move, the campaigning season had already ended.[55] As the committee prepared its report, Congress passed a series of laws that were closely linked to the vision for military industry proposed by Alexander Hamilton in his *Report on Manufactures*. In March, it passed the import and excise taxes proposed by Hamilton and raised the size of the regular army.[56] Then, in May, Congress passed the first federal framework for a national militia and transferred contracting authority from the War Department over to the Treasury Department.[57] Individually, each act might have addressed a very specific problem of governance in the early republic. But taken together, they gave the federal government greater oversight over the production and distribution of arms. The militia act, for instance, mandated that by 1797 each militiaman would have to arm himself with a musket based off of the French pattern. Given the demand for uniformity and the likely inability of acquiring arms from France, the measure all but ensured that the federal government, under the direction of Hamilton and supported with additional tax revenue, would have to begin its own arms program.

The legislative creation of the national armory system in 1794 was a direct outgrowth of the findings sparked by the Battle of the Wabash. Following Congress's rebuke, Knox and his associates offered up a full-throated defense of their conduct and began collecting information on the actual conditions of the arms in storage.[58] What they found did not bolster their case. At the meeting of Congress in late 1793, Washington submitted this return of the arms and ordnance then in possession at the country's arsenals and informed that body that despite the laws instituted the previous year, the weapons acquisition process still needed fundamental reforms "as it would leave nothing to the uncertainty of procuring warlike apparatus in the moment of public danger."[59] Of the approximately forty-five thousand small arms owned by the public listed in the return compiled by Knox, roughly one-third needed repair. The total number owned was also less than half of what the administration estimated that the country would need in case of a national emergency. As the failure of St. Clair's expedition had shown, the poor state of the country's armaments, now confirmed by the War Department's own investigation, crippled its ability to effectively deal with native forces. If the United States was forced into the concurrent wars of the French Revolution, an even greater disaster might result if soldiers were issued poor-quality weaponry.

The prospect of future disasters linked to the country's precarious arms supply forced Congress into actions that would both enshrine the national-ist state-building project of the 1780s and lead to a major transformation in American military power. The House committee tasked with responding to Knox's return of arms endorsed the view of the Washington administration that arms manufacturing was too important to leave to the private sector and recommended the creation of a national armory.[60] That April, after a brief debate in Congress, Washington signed into law an act that authorized him to establish up to four national armories for the fabrication of small arms.[61] After discussing the matter with Knox, Washington decided upon expanding the arsenal at Springfield into a full-fledged manufacturing enterprise and to establish a new institution at the meeting of the Potomac and Shenandoah Rivers in Virginia.[62] The Springfield armory, as it was already a federal facility, was in operation within a year producing muskets and cannon for the army—although it quickly abandoned the fabrication of brass artillery after more than half burst during in a public display of their proofing in New York City.[63] Harpers Ferry, starting in a much more rural area and separated from integrated networks for the supply of raw materials got a later start but was in operation by the end of the decade. Together, the Springfield and Harpers Ferry armories, working in conjunction with the private armories promoted by the Jefferson and Madison administrations, not only led to national self-sufficiency in the production of small arms but also introduced the first successful use of replaceable parts manufacture.[64]

The presidential administration of George Washington marked a significant development in the progress of his country's industrial and military capacity. When the United States declared its independence from Great Britain in 1776, it did so without the capacity to manufacture in large quantities its own small arms and munitions. During the 1780s a number of leading military and political minds addressed the problem and largely came to the same solution that virtually all early modern states came to: the nation itself would have to produce its own weapons. At the outset of the Washington administration, Congress tasked Alexander Hamilton to investigate the matter of domestic armaments production, and the treasury secretary eventually responded in his famous *Report on Manufactures* that the official policy of the administration was the creation of a national armory system. Thus, in the aftermath of Arthur St. Clair's defeat Congress embraced the view that only public institutions operated by the federal government were competent to provide arms for the country's military force. With revenues accruing to the Treasury Department through the restoration of public credit, the Federalist state-building project could move to a second issue of national consensus: arms manufacturing. Although the election of Thomas Jefferson in 1800 would alter the trajectory of the weapons acquisition process in the United States to emphasize private entrepreneurship, the precedents set by Washington were important for defining the system. Regardless of political party, the country's leaders sought to promote the manufacture of arms and munitions within the borders of the United States. Although Federalists and Jeffersonian Republicans would provide vastly different policy solutions, with correspondingly different social and economic outcomes, they did agree that arms production was the next great work confronting the United States.

Notes

1. Max M. Edling, *A Hercules in the Cradle: War, Money, and the American State, 1783–1867* (Chicago: University of Chicago Press, 2014), ch. 2.

2. Herbert E. Sloan, *Principle and Interest: Thomas Jefferson and the Problem of Debt* (Charlottesville: University Press of Virginia, 1995), 109–13.

3. Thomas Jefferson to John Brown, 28 May 1788, *The Papers of Thomas Jefferson*, ed. Julian P. Boyd et al., 44 vols. to date (Princeton, NJ: Princeton University Press, 1950–) 13:212 (hereafter *PTJ*). For Jefferson's long-standing interest in seeing the national government establish arsenals of some kind, see Jefferson to Edmund Pendleton, 18 January 1784, *PTJ*, 6:470–71.

4. Alexander Hamilton, *Report on Manufactures, The Papers of Alexander Hamilton*, ed. Harold C. Syrett, 27 vols., (New York: Columbia University Press, 1961–87), 10:291 (hereafter *PAH*).

5. For the broad contours of European history in this period see William H. McNeill, *The Pursuit of Power: Technology, Armed Force, and Society since A.D. 1000* (Chicago: University of Chicago Press, 1982), chs. 2 and 3; and David Parrott, *The Business of War: Military Enterprise and Military Revolution in Early Modern Europe* (Cambridge: Cambridge University Press, 2012), 300–304. For this process in Great Britain see Gordon E. Bannerman, *Merchants and the Military in Eighteenth-Century Britain: British Army Contracts and Domestic Supply, 1739–1763* (London: Pickering and Chatto, 2008), 146–50; Jenny West, *Gunpowder, Government, and War in the Mid-Eighteenth Century* (London: Royal Historical Society, 1991), ch. 1; Gareth Cole, *Arming the Royal Navy, 1793–1815: The Office of Ordnance and the State* (London: Pickering and Chatto, 2012), chs. 3 and 4. For similar developments in the French military bureaucracy in the eighteenth century see Ken Alder, *Engineering the Revolution: Arms and Enlightenment in France, 1763–1815* (Princeton, NJ: Princeton University Press, 1997), ch. 5; Jeff Horn, *The Path Not Taken: French Industrialization in the Age of Revolution, 1750–1830* (Cambridge, MA: MIT Press, 2006), ch. 5. For Prussia see W. O. Henderson, *Studies in the Economic Policy of Frederick the Great* (London: F. Cass, 1963), ch. 1; Dennis E. Showalter, "Manifestation of Reform: The Rearmament of the Prussian Infantry, 1806–13," *Journal of Modern History* 44 (1972): 364–80. For Russia see Alexander Trapeznik, "The State as an Agent of Industrial Development: The Tula Imperial Armaments Factory in Russia," *Journal of Slavic Military Studies* 22, no. 4 (2009): 549–73.

6. For China see Kenneth Chase, *Firearms: A Global History to 1700* (Cambridge: Cambridge University Press, 2003), chs. 2 and 6; Tonio Andrade, *The Gunpowder Age: China, Military Innovation, and the Rise of the West in World History* (Princeton, NJ: Princeton University Press, 2016), chs. 16–18. For Japan see Noel Perrin, *Giving Up the Gun: Japan's Reversion to the Sword, 1543–1879* (Boston: David R. Godine, 1979). For South Asia see Iqtidar Alam Khan, "Nature of Gunpowder Artillery in

India during the Sixteenth Century: A Reappraisal of the Impact of European Gun-nery," *Journal of the Royal Asiatic Society* 9, no. 1 (April 1999): 27–34; Pradeep Barua, "Military Developments in India, 1750–1850," *Journal of Military History* 58, no. 4 (October 1994): 599–616. For arms production in the Ottoman Empire see Gábor Ágoston, *Guns for the Sultan: Military Power and the Weapons Industry in the Ottoman Empire* (Cambridge: Cambridge University Press, 2008).

7. For the import of weapons into West Africa see J. E. Inikori, "The Import of Firearms into West Africa 1750–1807: A Quantitative Analysis," *Journal of African History* 18, no. 3 (July 1977): 339–68; W. A. Richards, "The Import of Firearms into West Africa in the Eighteenth Century," *Journal of African History* 21, no. 1 (January 1980): 43–59. For Egypt see John Dunn, "Egypt's Nineteenth-Century Armaments Industry," *Journal of Military History* 61, no. 2 (April 1997): 231–54. For Madagascar see Gwyn Campbell, "An Industrial Experiment in Pre-Colonial Africa: The Case of Imperial Madagascar, 1825–1861," *Journal of Southern African Studies* 17, no. 3 (1991): 525–59.

8. On Jeffersonian governance and the American weapons industry see Andrew J. B. Fagal, "Terror Weapons in the Naval War of 1812," *New York History* 94, no. 3–4 (Summer/Fall 2013): 221–40; A. J. B. Fagal, "American Arms Manufactur-ing and the Onset of the War of 1812," *New England Quarterly* 87, no. 3 (September 2014): 526–37; A. J. B. Fagal, "The Mills of Liberty: Foreign Capital, Government Contracts, and the Establishment of DuPont, 1790–1820," *Enterprise & Society* 19, no. 2 (June 2018): 309–51.

9. Merrit Roe Smith, *Harpers Ferry Armory and the New Technology: The Chal-lenge of Change* (Ithaca, NY: Cornell University Press, 1977); David A. Hounshell, *From the American System to Mass Production, 1800–1932* (Baltimore: Johns Hop-kins University Press, 1984), 32–46; David R. Meyer, *Networked Machinists: High Technology Industries in Antebellum America* (Baltimore: Johns Hopkins Univer-sity Press, 2006), 73–103; Robert Martello, *Midnight Ride, Industrial Dawn: Paul Revere and the Growth of American Enterprise* (Baltimore: Johns Hopkins Univer-sity Press, 2010), ch. 6. The main exception to this trend is the work, fully encom-passing the development of the American state, of Lindsay Schakenbach Regele. see Lindsay Schakenbach Regele, *Manufacturing Advantage: War, the State, and the Origins of American Industry, 1776–1848* (Baltimore: Johns Hopkins University Press, 2019).

10. Charles Tilly, "War Making and State Making as Organized Crime," in *Bringing the State Back In,* ed. Peter B. Evans, Dietrich Rueschemeyer and Theda Skocpol (Cambridge: Cambridge University Press, 1984), 169–89; and Charles Tilly, *Coercion, Capital, and European States, AD 990–1992* (Cambridge: Blackwell, 1992), 20–28; Geoffrey Parker, *The Military Revolution: Military Innovation and the Rise of the West, 1500–1800* (Cambridge: Cambridge University Press, 1996), 3; John Brewer, *The Sinews of Power: War, Money and the English State, 1688–1783* (Cam-bridge, MA: Harvard University Press, 1988), xx; Ira Katznelson, "Flexible Capacity: The Military and Early American Statebuilding," in *Shaped by War and Trade: Inter-national Influences on American Political Development,* ed. Ira Katznelson and Martin Shefter (Princeton, NJ: Princeton University Press, 2002), 82–86; Max M. Edling, *A Revolution in Favor of Government: Origins of the U.S. Constitution and the Making of the American State* (Oxford: Oxford University Press, 2003), 9–10; and Edling, *A Hercules in the Cradle,* 4–7.

11. William J. Novak, "The Myth of the 'Weak' American State," *American Historical Review* 113, no. 3 (June 2008): 752–72; John Fabian Witt, "Law and War in American History," *American Historical Review* 115, no. 3 (June 2010): 768–78; William J. Novak, "Long Live the Myth of the Weak State? A Response to Adams, Gerstle, and Witt," *American Historical Review* 115, no. 3 (June 2010): 792–800. Recent scholarship on the development of the American state and national institutions has tended to focus on areas outside of the military. See Richard R. John, *Spreading the News: The American Postal System from Franklin to Morse* (Cambridge, MA: Harvard University Press, 1995); William J. Novak, *The People's Welfare: Law and Regulation in Nineteenth-Century America* (Chapel Hill: University of North Carolina Press, 1996); Robin L. Einhorn, *American Taxation, American Slavery* (Chicago: University of Chicago Press, 2006); Douglas Bradburn, *The Citizenship Revolution: Politics & the Creation of the American Union, 1774–1804* (Charlottesville: University of Virginia Press, 2009); Brian Balogh, *A Government Out of Sight: The Mystery of National Authority in Nineteenth-Century America* (Cambridge: Cambridge University Press, 2009); Peter Thompson and Peter Onuf, eds., *State and Citizen: British America and the Early United States* (Charlottesville: University of Virginia Press, 2013); Gautham Rao, *National Duties: Custom Houses and the Making of the American State* (Chicago: University of Chicago Press, 2016).

12. Michael Mann, "The Autonomous Power of the State: Its Origins, Mechanisms, and Results," *European Journal of Sociology* 25, no. 2 (November 1984): 196; on the importance of US-native relations for the process of American state building see Gautham Rao, "The New Historiography of the Early Federal Government: Institutions, Contexts, and the Imperial State," *William and Mary Quarterly*, 3rd. ser., 77, no. 1 (January 2020): 97–128.

13. David Hackett Fischer, *Paul Revere's Ride* (New York: Oxford University Press, 1994), 43; Peter Charles Hoffer, *Prelude to Revolution: The Salem Gunpowder Raid of 1775* (Baltimore: Johns Hopkins University Press, 2013); J. L. Bell, *The Road to Concord: How Four Stolen Cannon Ignited the Revolutionary War* (Yardley, PA: Westholme, 2016); Michael A. McDonnell, *The Politics of War: Race, Class, and Conflict in Revolutionary Virginia* (Chapel Hill: University of North Carolina Press, 2007), 49–50.

14. Robert H. Churchill, "Gun Ownership in Early America: A Survey of Manuscript Militia Returns," *William and Mary Quarterly*, 3rd. ser., 60, no 3 (July 2003): 626; Kevin M. Sweeney, "Firearms, Militias, and the Second Amendment," in *The Second Amendment on Trial: Critical Essays on District of Columbia v. Heller*, ed. Saul Cornell and Nathan Kozuskanich (Amherst: University of Massachusetts Press, 2013), 310–82.

15. E. James Ferguson, *The Power of the Purse: A History of American Public Finance, 1776–1790* (Chapel Hill: University of North Carolina Press, 1961); E. Wayne Carp, *To Starve the Army at Pleasure: Continental Army Administration and American Political Culture, 1775–1783* (Chapel Hill: University of North Carolina Press, 1984); Brian N. Morton and Donald C. Spinelli, *Beaumarchais and the American Revolution* (Lanham, MD: Lexington Books, 2003), ch. 3. For the success of the Military Stores Department in the domestic production of essential military goods see Robert F. Smith, *Manufacturing Independence: Industrial Innovation in the American Revolution* (Yardley, PA: Westholme, 2016).

16. "Proceedings of Thirty-Second Day of Session," Third Virginia Convention, 25 August 1775, *Revolutionary Virginia: The Road to Independence*, ed. Robert L.

Scribner and Brent Tarter, 7 vols. (Charlottesville: University Press of Virginia, 1977), 3:487, 503–4; *The Statutes at Large; Being a Collection of All the Laws of Virginia, from the First Session of the Legislature, in the year 1619*, ed. William Waller Hening, 13 vols. (Richmond: J. and G. Cochran, 1821), 9:71–72.

17. Fielding Lewis to George Washington, 14 November 1775, *The Papers of George Washington: Revolutionary War Series*, ed. W. W. Abbot et al., 26 vols. to date (Charlottesville: University Press of Virginia, 1985–present), 2:373 (hereafter *PGW: Rev. War Ser.*); Fielding Lewis to George Washington, 4 February 1776, *PGW: Rev. War Ser.*, 3:246; Fielding Lewis to George Washington, 6 March 1776, *PGW: Rev. War Ser.*, 3:419.

18. Thomas Harris to Thomas Jefferson, 7 September 1805, Library of Congress, Papers of Thomas Jefferson.

19. Smith, *Manufacturing Independence*, 17–20.

20. Benjamin Lincoln, Memorandum Regarding Arsenals, 3 March 1783, *Papers of the Continental Congress*, microfilm edition, 204 reels (Washington, DC: National Archives, 1957–59), 45:289.

21. Ibid., 45:289–90.

22. Alexander Hamilton to George Washington, 8 April 1783, *PAH*, 3:317–21; Washington to Hamilton, 16 April 1783, ibid., 3:329–31; Washington to Hamilton, 2 May 1783, ibid., 3:346–47; Lincoln to Hamilton, May 1783, ibid., 26:438–43.

23. Richard H. Kohn, *Eagle and Sword: The Federalists and the Creation of the Military Establishment in America, 1783–1802* (New York: Free Press, 1975), 45–47; Lawrence D. Cress, *Citizens in Arms: The Army and the Militia in American Society to the War of 1812* (Chapel Hill: University of North Carolina Press, 1982), 84; Edling, *A Revolution in Favor of Government*, 142–43. For the full text of Washington's plan see "Sentiments on a Peace Establishment," *The Writings of George Washington*, ed. John C. Fitzpatrick, 39 vols. (Washington, DC: Government Printing Office, 1931–44), 26:374–98 (hereafter *WGW*).

24. "Sentiments," *WGW*, 26:396.

25. Ibid., 26:396.

26. Kohn shows that on most points, Hamilton largely copied Washington's recommendations. However, on the crucial subject of armaments, Hamilton went much further. See Kohn, *Eagle and Sword*, 47; "Continental Congress Report on a Military Peace Establishment," 18 June 1783, *PAH*, 3:378–97.

27. "Continental Congress Report on a Military Peace Establishment," 18 June 1783, *PAH*, 3:378–97.

28. For a full accounting of the national debate over the tariff in 1783, see Roger H. Brown, *Redeeming the Republic: Federalists, Taxation, and the Origins of the Constitution* (Baltimore: Johns Hopkins University Press, 1993), 22–31.

29. Ferguson, *Power of the Purse*, 129; Nathaniel Greene to Robert Morris, 11 July 1783, and Greene to Benjamin Lincoln, 2 August 1783, *The Papers of Nathaniel Greene*, ed. Richard K. Showman et al., 13 vols. (Chapel Hill: University of North Carolina Press, 1976–2005), 13:59, 79.

30. Edling, *Revolution in Favor of Government*.

31. Henry Knox's Notes on the State of the Frontier (January 1790), *The Papers of George Washington: Presidential Series*, ed. W. W. Abbot et al., 21 vols. (Charlottesville: University Press of Virginia, 1987–2020), 5:79 (hereafter *PGW: Pres. Ser.*).

32. "To the United States Senate and House of Representatives," 8 January 1790, *PGW: Pres. Ser.*, 4:544.

33. "House of Representatives Journal," *Documentary History of the First Federal Congress of the United States of America*, ed. Linda Grant De Pauw et al., 22 vols. (Baltimore: Johns Hopkins University Press, 1972–2017), 9:265.

34. Hamilton's *Report on Manufactures* holds a significant, and contested, place in the historiography on the early republic and the history of American economic thought. The principal question at stake for this scholarship regards the extent of protectionism versus free trade in Alexander Hamilton's report. Curtis P. Nettels, Jacob E. Cooke, Drew McCoy, Keiji Tajima, Doron Ben-Atar, and Songho Ha all present Hamilton's report as one that was fundamentally protectionist in its political economy toward American manufactures: Curtis P. Nettels, *The Emergence of a National Economy, 1775–1815* (New York: Holt, Rinehart, and Winston, 1962), 106–8; Jacob E. Cooke, "Tench Coxe, Alexander Hamilton, and the Encouragement of American Manufactures," *William and Mary Quarterly*, 3rd ser. 32, no. 3 (July 1975): 369–92; Drew McCoy, *The Elusive Republic: Political Economy in Jeffersonian America* (Chapel Hill: University of North Carolina Press, 1980), 148–65; Keiji Tajima, "Alexander Hamilton and the Encouragement of Manufactures: An Interpretation of the Hamiltonian System," *Japanese Journal of American Studies* 2 (1985): 127–55; Doron Ben-Atar, "Alexander Hamilton's Alternative: Technology Piracy and the Report on Manufactures," *William and Mary Quarterly*, 3rd Ser., 52, no. 3 (July 1995): 389–414; Songho Ha, *The Rise and Fall of the American System: Nationalism and the Development of the American Economy, 1790–1837* (London: Pickering and Chatto, 2009), 18–19. The contrasting view, that Hamilton's report was primarily designed to raise revenue can be found in William Appleman Williams, "The Age of Mercantilism: An Interpretation of the American Political Economy, 1763 to 1828," *William and Mary Quarterly*, 3rd ser., 15, no. 4 (October 1958): 419–37; John R. Nelson Jr., *Liberty and Property: Political Economy and Policymaking in the New Nation, 1789–1812* (Baltimore: Johns Hopkins University Press, 1987), 37–51; Douglas A. Irwin, "The Aftermath of Hamilton's 'Report on Manufactures,'" *Journal of Economic History* 64, no. 3 (September 2004): 800–821; Lawrence Peskin, "How the Republicans Learned to Love Manufacturing: The First Parties and the 'New Economy,'" *Journal of the Early Republic* 22, no. 2 (Summer 2002), 235–37; Andrew Shankman, "'A New Thing on Earth': Alexander Hamilton, Pro-Manufacturing Republicans, and the Democratization of American Political Economy," *Journal of the Early Republic* 23, no. 3 (Autumn 2003), 323–36.

35. Nelson, *Liberty and Property*, 48.

36. For Coxe as an arms merchant see, Harris and Nickols to Tench Coxe, 12 November 1785, Coxe Family Papers, Collection 2049, Historical Society of Pennsylvania, Box 24, Folder 4 (hereafter CFP). The 1784 reforms in the Virginia militia law held the requirement that the militia would eventually need weapons of a uniform size and caliber but in the meantime allowed for militiamen to "keep by them the best arms and accoutrements they can get"; see "An Act for Amending the Several Laws for Regulating and Disciplining the Militia, and Guarding against Invasions and Insurrections," in *The Statutes at Large; Being a Collection of All the Laws of Virginia, from the First Session of the Legislature in the Year 1619*, ed William Waller Hening, 1819–23, 13 vols. (Charlottesville: University Press of Virginia, 1969), 11:485. Invoices indicate that Coxe was one of the major arms dealers of the

1780, dealing with arms shipments of in the thousands of muskets; see for example, Clark and Nightingale to Coxe and Frazier, 20 July 1786, CFP, Box 25, Folder 7; "Sale of Musquets by Coxe and Frazier," 27 January 1787, CFP, Box 26, Folder 3. For Jefferson's efforts to acquire a substantial shipment of arms from the French Royal Manufactory at Tulle see Patrick Henry to Thomas Jefferson, 30 March 1785, *PTJ*, 8:68; Thomas Jefferson to the Governor of Virginia, 16 June 1785, ibid., 8:213; Patrick Henry to Thomas Jefferson, 10 September 1785, ibid., 8:507.

37. "Tench Coxe's Draft on the Report on the Subject of Manufactures," *PAH*, 10:16–17.

38. George Washington to Alexander Hamilton, 14 October 1791, *PGW: Pres. Ser.*, 9:78–79; Henry Knox's Minutes for the President's Speech, 18 October 1791, *PGW: Pres. Ser.*, 9:99–101.

39. Alexander Hamilton, *Report on Manufactures, PAH*, 10:283.

40. Ibid., 10:291.

41. Ibid., 10:291.

42. Ibid., 10:317.

43. Ibid. 10:317.

44. Ibid., 10:317.

45. For the armament of Native Americans in the Northwest see David Silverman, *Thundersticks: Firearms and the Violent Transformation of Native America* (Cambridge, MA: Harvard University Press, 2016), 153–54; Colin G. Calloway, *The Victory with No Name: The Native American Defeat of the First American Army* (Oxford: Oxford University Press, 2015), ch. 5.

46. Kohn, *Eagle and Sword*, 108–16.

47. George Washington to the US House of Representatives, 12 December 1791, *PGW: Pres. Ser.*, 9:274–79.

48. The first publication of the captivity narrative was in *Beer's Almanac and Ephemeris of the Motion of the Sun and Moon, the True Places and Aspects of the Planets: The Rising, Setting and Southing of the Moon, for the Year of our Lord 1793* (Hartford, CT: Hudson and Goodwin, 1792). The narrative was then republished in both book and pamphlet form. Between 1793 and 1816, nine separate editions of the narrative were published across the union. More significantly for the reading public, the narrative was included in Mathew Carey's 1794 *Affecting History*, a compilation of captivity narratives.

49. *Boston Independent Chronicle*, 22 December 1791; Benjamin Hawkins to George Washington, 10 February 1792, *PGW: Pres. Ser.*, 9:556.

50. Otho H. Williams to Alexander Hamilton, 5 March 1792, *PAH*, 11:108–9; Henry Lee to James Madison, 17 January 1792, *The Papers of James Madison*, ed. William T. Hutchinson et al., 17 vols. (Chicago: University of Chicago Press, 1962–91), 14:189; Lee to Madison, 29 January 1792, ibid., 14:203–5. For Henry Lee's forwarding of information to Washington regarding the army's defeat, which makes no mention either of the army's late start or of supply deficiencies and instead focused on the course of battle, see Lee to Washington, 4 December 1791, *PGW: Pres. Ser.*, 9:249–50; Washington to Lee, 14 December 1791, ibid., 9:285–86.

51. The committee had a proadministration bent with Federalists Thomas Fitzsimons, John Steele, John Vining, Theodore Sedgwick, and Abraham Clark. Antiadministration members were William Branch Giles, who had first proposed the inquest, and John F. Mercer. Although there are no records showing that Hamilton

influenced the committee behind the scenes, many of the Federalists on the committee had a strong personal relationship with the treasury secretary, and it is possible that they would have discussed matters with him. See Alexander Hamilton to John Steele, 15 October 1792, *PAH*, 12:567–68; Hamilton to Thomas Fitzsimons, 27 November 1794, ibid., 17:394–95; Theodore Sedgwick to Hamilton, 26 August 1793, ibid., 15:285–86.

52. For the full text of St. Clair's memorandum see Arthur St. Clair, *A Narrative of the Campaign against the Indians, under the Command of Major General St. Clair* (Philadelphia: Jane Aiken, 1812), 1–58.

53. Ibid., 13.

54. George C. Chalou, "St. Clair's Defeat, 1792," in *Congress Investigates: A Documented History, 1792–1974*, ed. Arthur M. Schlesinger Jr., and Roger Bruns, 5 vols. (New York: Chelsea House, 1975), 1:11.

55. "Causes of the Failure of the Expedition Against the Indians, in 1791, under the Command of Major General St. Clair," in *American State Papers: Documents, Legislative and Executive, of the Congress of the United States*, 38 vols. (Washington, DC, 1832–61), *Military Affairs*, 1:36–39 (hereafter *ASP: MA*).

56. "Protection of the Frontiers of the United States by Raising Additional Troops," in *The Public Statutes at Large of the United States . . . 1789 to March 3, 1845*, ed. Richard Peters, 8 vols. (Boston, 1855–56), 1:241–43 (hereafter *Statutes at Large*); "Duties on Merchandise," *Statutes at Large*, 1:259–64; "Duties on Spirits distilled within the United States," *Statutes at Large*, 1:267–71. For an analysis of the congressional debate over the tariff see Gerald Clarfield, "Protecting the Frontiers: Defence Policy and the Tariff Question in the First Washington Administration," *William and Mary Quarterly*, 3rd ser., 32, no. 3 (July 1975): 459–63. For an analysis of the effects of the *Report on Manufactures* upon the 1792 tariff rates see Irwin, "Aftermath of Hamilton's 'Report on Manufactures,'" 808–12.

57. "Militia of the United States," and "Alterations in the Treasury and War Departments," *Statutes at Large*, 1:271–74, 279–81.

58. William Knox to Samuel Hodgdon, 12 May 1792, *The Papers of the War Department, 1784 to 1800*; Hodgdon to Knox, June 29, 1792, ibid.; Memorial of Samuel Hodgdon, November 1792, in Schlesinger and Bruns, *Congress Investigates*, 1:54–63.

59. George Washington to the US Senate and House of Representatives, 3 December 1793, *PGW: Pres. Ser.*, 14:464; "Return of Ordnance, Arms, and Military Stores," 14 December 1793, *ASP: MA*, 1:44–60.

60. "Arsenals and Armories," 5 March 1794, *ASP: MA*, 1:65–66.

61. "An Act to Provide for the Erecting and Repairing of Arsenals and Magazines," *Statutes at Large*, 1:352; Henry Knox to George Washington, 10 April 1794, *PGW: Pres. Ser.*, 15:556–61.

62. Smith, *Harpers Ferry Armory and the New Technology*, ch. 1.

63. *New York Herald*, 16 May 1795; *Philadelphia Aurora General Advertiser*, 18 May 1795; "Military Force, Arsenals, and Stores," *ASP: MA*, 1:110.

64. David R. Meyer, *Networked Machinists: High-Technology Industries in Antebellum America* (Baltimore: Johns Hopkins University Press, 2006), 75–84; Fagal, "American Arms Manufacturing and the Onset of the War of 1812."

From Constitution Making to State Building

The Washington Administration and the Law of Nations

DANIEL J. HULSEBOSCH

> To constitute a well poised political Machine is the Task of us common Workmen; but to set it in Motion requires still greater Qualities. When once agoing, it will proceed a long time from the original Impulse. Time gives to primary Institutions the mighty Power of Habit and Custom, the Law both of wise Men and Fools serves as the great Commentator of human Establishments, and like other Commentators as frequently obscures as it explains the Text. No Constitution is the same on Paper and in Life.
> —Gouverneur Morris to George Washington, October 30, 1787

When Gouverneur Morris observed in a letter to George Washington that "no constitution is the same on paper as in life," he sent a warning and a call to action. The Philadelphia convention had submitted the proposed constitution to the states one month earlier. States were just beginning to organize conventions to consider whether to ratify it. Already, however, Morris was looking beyond debates about the document's meaning and toward actual governance. It was a plea, of course, for Washington to hold himself up for the office of the president. But Morris's goal was not just to place the right man in the right office. Federal officials would also have to share the right goals when turning the Constitution into a government. Strong text was not enough. Neither was good personnel. State building required establishing habits, customs, and precedents that would embed the constitution makers' purposes into the institutions of the federal government.

There was a large consensus about the most general purposes, and not just among Federalists. Twin goals widely shared across the revolutionary generation were to keep true to republican government while also forming a "civilized nation" that would be respected abroad, across Europe of course, but especially by the foreign polities surrounding the United

States. The desire for respect was partly instrumental: diplomats and merchants across the Atlantic world closely monitored government developments in America to gauge the faith and reliability of the revolutionary states. It was also, however, existential: many revolutionaries, Federalists especially, sought "recognition" under Enlightenment standards for their new nation, as well as for themselves. The standards of that civilization and many means for achieving it were located in the law of nations: in treaties, such as the United States had by 1787 negotiated with France, Britain, and several Native American nations, as well as in the customary law of nations. Together they formed, as Federalist jurist James Kent instructed his law students at Columbia College in 1794, "that system of rules which reason and custom have established among the civilized nations of Europe."[1]

The Washington administration repeatedly invoked those rules to make good on the promise of "civilized" governance. A primary goal was to answer long-standing European criticism of its faithless behavior and, having done so, then demand full recognition and respect for its equal status as a nation. A related failure was the confederation's inability to negotiate effectively with Native American nations. Here too, treaties could be made but not kept. In both cases—European and Native American diplomacy—the state governments were not the only source of the problem. British merchants and consular officials routinely faced harassment in the seaports, adding support for hard-line approaches to American commerce among policy makers in London. Deadlier violence characterized the West, where American citizens streamed onto land held and claimed by Native American nations. To manage both of these problems, the administration strove to rely on conventional rules and norms of the law of nations to demonstrate American compliance, complain about European and Native American violations of American rights, and enjoy all the powers to carry out war and commerce as well as, in the words of the Declaration of Independence, "all other Acts and Things which Independent States may of right do."[2]

The reverse side of national self-discipline was, therefore, federal strength. The agents enforcing compliance with treaties and the customary law of nations were federal officers, and the primary targets were American citizens as well as representatives of foreign powers. All this fit a larger trend of the nationalization of power for the purpose of demonstrating American competence and respectability as a nation, secure the territory ceded by Britain, and gain the commercial benefits of Atlantic trade and financing. The Constitution's text was not a cipher. It provided key scripts and directions. But much actual state building was improvised. The text did not provide answers for many of the questions that bombarded the federal government. It did not always even clarify who should answer those questions. Because problems often landed first on the desks of the only federal officials always in session—the executive—President Washington and his advisors took the lead. And while striving to act and be seen like a nation, federal officials in the Washington administration engineered innovations that further entwined the new Constitution with the law of nations.

Improvisation in pursuit of respect and prosperity within the Atlantic world was not the only motive driving American state builders to innovate on the law of nations during the 1790s. Some sought a revolution in the way nations interrelated that would extend their own struggle against imperial restraint to the entire Atlantic world, change what it meant to be a civilized nation, and yield even greater prosperity.[3] Like the earlier revolution, this one targeted the British Empire. Thomas Jefferson and James Madison, in particular, viewed Britain as a stronghold of retrograde and dubious interpretations of the law of nations. They championed instead innovations that drew on Enlightenment-era trends in the law of nations as well as undertheorized imperial practices to reform that law, including what Jefferson called "a jus gentium for America." Two examples included liberal commercial rules in war and peace that would foster free trade and a countervailing claim to enjoy a monopoly on commercial and diplomatic relations with indigenous people within US territory—the context for Jefferson's claim that there was in fact an American law of nations.

These two strands of American argument about the law of nations—the pursuit of full national recognition under the existing regime and revolutionary challenges to that regime—were tightly entwined in early federal statebuilding projects. All the leading state builders, whether they leaned toward conventional or revolutionary approaches to the law of nations, referred to the same sources of authority: European treatises and admired treaties, as well as a transnational stock of legal understandings, or customs, about how governments were supposed to operate at home and abroad. Similarly, some of them, like Jefferson, invoked both strands, sometimes at the same time but with different people. Finally, the law of nations had legitimating power not just within the new, relatively weak United States. It provided the idioms and grammar of power across the Atlantic world, and foreign nations demanded that the Washington administration comply with it. But Washington and his officials could also use the law of nations to defend themselves against encroachments on their independence and then frame their own imperial projects within its terms. The law of nations, old and new, permitted the United States to harness the energy of its revolution while forging what was supposed to pass as a "civilized" nation.

Constituting Union, among the States and with Foreign Nations

The great constitutional debate of the 1780s was a contest over what sort of government—what type of *state*—the revolutionaries had meant to create. Their political goal was never limited just to escaping the British Empire. They also wished to build republican governments at home that would thrive diplomatically and commercially in the Atlantic world of nations. Yet only a few years after winning independence, many Americans believed that the new American governments, collectively in their confederation, risked losing the peace. Formally, the United States had been recognized as an international state. Practically, however, it could not realize some basic goals of the Revolution: plentiful credit, robust land sales, and a stream of immigrant free labor.

The confederation shared many hallmarks of what some scholars today would call a "failed state." That was the language that Federalists used. And, like today, it was a language of argument and reform, not of neutral observation. "We may indeed with propriety be said to have reached almost the last stage of national humiliation," Alexander Hamilton warned ratification voters in *The Federalist*. "There is scarcely anything that can wound the pride or degrade the character of an independent nation which we do not experience." Treaties were violated, debts went unpaid, and American land was occupied by the British military. Because of the "imbecility of our government," foreign nations refused even to negotiate treaties. "Our ambassadors abroad," he concluded, "are the mere pageants of mimic sovereignty."[4]

Opponents of the new Constitution disputed that criticism, admitting difficulties with foreign relations and especially commerce, but believing that amendments to the Articles of Confederation would suffice. "It was found that our national character was sinking in the opinion of foreign nations," the Dissent of the Pennsylvania Minority at that state's ratification convention admitted, and "all now agreed that it would be advantageous to the union to enlarge the powers of Congress." But Anti-Federalists preferred a stronger confederation, not "consolidation" into a national government that might endanger the republicanism itself.[5] Some Anti-Federalists went further and doubted whether the conventional measurements, calculated for monarchies, fit an intentionally loose confederation of republics. What, after all, counted as success or failure for a revolutionary state? Anti-Federalist Thomas Tredwell complained at New York's ratification convention that the debate was "not between little states and great states," but rather "between little folks and great folks, between patriotism and ambition . . . not so much between navigating states and non-navigating states, as between navigating and non-navigating individuals."[6] It was about the purposes of statehood. Just how much state power, glory, and trade was consistent with republican government? And in what ways should the United States reintegrate into the Atlantic world? In the end, the Federalists succeeded in persuading enough ratifiers that the new federal Constitution—at least with some amendments—would vindicate the promise of the Revolution, safeguarding republican government and participating on an equal footing in the world of "civilized" states.

Viewed in its international and diplomatic context, it becomes clear that the Constitution was conceptualized, drafted, and implemented for not only domestic but also foreign audiences.[7] Some of the most vocal critics of the states during the so-called critical period had been European. So were the laws and norms beneath their critique: the customary law of nations and treaties, which they believed American states and citizens had routinely breached. These rights and duties were worked out in the law of nations: in its literature, institutions, and diplomatic practices. Though dynamic and contested, this law nonetheless provided standards for the proper behavior of nations. The stated goal of the law of nations was peace, the means were supposed to be international commerce, and the first-line mechanism of enforcement was reputation, or the pursuit of national honor and the avoidance of embarrassment. The last line of enforcement was war. This was conventional Enlightenment thinking and common among the *bien pensants*—very much what most Federalists imagined themselves to be. They might have learned about the law of nations in college moral philosophy courses, during legal apprenticeships, and from treatises on the law of nations. Like James Kent's law students in the 1790s, they learned about "the immense moral and political advantages, which have been gained in two centuries past, by the spirit of commerce over the spirit of military rapacity."[8] What the Constitution was supposed to create was forward-looking commercial republic, not a backward-facing fiscal-military state. All of this was reinforced by self-appointed impartial spectators, including actual foreign spectators in the 1780s. To gain full independence, a nation had to subject itself to law.[9]

To enable the United States to meet its international obligations, the new Constitution not only centralized foreign affairs in the federal government, for example, by giving Congress the power to regulate commerce between the states, with foreign nations, and with Native American nations. It also distributed those foreign affairs powers across the federal government and insulated some aspects of foreign relations from the relatively democratic House of Representatives. Examples include the president's powers to execute all laws and carry out diplomacy, vesting the treaty power in the president and Senate and creating a federal judiciary with jurisdiction over most cases that would arise under the law of nations and enjoined to enforce treaties as the supreme law of land. The major exception to this insulation was the power to declare war. The drafters, developing an Enlightenment strand of thought about how to attain "perpetual peace," glossed most recently by Adam Smith, believed that the people would hesitate to go to war because they would bear its cost in taxes and lives. Vesting this power in the people, through their direct representatives, was one of the most radically republican features of the Constitution. It distinguished the new government from those in Europe while also contributing to the professed Enlightenment project of reducing war. Through these innovative structures, the Constitution was supposed to reconcile the twin goals of the Revolution announced in the Declaration of Independence: popular sovereignty and international recognition.

Amid contentious disagreement about the wisdom and effect of the Constitution, there remained broad consensus at least about one principle and one person. The principle was that the federal government should conduct foreign relations to gain the world's respect. There was also consensus about which person should become the first president: George Washington. The principle and the man were related. Washington had been a transatlantic celebrity for over thirty years, known in Britain for his daring skirmish in the Ohio valley that helped ignite the Seven Years War and then celebrated across Europe for outfoxing the British military during the Revolution. Like the Constitution itself, Washington's reputation circulated widely at home and abroad. But how exactly would the two work together?

The Law of Nations as Transatlantic Standard of Statehood

Nothing demonstrates more clearly than executive decision making in Washington's administration that the first American nation builders viewed the Constitution as a project rather than just a text. Not even the Federalists believed that the Constitution itself, by dint of its publication and ratification, would by its own terms solve all the nation's problems. When federal administrators faced a difficult problem, they rarely turned first to the Constitution as a guide for what they should do. When they did do so, the spare text rarely answered their questions. Even Gouverneur Morris, who had helped pen the final version of the Constitution, believed that practical construction would determine more about the meaning of the Constitution than its plain text. Yet those first constructions would create lasting precedents, influential if not binding. The textual limits of the

Constitution was one reason why it was so contentiously debated during the ratification period.[10] Everyone knew that much would turn on how it was used—what it could be made to do.

Repeatedly, those who administered the Constitution recurred to the law of nations. Not only judges and executive officials did so. Even legislators debated its meaning. It was a common resource and idiom of self-governance. Consequently, analysis of the law of nations pervaded Washington's cabinet as it grappled with problems of governance, those foreseen and those not.

In the fall of 1789, Spanish colonial officials detained a few British ships and their crews anchored in the Nootka Sound, on the Pacific coast of North America near present-day Vancouver Island, on charges of violating Spain's territorial and navigational rights on the continent's western shore. Britain prepared for war. One point of contention between the two empires had not changed for centuries: Spain claimed the entire Pacific as its sphere of colonial influence, based on the law of nations doctrine of discovery as well as papal grants. Britain, by contrast, argued that all colonial claims must rest on actual possession, and Spain had no dense settlements on the Pacific coast.[11] The president's advisors all assumed that if war ensued, Britain would try to capture New Orleans to control the Mississippi River. They feared that, to do so, it would march troops from Canada to the Mississippi, across the Ohio valley. When Britain asked permission, how should Washington respond? And if troops crossed American territory without permission, what should he do?

The Constitution did not specify that the president should monitor geopolitical developments, anticipate threats to American territorial sovereignty, and develop contingency plans—and do all this while consulting the law of nations. But that is what Washington and his closest advisors thought he should do. All agreed that the main imperative was to avoid being embroiled in war. Neither belligerent was an ally with claims on US assistance. Both, however, possessed large colonies bordering the United States. Britain, especially, might want to march troops from Canada, down the Mississippi valley, to engage Spanish forces in Louisiana. The cabinet prepared for this possibility by working through various scenarios, including a formal request for permission to transit troops from Britain, as well as transit without permission. The latter possibility was further divided into transit without asking for permission, and transit in defiance of American refusal to permit transit. The larger stakes were defined in terms of which empire, if it succeeded in ousting the other, was a more dangerous neighbor.

The practical advice varied, but the starting point was the same for each: the law of nations concerning the rights and duties of a neutral nation caught between two neighboring nations at war. Thomas Jefferson, John Jay, and Alexander Hamilton combed through several early modern treatises, including those by Emer de Vattel, Hugo Grotius, Samuel von Pufendorf, and Jean Barbeyrac, to discover the rights and responsibilities of neutral nations. John Adams and Henry Knox also referred, without citation, to what the former termed "an honest neutrality" under the law of nations.[12] They all arrived at the same conclusion: a sovereign nation had the right to refuse another nation's request to march troops through its territory for hostile purposes. If the United States gave Britain permission, Spain could construe it as a violation of American neutrality, which could justify its own attack on the United States. In short, giving permission would likely result in war. Similarly clear was the legal position of a neutral nation that refused permission and suffered an invasion: it was justifiable, possibly required as a matter of honor, for it to respond with force. That would mean war with Britain. The choice, then, was whether to risk war with Spain or Britain, with the possibility that the United States could end up losing territory to either or both.

Although his advisors cautioned Washington to avoid war, they also worked through myriad possibilities, many outside American control, to gauge which course of action (or reaction) would be best for the United States. Their strategies for playing within the parameters of the law of neutrality differed in revealing ways. Jefferson suggested that the United States approach France and Spain with the possibility of coordinating against Britain. Hamilton, on the other hand, argued that the United States owed no "gratitude" to Spain for its indirect support during the Revolution and that it was in the American interest to seek cooperative commercial relations with Britain. In the end, Spain and Britain resolved their dispute peacefully, and the cabinet never had to put its contingency planning to use. Nonetheless, this first risk of war with a European empire revealed how the federal government's administrators viewed their constitutional power. To begin with, they assumed that the executive branch should make such contingency plans. They also assumed that they would have to respond to Britain if it either requested permission to pass through American territory or did so without permission. The cabinet did not consult Congress. It did not publicize its discussion. Most important, all agreed that the law of nations governed the key issues, and they agreed that the United States should avoid war if possible. But they disagreed about the geopolitical dynamics and opportunities surrounding the conflict.

The reflexive use of the law of nations was not just the ploy of a "weak state" attempting to leverage law where it lacked power. First, the debate was internal. The cabinet members sought guidance for a new problem from authority that they assumed would be respected among themselves and abroad. They were not arguing with anyone. They were predicting how the belligerents would go about waging their war and what sorts of American arguments might affect their actions. Second, the prediction that Britain and Spain would likewise frame their appeals in terms of the law of nations was accurate. The law of nations was a transatlantic idiom of diplomacy. Britain, arguably the most powerful empire in the Western world by the 1790s, invoked the law of nations throughout the crisis, both in its contest with Spain over access to the Pacific coast and when it sought cooperation from the United States. Britain's legal argument was that Spain's claim to the Pacific coast was invalid under the best interpretation of the international law of discovery. The British drew on the Protestant tradition, epitomized in Vattel's treatise, that mere discovery of an uninhabited land, and even sparse occupation of that land, was not enough to establish a sovereign claim. What was necessary was possession: actual settlement and use of that land, along with an ability to defend its borders. The Americans agreed with this interpretation. They soon wielded it against Spain themselves, to claim a swath of West Florida, and they refined the argument that the doctrine of discovery required productive use in the process of dispossessing Native Americans. Nonetheless, the belief that one belligerent had the better legal argument in its dispute with another—that its cause was more just—did not affect a neutral's duty. If a third party wished to remain neutral, it could not choose sides.

Although the preparation during the Nootka Sound controversy in 1790 was all for naught, many of the same issues arose again in early 1793. The execution of Louis XVI ignited a quarter century of war across Europe and much of the globe. Consequently, the meaning of American neutrality became the leading problem of federal foreign policy for a generation. One important difference this time, however, was that the French regime in power from 1792 to 1793 did not adhere closely to the conventional law of nations. Instead, it expected the United States to assist its effort as a quasi-neutral power. Meanwhile, Britain launched an effort to search and seize all manner of American shipping, and although it relied on arguments sounding in the law of nations, Americans disputed British reasoning on key issues. Both belligerent powers tugged at different ends of the laws of war and peace. The British and French ministers to the United States, George Hammond and Citizen Genet, pressed executive officials to answer their complaints, avoid support for their enemies, and compensate them for violations of neutrality. The cabinet's response was a full-time and evolving pursuit. Yet as contentious as the politics of the global war were at home, Washington's leading advisers were unanimous in their analysis of most of the crucial legal and diplomatic problems.

Neutrality was a term of art filled with ambiguity. It was easy enough to state the principle: nations not at war, Vattel enjoined in his widely circulating treatise on the law of nations, should "remain common friends to both parties, without favoring the arms of the one to the prejudice of the other."[13] Favoring one side would empower the other to answer with reprisal and possibly lead to war. Vattel also recognized that preexisting treaty commitments might create an exception to the customary law of neutrality, and the United States did have a treaty of alliance with France dating from 1778. One major uncertainty concerned Article XI in that treaty, in which the United States promised to "guarantee . . . the present Possessions of the Crown of france in America," which meant France's Caribbean colonies.[14] Did that provision obligate the United States to go to war against Britain? To join the war if France expressly requested assistance? To do so only if France was involved in a "defensive" war? As Washington's advisors debated these questions, European legal treatises played a large role. Hamilton invoked an obscurely worded section of Vattel to argue that, because the United States had made the treaty with a different French regime, under the now executed Louis XVI, it was not bound to fulfill its duties under the treaty, at least until the new form of government was settled. Jefferson immediately doubted the proposition, dismissing Hamilton's gambit as based on "an ill-understood scrap in Vattel."[15] Hamilton's error was not, however, that he relied on treatise authority to make sense of the duties of a neutral nation. Jefferson soon marshalled a series of quotations from Vattel and other treatises supporting the contrary argument—that treaties with a nation remained binding even after a change in the form of its government. Nations, not particular governments, made treaties. Presented with Hamilton's argument, however, Attorney General Edmund Randolph asked the president to delay a decision until he had an opportunity to peruse Vattel himself. The cabinet adjourned, Randolph consulted Vattel, and he returned supporting Jefferson's interpretation rather than Hamilton's. The treaty, Washington decided, remained binding.[16]

France never did ask the United States to join the war effort—openly, at least. The revolutionary regime calculated that the United States was less valuable as a military ally than as a formally neutral nation—with neutral seaports, neutral commercial carriers on the ocean, and neutral bases for invading Spain's American colonies. Its neutral ports would be safe harbors in which to escape from the British navy, sell prizes captured on the high seas, and refit. Neutral American ships could transport valuable sugar from the Caribbean to Europe. And its western settlements, already chafing at Spanish control of the Mississippi, would offer safe havens for attacks against New Spain. These calculations presumed that the United States would assume the posture of something less than "perfect," or impartial, neutrality. The cabinet agreed, however, that the nation should remain perfectly neutral, though Jefferson and Madison did not believe that included full impartiality.[17] The difference between perfect neutrality and impartiality did not manifest itself in policy differences among Washington's closest advisors, however. They all agreed on a neutral stance toward the belligerents. Instead, the distinction between neutrality and impartiality mattered when shaping the federal government's disciplinary posture toward its citizens. Even here there was an underlying consensus that citizens should avoid forms of involvement that risked reprisal from either of the belligerents. That really meant reprisal by Britain.

Many Americans believed that they owed their independence to France, and it appeared to them that France was now following the American example by escaping monarchy and becoming a republic.[18] The conversion of public sympathy into popular support was the danger. The cabinet therefore agreed that President Washington should issue a series of rules for neutral conduct, along with a proclamation that, while studiously avoiding the term "neutrality," reminded American citizens that the nation was at peace with all the European belligerents and required them to avoid participating in arming, supplying, or sailing on the ships of any nation at war. Prosecutions for breach of these neutral duties followed immediately. These criminal cases were not based on any congressional statute. Instead, they alleged violations of existing treaties and the customary law of nations. The cabinet not only unanimously supported the prosecutions but also helped identify a key defendant. Then Attorney General Randolph and Treasury Secretary Hamilton assisted the local federal district attorney in drafting the indictments.[19] The substantive offenses derived from the law of nations. The classification and penalties came from the common law: the courts classified the crimes as misdemeanors, the punishment for which was not capital.[20] But controversy swirled around the cases because there was no clear ground for federal judicial jurisdiction. Nonetheless, the cabinet, federal attorneys, and judges all forged ahead. Juries, on the other hand, balked. Why they refused to find guilt was unclear, as the jurors did not explain their verdicts. Secretary of State Thomas Jefferson, who was not bothered by the verdicts, ascribed them to the jurors' belief that the defendants were not aware, when they set sail, that they were engaged in criminal conduct, rather than to any doubt about the applicability of the law of nations to individual citizens.[21]

Just as controversial as these criminal prosecutions was litigation over disputed prizes hauled into American seaports. The structure of this controversy was similar to that concerning crimes. Most agreed that the law of nations prescribed the substantive rules of lawful capture of ships and cargo on the sea, as well as for adjudicating the disposition of those resulting prizes. But who, or which institution, was supposed to make such decisions? It was again a question of jurisdiction. These disputes typically involved a privateer with a commission from one of the belligerents, usually France, and the owner of the ship or cargo that had been captured, very often British. The most fundamental rule in the laws of war governing captures on the seas was that the question of whether a capture was legal or not under the law of nations—prize or no prize, in the locution of the day—was reserved for the admiralty courts of the captor's nation alone. The conceit beneath admiralty jurisdiction was that such courts, although staffed by judges from the belligerent nation, did not apply local rules but instead applied a branch of international law—the laws of war. The only exception to exclusive prize jurisdiction by the courts of the captor's own nation was when a capture violated a nonbelligerent nation's neutrality. Examples included captures that occurred within the neutral nation's territorial waters rather than on the high seas as the laws of war required. The customary remedy in such instances, however, was a diplomatic appeal to the neutral nation to return the wrongly captured prize: an appeal directly to executive officials rather than to the courts. Accordingly, in a handful of instances Washington's cabinet instructed some state officials to return prizes that it determined were captured in violation of American neutrality.

But the cabinet, speaking through Secretary of State Jefferson, also advised foreign diplomats and property owners to bring suit for recovery in federal courts on the basis of breaches of American neutrality. The lower federal courts that first heard these legal claims for repossession of captured property demurred. After reviewing the European custom surrounding such controversies in the available treatise literature, one federal judge explained that "the party whose property is taken in a neutral country calls on the neutral sovereign to assert these rights, for the protection those within the territory. If this cannot be done by negotiation, it resorts to force."[22] In short, *judicial* remedy for wrongly captured property was not available in a neutral nation. The Supreme Court ultimately disagreed. It held, in the spring of 1794, that the federal courts did have jurisdiction in such cases, thereby unleashing a flood of litigation by British claimants against French privateers for violating American neutrality.[23] Faced with the familiar problem of how and when to restore prizes seized in violation of a nation's neutrality, the federal judiciary, at the executive's prompting, engineered a new remedy.

The federal courts then proceeded to broaden the category of violations that justified returning prizes from the captor to the original owners. In addition to captures made within US territory, it added captures made on the high seas by ships that were "fitted out"—built or armed—in American ports, and also captures made by ships crewed by US citizens. The effect was to penalize French privateers that recruited men, ships, and supplies in American seaports. Although the federal courts returned relatively few prizes to British claimants, each litigation typically lasted many months and, by tying up ships and resources, hampered the French campaign. With the addition in mid-1794 of a congressional statute further expanding the courts' power to redress violations of American neutrality, their jurisdiction now explicitly covered American citizens who joined such efforts and deterred the participation of many more.[24] This was part of what the Washington administration thought was necessary to protect national neutrality, particularly from the most immediate threat: many Americans' enthusiasm for France and its antimonarchical revolution. The goal, in short, was to protect the United States from its own citizens.

Toward the end of 1793, Jefferson indicated his desire to resign from the cabinet. The trajectory of events, and the rest of the cabinet's evident frustration with France, confirmed his choice. Just before he left, he participated in a particularly difficult decision: requesting that France recall its minister to the United States, Citizen Genet. The problem was that Genet breached all manner of diplomatic protocols and dismissed the strictures of the law of nations. "His ignorance of every thing written on th[at] subject," Jefferson marveled in a letter to Madison, "is astonishing. I think he has never read a book of any sort in that branch of science."[25] Innovating at the margins of the law of nations was one thing; acting in open violation or simple ignorance of that law was another. Genet was also ignorant of the Constitution, particularly as the cabinet had interpreted it for four years: all diplomatic communication was supposed to flow through the president. But Genet, who began his career as a government propagandist under the ancién regime, reveled in his popularity, and he threatened to ask the American people, or at least the House of Representatives, to support the French Revolution in every way short of declaring war. Going around Washington and appealing directly to the people was the last straw. The president—and now the executive as an institution—was simply too popular to be humiliated in that way. Genet *will sink the republican* interest," Jefferson lamented. Suddenly it was Hamilton who suggested that the president make his own appeal to the people and excoriate French machinations.[26] The French Revolution's representative had become a liability to the republican cause across the Atlantic. He had succeeded in demonstrating to Federalists that the people were a resource who could be mobilized for or against the federal government. It was a lesson in extratextual constitutional interpretation that endured, one that figured large in the popular debate over the Jay Treaty with Britain in the final year of Washington's presidency.[27]

"Jus Gentium for America"

The Constitution contained structures designed to commit the federal government, states, and citizens to comply with treaties and the law of nations. Yet the text mentions the "the law of nations" only once, when giving Congress the power to define and punish violations of the law of nations.[28] One reason the drafters did not give Congress more authority over the law of nations is that, according early modern legal theory, nations could not make the law of nations unilaterally. It was a collective, civilizational project resting on a combination of natural law and bilateral agreements, with custom occupying an ambiguous space between them. The law of nations provided that nations only had criminal jurisdiction over crimes committed in their own territory or by their own subjects, with stateless pirates (*hostis humani generis*) constituting a possible exception.[29] That helps explain the congressional power to define and punish such crimes. Otherwise, a nation alone could not change that law.

Still, that law did change. Two areas in which early Americans sought to accelerate that change was commerce and the transnational law respecting control over indigenous populations.

Across the eighteenth century, diplomatists and legal writers imagined that the law of nations was becoming more liberal and more oriented toward peaceful and multilateral commerce and less toward war and military alliances. The celebrated and interlocking Treaties of Utrecht in 1713 provided one model; the dream of universal peace was another. Both were premised on the presumed reciprocity of interests among nations. When the revolutionaries fought to escape the mercantile restraints of the British Empire, they believed that they would enter a new world of free international trade. That progressive image of international progress was foundational to revolutionary diplomacy, especially the Model Commercial Treaty of 1776.[30] No nation agreed to that draft as written. But Americans diplomats kept tendering the offer. Perhaps no one struggled harder than Jefferson in France. He made himself a master of the tumultuous transatlantic tobacco trade, the dynamic and peripatetic whaling industry, and other economic sectors in his effort to obtain a liberal trade agreement. He left disappointed. The Model Treaty project had failed. In the face of what he saw as the reactionary Jay Treaty of 1794, it was as if he gave up on negotiated treaties altogether. Instead, he doubled down on natural law.[31] The type of natural law he embraced, however, was not the divine or providential law of the early modern treatise writers. Jefferson imagined a natural law of trade. Left alone, without the artificial restraints of nations, and apart from diplomatic tinkering, the commercial world would seek its natural equilibrium. And with that equilibrium, American commodity production would flourish.

All that was necessary was the application of some political leverage, a peaceful nudge. Jefferson and Madison called it "peaceable coercion."[32] Turning the notion of international reciprocity almost on its head, Jefferson argued that nations trading in the Atlantic world were now so interdependent, or at least so dependent on American trade, that boycotts and embargoes would almost instantly force France and Britain to respect US grievances. Peaceable coercion was an alternative to war. "I think it would furnish us a happy opportunity of setting another example to the world," Jefferson wrote to Madison in the thick of the Neutrality Crisis of 1793, "by shewing that nations may be brought to do justice by appeals to their interests as well as by appeals to arms." He then recommended that Congress initiate trade embargoes with belligerent nations, a proposal that would have gotten nowhere had he suggested it in President Washington's cabinet at that time. "I should hope that Congress instead of a denunciation of war," he continued, "would instantly exclude from our ports all the manufactures, produce, vessels and subjects of the nations committing this aggression, during the continuance of the aggression and till full satisfaction made for it. This would work well in many ways, safely in all, and introduce between nations another umpire than arms. It would relieve us too from the risks and the horrors of cutting throats."[33]

Jefferson had fingered the perennial criticism of the law of nations: there was no "umpire" between nations other than diplomacy and war. To him and many Republicans, the increasing economic interdependence among nations offered a new kind of weapon, socially wounding but not bloody. Reciprocity was no longer an ideal: it was a fact, an economic law replacing the Enlightenment mechanism of a balance of powers achieved through negotiation. Even if nations were not balanced by gross political or economic power, they were nonetheless mechanically balanced by virtue of their need for each other's trade. Jefferson was convinced that the large European trading nations were *especially* dependent on American commerce. The United States, he believed, supplied Europe with indispensable produce, as well as a necessary market for manufactured goods.

As secretary of state, Jefferson relentlessly defended American neutral rights against the perceived depredations of both France and Britain, especially the latter. In defense of American neutral rights, he maintained that "free ships made free goods": any goods carried on neutral ships in time of war, even goods owned by one belligerent nation, should be, legally, neutral and therefore immune from capture by the other belligerent. He argued that the modern customary law of nations protected that principle, even in the absence of express protection in a treaty. Britain disagreed: under the customary law of nations, an enemy's goods were liable to capture wherever found on the high seas. Jefferson also maintained that food could not be considered contraband. Again Britain refused to concede the point. Outside the laws of war, he pushed for retaliation against British barriers to trade with its colonies, to persuade it to open them to American trade. But Treasury Secretary Hamilton resisted promoting these causes too strongly, and the United States gave up most of them by the terms of the Jay Treaty with Britain in 1794. That did not stop Jefferson and other Republicans from defending them as law in fact. All these principles would be central to the diplomacy of his own presidency a decade later.

Jefferson was also an innovator on the law of nations in relation to Native Americans. Following the precedent of the British Empire, the Continental Congress and then the Washington administration gave primary jurisdiction over Indian affairs to the secretary of war rather than to the secretary of state. Diplomacy with Native American polities nonetheless regularly arose in negotiations with Britain and Spain. Although Native Americans were not present, their legal rights and interests were negotiated, and sometimes established, in the course of European-American diplomacy. Jefferson, for example, explored the rights and duties of the United States, in relation to Native Americans resident within the borders established by the Treaty of Peace of 1783, when negotiating with George Hammond, the British minister plenipotentiary who arrived in 1791. The two diplomats groped through legal arguments that reveal a moment of creativity in the status of indigenous polities within the law of nations, at least as conceived by the Atlantic powers. At stake was the meaning of nationhood: for Native American polities and also for the United States.

Several complications surrounded the diplomatic status of Native American nations (or, as the Constitution pointedly referred to them, "tribes"). The degree of their "sovereignty"—already a charged legal keyword in the early modern world—was hotly debated, often in juristic writings. Its practical meaning, however, was worked out in diplomatic interactions between the federal government, the states, and the Native Americans.[34] But those were never the only participants in that struggle during the Washington administration. The British and Spanish empires not only surrounded the American "neighborhood."[35] They were also *inside* it: British troops were stationed within American territory, and Spain claimed a swath of what Americans considered their southwestern territory. Both empires had extensive military and commercial relations with Native American nations within the United States. Washington and his advisors believed that those relationships posed threats to United States security and commerce.

A central measure of the relative autonomy of the Native American nations was the degree to which they could carry out their own foreign policy. At times, the Washington administration conceded that the Native Americans were free to make war and peace and regulate their own commerce as they pleased.[36] The trend of policy, however, was decidedly toward constricting that choice, and the strategy to realize the policy was to prevent the other empires from negotiating with Native Americans within US borders. Here as elsewhere, early Americans tried to embed policy in law.

One example is the first Trade and Intercourse Act (1790), soon known as the Nonintercourse Act. That statute is remembered for manifesting a federal monopoly over land purchases from Native Americans, a centralizing policy adopted from the British Empire. It also provided that "no person shall be permitted to carry on any trade or intercourse with the Indian tribes, without a [federal] license," and it criminalized any such trade carried on without such license.[37] The administration sought this statute from Congress in the summer of 1790, at the height of the Nootka Sound controversy, in expectation that a war between Spain and Britain would destroy existing trading relations in western territories—relations that Spanish and British traders monopolized. The statute and its administration were supposed to prevent British traders from taking the old Spanish trading networks as their own, if Britain ejected Spain from the Mississippi valley. Because the canny Alexander McGillivray, a Creek chief, was also concerned about the disruption of this trade, he supported the development of new American trading networks. As Jefferson explained to Washington, the federal government could not force the Creeks to trade with specific American merchants. The Creeks, or at least McGillivray, would likely claim their own monopoly within Creek territory. But the government could foreclose external options, making it probable that "we shall even gain some advantage in substituting citizens of the US instead of British subjects, as associates of Colo. McGillivray, & excluding both British & Spaniards from the country."[38] The following month, when seeking the Senate's consent for new treaty negotiations with the Creeks, Washington explained that "the trade of the Indians is a main mean of their political management," which made it "obvious, that the United States cannot possess any security for the performance of treaties with the Creeks, while their trade is liable to be interrupted or withheld, at the caprice of two foreign powers."[39] The point of the statute, in short, was to imagine and then build an American monopoly over the "political management" of Native Americans located within the United States' borders—those borders, at least, as recognized by the European nations. The native nations would retain the autonomy to make war, sell land, and carry out commerce. But they could exercise those sovereign powers only in relation to the United States.

Even without an Anglo-Spanish war, the Washington administration's project of monopolizing relations with Native Americans accelerated. Amid the long-running American war with Native American nations in the North-west Territory, Britain repeatedly offered to mediate a peace. The British peace plan imagined the establishment of a separate, self-governing Native American buffer state between the United States and the remaining British colonies. The Washington administration rejected the offer and the plan. First, it would not recognize that a European empire had any valid diplomatic interest in what the Americans considered a war within their own territory. Second, it would not consider giving up any of the territory it received in the Treaty of Peace to form a separate nation, even an indigenous nation whose foreign relations might be governed jointly by Britain and the United States. When George Hammond floated the ideas of British "mediation" as well as a "barrier" state filled with Native Americans in 1792, Hamilton rejected the proposals and declared that "a part of the Indians, now engaged in war with the United States, lived within their territory and were considered in some measure as their subjects, and that upon that ground no external interven-tion could be allowed." In addition, a three-way negotiation "would degrade the United States in the estimation of the Indians, and sow the seeds of future dissension, as the latter would be tempted to aggression by the expec-tation of a similar interference on any other occasion."[40] That was the same response that the administration gave to Spain when it similarly proposed filling the disputed territory between New Spain and the United States—part of the Southwest Territory—with a Native American–controlled buffer zone.[41] The United States needed respect and recognition from the Native American nations too, and that required ejecting the European empires from territories it claimed as its own. Washington's cabinet considered pro-posals for indigenous states—for Native American sovereignty—as assaults on their own sovereignty. A civilized nation, they began to argue, had super-visory power over the indigenous people within its territory.

Jefferson made the legal argument for federal domination over the Native Americans most coherently. While discussing the contested border between the Northwest Territory and Britain's Canadian provinces, Ham-mond asked Jefferson what right the United States believed it had to "Indian soil." Jefferson replied that the United States enjoyed a "right of preemp-tion of their lands, that is to say the sole and exclusive right of purchasing from them whenever they should be willing to sell" as well as "a right of regulating the commerce between them and the Whites." He argued that an exclusive right to purchase Native American land was "established by the usage of different nations, into a kind of Jus gentium for America, that a White nation setting down and declaring that such and such are their limits, makes an invasion of those limits by any other White nation an act of war, but gives no right of soil against the native possessors."[42] Jefferson transformed a common imperial practice into a binding rule of the law of nations. The goal was to exclude other nations from interfering in the process by which the government purchased land from the Native Americans.

When it came to commercial relations, Jefferson maintained that the United States could "prohibit the British traders from coming into the Indian territory." British merchants had been supplying the Native Americans with guns, which led Hammond to conclude that the United States intended to block that trade and then "exterminate the Indians and take the lands." Jefferson demurred. The goal instead was to open trade with them and purchase no more land than was necessary. Rather than setting up Native American nations as "an independent nation," as Hammond proposed, "We consider them as a Marechaussee, or police, for scouring the woods on our borders, and preventing their being a cover for rovers and robbers."[43] Under the jus gentium for America, as the Washington administration began to conceive it, the "Indians" were American subjects, though not citizens, and they served to protect the American marchlands. No European nation or its citizens had a legal right to deal with them directly. The administration even adopted the concept of a barrier. But it was a marchland barrier—a barrier within federal jurisdiction. The Native Americans formed "a barrier," Washington explained to the Senate, "against the Colonies of an European power."[44]

That at least was the plan—Jefferson's plan especially. Britain pushed back. In the Jay Treaty, Britain agreed to evacuate its military from its forts within American territory. However, Lord Grenville obtained a provision that preserved the right of British colonial merchants to trade directly with Native Americans in the United States, while allowing Americans a reciprocal right in Canada. Similarly, the Native Americans themselves could pass and trade freely across the international boundary. The treaty also provided that British settlers and traders around those forts could remain, with their property rights, without naturalizing as American citizens. These provisions combined to safeguard the existing "Indian trade" of the British Empire while creating a reciprocal opportunity for American traders to initiate new trade with Natives Americans in Canada. It was an innovative attempt to create an international trading condominium in the Northwest Territory, one that Britain and the United States would attempt to create again a generation later in the Pacific Northwest. Hamilton thought the gains would tilt in favor of American commerce. Jefferson and the Republicans, however, never reconciled themselves to the presence within the American West of foreign interlopers on national trade.[45]

Worse for Jefferson was the treaty's seeming renunciation of the free trade principles that he believed were embedded in the Enlightenment-era law of nations. The treaty provided only symbolic access of free trade to Britain's Caribbean colonies, and the symbol was weighed down by heavy restrictions—so heavy that the Senate rejected that article, and it was not included in the ratified version of the treaty. In addition, the treaty forbade economic sanctions, denying the Jeffersonians the retaliatory tool they thought would supplant traditional diplomacy and war, while opening the world for American trade. They concluded, therefore, that the treaty forsook free trade in peace.

Similarly, in war, the Jay Treaty did not provide that all cargo carried in neutral commercial vessels would be free from confiscation, or, in the Enlightenment trope, that free ships made free goods. Instead, the treaty embraced the older rule that one belligerent could seize the goods of its enemy on the high seas, wherever found. This concession created an asymmetry between France and Britain: France had agreed to the principle of free ships, free goods in its 1778 treaty with the United States. Consequently, it could not seize British goods on American ships. Britain, however, would be able to seize French goods on those same ships. France protested the asymmetry, and the issue contributed to the poor relations between the two nations that would end in the Quasi War a few years later.

The larger lesson for Jefferson was to confirm his loss of faith in traditional diplomacy and bolster his confidence that unilateral action would extract concessions from other nations. It is revealing that the only European treaty that Jefferson signed during his two-term presidency was the Louisiana Purchase Treaty, greatly increasing land available for commodity production. And his most famous domestic initiative was the Embargo Act, which he hoped would vindicate neutral trade without necessitating traditional diplomacy or risking war. A new generation of Republicans soon embraced Jefferson's liberal international principles, but not his aversion to war.

The Washington administration turned reflexively to the law of nations to establish the nation's legitimacy. The administration encountered many complex problems of practical governance, at home and abroad—more than it had anticipated. The Constitution's text provided some guidance but not precise instructions. Instead, when facing these challenges the administration returned to the law of nations. That law offered general principles and specific rules, and it shaped the administration's sense of what American interests ought to be. The law of nations was also dynamic and open to change. Some of those changes were contested among nations and difficult to realize—the doctrines of free trade, for example. Americans contributed to the substantial change of others. The principle of a complete monopoly of a "civilized" nation over the management of indigenous polities within its borders offers a stark example. It was a sign of the diplomatic power of the law of nations that such an obviously self-interested principle, framed within that law, had at least some persuasive effect in Europe. It was also, however, a sign of the confines of a body of law that was supposed to produce a "civilized" world.[46]

Notes

1. James Kent, *Dissertations: Being the Preliminary Part of a Course of Law Lectures* (New York, 1795), 51.

2. Declaration of Independence (1776). On the foreign and diplomatic imperatives behind constitution making, see David M. Golove and Daniel J. Hulsebosch, "A Civilized Nation: The Early American Constitution, the Law of Nations, and the Pursuit of International Recognition," *New York University Law Review* 85 (2010): 932–1066; Max M. Edling, *A Revolution in Favor of Government* (New York: Oxford University Press, 2003); Leonard J. Sadosky, *Revolutionary Negotiations: Indians, Empires, and Diplomats in the Founding of America* (Charlottesville: University of Virginia Press, 2009); Gregory Ablavsky, "The Savage Constitution," *Duke Law Journal* 63 (2014): 999–1089; Frederick W. Marks III, *Independence on Trial: Foreign Affairs and the Making of the Constitution* (Baton Rouge: Louisiana State University Press, 1973). See also Eliga Gould, *Among the Powers of the Earth* (Cambridge, MA: Harvard University Press, 2012); David Armitage, *The Declaration of Independence: A Global History* (Cambridge, MA: Harvard University Press, 2006); Douglas Sylvester, "International Law as Sword or Shield? Early American Foreign Policy and the Law of Nations," *New York University Journal of International Law and Politics* 32 (1999): 1–87.

3. Peter Onuf and Nicholas Onuf, *Federal Union, Modern World: The Law of Nations in an Age of Revolutions, 1776–1814* (Madison, WI: Madison House, 1993); David M. Golove, "The American Founding and Global Justice: Hamiltonian and Jeffersonian Approaches," *Virginia Journal of International Law* 57 (2018): 621–56.

4. Alexander Hamilton, *The Federalist*, no. 15. For a recent, critical analysis of the concept of "failed states," see Susan L. Woodward, *The Ideology of Failed States: Why Intervention Fails* (Cambridge: Cambridge University Press, 2017). For a recent survey of the Confederation's failings from a Federalist perspective, see George Van Cleve, *We Have Not a Government: The Articles of Confederation and the Road to the Constitution* (Chicago: University of Chicago Press, 2017).

5. *The Address and Reasons of Dissent of the Minority of the Convention of the State of Pennsylvania, to Their Constituents, in Documentary History of the Ratification of the Constitution Digital Edition,* ed. John P. Kaminski, Gaspare J. Saladino, Richard

Leffler, Charles H. Schoenleber and Margaret A. Hogan (Charlottesville: University of Virginia Press, 2009). See generally Saul Cornell, *The Other Founders: Anti-Federalism and the Dissenting Tradition in America, 1788–1828* (Chapel Hill: University of North Carolina Press, 1999).

6. Quoted in Daniel J. Hulsebosch, *Constituting Empire: New York and the Transformation of Constitutionalism in the Atlantic World, 1664–1830* (Chapel Hill: University of North Carolina Press, 2005), 230.

7. The next few paragraphs are derived from Golove and Hulsebosch, "A Civilized Nation"; Daniel J. Hulsebosch, "Being Seen Like a State: How Americans (and Britons) Built the Constitutional Infrastructure of a Developing Nation," *William and Mary Law Review* 59 (2018): 1239–319; David M. Golove and Daniel J. Hulsebosch, "'The Known Opinion of the Impartial World': Foreign Relations and the Law of Nations in The Federalist," in *The Cambridge Companion to the Federalist*, ed. Jack N. Rakove and Colleen Sheehan (Cambridge: Cambridge University Press, 2020), 114–63.

8. Kent, *Dissertations*, 79.

9. Cf. Onuf and Onuf, *Federal Union, Modern World*, arguing that early Americans helped make international diplomacy more legalistic.

10. See Jack N. Rakove, *Original Meanings: Politics and Ideas in the Making of the Constitution* (New York: Knopf, 1996); Jonathan Gienapp, *The Second Creation: Fixing the American Constitution in the Founding Period* (Cambridge, MA: Belknap Press of Harvard University Press, 2018).

11. On these competing modes of claims making, see Anthony Pagden, *Lords of All the World: Ideologies of Empire in Spain, Britain and France c. 1500–c. 1800* (New Haven, CT: Yale University Press, 1995).

12. The various opinions are in Washington's papers: John Jay to George Washington, 28 August 1790, Founders Online, National Archives, https://founders.archives.gov/documents/Washington/05-06-02-0170 (citing Vattel); Thomas Jefferson to George Washington, 28 August 1790, Founders Online, National Archives, https://founders.archives.gov/documents/Washington/05-06 -02-0171; John Adams to George Washington, 29 August 1790, Founders Online, National Archives, https://founders.archives.gov/documents/Adams/99-02-02 -1065; Henry Knox to George Washington, 29 August 1790, Founders Online, National Archives, https://founders.archives.gov/documents/Washington/05-06 -02-0175; Alexander Hamilton to George Washington, 15 September 1790, Founders Online, National Archives, https://founders.archives.gov/documents/Washington /05-06-02-0212-0001 (citing Barbeyrac, Grotius, Pufendorf, and Vattel).

13. Emer de Vattel, *The Law of Nations*, ed. Béla Kaposy and Richard Whatmore (1758; Indianapolis: Liberty Fund, 2008), book III, ch. 7.

14. The Franco-American Treaty of Alliance, 6 February 1778, art. 11.

15. Thomas Jefferson to James Madison, 28 April 1793, Founders Online, National Archives, https://founders.archives.gov/documents/Jefferson/01-25-02-0563.

16. See "Thomas Jefferson's Notes on a Cabinet Meeting, 6 May 1793," Founders Online, National Archives, https://founders.archives.gov/documents/Washington /05-12-02-0426. See also Robert J. Reinstein, "Executive Power and the Law of Nations in the Washington Administration," *University of Richmond Law Review* 46 (2011): 373–456.

17. "I should still doubt whether the term impartial in the Proclamation is not stronger than was necessary, if not than was proper. Peace is no doubt to be

preserved at any price that honor and good faith will permit." James Madison to Thomas Jefferson, 8 May 1793, Founders Online, National Archives, https://founders.archives.gov/documents/Jefferson/01-26-02-0056.

18. See Stanley Elkins and Eric McKitrick, *The Age of Federalism* (New York: Oxford University Press, 1993).

19. See Golove and Hulsebosch, "A Civilized Nation," at 1032–35.

20. Memorandum from Edmund Randolph, 17 May 1793, Founders Online, National Archives, https://founders.archives.gov/documents/Washington/05-12-02-0474.

21. Thomas Jefferson to Gouverneur Morris, 16 August 1793, Founders Online, National Archives, https://founders.archives.gov/documents/Jefferson/01-26-02-0629-0005 ("But it appeared on the trial that the crime was not knowingly and wilfully committed; that Henfield was ignorant of the unlawfulness of his undertaking; that in the moment he was apprised of it, he shewed real contrition; that he had rendered meritorious services during the late war, and declared he would live and die an American. The Jury, therefore, in absolving him, did no more than the constitutional authority might have done, had they found him guilty").

22. *Moxon v. The Fanny*, 17 F.Cas. 942, 946–47 (D. Pa. 1793).

23. *Glass v. The Sloop Betsey*, 3 US (3 Dall.) 6 (1794).

24. See David Sloss, "Judicial Foreign Policy: Lessons from the 1790s," *St. Louis University Law Journal* 53 (2008): 145–96; Kevin Arlyck, "The Courts and Foreign Affairs at the Founding," *Brigham Young University Law Review* 1 (2017): 1–65.

25. Thomas Jefferson to James Madison, 3 August 1793, Founders Online, National Archives, https://founders.archives.gov/documents/Jefferson/01-26-02-0548.

26. Ibid.

27. Todd Estes, *The Jay Treaty Debate, Public Opinion, and the Evolution of Early American Political Culture* (Amherst: University of Massachusetts Press, 2006).

28. US Constitution, art. I, sec. 8, cl. 10.

29. See Lauren Benton, "Toward a New Legal History of Piracy: Maritime Legalities and the Myth of Universal Jurisdiction," *International Journal of Maritime History* 23 (2011): 225–40; Christopher Harding, "'Hostis Humani Generis'—The Pirate as Outlaw in the Early Modern Law of the Sea," in *Pirates? The Politics of Plunder, 1550–1650*, ed. Claire Jowitt (Basingstoke: Palgrave Macmillan, 2007), 20–38.

30. Still foundational is Felix Gilbert, *To the Farewell Address: Ideas of Early American Foreign Policy* (New York: Harper and Row, 1961). For the legal innovations embedded in the Model Treaty, see Daniel J. Hulsebosch, "The Fulfillment Revisited: Political Experience, Enlightenment Ideas, and the International Constitution," *New England Quarterly* 91 (2018): 209–39.

31. Cf. Onuf and Onuf, *Federal Union, Modern World* (arguing that the Republicans carried forward the project of the Model Treaty).

32. See, e.g., Thomas Jefferson to Robert R. Livingston, 9 September 1801, Founders Online, National Archives, https://founders.archives.gov/documents/Jefferson/01-35-02-0185 (instructing his minister to France that the best way to protect neutral commerce under the law of nations was to apply "those peaceable coercions, which are in the power of every nation, [and] if undertaken in concert, & in time of peace, are more likely to produce the desired effect").

33. Thomas Jefferson to James Madison, [24 March 1793,] Founders Online, National Archives, https://founders.archives.gov/documents/Jefferson/01-25-02-0408.

34. Richard White, *The Middle Ground: Indians, Empires, and Republics in the Great Lakes Region, 1650–1815* (New York: Cambridge University Press, 1991); Colin G. Calloway, *The Indian World of George Washington: The First President, The First Americans, and the Birth of the Nation* (New York: Oxford University Press, 2019); Francis Paul Prucha, *The Great Father: The United States Government and the American Indians*, vol. 1 (Lincoln: University of Nebraska Press, 1984); Gregory Ablavsky, "Sovereign Metaphors in Indian Law," *Montana Law Review* 80 (2019): 11–40; Gregory Ablavsky, "Beyond the Indian Commerce Clause," *Yale Law Journal* 124 (2015): 1012–90. For "sovereignty" in imperial settings, see Lauren Benton, *A Search for Sovereignty: Law and Geography in European Empires, 1400–1900* (Cambridge: Cambridge University Press, 2010).

35. James E. Lewis, *The American Union and the Problem of Neighborhood: The United States and the Collapse of the Spanish Empire, 1783–1829* (Chapel Hill: University of North Carolina Press, 1998).

36. Opinion on McGillivray's Monopoly of Commerce with Creek Indians, 29 July 1790, Founders Online, National Archives, https://founders.archives.gov /documents/Jefferson/01-17-02-0059 ("The [Creek] nation has a right to give us their peace, and to withhold their commerce, to place it under what monopolies or regulations they please").

37. An Act to Regulate Trade and Intercourse with the Indian Tribes, 22 July 1790.

38. Opinion on McGillivray's Monopoly of Commerce with Creek Indians, 29 July 1790, Founders Online, National Archives, https://founders.archives.gov /documents/Jefferson/01-17-02-0059. For McGillivray's commercial diplomacy, see Claudio Saunt, *A New Order of Things: Property, Power, and the Transformation of the Creek Indians, 1733–1816* (Cambridge: Cambridge University Press, 1999), 17–89; Ray Allen Billington with James Blaine Hedges, *Westward Expansion: A History of the American Frontier* (New York: Macmillan, 1949), 234–35.

39. George Washington to the US Senate, 4 August 1790, Founders Online, National Archives, https://founders.archives.gov/documents/Washington/05-06 -02-0084-0001.

40. George Hammond to Lord Grenville, 8 June 792, FO 4/15, National Archives of the United Kingdom.

41. François Furstenberg, "The Significance of the Trans-Appalachian Frontier in Atlantic History," *American Historical Review* 113 (2008): 647–77; Arthur P. Whitaker, *The Spanish-American Frontier, 1783–1795: The Westward Movement and the Spanish Retreat in the Mississippi Valley* (Boston: Houghton Mifflin, 1927), 102.

42. Thomas Jefferson, "Notes of a Conversation with George Hammond, 4 June 1792," Founders Online, National Archives, https://founders.archives.gov /documents/Jefferson/01-24-02-0023.

43. Thomas Jefferson, "Notes of a Conversation with George Hammond, 4 June 1792," Founders Online, National Archives, https://founders.archives.gov /documents/Jefferson/01-24-02-0023.

44. George Washington to the US Senate, 22 August 1789, Founders Online, National Archives, https://founders.archives.gov/documents/Washington/05-03 -02-0303.

45. Alexander Hamilton, "Remarks on the Treaty of Amity Commerce and Navigation Lately Made between the United States and Great Britain, [9–11 July 1795],"

Founders Online, National Archives, https://founders.archives.gov/documents /Hamilton/01-18-02-0281. For Jeffersonian resistance, cf. Lawrence Hatter, *Citizens of Convenience: The Imperial Origins of American Nationhood on the U.S.-Canadian Border* (Charlottesville: University of Virginian Press, 2016).

46. For a recent analysis of these two sides of the early modern law of nations, see Jennifer Pitts, *Boundaries of the International: Law and Empire* (Cambridge, MA: Harvard University Press, 2018).

The Legislative Output of Congress

MAX M. EDLING

The representatives and senators elected to the first federal Congress took their good time to arrive in New York City. In a bid to remain the capital of the American union, the city had contracted Pierre L'Enfant to redesign city hall on the corner of Wall Street and Nassau Street into an elegant, if modestly sized, legislative building that was renamed Federal Hall. Here the new Congress was set to convene on March 4, 1789. But as had often been the case with the old Congress, neither chamber had reached a quorum when the day arrived. Somewhat inauspiciously, the House of Representatives did so only four weeks later, on All Fools' Day. The Senate required yet another week to reach its minimum number of twelve senators. By early April, Congress could at long last begin to count the electoral votes for president and soon after inform George Washington that, to nobody's surprise, he had been unanimously elected the first president of the United States.[1]

Washington was inaugurated on April 30. The chancellor of New York State, Robert Livingston, administered the oath of office on the second-story balcony of Federal Hall. His cry of "Long live George Washington, President of the United States," was reportedly answered with cheers from the crowd assembled below and by a thirteen-gun salute. The president then retired to the Senate chamber to deliver the first ever inaugural address, a performance that the surly William Maclay, senator for Pennsylvania, described as singularly uninspiring. Washington's address noted that the new Constitution instructed the executive to recommend "necessary and expedient" measures for the consideration of Congress. He therefore suggested that the legislature contemplate constitutional amendments to still the disquiet that had been so much in evidence in state conventions and print discourse during the recent ratification struggle. But Washington otherwise refrained from any "recommendation of particular measures" and instead passed the buck to the assembled legislators, expressing his faith in "the talents, the rectitude, and the patriotism" of the representatives and senators in the audience. His only hint about the business facing the new Congress was an opaque reference to the Constitution, "which in defining your powers, designates the objects to which your attention is to be given."[2]

The reference to "the Great Constitutional Charter" indicates that Washington believed that the first Congress would strive to realize an agenda that had been formulated by the Philadelphia convention. In this he was far from alone. The previous summer, James Iredell had said that "the first session of Congress" would put in execution "every power contained in the Constitution." Samuel Osgood, who would become postmaster general under Washington, simply described the first Congress as "a second convention." The composition of the federal government meant that Congress could seamlessly continue the work of the convention. Knowledge of the past proceedings in Philadelphia, which had taken place behind closed doors, was widespread in all branches of the new government. Nine representatives and ten senators in the first Congress had been members of the Constitutional Convention. In the executive branch, the president, treasury secretary, and attorney general had also been at the convention, as had three of the six justices on the Supreme Court. Although opposition to the Constitution from so-called Anti-Federalists had been strong in many of the states, the first Congress was controlled by men who had favored the Constitution. With forty-nine of fifty-nine representatives and twenty of twenty-two senators supporting the Constitution, effective opposition to the Federalists' political program was ruled out.[3]

The Constitutional Convention was summoned to amend the Articles of Confederation so as to "render the federal constitution adequate to the exigencies of government and the preservation of the Union." Although the inadequacies were not spelled out, years of reform attempts in the Confederation Congress demonstrate that even if the flaws in the articles were considered to be serious, they were relatively few in number. These flaws prevented Congress from regulating commerce, from raising revenue to pay the running costs of government and charges on the public debt, and from administering the western lands. In order to address these shortcomings, the convention exceeded its mandate and replaced the articles with a completely new Constitution that created a tripartite national government capable of acting directly on the citizens and inhabitants of the United States independent of the state governments. Yet the record of the convention suggests that the majority of delegates did not envisage any dramatic broadening of the remit of the national government beyond the management of international and interstate affairs. The brief report that conveyed the finished Constitution to Congress instead presented the new compact of union as the answer to a long-standing desire among "the friends of our country . . . that the power of making war, peace and treaties, that of levying money and regulating commerce, and the correspondent executive and judicial authorities should be fully and effectually vested in the general government of the Union."[4]

Preparing to accept the presidency in January 1789, Washington expected that the new government would pursue a narrow agenda of reforming the public finances in order "to extricate my country from the embarrassments in which it is entangled, through want of credit; and to establish, a general system of [commercial] policy, which, if pursued will insure permanent felicity to the Commonwealth." James Madison, who had been the leading light in the Constitutional Convention, also expected questions of commerce and revenue to require "our first attention, and our united exertions" in Congress. He explicitly linked the question of revenue to the ability of the government to resume payments on the debt and thereby to restore public credit. Referring to the United States' debt obligations, Madison's first speech in the House of Representatives declared that "the union, by the establishment of a more effective government having recovered from the state of imbecility, that heretofore prevented a performance of its duty, ought, in its first act, to revive those principles of honor and honesty that have too long lain dormant." A few weeks later he claimed that the Constitution's origins lay in the need to retaliate against British commercial discrimination.[5]

Debate on measures that would become the Impost, Tonnage, and Collection Acts in fact came to dominate the House agenda for its first three months. Later, the first Congress would tackle the restructuring of the national debt and vote to incorporate a national bank. At first sight, the regulation of commerce and the reform of the public finances may seem like highly technical questions unlikely to generate much political passion. Yet over the course of the Congress these issues came to generate disagreement that would grow into an organized opposition to administration policies from within the ranks of former Federalist sympathizers in Congress. Having worked closely to secure the adoption of the Constitution, Madison and Alexander Hamilton fell out over its application. As treasury secretary, Hamilton's financial and fiscal policies included the restructuring of the national debt, the creation of the Bank of the United States, and appeasement toward Britain. Madison believed that Hamilton's program enhanced the power of the federal government to the point where it threatened to overpower the states. He also wished the United States to stand up to British trade restrictions.

Scholarship on the first and subsequent Congresses during the Washington administration has concentrated on the unfolding of the events that began with the dissolution of the Hamilton-Madison alliance and ended with the formation of political parties in the legislative assembly. There are good reasons for this. Hamilton and Thomas Jefferson, Madison's mentor, have been cast as the original exponents of two competing visions of the destiny of the United States, which have remained in tension over the course of American history. Nevertheless, this focus has fostered a one-sided view of the early Congresses as primarily a site for ideological conflict and party formation. Few scholars have taken an interest in the main activity of this political institution: the enactment of legislation.

For those familiar with the literature on "the Age of Federalism" (i.e., the presidencies of Washington and John Adams), this may sound like an exaggerated, perhaps even false claim. It is true that there are many studies of specific acts of legislation and that every survey of the period highlights the major legislative achievements of at least the first Congress (e.g., the adoption of the Bill of Rights, the funding and assumption of the national debt, the creation of the Bank of the United States, the establishment of the federal judiciary, and the decision to locate the capital on the Potomac River). What is missing is rather a *systematic* analysis of the total body of legislation adopted by the early Congresses, an analysis that places landmark legislation alongside the more mundane actions of the legislature. This essay aims to provide such a systematic study by means of a quantitative analysis of the legislation of Congress under Washington.[6]

The purpose is not to supplant but rather to complement existing scholarship on the early Congress and its role in the federal government. It is obvious that no political history of the early United States can ignore the milestone acts just listed, and it would be absurd to claim that all laws are equally salient. Few historians would argue that the construction of a lighthouse on Portland Head mattered as much to the nation's development as did the incorporation of the Bank of the United States. Because a quantitative analysis cannot measure the relative significance of laws either in terms of contemporary controversy or long-term significance, it is ill-equipped to capture the dramatic turning points in political development that often structure historical narratives. But such weakness is also a strength. For although much is learned about politics from controversy and adversity, the majority of actions undertaken by any political institution consists of routine tasks that give rise to limited or no contention. A single-minded focus on ideological clashes and party formation will direct attention away from the day-to-day operations that form an equally important part of the history of the early federal government.

To understand the legislative activities of Congress, the federal legislature cannot be analyzed in isolation from the state governments. The men who wrote the Constitution expected that the national legislature would do some things, the state legislatures other things. To find out if the Constitution realized their idea of a division of labor between the federal and state governments, it is necessary to study the activity of state legislatures alongside the activity of Congress. To reach a provisional answer to this question it is not necessary to investigate the legislative output of all of the eleven states that made up the union when the first Congress convened in 1789, or of all of the sixteen states in existence when the fourth Congress adjourned, however. If the Constitution established the division of labor intended by its framers, whereby the national government looked after external matters and the state governments took care of their own internal affairs, a clearly discernable pattern of legislation ought to be present in every single one of the state legislatures in the union, albeit with some local variation. In this essay, Congress will be compared to the assembly of the Commonwealth of Pennsylvania, a state that shared both its capital and its capitol with the national government from 1791 to 1800.[7]

A quantitative analysis of congressional and state legislation in the 1790s faces significant methodological challenges. To discover patterns in legislative output requires classification of individual acts. Such class categories can either be analytical or already inscribed in the sources. Because historians of the early United States have "been remarkably inattentive to the legislature," as William Novak points out, there have been no quantitative analyses of legislation in the early United States at either federal or state level. The situation is different in European historiography, where the state has always appeared a decisive force in the shaping of society and therefore a legitimate object of study. In England before the union with Scotland, and in Britain from 1707, Parliament was the core governmental institution in the centuries that followed the Glorious Revolution and the parliamentary statute an essential governmental instrument. In the early 1990s, a group of British historians led by Julian Hoppit and Joanna Innes collected and classified the approximately 13,600 acts passed by Parliament between 1688 and 1800, together with several thousand failed legislative attempts. Dealing with such numbers over an extended time period required a classification schema that could be easily imposed on the legislative record, often only on the basis of the statute title. The only classification used by Parliament in the eighteenth century was the distinction between public and private acts, a distinction of limited analytical value. Because Hoppit and his collaborators were interested in the "purposes of legislation," they instead developed analytical categories that took into account "the subject matter of acts and failed initiatives." The result was a classification schema made up of 10 main categories, divided into 31 subcategories, which were further subdivided into 177 particular categories.[8]

Applying the same categories to the record of the first four Congresses and the Pennsylvania assembly makes it possible to compare the actions of the American and British legislative assemblies, thereby highlighting specificities about the early federal government that stand out less clearly when Congress is investigated on its own. Using Parliament as a reference point has the added advantage of making possible an assessment of the early federal government's actions against the benchmark of an actual eighteenth-century state rather than against the benchmark of an ahistorical concept of the state taken from the social sciences. Britain is a relevant point of comparison because it was both the nation out of which independent America sprang and an unusually successful eighteenth-century state. In the eyes of Britons and foreigners alike, the British eighteenth-century state appeared to be more resourceful and more efficient than any of its competitors.[9]

Historians have written much about Britain's ability to engage in frequent and costly wars and to dictate the rules of international commerce thanks to its powerful *fiscal-military state:* a war machine singularly effective in raising revenue from loans and taxation to be spent on soldiers, warships, and foreign subsidies. Less prominent in the literature is the concept of Britain's *reactive state,* a term coined by historians of Parliament. The concept points to Parliament's role in reacting or responding to demands by individuals and small interest groups for legislation aimed to enable economic and social projects that were typically personal or local rather than national in scope. The process involved a systematic and often radical redefinition of different types of property rights by Parliament, and the "reactive state" was to that extent a constitutive as much as a reactive governmental institution. In the long eighteenth century, Parliament was primarily concerned with meeting demands for landed property regulation, improved transportation, and the promotion of agriculture by means of enclosure. Much more than a cog in Britain's war machine, Parliament was an institution that allowed the landed nobility and gentry to promote their material interests. In terms of the volume of legislation, the reactive state outdistanced the fiscal-military state by a long stretch.[10]

The British *reactive* and *fiscal-military state* provide two analytical concepts that can be fruitfully used to discuss the nature of the early federal government. Britain's reactive state was concerned with domestic economic regulation and promotion, broadly construed. The raison d'être of the British fiscal-military state, in contrast, was to provide for the security of the nation and its overseas possessions and to promote British interests relative to other nations, including the regulation of international trade. A comparison of the legislative output of the American and the British legislatures has to be sensitive to the considerable geopolitical and socioeconomic differences between the United States and Britain in the late eighteenth century. The United States was a young, peripheral, and weak nation removed from European great power politics, whereas Britain, despite the loss of the thirteen colonies, remained arguably the most powerful state in the world and carried great weight in the European balance of power. Economic differences also abounded. Agriculture dominated in both nations, but there was great disparity in the distribution of wealth, the supply and price of farmland, the predominant labor regimes, and the nature of property rights—freehold in America, leasehold in Britain. Geographic dissimilarities were equally pronounced. England was a compact and densely populated nation. With only half the population of England, the United States was almost eighteen times its size. A final difference was evident in legal and governmental institutions. Both nations were common law jurisdictions. But the United States was a federal union of republics, whereas the composite monarchy of Great Britain was a much more centralized regime.

England's Glorious Revolution was followed by a dramatic upsurge in parliamentary activity. In the two centuries before 1688, Parliament passed around twenty-seven hundred acts. Between 1688 and 1800, it passed more than 13,600 acts and turned down some 5,600 legislative proposals. The volume of legislation increased gradually as the eighteenth century progressed. Between 1689 and 1714 (i.e., before the accession of George I) Parliament passed around forty-five acts every year. In the 1790s, the annual average had jumped to 275 acts. The growth in legislation was caused by the constitutional changes following the events of 1688. In the seventeenth century, the monarch and the courts regulated and governed society. In the eighteenth century, Parliament became the principal institution of the British government and the act of Parliament became the principal instrument of government.[11]

Parliament's rise in importance was a boon to the social classes that elected it (i.e. the landowning gentry and, to a lesser extent, the merchant class). These groups made use of parliamentary legislation to meet the demands of a changing society. The vast majority of legislation in the eighteenth century originated with individuals and small groups seeking the authority of an act of Parliament to further their specific and local interests. Most legislative activity can be described as economic and domestic in nature, directly or indirectly concerned with wealth and income. An act of Parliament bestowed authority on local bodies of diverse kinds: turnpike trusts, poor law authorities, charities, improvement commissioners, etc., and the central government did not pursue national policy as much as it invested local bodies with the power to do so. This defused a long-standing tension between the center and the localities, as Parliament became a resource rather than a threat or competitor to local power magnates. "For many within the upper echelons of society, the expansion of legislation was central to their financial hopes and commercial aspirations," Hoppit writes. "Without the changes that followed 1689 we might doubt whether estate settlements could so readily have been altered, turnpikes built and fields enclosed."[12]

Hoppit found that between 1688 and 1800 parliamentary legislation belonged overwhelmingly to the categories *personal legislation, communications,* and *the economy* (see table 1 for classes of legislation). *Personal legislation* refers to private matters, primarily estate and inheritance legislation. Laws pertaining to *the economy* were primarily concerned with enclosures. In the period 1688–1714, slightly more than three-fifths of all acts fell in these three categories. In the four decades between 1760 and 1800, the figure rose to just above 70 percent of the total. The relative importance of the three categories shifted over time, however. In the period to 1714, close to half the total number of acts belonged in the personal class. The economy and communications accounted for only 7.7 and 5.1 percent, respectively, of all legislation in these years. Both were dwarfed by financial legislation, which made up 13.9 percent of the total. In the period 1760–1800, however, personal legislation had fallen from half to less than a fifth of all acts, whereas the economy and communications had jumped to, respectively, 30.9 and 21.6 percent. Communications legislation increased sharply in the middle and economic regulation toward the end of the century. Thus, it is evident that Parliament's interest in promoting the economy and transportation began in earnest only in the second half of the eighteenth century.[13]

Legislation in all three categories had bearing on private income and wealth accumulation. In the *personal* category, the laws were predominantly estate acts. Put simply, these were a means to free landed property from restrictions imposed by legal settlements. Settlements were introduced to protect the interests of the landowner's family at the expense of the individual landowner, primarily to preserve the property intact for coming generations. But settlements also distributed family property among a broader circle of family members beyond the estate holder and his heir, for instance by providing annual incomes for younger sons and dowries for daughters. Essentially, a settlement made the landholder a tenant for life rather than a freehold property owner and could impose extensive restrictions on the use of the property. Cutting down trees, draining peat bogs, and opening mines, for example, could all be proscribed in legal settlements. In particular, the sale of the property, in whole or in part, was not permitted. An estate act removed these restrictions and transformed the estate into property that

TABLE 1. British, US, and Pennsylvania legislation by category (percentage)

	British acts, 1789–1797	US statutes, 1789–1797	PA acts, 1790–1797
Personal	16.6	16.3	13.4
Government	2.4	24.4	27.8
Finance	11.5	32.2	17.2
Law and order	2.3	7.5	4.6
Religion	2.4	—	0.4
Armed services	4.0	9.5	2.2
Social issues	5.5	0.8	8.8
Economy	31.0	1.8	13.7
Communications	24.2	7.5	11.9
Miscellaneous	0.2	—	—

Source: UK: Julian Hoppit et al., "Parliamentary Acts, 1660–1800," Excel file in author's possession. US: *The Public Statutes at Large of the United States of America* (Boston: Charles C. Little and James Brown, 1845–67) 1:23–519, 6:1–30, 7:1–60, 8:116–56. PA: *The Statutes at Large of Pennsylvania, From 1682-1801, Compiled under the Authority of the Act of May 19. 1887, by James T. Mitchell and Henry Flanders,* 17 vols. (Harrisburg: Clarence M. Busch, 1896-1915), vols. 13-15, http://www.palrb.us /stlarge/.

Note: US laws includes both public and private statutes as well as the five international treaties and the nine treaties with American Indian nations ratified in this period.

could be developed, mortgaged, or sold. One study reports that of the thirty-five hundred estate acts passed between 1660 and 1830, more than half authorized the sale of property and close to three-quarters the sale, lease, or exchange of property. Estate acts could therefore allow property holders to take advantage of opportunities brought about by economic change.[14]

Economic legislation was heavily dominated by enclosure acts. According to Hoppit, for the whole of the period 1660 to 1800, around 70 percent of economic legislation consisted of such acts. In the middle years of the 1790s that figure was 75 percent. The enclosure movement began in earnest in the 1750s, and the rise of enclosure acts explains why economic legislation rose so sharply in the second half of the eighteenth century. Typically, enclosure allowed for the consolidation of strips of open field into compact farms or for the privatization of land previously held in common. Economic historians debate the effect this had on agricultural productivity, whereas social historians have been much more concerned with the social upheaval and dispossession of the rural poor that followed in the wake of the enclosure movement. The second most important subcategory of economic legislation was the regulation of external trade, which amounted to about 16 percent of legislation in this period. Next in size was the regulation of internal trade. These were measures that eighteenth-century commentators placed under the rubric of *internal police* regulations, dealing with weights and measures, consumption, and middlemen, for example. Hoppit and the other investigators also counted laws promoting agricultural production and manufactures as economic legislation, although such statutes were few in number.[15]

Turnpike acts were by far the most common type of legislation affecting communications. Over the 1660 to 1800 period, almost three-quarters of communications acts either incorporated new turnpike trusts or extended already existing corporation charters. Other acts were concerned with bridge construction, canals and river improvements, and harbor developments. By the middle of the 1790s, turnpike acts accounted for a little over 60 percent, and legislation incorporating canal companies or regulating canals for slightly more than a fifth of all communications legislation. A turnpike act gave a trust the right to build or improve a road and to charge users of the road a fee. Fees were intended to cover road repair and maintenance only, because turnpike trusts were prohibited from turning a profit from road management. Economic historians have nevertheless shown that there were very significant indirect profits to be made from road construction, which made it worthwhile to petition for incorporation of a turnpike trust. Trusts were normally made up of property owners who owned the land on which the road ran, and there is a strong correlation between the construction of turnpikes and the rise in the value of land and the income from landed estates located within easy reach of turnpike roads. Corporations chartered for the purpose of bridge building had a similar composition, whereas legislation for river improvements and canals were often backed by manufacturing and mining corporations. Both bridges and improved water communications generated the same advantages to investors as turnpike trusts did.[16]

In the course of the seventeenth century all English colonies in America acquired representative assemblies, and during the eighteenth century the North American colonial assemblies took on several of the features of the British Parliament. Like Parliament, the assemblies passed a growing number of laws per session, reflecting "their developing ability to handle the legislative needs of their constituents." There are therefore indications that the same trend toward "demand-led" legislation that can be observed in the mother country also existed in the colonies. In North America, rapid demographic, geographic, and economic growth generated demands from the population for more and better provisions for defense, mediums of exchange, American Indian relations, and transportation, for adjudication between competing interest groups, and for the creation of more accessible governmental institutions and officers, such as county courts and justices of the peace. When local government at town and county level could no longer meet these demands, the colonists turned to their assemblies for assistance.[17]

The American Revolution enhanced the colonial assemblies' ability to respond to constituency demands. The collapse of the empire that resulted from the refusal of the American colonists to go along with Britain's far-ranging reforms created a vacuum that was soon filled by the new states. Although the colonists had vehemently opposed Parliament's legislation over the colonies, they were not averse to government as such. In fact, historians have argued that they wanted more, not less, government intervention in social and economic affairs, but they wanted governments that were under their own control. With independence the Privy Council's power to review and overrule colonial legislation and Parliament's contested right to legislate for the colonists were terminated. As a consequence, the obstacles to the assemblies' ability to legislate on economic and social matters were removed.[18]

The revolutionary transformation of government that turned colonial dependencies into sovereign states and privileged the legislature over the executive in the new state constitutions meant that there were few restrictions on the actions that could be undertaken by the state assemblies after the Revolution. This development laid the foundation for the nineteenth-century regulatory regime that has been so carefully mapped in Novak's *The People's Welfare*. As Novak shows, the notion that antebellum United States was a stateless laissez-faire society, where government intervention in social and economic affairs was shunned, is incorrect. At the state and local level, government was busy bringing about the well-ordered and opulent society.[19]

In the Continental Congress the Revolution produced an anomalous central government that was a hybrid between a legislature and a diplomatic congress with executive functions, "formed to coordinate rather than direct the exertions of the states, and with primary responsibility for deliberating on war, peace, treaties, and alliances." The deliberations in the Constitutional Convention and the initial business of the first Congress suggest that the federal government was designed to manage a similarly limited agenda emanating from the aftereffects of the War of Independence. Yet a legitimate claim to an almost unlimited right to legislate could be based on the broad grant to Congress to "promote the general Welfare" found in the Constitution's preamble, and in the "necessary and proper" clause of Article I, Section 8. Such, at least, were the fears voiced by the Anti-Federalist critics of the Constitution in the struggle over ratification.

Given the trend witnessed in both the British Parliament and the American eighteenth-century legislatures before independence, it seems at least conceivable that the new federal government would be eager to try its hand at social and economic reform. However, the legislative agenda of the national assembly turned out to be much narrower as Congress under Washington pursued a course that largely left social and economic regulation alone.[20]

Even a casual glance at the legislative output of the early Congress indicates that it was a different institution from the British Parliament. The volume of legislation was considerably lower. Whereas the annual average of Parliament was around 275 acts in the 1790s, the first four Congresses managed less than 400 in eight years. Instinctively, one is led to believe that the business of setting up a new government—dealing with everything from the judiciary to the revenue system—was vastly more time consuming than the routine matters facing Parliament. But this explanation does not stand up to closer scrutiny. The average number of statutes enacted by each Congress stayed at less than a hundred up to the War of 1812. Between the War of 1812 and the Civil War the average hovered at 150, still very much below Parliament's output in the 1790s. It was not until the Harding administration that congressional output remained consistently above five hundred statutes per Congress. It is much more likely that the United States differed from Britain because the vast mass of legislation that kept Parliament busy in the final decade of the eighteenth century simply was not on the agenda of Congress.[21]

A comparison of the main classes of legislation adopted by Congress during the Washington administration and by Parliament in the corresponding time period supports this assumption (see table 1). The first four Congresses passed 319 public and 66 private statutes. In addition to this, the Senate ratified five international treaties and nine treaties with American Indian nations. Congressional legislation belonged overwhelmingly in the classes *government* and *finance,* which together accounted for 56.6 percent of all legislation. The former category includes legislation concerned with the executive and legislative branches of the national government, with local government, and with *the colonies,* which in the US context has been interpreted as legislation related to the federal territories. In the classification of Parliamentary statutes, the *finance* category includes not only public finance but also private financial measures such as laws on banking and money. Congress's ventures into private finance were limited to only three statutes governing insolvent debtors, however. Almost all financial legislation concerned appropriations, taxation, and debt management, including the creation of the Bank of the United States. These were areas where Parliament was relatively inactive in the 1790s and indeed in the last four decades of the eighteenth century generally. Conversely, Congress did little to regulate the economy or promote transportation. Less than one statute in ten belonged to these classes, whereas in Britain they dominated Parliament's agenda, accounting for 55.2 percent of the total number of acts passed in the 1789–97 period.[22]

The record of Congress and Parliament converge only in the area of *personal legislation*. About a sixth of all acts passed in both assemblies fall in this category. But beyond a superficial similarity, it is once again the differences that stand out. Parliament passed estate acts, naturalization acts, and a smattering of acts granting name changes and divorces. Congress, in contrast, passed laws granting relief to merchants, on the one hand, and compensation for goods supplied and services rendered during the War of Independence, on the other hand. In fact, there was virtually no overlap between the activities of the two legislatures in the category of personal legislation. The handful of US statutes dealing with landed property all concerned land grants in the Northwest Territory, located on the extreme geographical periphery of the United States.

The categories *social issues, the economy,* and *communications* made up more than three-fifths of the total legislation in Parliament. Enclosure acts and the incorporation of turnpike and canal companies were by far the most common types of laws passed. In contrast, apart from running the post office, Congress hardly made any attempt to directly promote the economy or transportation. The only social issue legislation was a naturalization act and an act regulating quarantines. Economic legislation was restricted to one act each addressing the exchange rate of a Danish coin, the fisheries, and the slave trade and two acts prohibiting the exportation of arms and ammunition. The communications category, finally, was by far the largest of the three. There were seven acts regulating the post office and post roads, fifteen acts for the construction of lighthouses and the placement of buoys, and eight acts adjusting the shipping register, issuing passports for US ships, and governing the coastal trade. With the exception of the post office legislation, which dealt with the relationship between the states of the American union, the common denominator of all legislation in these three categories is plain to see: they all regulated relations between the United States and the outside world, by dealing with immigrants, international commerce, and shipping.[23]

The pattern of congressional legislation reveals a national assembly confined to a very narrow remit. It is indeed striking that so many of the classes that historians of Parliament needed to categorize British eighteenth-century legislation do not apply to the legislative output of Congress. No laws passed in the period 1789–97 fit categories such as *banks, lenders; law of property; rivers; canals; bridges, ferries, and tunnels; roads, general;* or *roads, specific,* for example. Nor were there any estate acts or enclosure acts. Only a small trickle of laws had anything do to with landed property. The reason for this is obvious. Property titles were held under state governments and were governed by state laws and regulated by state courts. The federal government and the federal courts had little to do with private property in land. Once the sale of lands in the Northwest Territory began, this would change, but only for people who bought land and settled in the federal territories.[24]

In contrast to political historians of early America, political scientists working in the subfield of American political development have taken more of an interest in the substance of legislation, often in an attempt to better understand party behavior, polarization, and leadership in Congress. Ira Katznelson and John Lapinski have developed a detailed coding schema to allow for the classification of US legislation over time, and Lapinski has applied it to the period after 1877. Table 2 presents the legislation of Congress under Washington coded according to the Katznelson-Lapinski

TABLE 2. US legislation 1789–1797 by modern policy categories

Tier 1	Tier 2	Tier 3	Acts
Sovereignty	Liberty	Loyalty and expression	1
		Religion	
		Privacy	
	Membership and nation	Commemorations and national culture	1
		Immigration and naturalization	2
	Civil rights	African Americans	
		Native Americans	
		Other minority groups	
		Women	
		Voting rights	
	Boundaries	Frontier settlement	3
		Indian removal and compensation	18*
		State admission / union composition	3
		Territories and colonies	10

(continues)

TABLE 2. (*continued*)

Tier 1	Tier 2	Tier 3	Acts
Organization and scope	Government organization	Congressional organization, administration and personnel	14
		Executive organization, administration and personnel	26
		Impeachment and misconduct	
		Judicial organization, administration and personnel	24
	Representation	Census and apportionment	4
		Elections	1
		Groups and interests	
	Constitutional amendments	Federalism and terms of office	
		Political participation and rights	
		Other	
International relations	Defense	Air force organization and deployment	
		Army organization and deployment	12
		Conscription and enlistment	
		Militias	7
		Naval organization and deployment	3
		General military organization	
		Military installations	4
		Civil and homeland defense	
	Geopolitics	Diplomacy and intelligence	6**
		Foreign aid	
		International organizations	
	International political economy	Maritime	25
		Trade and tariffs	37
		Economic international organizations	

Tier 1	Tier 2	Tier 3	Acts
Domestic affairs	Agriculture and food	Agricultural technology	
		Farmers and farming support	
		Fishing and livestock	
	Planning and resources	Corporatism	
		Environment	
		Infrastructure and public works	
		National resources	
		Social knowledge	
		Post office	6
		Transportation	
		Wage and price controls	
		Interstate compacts and federalism	21
		Urban, rural and regional development	
	Political economy	Appropriations	36
		Omnibus legislation	
		Business and capital markets	
		Fiscal and taxation	36
		Labor markets and unions	1
		Monetary	10
		Economic regulation	7
	Social policy	Children and youth	
		Crime	4
		Disaster	
		Education	
		Handicapped and disabilities	
		Civilian health	1
		Housing	
		Military pensions, benefits, and civilian compensation	9
		Public-works employment	
		Social regulation	
		Social insurance	

(continues)

TABLE 2. (*continued*)

Tier 1	Tier 2	Tier 3	Acts
District of Columbia			1
Housekeeping			1
Quasi-private			2

Sources: US statutes and treaties, see sources cited in table 4.1.; Ira Katznelson and John S. Lapinski, "The Substance of Representation: Studying Policy Content and Legislative Behavior," in *The Macropolitics of Congress*, ed. John S. Lapinski and E. Scott Adler (Princeton, NJ: Princeton University Press, 2011), table 4.1, 114–15.

Notes: The table excludes all private acts but includes nine Indian treaties and five international treaties. One act continued earlier legislation passed to regulate "Maritime" matters, "Trade and tariffs," and "Federalism" and has been counted as three statutes (An act to continue in force for a limited time the acts therein mentioned. [Obsolete.] March 2, 1795, ch. 38, *US Statutes at Large* 1:425). One act continued earlier legislation passed to regulate "Appropriations" and "Trade and tariffs" and has been counted as two statutes (An act to continue in force, for a limited time, the acts therein mentioned, 30 May 1796, ch. 43, *US Statutes at Large* 1:488). All acts with the word "appropriations" in the title, and acts that make clear that the purpose was to appropriate money to meet specific costs, have been classed as "Appropriations" regardless of the use of appropriations, for example military, treaties, or government. Acts dealing with the Bank of the United States have been coded as "Fiscal and taxation" rather than "Monetary." The three acts classed as "Economic regulation" are legislation regulating bankruptcies. The single act coded as "Labor markets and unions" addressed sailors. "Monetary" legislation refers to coinage and the value of foreign coins in the US.

* Includes nine Indian treaties.

** Includes five international treaties.

classification schema. Because it adheres quite closely to the structure of legislation of the modern Congress, the schema can be used to compare the activities of the early Congress to that of the twentieth-century Congress.[25]

The many gaps in the legislative activity of the early Congress is the most striking feature of table 2. The first four Congresses passed 94 acts that can be classed as dealing with international relations and 131 that can be classed as dealing with domestic affairs. But the vast majority of acts in the latter category concerned federal matters, appropriations, and taxation. Once these laws are subtracted, the total number of domestic affairs laws falls to a modest thirty-eight. Half of these dealt with monetary matters (i.e., the mint and the valuation of foreign coin and military pensions). The seven acts in the *economic regulation* class concerned bankruptcy (three) and patents and copyrights (four). The virtual absence of activity in the tier 2 areas of *agriculture and food, planning and resources,* and *social policy* is of course significant. It would be a mistake to explain this difference by pointing to the obvious differences between the late eighteenth-century warfare state and the late twentieth-century welfare state, however. Although it would be a gross exaggeration to label them welfare states, the late eighteenth-century "reactive state" in both Britain and Pennsylvania were nevertheless active in many of the areas that the federal government left alone.

Table 3 provides yet another analysis of the pattern of congressional legislation under the Washington administration. Rather than comparing the output to that of Parliament or applying modern policy categories, it identifies legislation as belonging in one of three jurisdictional spaces in an attempt to highlight *where,* in spatial terms, Congress was most active: in the heartland of the American union made up of the original thirteen—by 1797, sixteen—republics; in the western borderlands of the trans-Appalachian national domain that was organized as federal territories; or in the Atlantic world of diplomatic and commercial interaction with

TABLE 3. US legislation and treaties by jurisdictional space

Heartland (117)	*Atlantic (87)*
Federal-state relations (27)	Customs duties (32)
Judiciary (25)	Trade regulations; shipping;
Debt and BUS (23)	fisheries (20)
Excise (11)	Lighthouses, etc. (16)
Pensions (9)	Diplomacy (12)
Post office (7)	Navy (3)
Mint (6)	Naturalization (2)
Patents, copyright (4)	Coastal defense (2)
Insolvent individuals (3)	
Other (2)	
Borderlands (52)	*Government (77)*
Army (19)	Salaries, compensation (28)
Indian affairs (17)	Appropriations (26)
Land sales and grants (10)	Seat of government; Congress (13)
Organization of territorial	Central executive departments (6)
government (4)	Other (4)
State land cessions (2)	

Source: See table 4.1.

Note: The table excludes private acts but includes international and American Indian treaties.

European nations. Because the many statutes concerned with the internal operations of government were not geographically determined, they have been allocated to a residual class of *government* legislation.

Invariably, there is a certain arbitrariness to all classification attempts, including table 3. The army did not guard only the Indian frontier but was posted in coastal forts. Appropriations were made for many specific outlays, such as defense and diplomacy. Customs duties were intended to raise revenue but also to protect domestic manufactures. Nevertheless, placed alongside the comparison with the British Parliament presented in table 1, table 3 sheds additional light on the major focus of the legislative activities of Congress under the Washington administration. The first thing to note is that Congress passed more laws to govern the thirteen republics than to govern the western territories or to regulate international relations. Nevertheless, legislation pertaining to the borderlands and the Atlantic combined was more frequent than legislation governing the heartland.[26]

Contrary to first impressions, the long list of acts in the *heartland* category in fact bears out the conclusion that the federal government did very little to directly shape society or the economy by means of legislation. The most common type of legislation in this category was statutes governing intraunion relations between the federal government and the states, such as federal government assent to state laws, the settlement of accounts between the federal government and the states, and the addition of two stripes and two stars to the national flag. These laws had to do with the American union rather than the internal affairs of the states. This is true also of legislation relative to the post office, the mint, and patents and copyrights. On average six laws per Congress were passed to organize and reorganize the judiciary. But these acts were primarily administrative in nature, creating circuit courts and determining fees, for example. Congress also passed many laws to regulate the national debt and, starting in earnest with the third Congress, to implement a program of internal taxation. Although this legislation had consequences for manufactures, private credit, and the consumption of households, they were enacted to generate revenue rather than to regulate or promote the economy. Pensions were paid to soldiers of the War of Independence and their widows and children. The three laws that specified the terms of imprisonment for debt were of a highly specific and limited nature and did not amount to an attempt to introduce a national law of bankruptcy.[27]

The overall picture that emerges from the analysis of the legislative output of the first Congress is that of a federal government concerned with the management of the common domain in the West, relations to the outside world, primarily in the sphere of foreign commerce and coastal navigation, and interstate relations. The Constitution of 1787 was intended to allow for the creation of a federal government designed to deal with international relations, including commerce, intraunion affairs, and the management of the West, including so-called Indian diplomacy. The record of congressional legislation shows that the framers' intention was realized. In addition to such concerns, it also fell to the federal government to employ the customs service, the federal judiciary, the post office, the mint, and the Patent Acts to maintain the common market and customs union created by the American union. The federal government undoubtedly had an indirect impact on the economic fortunes of most American households in the 1790s due to its commercial policies, western land management, and fiscal and financial legislation. But the early Congresses were not involved with the direct regulation of the domestic economy in the manner of the British legislature. Congress neither redefined nor redistributed landed property. Apart from the creation of the Bank of the United States, it incorporated no business companies. It did not invest in, initiate, or manage any internal improvement projects within state borders. Although there were designated postal roads, there were no federal turnpikes or canals. Nor did Congress tamper with the religious establishments or the internal police of the states.[28]

The comparison between British and American legislation in the 1790s shows that Congress had different priorities than Parliament. In particular, the American national legislature was not involved in the routine business of regulating private property, promoting communications, and enclosing land, the activities that preoccupied Parliament. Nor is there any indication that congressmen tried their hand at what contemporaries called internal police regulation. Congressional inaction in such fields raises the bigger question about the nature of the early American state and its relation to society. As Novak's polemical intervention suggests, it has long been customary to describe early America as a virtually stateless society, a social condition that many historians believe lasted to the Civil War, or possibly even to the days of the New Deal. Yet, just as Novak argues, this is a misconception brought about by what Louis Hartz long ago called a "disproportionate degree of attention" to national matters in an era when in fact "by far the greatest amount of governmental activity in economic life was initiated not by the national government but by the state governments." Above all this is true of almost everything that eighteenth-century governments did in the domestic sphere. For this reason, Thomas Jefferson insisted in his first annual message to Congress that it was the states rather than the national government that had the "principal care of our persons, our property, and our reputation, constituting the great field of human concerns."[29]

Hartz made his observation in a book analyzing economic policy in Pennsylvania between the Revolution and the Civil War. The Commonwealth of Pennsylvania adopted a new state constitution in September 1790 in response to the reorganization of the American union under the federal constitution of 1787. From that point and throughout the 1790s, the Pennsylvania General Assembly began its major session in December and met on occasion for an extra session in August or September. The ten sessions between December 1790 and April 1797 adopted a total of 454 acts and resolutions, a figure that comes fairly close to the 373 statutes adopted and the 14 treaties ratified by Congress between 1789 and 1797.[30]

The legislation passed by the first session of the General Assembly under the new Constitution at first look appears strikingly similar to that of the early Congress. No less than 55 percent of the laws adopted concerned government and finance, exactly the same figure as in the first four Congresses. In the *finance* category, half the acts dealt with the public debt, and close to a quarter dealt with taxation. All acts addressed public, none private, finance. Personal legislation accounted for 18.1 percent, which corresponds closely to the figure of 16.8 percent of federal laws. As was the case with Congress, the Pennsylvania assembly legislated primarily to offer relief to soldiers and suppliers who had served the commonwealth during the War of Independence. And just as in Congress, there was very limited legislative activity in the areas of social, economic, and communications regulation. One in five laws adopted by the Pennsylvania assembly dealt with such matters, compared to one in ten of the laws adopted by the early Congresses. A cursory investigation therefore suggests that similarities rather than differences characterize the Pennsylvania and the national legislatures. But such a conclusion would be premature. Closer inspection reveals the 1790–91 winter session to be an anomaly when Pennsylvania was dealing with the fallout from the War of Independence and with the changes in the American union and in the organization of the commonwealth caused by the adoption of the federal and state constitutions. Over the next six years, a different pattern of legislation emerged.

The share of *personal, government,* and *finance* legislation of the General Assembly's total legislative output dropped off over time. In the final two sessions studied (i.e., the sessions beginning in December 1795 and December 1796), these classes accounted for 45.3 percent of the total, compared to 73.3 percent in the 1790–91 session. Instead, legislation pertaining to *social issues, the economy,* and *communications* grew. In 1790–91, 20 percent of all legislation belonged in these categories. For 1795–97, the figure is 46.3

percent. Although the latter figure still falls short of the share of such legislation in the overall legislative output of Parliament, where it accounted for 60.7 percent of total output, the trend is for the activity of the Pennsylvania General Assembly to resemble the British Parliament more and Congress less. Even if the General Assembly did not pass either estate or enclosure acts, it shared with Parliament the impulse to promote the economy and reform society in accordance with the wishes of its constituents.

Beginning in the late colonial period, the Pennsylvania electorate made increasing demands on the assembly to provide law courts and justices of the peace to manage local government, and more representatives to the assembly to represent electors in the legislature. In a society where the state took on an increasing role in economic intervention and social regulation, influence over the government became more important. Although some historians have claimed that the Pennsylvania constitution of 1790 represents a conservative and antidemocratic turn in the politics of the state, it is clear that the assembly continued to respond to local demands also under the new constitution. Around 42 percent of legislation in the *government* category consisted of laws establishing or altering election districts, highlighting the fact that a major impediment preventing electors from exercising their right to vote was their geographic distance to the polling place. Another significant subclass of legislation in this category was the many incorporation acts that created counties and boroughs. No less than thirteen counties and twenty-three boroughs were incorporated between 1790 and 1797, accounting for close to 30 percent of the total number of *government* laws. In other words, more than 70 percent of *government* legislation aimed at establishing working local governments on the one hand and to give outlying communities a voice in the assembly on the other hand. This record is in marked contrast to both Parliament and Congress. The British Reform Act was adopted only in 1832, and in Congress *government* legislation was dominated by salaries and compensation and the location and workings of the legislature.[31]

Whereas Congress passed only public finance legislation, save for the three statutes dealing with the imprisonment of insolvent debtors, thirteen of the seventy-eight finance acts passed by the General Assembly between 1790 and 1797 concerned private finance. Five of them addressed the problem of bankruptcy and debtors. A single act prohibiting private lotteries is a typical example of the exercise of eighteenth-century police powers. But the assembly also incorporated a bank—the Bank of Pennsylvania (1793)— and two insurance companies—the Insurance Company of North America (1794) and the Insurance Company of the State of Pennsylvania (1794). The incorporation of private business companies was a new phenomenon.

In the entire colonial period only a single business venture was chartered by the Pennsylvania legislature. But from the 1790s, the assembly incorporated several companies every year. The actions of the General Assembly in fact represent the beginnings of a broad trend in the early United States of state legislatures making increasing use of their power of incorporation. Between 1790 and 1860, more than twenty-three hundred business charters were granted in Pennsylvania alone, although the share of the banking and insurance sectors was less than a fifth of the total.[32]

The first Pennsylvania assembly to meet under the constitution of 1790 spent little time on internal improvements, but it did enact a general law that outlined a broad commitment to the improvement of roads and waterways and appropriated money, partly from the sale of the commonwealth's appreciated federal bonds, to build twenty-five designated roads and to build and improve nineteen designated waterways. The state also reserved £5,000 annually from the interest Pennsylvania received on its 3 percent US bonds for the maintenance of roads. On the back of this act, subsequent assemblies passed a large number of specific laws for the construction of roads, canals, and bridges and to declare rivers public highways. Once more the actions of the General Assembly in this field heralded a broad nineteenth-century trend in American political and economic life, although the so-called transportation revolution took off in earnest only a few decades into the next century. It should be noted that many of the statutes passed in the 1790s, and in later periods, never resulted in the construction of roads or the improvement of waterways. The legislation that was passed in the 1790s is a reliable guide to the aspirations and remit of the state legislature. But on its own it cannot be used to determine the state's impact on society and the economy.[33]

Nine acts were passed to declare various waterways public highways, thereby allowing for the legal removal of any natural or artificial obstructions to the passage of boats and rafts. The purpose was to facilitate riverine transportation, but because of the frequency of dams along the creeks of Pennsylvania, these laws impacted the private property rights of dam owners. The General Assembly was therefore careful to stipulate that the locks and slopes, which would be constructed to make transportation by rafts and boats across mill dams possible, would not damage the operations of existing waterworks. Transportation of livestock and goods was also the primary rationale behind the surveying and construction of roads. Many of the laws were for rather limited improvements and made appropriations for sums of only a few hundred or at most a couple of thousand dollars. But the assembly also incorporated four turnpike companies: the Philadelphia and Lancaster Turnpike Road Company (1792), the Lancaster and Susquehanna Turnpike Road Company (1794), the Lancaster, Elizabethtown, Middletown, and Harrisburg Turnpike Road Company (1796), and the Gap Newport and Wilmington Turnpike Road Company (1796). The construction of these roads was a major undertaking that went far beyond what local governments could achieve with their limited resources. The actions of the Pennsylvania assembly should be seen in the wider context of a huge increase in the incorporation of transportation companies in the early United States. According to one calculation 10,800 transportation corporations were formed between 1790 and 1860 under special acts of incorporation. The real number is higher because from the middle of the nineteenth century, many states passed general incorporation acts that made the special act redundant. A little over two-fifths of the transportation corporations were turnpike companies. Bridge companies accounted for slightly more than 12 percent and canal and navigation companies for slightly less than 13 percent of the total. In the decades after 1790, before the advent of the railroad, these figures would have been significantly higher.[34]

Legislation providing for the creation of ferries, bridges, and canals and for the clearing of waterways were other means by which the General Assembly promoted communications but also created property rights. Between 1790 and 1797 four acts gave individuals a monopoly on the operation of ferries where busy roads crossed rivers. In a similar manner, three acts granted individuals or partnerships the right to erect toll bridges. These rights were granted in perpetuity and could be willed to descendants or assigned to other parties. Larger construction works were beyond the means of individuals and required a different response from the legislature. The Pennsylvania assembly incorporated two bridge companies to build stone bridges over the Lehigh River at Northampton and over the Delaware River at Easton. Other bridge-building initiatives originated in the counties but were supported by the assembly by granting permission for lotteries to raise additional money. The Pennsylvania assembly also launched four navigation companies in the early and middle years of the 1790s. The Schuylkill and Susquehanna Navigation Company (1791) and the Delaware and Schuylkill Canal Company (1792) were intended to construct a waterway between Philadelphia and the Susquehanna River, the Conewago Canal Company (1793) was chartered to create a waterway that would bypass Conewago Falls and allow for riverine transportation up the Susquehanna, and the Brandywine Canal Company (1793), finally, was intended to make possible water transportation to the point where Brandywine Creek intersected with the Lancaster turnpike. The legislative program was based on the optimistic but flawed notion that

existing rivers could be made navigable. Real improvements of water transportation had to await the canal era that began with the construction of the
Eerie Canal in the late 1810s.[35]

The scale of these prospective communications undertakings is striking. The Susquehanna and Schuylkill companies were to be capitalized at
$400,000 and the Brandywine company at $300,000. In a separate act,
the Susquehanna Company was granted the right to raise an additional
$400,000 to meet construction costs. The Conewago Falls Company was
entitled to hold property not exceeding $1 million. Slightly smaller, the turn-
pike companies were capitalized at sums from $50,000 to $300,000. In an
age where businesses and individual fortunes were small, these corporate
bodies represent significant concentrations of capital. With shares cost-
ing $300 a piece, investment in transportation companies was restricted
to individuals with wealth or access to credit. Although turnpike companies would turn out to be notoriously unprofitable, the assembly tried to
make initial investment attractive by providing for a minimum 6 percent
dividend and holding out the prospect of 15–20 percent profits on capital
invested in road and bridge companies.[36]

Most Pennsylvania legislation dealing with social issues fit under the
rubric of internal police regulations of the kind that would bring about a
well-ordered society. As the use of the term *internal police* in late eighteenth-
century American newspapers shows, such police regulations were most
frequent in cities. It therefore comes as no surprise that the concentra-
tion and growth of population and the increase in commercial transactions
in Philadelphia spurred the Pennsylvania assembly to pass measures to
impose and maintain order in the city. Much internal police legislation
concerned mundane matters such as the direction, paving, and lightning
of streets; the repair of wharfs; the organization of the night watch; fire
regulations; the creation and regulation of market places; and prohibitions
against prostitution, gambling, and "disorderly sports and dissipation."
William Novak has shown that Americans in the early national and antebellum period generally expected their governments to provide such regulation. In cities this expectation was present already in the colonial era.
Other police legislation dealt with poor relief and orphans. The Pennsylvania assembly also supported Dickinson College and the Pittsburgh and
Washington academies, and it created the University of Pennsylvania by
merging two existing educational institutions. The assemblymen's broader
interest in education and social mores led to specific legislation for the
Library Company and a general incorporation act to facilitate the establishment of religious, charitable, and educational societies. In the aftermath of
a deadly yellow fever epidemic, the assembly also passed several laws that

created and reformed a health office in Philadelphia and introduced routines to prevent European immigrants from bringing contagious diseases into the city.[37]

Although the vast majority of police legislation appearing on the Pennsylvania statute books concern Philadelphia, indirectly the General Assembly also shaped the regulation of internal police outside city limits. Returning to the *government* category of legislation, the principal purpose of incorporating a borough was to invest the local community with police powers. As Novak points out, "In contrast to the modern ideal of the state as a centralized bureaucracy, the [ideal of the] well-regulated society emphasized local control and autonomy." He is correct to stress that local autonomy was considered essential to the realization of the well-regulated society, but at least in Pennsylvania such local control and autonomy was always exercised under the supervision of the state government. Incorporation acts defined the geographic boundaries of the borough and gave resident freeholders and "house-keepers" the right to elect local government officers and supervisors of streets and highways, who were responsible for looking after borough affairs. Like all incorporation acts, incorporation made the borough a legal person that could own land and buildings and could sue and be sued in courts. Boroughs could also levy taxes on the inhabitants to meet the costs of road maintenance and other items of expenditure.[38]

Boroughs were incorporated for the purpose of "regulating the buildings, preventing nuisances and encroachments on the commons, squares, streets, lanes and alleys of the same." Most Pennsylvania incorporation acts used the incorporation of Reading, Berks County, in 1783, as the template for the "powers, jurisdictions, exclusions, authorities and privileges" of newly incorporated boroughs and for the "qualifications, restrictions, penalties, fines and forfeitures" that limited such boroughs and their inhabitants. The Reading Act ran to twenty-three pages and contained very detailed instructions about the police regulations that the burgesses and other officers were expected to oversee. It addressed what to do about such diverse matters as clay and shavings thrown into the street, oversized doorsteps, the unhygienic disposal of rotting carcasses and excrement, storage of gunpowder in houses and dwellings, and "foul or nauseous liquor" coming from distillers, soap boilers, and tallow chandlers. In addition to the power to regulate the police of the borough, incorporation acts also had economic implications because they typically gave boroughs the right to hold two markets per week and two annual two-day fairs. Boroughs were required to appoint a clerk of the market, who had "the assize of bread, wine, beer, wood, coals, hay, corn, and other provisions, brought for the use of the inhabitants."[39]

Although social regulation and communications had economic consequences, in their classification of legislation, Hoppit et al. treat economic
legislation as a separate category. In the case of Pennsylvania, roughly half
the economic legislation concerned the regulation of real estate in the form
of land. These laws were different from Parliament's legislation in the same
period because the practice of holding land in fee simple in Pennsylvania
meant that there was no need for estate acts. Christopher Pearl explains
that a main concern of the state's landowners was instead to ensure that
they had clear and undisputed title to their property. The state constitution
of 1776 responded to this request by establishing a Register's Office for
the Probate of Wills and Granting Letters of Administration and an Office
for the Recording of Deeds. Five years later, the government created a new
court, the Board of Property, that would arbitrate land disputes, and a Public Land Office, which "surveyed land, developed standard forms, gathered
preexisting land documents, and housed all land records for easy access."
The concern of the landholders is reflected in the fact that the most common economic legislation in the early and mid-1790s regulated boundaries
and land claims. But the assembly also passed the occasional act dealing
with land improvements.[40]

The second most important group of laws in the *economy* category was
the twenty-one acts authorizing individuals to erect dams. Such authorization was necessary because dams were a potential infringement of transportation on rivers and waterways that the assembly had declared public
highways. It was rare for these acts to spell out the type of mills or waterworks that the dams would power, and they therefore give no indication
about the economic activities that the lawmakers wished to promote. A
final and smaller group of acts in the *economy* category, finally, belongs to
an important branch of police regulation: the inspection of the quality and
price of goods produced in the state. The Pennsylvania assembly passed
five such acts related to things like auctions, the assize of bread, and the
quality of gunpowder and exported flour.

The legislative record of the first Congresses shows that under the Washington administration the federal legislature concentrated on building new
governmental institutions and managing the public finances. It also acted
to harmonize relations within the American union and to organize the
western domain, and it passed legislation addressing naturalization, international commerce, and coastal navigation. Apart from the reform of the
public debt and the incorporation of the Bank of the United States, which
certainly were major reforms with far-reaching consequences, the first

Congress did next to nothing to promote the domestic economy or to regulate society. It created the post office and a common market, which involved regulating the coin and the weights and measures of the nation. But with these exceptions, Congress left the wide field of internal police regulation alone. It passed no legislation to promote transportation projects, it redistributed no land, and it incorporated no business ventures other than the Bank of the United States—a joint private-public venture. This inaction is best explained by the fact that the duties of the federal government lay elsewhere than in economic and social regulation. The laws passed by the early Congresses show that the principal concerns of the national government were to manage the common domain in the West, relations with the outside world, primarily in the sphere of foreign commerce, and interstate relations between members of the American union. The federal republic and the federal government were created to provide security to the American states from both external threats and civil war and to promote the material interests of their citizens in the trans-Appalachian West and in the Atlantic marketplace.

To understand the nature and function of the early American union it is important to recognize that the relatively narrow set of activities of the federal government was not typical of eighteenth-century states. Providing national security and looking after the national interests were certainly among the most important tasks of the British government. But members of Parliament spent far more time promoting the domestic economy by incorporating transportation companies and other businesses ventures, liberating landed estates from legal restrictions on sale and development, and turning common land into private property. In the American system of government, such tasks were not neglected, but they fell to the state governments rather than to Congress. The record of the Pennsylvania assembly shows a legislature with an agenda quite similar to that of Parliament, especially once the significant differences in the geography, demography, and economy of Pennsylvania and Great Britain are taken into account.

The limited scope of the investigation cautions against making too sweeping conclusions. Only eight years of federal legislation have been studied, only one state assembly scrutinized. It goes without saying that Congress under the Washington administration may not be representative of Congress in the nineteenth century and that Pennsylvania may not be representative of all the other states in the union. Conclusions about the respective roles of Congress and the state assemblies in the early American union can therefore only be tentative at this stage. Nevertheless, as an invitation to further discussion, it is possible to use the two concepts of the

British eighteenth-century state introduced by historians of Parliament to propose that whereas the fiscal-military and the reactive state were merged in the same government in Britain, in the United States they existed at different levels of the federal structure. Congress was central to the American fiscal-military state. The General Assembly of Pennsylvania was central to the American reactive state.[41]

Contemporary writers who commented on the nature of the federal government would have been quite comfortable with this description of the early United States. In his *Lectures on Law,* James Wilson described the General Assembly of Pennsylvania as "vested with every power necessary for a branch of the legislature of a free state," whereas Congress was a legislature of only "enumerated powers." These enumerated powers, said Wilson, were confined to foreign affairs and commerce, relations between the members of the union, and Indian diplomacy. The domestic duties of the federal government, in contrast, were essentially reduced to the creation and supervision of the common market, or customs union, the management of the national post office, and the promotion of arts and sciences by granting copyrights and patents. Wilson was a Federalist. On the other side of the party divide, St. George Tucker argued in his law lectures that governmental power could be divided into internal power, "or such as are to be exercised among the citizens of a state, within the state itself," and external power, "or such as may be exercised towards foreign nations, or different and independent states." "These powers," Tucker continued, "which in all great empires, and monarchies, and even in smaller states, are generally united in one and the same man, or body of men, according to the system adopted by the states of the American confederacy, are . . . separated from each other; the former branch, being with some exceptions, confided to the state-governments, the latter to the federal government."[42]

Notes

1. Charlene Bangs Bickford and Kenneth Bowling, *Birth of the Nation: The First Federal Congress, 1789–1791* (Madison, WI: Madison House, 1989), 9–13.

2. George Washington, First Inaugural Address to Congress, in *A Compilation of the Messages and Papers of the Presidents, 1789–1797,* ed. James D. Richardson, 10 vols. (New York: Bureau of National Literature, 1897) 1:44–45.

3. Bickford and Bowling, *Birth of the Nation,* 5, 107–10, Iredell and Osgood quoted at 5; Kenneth Bowling, *Politics in the First Congress, 1789–1791* (New York: Garland, 1990), 16–17; Gordon S. Wood, *Empire of Liberty: A History of the Early Republic, 1789–1815* (New York: Oxford University Press, 2009), 57–58.

4. "Confederation Congress Calls the Constitutional Convention," in *The Documentary History of the Ratification of the Constitution,* ed. Merrill Jensen, John P.

Kaminiski, and Gaspare J. Saladino, 34 vols. to date (Madison: State Historical Society of Wisconsin, 1976–) 1:187; "The President of the Convention to the President of Congress," in ibid., 305. On attempts to reform the Articles of Confederation, see Merrill Jensen, *The New Nation: A History of the United States during the Confederation, 1781–1789* (New York: Knopf, 1950); Jack N. Rakove, *The Beginnings of National Politics: An Interpretive History of the Continental Congress* (New York: Knopf, 1979); and George W. Van Cleve, *We Have Not a Government: The Articles of Confederation and the Road to the Constitution* (Chicago: University of Chicago Press, 2017). I discuss the rationale behind the framing and adoption of the Constitution in Max M. Edling, *A Revolution in Favor of Government: Origins of the US Constitution and the Making of the American State* (New York: Oxford University Press, 2003) and Max M. Edling, *Perfecting the Union: National and State Authority in the US Constitution* (New York: Oxford University Press, 2021).

5. "From George Washington to Lafayette, January 29, 1789," *The Papers of George Washington: Presidential Series*, ed. Dorothy Twohig, 19 vols. to date (Charlottesville: University Press of Virginia, 1987), 1:262–64; "From James Madison to Edmund Pendleton, April 8, 1789," *The Papers of James Madison*, ed. Charles F. Hobson and Robert A. Rutland, 17 vols. (Charlottesville: University Press of Virginia, 1979), 12:51–52; "Import and Tonnage Duties, [8 April] 1789," ibid. 12:64–66; Debates in the House of Representatives, April 8 and 25, 1789, in *Documentary History of the First Federal Congress of the United States of America, March 4, 1789–March 3, 1791*, ed. Linda Grant DePauw et al., 20 vols. (Baltimore: Johns Hopkins University Press, 1972–2012), 10:4–5, 313–14.

6. Bowling, *Politics in the First Congress*, and Bickford and Bowling, *Birth of the Nation*, are the major treatments of the first Congress. See also Kenneth R. Bowling and Donald R. Kennon, eds., *The House and Senate in the 1790s: Petitioning, Lobbying, and Institutional Development* (Athens: Ohio University Press, 2002). David P. Currie and Jonathan Gienapp have written about the interpretation and development of constitutional law in the first Congresses. See Currie, *The Constitution in Congress: The Federalist Period, 1789–1801* (Chicago: University of Chicago Press, 1997), and Gienapp, *The Second Creation: Fixing the American Constitution in the Founding Era* (Cambridge, MA: Belknap, 2018). Overviews of the Federalist era include Stanley Elkins and Eric McKitrick, *The Age of Federalism: The Early American Republic, 1788–1800* (New York: Oxford University Press, 1993); James Roger Sharp, *American Politics in the Early Republic: The New Nation in Crisis* (New Haven, CT: Yale University Press, 1993); and Wood, *Empire of Liberty*, 53–208. On the Bill of Rights, see Kenneth R. Bowling, "'A Tub to the Whale': The Founding Fathers and Adoption of the Federal Bill of Rights," *Journal of the Early Republic* 8, no. 3 (Fall, 1988): 223–51; on the reform of the debt, Max M. Edling, *A Hercules in the Cradle: War, Money, and the American State, 1783–1867* (Chicago: University of Chicago Press, 2014), 81–107; on the location of the capital, Jacob E. Cooke, "The Compromise of 1790," *William and Mary Quarterly*, 3rd ser., 27, no. 4 (October 1970): 523–45; Kenneth R. Bowling with a rebuttal by Jacob E. Cooke, "Dinner at Jefferson's: A Note on Jacob E. Cooke's 'The Compromise of 1790,'" *William and Mary Quarterly*, 3rd ser., 28, no. 4 (October 1971): 629–48. The literature on party formation in the early Congress is substantial, e.g. Noble E. Cunningham, *The Jeffersonian Republicans: The Formation of Party Organization, 1789–1801* (Chapel Hill: University of North Carolina Press, 1957); Norman K. Risjord, *The Early American*

Party System (New York: Harper and Row, 1969); Rudolph M. Bell, *Party and Faction in American Politics: The House of Representatives, 1789–1801* (Westport, CT: Greenwood, 1973); John F. Hoadley, *Origins of American Political Parties, 1789–1803* (Lexington: University Press of Kentucky, 1986); John H. Aldrich and Ruth W. Grant, "The Antifederalists, the First Congress, and the First Parties," *Journal of Politics* 55, no. 2 (May 1993): 295–326; John H. Aldrich, *Why Parties? A Second Look,* 2nd ed. (Chicago: University of Chicago Press, 2011).

7. North Carolina and Rhode Island initially rejected the Constitution and joined the union only in 1789 and 1790, respectively. Vermont joined the union in 1791, Kentucky in 1792, and Tennessee in 1796. On the framers' vision of the future division of labor between the federal government and the states, see Edling, *Perfecting the Union.*

8. William J. Novak, "A State of Legislatures," *Polity* 40, no. 3 (July 2008): 342; Julian Hoppit, "Patterns of Parliamentary Legislation, 1660–1800," *Historical Journal* 31, no. 1 (March 1996): 116, 118. Julian Hoppit and Joanna Innes, introduction to *Failed Legislation, 1660–1800: Extracted from the Commons and Lords Journal,* ed. Hoppit (London: Hambledon, 1997), 30–32, presents the subject classifications used by the project. American political scientists have studied US legislative output in the twentieth century; see for example David Mayhew, *Divided We Govern: Party Control, Lawmaking, and Investigations, 1946–2002,* 2nd ed. (New Haven, CT: Yale University Press, 2005), and John S. Lapinski, *The Substance of Representation: Congress, American Political Development, and Lawmaking* (Princeton, NJ: Princeton University Press, 2013). Innes has employed the parliamentary legislation database to analyze Parliament and legislation in numerous publications discussing the relationship of economic and social developments to the politics of the British union; see Innes, "Parliament and the Shaping of Eighteenth-Century English Social Policy," *Transactions of the Royal Historical Society,* 5th series, 40 (1990): 63–92; Innes, "The Domestic Face of the Military-Fiscal State: Government and Society in Eighteenth-Century Britain," in *An Imperial State at War: Britain from 1689 to 1815,* ed. Lawrence Stone (London: Routledge, 1994), 96–127; Innes, "The Local Acts of a National Parliament: The Role of Parliament in Sanctioning Local Legislation," *Parliamentary History* 17, no. 1 (1998): 23–47; Innes, "Legislating for Three Kingdoms: How the Westminster Parliament Legislated for England, Scotland and Ireland, 1707–1830," in *Parliaments, Nations and Identities in Britain and Ireland, 1660–1860,* ed. Julian Hoppit (Manchester: Manchester University Press, 2003), 15–47. Hoppit reports his findings in *Britain's Political Economies: Parliament and Economic Life, 1660–1800* (Cambridge: Cambridge University Press, 2017).

9. Novak makes the point that the study of the American state has suffered from the use of abstract theories and concepts of the state drawn from a theoretical model developed from European historical experiences; William J. Novak, "The Myth of the 'Weak' American State," *American Historical Review* 113, no. 3 (June 2008): 761–65.

10. John Brewer, *The Sinews of Power: War, Money, and the British State, 1688–1783* (Boston: Unwin Hyman, 1989); Patrick K. O'Brien, "The Political Economy of British Taxation, 1660–1815," *Economic History Review,* 2nd ser., 41, no. 1 (February 1988): 1–32; Hoppit, "Patterns of Parliamentary Legislation," 125–27; Bob Harris, "Parliamentary Legislation, Lobbying and the Press in Eighteenth-Century Scotland," *Parliamentary History* 26, no. 1 (2007): 76, citing Lee Davison et al., eds., *Stilling the Grumbling Hive: The Response to Social and Economic Problems in England,*

1689–1750, (Stroud: Allan Sutton, 1992); Innes, "The Local Acts of a National Parliament"; Julian Hoppit, "Compulsion, Compensation and Property Rights in Britain, 1688–1833," *Past and Present* 210 (February 2011): 93–128.

11. Hoppit, "Patterns of Parliamentary Legislation," 109, and table 1, 117; Julian Hoppit, "The Nation, the State, and the First Industrial Revolution," *Journal of British Studies* 50, no. 2 (April 2011): 316.

12. Hoppit, "Patterns of Parliamentary Legislation," 126–27, quotation at 127; Innes, "The Local Acts of a National Parliament"; Hoppit, "Compulsion, Compensation and Property Rights," 99–103.

13. Hoppit, "Patterns of Parliamentary Legislation," table 3, 119.

14. Dan Bogart and Gary Richardson, "Making Property Productive: Reorganizing Rights to Real and Equitable Estates in Britain, 1660–1830," *European Review of Economic History* 13, no. 1 (April 2009): 3–30.

15. Hoppit, "Patterns of Parliamentary Legislation," 121–22; Julian Hoppit et al., "Parliamentary Acts, 1660–1800," Excel file in author's possession; Robert C. Allen, "Agriculture during the Industrial Revolution, 1700–1850," in *The Cambridge Economic History of Modern Britain,* vol. 1, *Industrialisation 1700–1860,* ed. Roderick Floud and Paul Johnson (Cambridge: Cambridge University Press, 2004), 96–116. On the enclosure movement, see Michael Turner, *Enclosures in Britain, 1750–1830* (London: Macmillan, 1984). On *internal police,* see Edling, *Perfecting the Union,* ch. 3.

16. Hoppit, "Patterns of Parliamentary Legislation," 121; Dan Bogart, "Turnpike Trusts and Property Income: New Evidence on the Effects of Transport Improvements and Legislation in Eighteenth-Century England," *Economic History Review* 62, no. 1 (2009): 128–52. On turnpikes, canals, and bridges, see William Albert, *The Turnpike Road System in England, 1663–1840* (Cambridge: Cambridge University Press, 1972); J. Ginarlis, and S. Pollard, "Roads and Waterways, 1750–1850," in *Studies in Capital Formation in the United Kingdom, 1750–1920,* ed. C. H. Feinstein and S. Pollard (Oxford: Oxford University Press, 1988), 182–224; D. F. Harrison, "Bridges and Economic Development, 1300–1800," *Economic History Review* 45, no. 2 (May 1992): 755–93; Simon Ville, "Transport," in *Cambridge Economic History of Modern Britain,* 1:295–331.

17. Jack P. Greene, *Peripheries and Center: Constitutional Development in the Extended Polities of the British Empire and the United States, 1607–1788* (Athens: University of Georgia Press, 1986); Alison G. Olson "Eighteenth-Century Colonial Legislatures and Their Constituents," *Journal of American History* 79, no. 2 (September 1992): 543–67, quotation at 566; Peverill Squire, "The Evolution of American Colonial Assemblies as Legislative Organizations," *Congress & the Presidency* 32, no. 2 (Autumn 2005): 109–31, reviews the literature on the colonial assembly.

18. Novak, "A State of Legislatures"; Douglas Bradburn, *The Citizenship Revolution: Politics and the Creation of the American Union, 1774–1804* (Charlottesville: University of Virginia Press, 2009), 47. For more on the rise of the state legislatures in the revolutionary period, see Christopher Tomlins, *Law, Labor, and Ideology in the Early American Republic* (New York: Cambridge University Press, 1993), 35–59; James Henretta, "Magistrates, Common Law Lawyers, Legislators: The Three Legal Systems of British America," in *The Cambridge History of Law in America,* ed. Christopher Tomlins and Michael Grossberg, 3 vols. (Cambridge: Cambridge University Press, 2008), 1:586–89; Bradburn, "The Rise of the States: Governance,

Institutional Failure, and the Causes of American Independence," unpublished paper presented at the Conference on Political Economy and Empire in the Early Modern World, Yale University, May 2013, 14–36; Christopher R. Pearl, *Conceived in Crisis: The Revolutionary Creation of an American State* (Charlottesville: University of Virginia Press, 2020).

19. William J. Novak, *The People's Welfare: Law and Regulation in Nineteenth-Century America* (Chapel Hill: University of North Carolina Press, 1996).

20. On the Confederation Congress, see Rakove, *Beginnings of National Politics*, 175; David C. Hendrickson, *Peace Pact: The Lost World of the American Founding* (Lawrence: University Press of Kansas, 2003), 135–36, quotation at 136; Benjamin H. Irvin, *Clothed in the Robes of Sovereignty: The Continental Congress and the People Out of Doors* (New York: Oxford University Press, 2011).

21. Donald L. Eilenstine, David L. Farnsworth, and James S. Fleming, "Trends and Cycles in the Legislative Productivity of the United States Congress, 1789–1976," *Quality and Quantity* 12 (1978): table 1, 22–23.

22. Note that table 1 presents my coding of US and Pennsylvania legislation together with the Hoppit team's coding of British legislation. In methodological terms table 1 does not present a comparative analysis because such analysis would require that the same researcher or team of researchers code all data.

23. James H. Kettner, *The Development of American Citizenship, 1608–1870* (Chapel Hill: University of North Carolina Press, 1978), 235–44; Aristides Zolberg, *A Nation by Design: Immigration Policy in the Fashioning of America* (Cambridge, MA: Harvard University Press, 2006), 24–98; Edwin Maxey, "Federal Quarantine Laws," *Political Science Quarterly* 23, no. 4 (December 1908): 617–19; Richard R. John, *Spreading the News: The American Postal System from Franklin to Morse* (Cambridge, MA: Harvard University Press, 1995); Allen S. Miller, "'The Lighthouse Top I See': Lighthouses as Instruments and Manifestations of State Building in the Early Republic," *Buildings & Landscapes: Journal of the Vernacular Architecture Forum* 17, no. 1 (Spring 2010): 13–34. On the Federalists largely unrealized visions of communications improvements, see John Lauritz Larson, *Internal Improvement: National Works and the Promise of Popular Government in the Early United States* (Chapel Hill: University of North Carolina Press, 2001), 9–38. The federal government's importance for the development of arms technology has long been noted; see Merrit Roe Smith, *Harpers Ferry Armory and the New Technology: The Challenge of Change* (Ithaca, NY: Cornell University Press, 1977), and Andrew Fagal's contribution to this volume. It should be noted that the quantitative analysis undertaken here concerns Congress only. The federal government promoted the economy in other ways than legislation. The patent and copyright administration and the rulings of the federal courts are two important examples of nonlegislative federal government action.

24. The full list of legislation categories is in Hoppit and Innes, introduction to Hoppit, *Failed Legislation*, 30–32. The pattern of legislative activity in Congress in the 1790s supports the argument about the early American state made in Ira Katznelson and Martin Schefer, eds., *Shaped by War and Trade: International Influences on American Political Development* (Princeton, NJ: Princeton University Press, 2002).

25. Ira Katznelson and John S. Lapinski, "The Substance of Representation: Studying Policy Content and Legislative Behavior," in *The Macropolitics of Congress,*

ed. John S. Lapinski and E. Scott Adler (Princeton, NJ: Princeton University Press, 2011), 100–26; Lapinski, *The Substance of Representation*.

26. On the army, see Richard H. Kohn, *Eagle and Sword: The Federalists and the Creation of the Military Establishment in America, 1783–1802* (New York: Free Press, 1975); on Indian Affairs, see Leonard J. Sadosky, *Revolutionary Negotiations: Indians, Empires, and Diplomats in the Founding of America* (Charlottesville: University of Virginia Press, 2009), 119–75; and Bernard W. Sheehan "The Indian Problem in the Northwest: From Conquest to Philanthropy," in *Launching the "Extended Republic": The Federalist Era*, ed. Ronald Hoffman and Peter J. Albert (Charlottesville: University of Virginia Press, 1996), 190–222; on the western lands see Malcolm J. Rohrbough, *The Land Office Business: The Settlement and Administration of American Public Lands, 1789–1837* (New York: Oxford University Press, 1968); on territorial government, see Bethel Saler, *The Settlers' Empire: Colonialism and State Formation in America's Old Northwest* (Philadelphia: University of Pennsylvania Press, 2014), 40–82; on the customs and revenue legislation, see Gautham Rao, *National Duties: Custom Houses and the Making of the American State* (Chicago: University of Chicago Press, 2016); on diplomacy, see David M. Golove and Daniel J. Hulsebosch, "A Civilized Nation: The Early American Constitution, the Law of Nations, and the Pursuit of International Recognition," *New York University Law Review* 85, no. 4 (2010): 932–1066; and Eliga H. Gould, *Among the Powers of the Earth: The American Revolution and the Making of a New World Empire* (Cambridge, MA: Harvard University Press, 2012).

27. Morgan Sherwood, "The Origins and Development of the American Patent System," *American Scientist* 71, no. 5 (September–October 1983): 500–506. The first congressional bankruptcy act was passed in 1800 but was only a temporary measure. The first stable act was passed in 1898; see Peter J. Coleman, *Debtors and Creditors in America: Insolvency, Imprisonment for Debt, and Bankruptcy* (1974; Washington, DC: Beard Books, 1999), 16–30. There is a very substantial literature on early American federalism, but it focuses on political principles and ideology rather than on administration and legislation. For key works see Cathy D. Matson and Peter S. Onuf, *A Union of Interests: Political and Economic Thought in Revolutionary America* (Lawrence: University Press of Kansas, 1990); Andrew C. Lenner, *The Federal Principle in American Politics, 1790–1833* (Lanham, MD: Madison House, 2001); and Hendrickson, *Peace Pact*.

28. There were roads built in the federal territories and the national road would later become a contentious exception; see Karl B. Raitz, ed., *The National Road* (Baltimore: Johns Hopkins University Press, 1996); Pamela L. Baker, "The Washington National Road Bill and the Struggle to Adopt a Federal System of Internal Improvements," *Journal of the Early Republic* 22, no. 3 (Autumn 2002): 437–64. My interpretation of the federal Constitution is presented in Edling, *Perfecting the Union*.

29. Louis Hartz, *Economic Policy and Democratic Thought: Pennsylvania, 1776–1860* (Cambridge, MA: Harvard University Press, 1948), 3; Thomas Jefferson, First annual message, *The Papers of Thomas Jefferson*, ed. Julian P. Boyd, 44 vols. to date (Princeton, NJ: Princeton University Press, 1950–), 36:60. More than any other scholar of the early republic, Richard John has stressed the importance of government to social, economic, and political development. In addition to John, *Spreading the News*, see Richard R. John, "Governmental Institutions as Agents of Change: Rethinking American Political Development in the Early Republic, 1787–1835,"

Studies in American Political Development 11, no. 2 (Fall 1997): 347–80, and John, "The State *Is* Back In: What Now?" *Journal of the Early Republic* 38, no. 1 (Spring 2018): 105–18.

30. There is a large literature on Pennsylvania politics in the period of the American Revolution and on the Pennsylvania constitutions of 1776 and 1790. For some key works, see Steven Rosswurm, *Arms, Country, and Class: The Philadelphia Militia and the Lower Sort in the American Revolution* (New Brunswick, NJ: Rutgers University Press, 1987); Owen S. Ireland, *Religion, Ethnicity, and Politics: Ratifying the Constitution in Pennsylvania* (Philadelphia: Pennsylvania State University Press, 1995); William Pencak, ed., *Pennsylvania's Revolution* (Philadelphia: Pennsylvania State University Press, 2010); and Pearl, *Conceived in Crisis*.

31. See Pearl, *Conceived in Crisis*, for a discussion of such claims.

32. Hartz, *Economic Policy and Democratic Thought*, 38–39. On the early American corporation and early American incorporation, see James Willard Hurst, *The Legitimacy of the Business Corporation in the Law of the United States, 1780–1970* (Charlottesville: University Press of Virginia, 1969); Pauline Maier, "The Revolutionary Origins of the American Corporation," *William and Mary Quarterly*, 3rd ser., 50, no. 1 (January 1993): 51–84; Novak, *People's Welfare*, 105–6; Andrew M. Schocket, *Founding Corporate Power in Early National Philadelphia* (DeKalb: Northern Illinois University Press, 2007); John Joseph Wallis, "The Other Foundings: Federalism and the Constitutional Structure of American Government," in *Founding Choices: American Economic Policy in the 1790s*, ed. Douglas A. Irwin and Richard Sylla (Chicago: University of Chicago Press, 2011), 177–213; Robert E. Wright, "Rise of the Corporate Nation," in ibid., table 7.1, 220–21; Robert E. Wright, *Corporation Nation* (Philadelphia: University of Pennsylvania Press, 2013).

33. An Act to Provide for the Opening and Improving Sundry Navigable Waters and Roads within This Commonwealth, 13 April 1791, in *Acts of the General Assembly of the Commonwealth of Pennsylvania, Passed at a Session which was Begun and Held at the City of Philadelphia on Tuesday, the Seventh Day of December, in the Year One Thousand Seven Hundred and Ninety, and of the Independence of the United States of America, the Fifteenth* (Philadelphia: Hall and Sellers, 1791), 77–81.

34. Robert E. Wright, "The Pivotal Role of Private Enterprise in America's Transportation Age, 1790–1860," *Journal of Private Enterprise* 29, no. 2 (Spring 2014): 3–4. Klein and Majewski report that turnpike corporations made up 27 percent of all business incorporations between 1800 and 1830 in the Northeast; Daniel B. Klein and John Majewski, "Economy, Community, and Law: The Turnpike Movement in New York, 1797–1845," *Law and Society Review* 26, no. 3 (1992): table 1, 470. On the development of transportation in the antebellum period, see George Rogers Taylor, *The Transportation Revolution, 1815–1860* (New York: Harper and Row, 1951), and John Majewski, *A House Dividing: Economic Development in Pennsylvania and Virginia before the Civil War* (New York: Cambridge University Press, 2000). On roads, see Joseph Durrenberger, *Turnpikes: A Study of the Toll Road Movement in the Middle Atlantic States and Maryland* (1931; Cos Cob, CT: John E. Edwards, 1968); Daniel B. Klein, "The Voluntary Provision of Public Goods? The Turnpike Companies of Early America," *Economic Inquiry* 28, no. 4 (October 1990): 788–812; and Klein and Majewski, "Economy, Community, and Law," 469–512.

35. For the background of the Pennsylvania initiatives, see Jessie L. Hartman, "Pennsylvania's Grand Plan of Post Revolutionary Internal Improvement,"

Pennsylvania Magazine of History and Biography 65, no. 4 (October 1941): 437–57. On canal building generally, see Carter Goodrich, *Government Promotion of American Canals and Railroads, 1800–1890* (New York: Columbia University Press, 1960); Carter Goodrich, ed., *Canals and American Economic Development* (New York: Columbia University Press, 1961); and Ronald Shaw, *Canals for a Nation: The Canal Era in the United States, 1790–1860* (Lexington: University Press of Kentucky, 1990).

36. For the unprofitability of turnpike companies, see Klein and Majewski, "Turnpike Movement in New York," 469–512.

37. Novak, *People's Welfare*, 1–50 and passim; Emma Hart, "City Government and the State in Eighteenth-Century South Carolina," *Eighteenth-Century Studies* 50, no. 2 (Winter 2017): 195–211. The University of Pennsylvania was created by merging the University of the State of Pennsylvania with the College, Academy and Charitable School of Philadelphia. On the nonbusiness corporation in the early United States, see Ronald Seavoy, *The Origins of the American Business Corporation, 1784–1855: Broadening the Concept of Public Service During Industrialization* (Westport, CT: Greenwood, 1982), 9–38; Johann Neem, *Creating a Nation of Joiners: Democracy and Civil Society in Early Massachusetts* (Cambridge, MA: Harvard University Press, 2008); Sarah Barringer Gordon, "The African Supplement: Religion, Race, and Corporate Law in Early National America," *William and Mary Quarterly*, 3rd ser., 72, no 3 (July 2015): 385–422. On health regulations in Philadelphia, see Simon Finger, *The Contagious City: The Politics of Public Health in Early Philadelphia* (Ithaca, NY: Cornell University Press, 2012). On internal police, see Edling, *Perfecting the Union*, ch. 3.

38. Novak, *People's Welfare*, 237. I am indebted to Christopher Pearl for information about the workings of borough government in Pennsylvania in the revolutionary period.

39. "A further Supplement to the Act, entituled 'An Act for erecting the town of Carlisle, in the county of Cumberland, into a borough, for regulating the buildings, preventing nuisances and encroachments on the commons, squares, streets, lanes and alleys of the same, and for other purposes therein mentioned,' passed the thirteenth day of April, one thousand seven-hundred and eighty-two," 19 April 1794, *Acts of the Commonwealth of Pennsylvania [3 December 1793]*, ch. 236, 543; "An Act to erect the town of Pittsburg, in the county of Allegheney, into a borough, and for other purposes therein mentioned," 22 April 1794, ch. 251, ibid., 590–91; "An Act for Erecting the Borough of Reading in the County of Berks Into a Borough; For Regulating the Buildings, Preventing Nuisances and Encroachments on the Squares, Streets, Lanes and Alleys of the Same, And for Other Purposes Therein Mentioned, September 12, 1783, *The Statutes at Large of Pennsylvania from 1682–1801*, vol. 11, ch. 1031, 123–46. On the incorporation of towns and the delegation of power in the system of early American government, see William J. Novak, "The American Law of Association: The Legal-Political Construction of Civil Society," *Studies in American Political Development* 15 (Fall 2001): 163–88; Novak, "A State of Legislatures," 340–47. Novak, *People's Welfare*, 51–233, deals with fire regulations, markets, public ways, prostitution and drunkenness, and health.

40. Pearl, *Conceived in Crisis*, 175, 179 (quotation).

41. There is a need for systematic investigations of state activity in the founding period. Although he takes a different approach to the analysis of Pennsylvania presented here, Gregory Scott King-Owen's investigation of petitions to the North Carolina assembly confirms the Pennsylvania pattern of a legislative output dominated

by the requests from communities and private individuals for local regulations and the protection of property. See Gregory Scott King-Owen, "The People's Law: Popular Sovereignty and State Formation in North Carolina, 1780–1805," unpublished PhD diss., Ohio State University, 2011.

42. James Wilson, *Lectures on Law, Delivered in the College of Philadelphia, in the Years One Thousand Seven Hundred and Ninety, and One Thousand Seven Hundred and Ninety One*, in *Collected Works of James Wilson*, ed. Kermit L. Hall and Mark David Hall (Indianapolis: Liberty Fund, 2007), 870–72, quotation at 870; St. George Tucker, "Of the Several Forms of Government," in George Tucker, *View of the Constitution of the United States. With Select Writings*, ed. Clyde N. Wilson (Indianapolis: Liberty Fund, 1999), 45.

Afterword

Reflections on the Political History
of the Early Republic

ROSEMARIE ZAGARRI

Although political commentators have sometimes called the government created by the Constitution "a machine that would go of itself,"[1] governance was never a self-sustaining operation. Particularly during George Washington's early years as president, when the new federal government was first being launched, countless decisions were made that determined the scope, extent, and nature of federal authority. As is well known, the US Constitution was a bare-bones document that left many decisions about the precise mechanisms of governance to be determined at a later date. It was up to the first officeholders during Washington's administration—ranging from the president to Congress to numerous lower-level functionaries—to fill in the blanks.

This is the story that *Washington's Government* seeks to tell: the story of how real people translated the Constitution's abstract framework for governing into a concrete reality. Moving beyond old-fashioned institutional history, the essays look at the federal government "from the inside out,"[2] to investigate the people and decisions that made the new government into a functioning entity. Some of the essays highlight the fact that many important questions—including apparently obvious ones, such as the origins of the president's cabinet, patterns of officeholding in the new federal bureaucracy, and the legislative output of Congress—have hardly been examined by previous generations of historians. Other essays take on familiar subjects, such as Native American policy or the collection of customs revenue, but bring incisive new analytical frameworks to bear, deploying insights from the literature on state formation, the law of nations, or the modern presidency. Several authors use a creative combination of top-down policy history and bottom-up social history to explore their topics. Instead of depicting early federal officeholders as staid bureaucrats with constricted visions, these essays depict a dynamic cohort of imaginative problem solvers who shaped the federal government into a functioning nation-state.

These are not the stories that historians have been much interested in telling in recent years. During the past few decades, political historians of the early national period have generally shied away from doing institutional or administrative histories. Instead, they have chosen to pursue different kinds of historical questions, using newer historical methodologies and approaches. Seeking to expand the boundaries of political history, some historians have redefined the meaning of "politics" itself, expanding the concept to include people, issues, and events that existed outside of the limits of formal electoral politics or official political institutions. Still other historians, seeking to redress past omissions or exclusions from the scholarly record, have turned their attention to hegemonic ideologies of race, class, and gender or to recovering the voices of women, free blacks, or the white working classes. Many other studies have highlighted the federal government's role in enforcing oppressive policies toward enslaved people or Native Americans. Such approaches have greatly enriched our understanding of early American history and politics, challenging whiggish notions of progress and undermining an uncritical belief in the benevolence of American institutions.[3]

Bearing these contributions in mind, now is a propitious moment to revisit the administrative history of the early federal government. As a field of study, administrative history has faced criticism that it is sometimes too insular or overly narrow in its focus. Historian John Brewer, in his classic work *The Sinews of Power: War, Money and the English State, 1688–1783*, challenges this supposition, Pointing to the source of historians' resistance, he notes, "Administrations thrive on routine. They abhor the stock in trade of the dramatist and the historian—change, disruption, violent action—[and] aspir[e] [instead] to the ubiquity of sameness." Administrative histories, he insists, have far more value than may casually be assumed. "The ability of government administrators," he said, to engage in "routine" or "quotidian" activities fosters the groundwork for building the entire nation-state. Critical but mundane activities such as collecting revenue, raising money, and requisitioning supplies allow a government to function effectively. If done successfully, these functions enable a nation to build armies, create navies, provide security, generate prosperity, and expand its influence. In the case of Great Britain, according to Brewer, the activities of "dullish" government clerks and low-level officials were its secret weapon. Their decisions, made at the bureaucratic level, created the infrastructure of a "fiscal-military state" that launched Britain's transformation into a major world power. Though small in size, Britain played an outsize role in conquering territory, dominating the seas, and influencing world events throughout much of the eighteenth century and well beyond.[4]

Brewer's insights inform the spirit of the essays in *Washington's Government*. In a sense, all of the essays in this volume are about power of some sort—demonstrating how the power of the new federal government was routinized, institutionalized, and put into practice by a variety of state actors. At another level, however, the essays address an even broader issue. In order to be successful, democratic governments must assert their authority and secure their legitimacy in the minds of the people. Authority and legitimacy are essentially about trust. These essays reveal the process by which the new federal government created institutions and policies that garnered the support and trust of the nation—not of all its inhabitants, by any means, but of white American citizens. Securing the people's trust and affirming the government's legitimacy made it possible for Washington and his successors to transform the experiment in republican government into an enduring and long-lasting nation-state. This accomplishment was possible, however, not only because of efforts of prominent officeholders such as George Washington and Alexander Hamilton but also because of the many subordinate clerks and minor officeholders discussed in these essays.

So how do the essays change our understanding of early American political history? How do we think about the Washington administration differently after reading this volume?

What is most striking, I think, is the strong sense in which the federal government in its earliest years should be understood as an exercise in improvisation, a large-scale experiment in pragmatic politics. Because the Constitution left so much to be decided at a later date, the burden fell on those holding office in the first years of the new republic to make decisions that had enormous long-term consequences. There was no handbook for putting this new government into operation. Although their decisions might seem to be narrow in scope, the first officeholders' decisions had a profound impact on the daily lives of many people, ranging from the merchants and customs collectors discussed by Gautham Rao to the arms manufacturers examined by Andrew Fagal to the federal officeholders studied by Peter Kastor to the Native Americans and land-hungry white settlers who were the objects of the policies explored by Stephen Rockwell. Although American officeholders drew on preexisting models and precedents for their policies, they were, in many ways, making it up as they went along.

At a deeper level, those holding office during the new government's first years were also creating the structural mechanisms that allowed the three branches of government to become operational. Though not called for within the Constitution, Washington himself created, as Lindsay Chervinsky observes, the first cabinet, a group of advisors that provided the president with critical advice, particularly on matters of foreign policy. Under

Secretary of the Treasury Alexander Hamilton's leadership, federal judges created a remitting process that intermingled executive and judicial powers in matters relating to customs duties. Although not officially sanctioned under the Constitution, the process facilitated what Kate Brown calls "collaborative state building,"[5] a mechanism that enhanced the government's revenue-collecting function.

In addition, even the new federal legislature had serious decisions to make. Daniel Hulsebosch explains how the US state-building project was shaped by the need to adhere to the law of nations to secure international recognition. Abiding by the international norms that governed relations between so-called civilized nations would both safeguard independence and secure material advantages. But far from being mere rule makers, the Washington administration used the law of nations innovatively as both a "sword and shield" to hold European powers and American Indian nations to account for their transgressions and to advance national interests. In addition, although the Constitution defined Congress's powers, members of the early Congresses still had to determine the scope of their legislative agenda. Their choices, as Max Edling tells us, were somewhat surprising. Instead of focusing on "reactive" legislation dealing with agriculture, transportation, or property rights, Congress chose instead to enact laws dealing with "fiscal-military" matters such as defense and taxation. In doing so, Congress differentiated itself from the British Parliament, which passed both kinds of legislation, and the Pennsylvania state legislature, which overwhelmingly passed "reactive" legislation.[6] In all of these policy domains, the practices described in the essays quickly became entrenched parts of the federal government.

Emphasizing the experimental, or improvisational, nature of the administrative state under George Washington does not suggest that what emerged was a "weak" state, somehow deficient in its ability to perform the essential functions of government. Rather, it indicates that the new government was a work in progress, whose powers were in the process of being understood, devised, and expressed. Jonathan Gienapp sees a similar process at work with regard to early legislators' understanding of the US Constitution. In his recent work, *The Second Founding: Fixing the American Constitution in the Founding Era,* Gienapp argues that the first generation of political leaders in Congress not only lacked a clear understanding of "what the Constitution meant but, far more fundamentally, [did not know] what the Constitution itself actually *was*."[7] These leaders, in other words, were not even certain about how they should govern according to the dictates of a written constitution: whether the document should be seen as fixed and complete or fluid and changing; whether the text should be regarded as the sole arbiter of meaning or viewed within the context of the ratification debates; and finally, whether the framers' intentions should be taken into account or not. As they passed the nation's first laws or formulated its first policies, political leaders were trying to ascertain not only how to apply the Constitution to particular situations but what it meant to govern under a written constitution. Office holders within the federal bureaucracy faced a comparable dilemma. They too struggled to determine how to create new institutions or policies under the Constitution—and more fundamentally, they struggled with what it meant to apply a written constitution to their particular policy domains.

Contrary to what one might expect, none of these decisions was fore-ordained. Nor were they simple extrapolations from wording of the Con-stitution. Nonetheless, they were decisions of enormous consequence. In his important article "American History in a Global Age," historian Johann Neem has discussed the continuing value of national histories at a moment in which the processes of globalization—and a push to produce global histories—are pressing issues. At their best, he suggests, nation-state his-tories can make us look with fresh eyes at the entire process of state for-mation. In the context of global history, the nation should be seen as a "conscious project." As Neem puts it, "Whereas once the nation was an assumption, it can [now] be seen as the product of specific historical pro-cesses." In other words, instead of assuming that the nation-state is a natu-ral, normal, or inevitable structure for organizing political relationships, the concept of the nation-state needs to be "denaturalized," as it were, scru-tinized and interrogated to determine its historical specificity.[8]

This volume does exactly what Neem suggests: it helps us see the spe-cific historical processes that produced the early American nation-state, uncovering the new institutions and emerging practices that made the fed-eral government viable. Collectively, the authors show us that through a combination of flexibility and pragmatism, officeholders in the Washing-ton administration were able to create a government that ordinary citizens could trust and depend upon. The nation they built began to fulfill the Con-stitution's promise to provide security, defend the union, and protect the general welfare. In doing so, it fostered trust and secured legitimacy.

Given the government's dismal failure under the Articles of the Con-federation, this was a major accomplishment—and one which was by no means certain at the outset. It must be acknowledged, however, that the federal government's newfound strength with respect to its white inhab-itants came at a cost—most notably with respect to Native Americans who were exterminated or deprived of their lands, and for enslaved Afri-can Americans, whose labor was systematically expropriated in order to bolster the prosperity of the new American state. This was no accident. These developments were, in fact, two sides of the same coin. "The federal government," as Gautham Rao has insightfully noted, "could appear potent to those who faced it down while seeming distant or useful [to] those who indirectly benefitted from its actions."[9]

As certain essays in this volume show, administrative historians are just beginning to recognize the need to investigate not only the accomplishments of the administrative state but also to recognize its dark underside. The bureaucratizing process produced winners and losers—but all too often it was the people of color who lost out. Thus, the charge for future historians is to continue to write administrative histories—but to write them in such a manner so as to account for the fate of all the country's inhabitants, not just its white male citizens. In doing what they do best, administrative historians can identify the precise structures of power and specific institutions of governance that emerged in the early United States. This process allowed the Washington administration and its successors to create a machinery of government that guaranteed liberty to the country's white inhabitants while systematically denying it to others. This is a process that is indeed worth studying.

Notes

1. Michael Kammen, *A Machine That Would Go of Itself: The Constitution in American Life* (New York: Knopf, 1986), 125. The quotation is originally from James Russell Lowell in 1888.

2. See the introduction to this volume, p. 16.

3. For examples of this kind of work, see the introduction to this volume, notes 2 and 3 as well as Simon P. Newman, *Parades and the Politics of the Street: Festive Culture in the Early American Republic* (Ithaca, NY: Cornell University Press, 1998); Catherine Allgor, *Parlor Politics in Which the Ladies of Washington Help Build a City and a Government* (Charlottesville: University Press of Virginia, 2000); Susan Branson, *These Fiery Frenchified Dames: Women and Political Culture in the Early National Philadelphia* (Philadelphia: University of Pennsylvania Press, 2001); Rosemarie Zagarri, *Revolutionary Backlash: Women and Politics in the Early American Republic* (Philadelphia: University of Pennsylvania Press, 2007); Colin G. Calloway, *The Indian World of George Washington: The First President, the First Americans, and the Birth of the Nation* (Oxford: Oxford University Press, 2018); Adam Rothman, *Slave Country: American Expansionism and the Origins of the Deep South* (Cambridge, MA: Harvard University Press, 2005); Matthew Mason, *Slavery and Politics in the Early American Republic* (Chapel Hill: University of North Carolina Press, 2009).

4. John Brewer, *The Sinews of Power: War, Money and the English State, 1688–1783* (Cambridge, MA: Harvard University Press, 1990), xv, xvi, xx.

5. See Kate Elizabeth Brown's essay in this volume, p. 109.

6. See Max M. Edling's essay in this volume, pp. 216–52.

7. Jonathan Gienapp, *The Second Creation: Fixing the American Constitution in the Founding Era* (Cambridge, MA: Harvard University Press, 2018), 1.

8. Johann N. Neem, "American History in a Global Age," *History and Theory* 50, no. 1 (February 2011): 41–70, quotes on 67.

9. Gautham Rao, "The New Historiography of the Early Federal Government: Institutions, Contexts, and the Imperial State," *William and Mary Quarterly,* 3rd ser., 77, no. 1 (January 2020): 97–128, quote on 127.

Contributors

KATE ELIZABETH BROWN is Assistant Professor of History at Western Kentucky University. She is the author of *Alexander Hamilton and the Development of American Law* (University Press of Kansas, 2017).

LINDSAY M. CHERVINSKY is Scholar in Residence at the Institute for Thomas Paine Studies and a Senior Fellow at the International Center for Jefferson Studies. She is the author of *The Cabinet: George Washington and the Creation of an American Institution* (Belknap Press, 2020).

MAX M. EDLING is Reader in Early American History at King's College London. An expert on the founding and the early federal government, he is the author of three books, most recently *Perfecting the Union: National and State Authority in the US Constitution* (Oxford University Press, 2021).

ANDREW J. B. FAGAL is an associate editor with *The Papers of Thomas Jefferson* at Princeton University. In addition to all things Jefferson, his specialties are in early American political, economic, and military history, with a focus on the nascent arms industry. His articles on the development and acquisition of armaments have appeared in *Enterprise & Society*, the *New England Quarterly*, and *New York History*.

DANIEL J. HULSEBOSCH is the Russell D. Niles Professor of Law and Associate Professor of History at New York University. He is the author of *Constituting Empire: New York and the Transformation of Constitutionalism in the Atlantic World, 1664–1830* (University of North Carolina Press, 2005) and a series of articles analyzing the international dimensions of early American law and constitutionalism.

PETER J. KASTOR is Samuel K. Eddy Professor at Washington University in St. Louis. He is the author or editor of six books, including *William Clark's World: Describing America in an Age of Unknowns* (Yale University Press, 2010).

GAUTHAM RAO is Associate Professor of History at American University in Washington, DC, and Editor in Chief of *Law and History Review*. He is the author of *National Duties: Custom Houses and the Making of the American State* (University of Chicago Press, 2016) and is currently working on a book about the history and legacy of fugitive slave laws.

STEPHEN J. ROCKWELL is Professor of Political Science at St. Joseph's College in New York. He is the author of *Indian Affairs and the Administrative State in the Nineteenth Century* (Cambridge University Press, 2010) and "Henry Knox and the Forging of Bureaucratic Autonomy," in *Federal History* (2018).

ROSEMARIE ZAGARRI is University Professor and Professor of History at George Mason University. A specialist in Early American political history, her most recent book is *Revolutionary Backlash: Women and Politics in the Early American Republic* (University of Pennsylvania Press, 2008). She was president of the Society for Historians of the Early American Republic in 2009–10.

Index

Page numbers in italics indicate illustrations.